HAPPINESS

#3

SHUZO OSHIMI

HAPPiNESS #3 CONTENTS

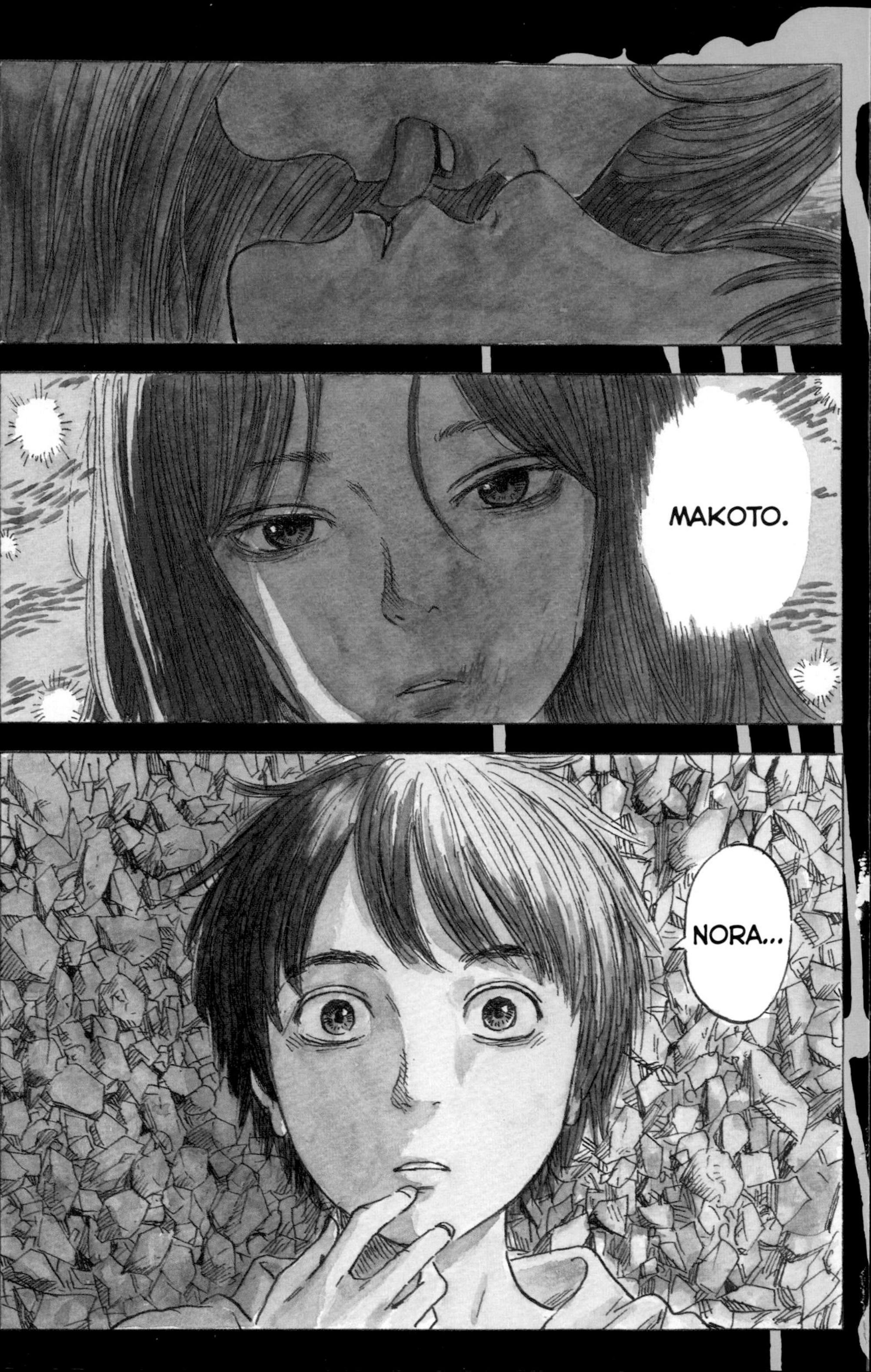
MAKOTO.
NORA...

Chapter 11: Yuuki

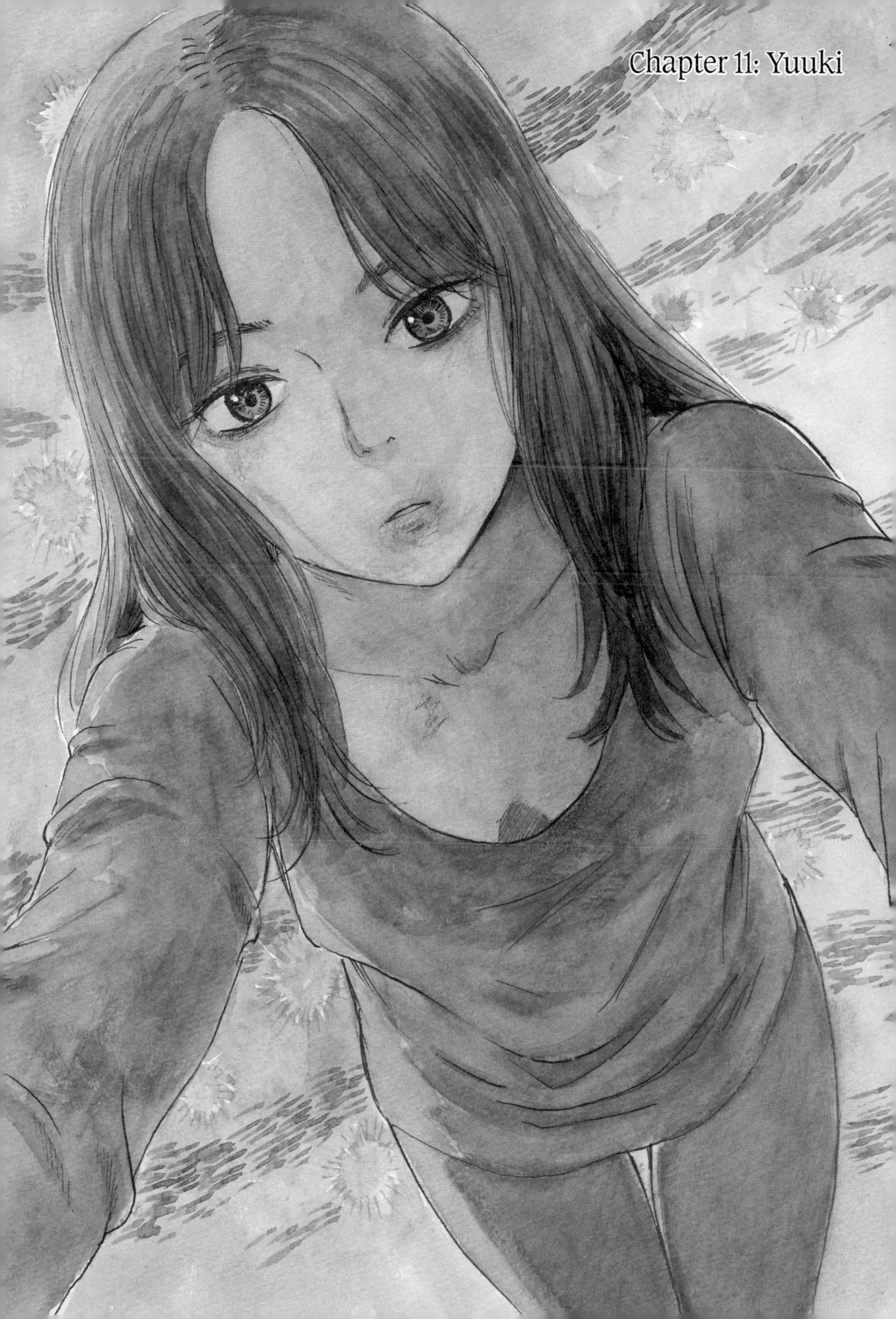

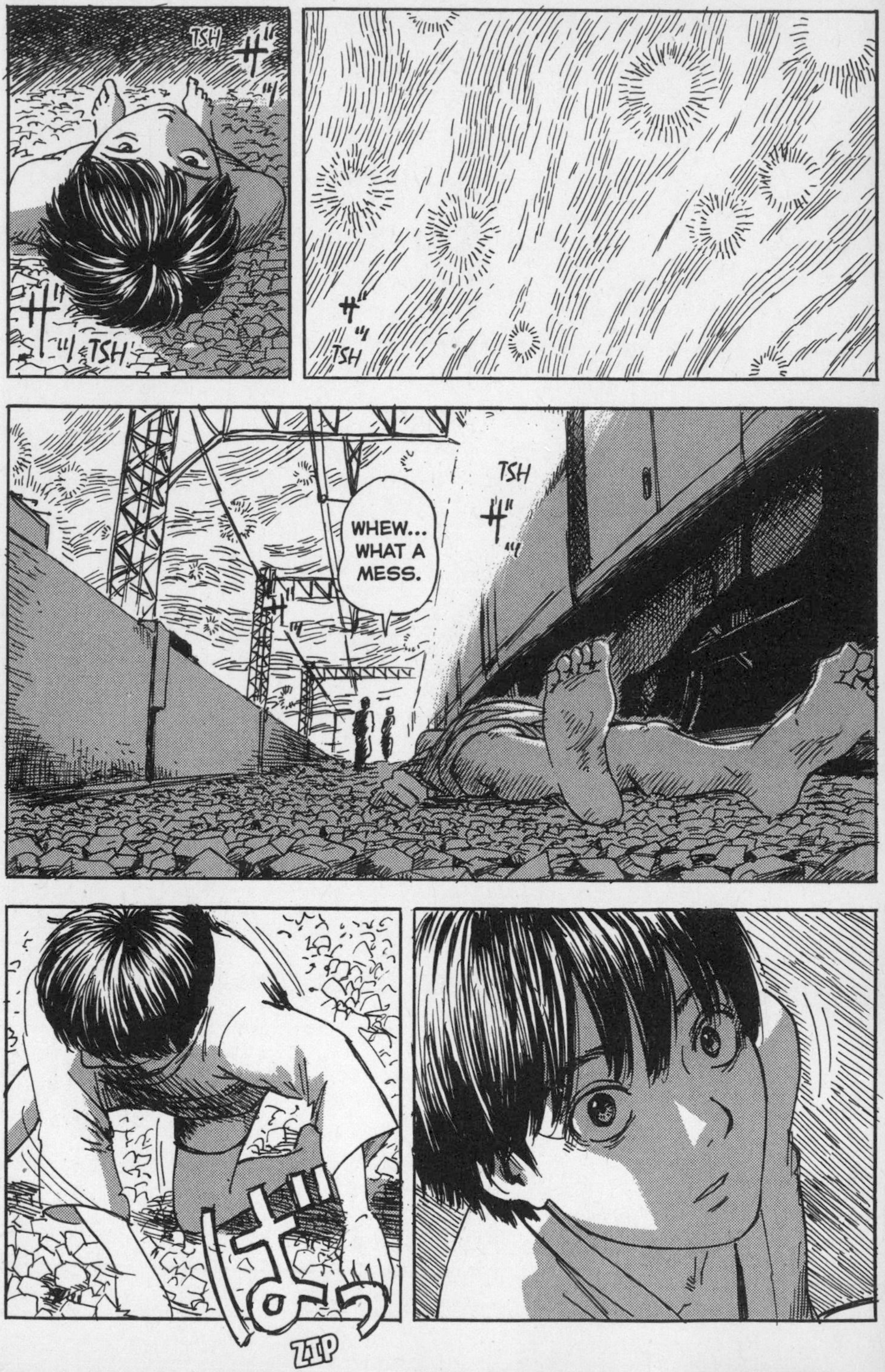
TSH
TSH
TSH
TSH
WHEW... WHAT A MESS.
ばっ
ZIP

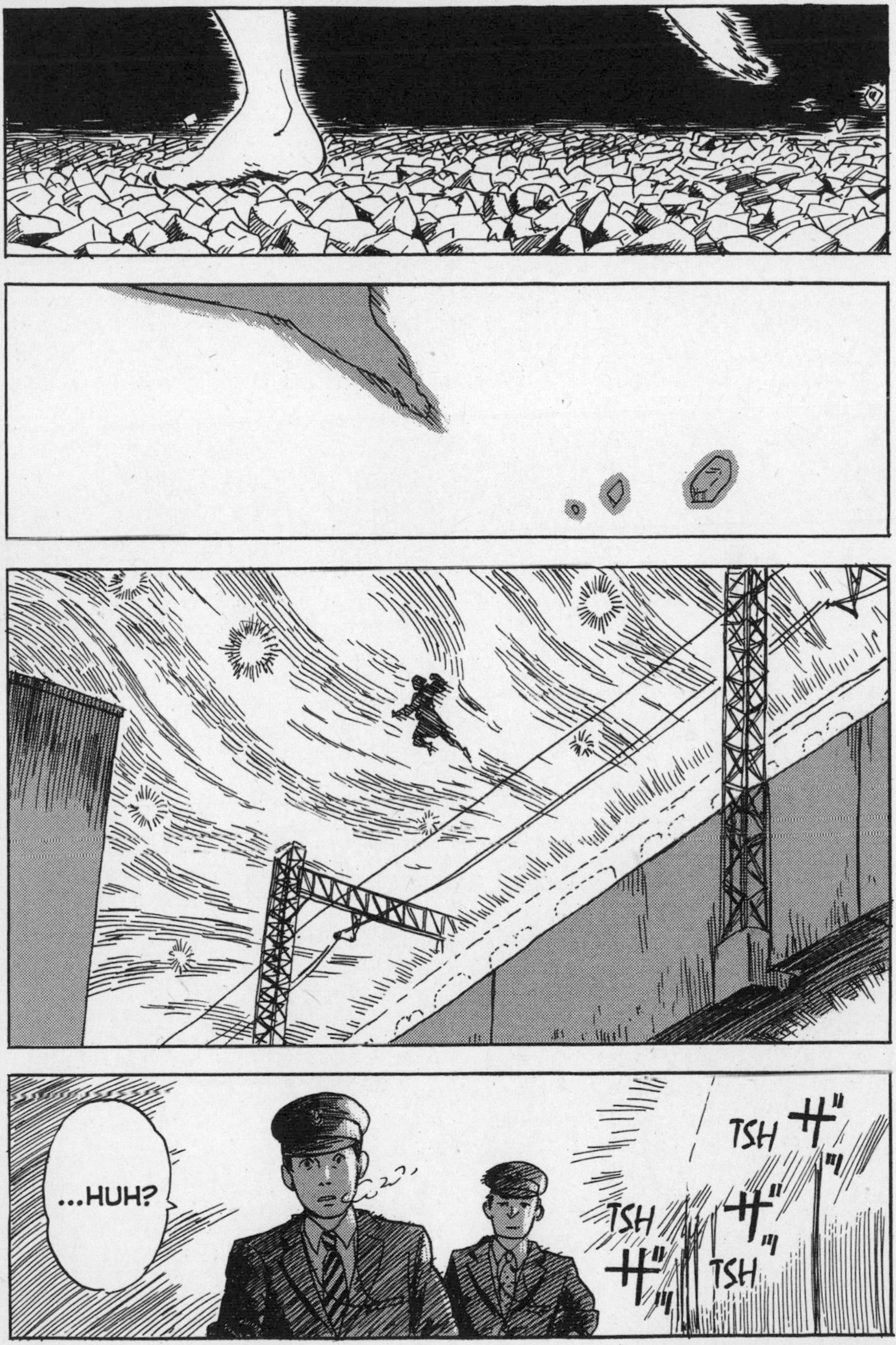
TSH
ザッ
TSH
ザッ
TSH
ザッ
...HUH?

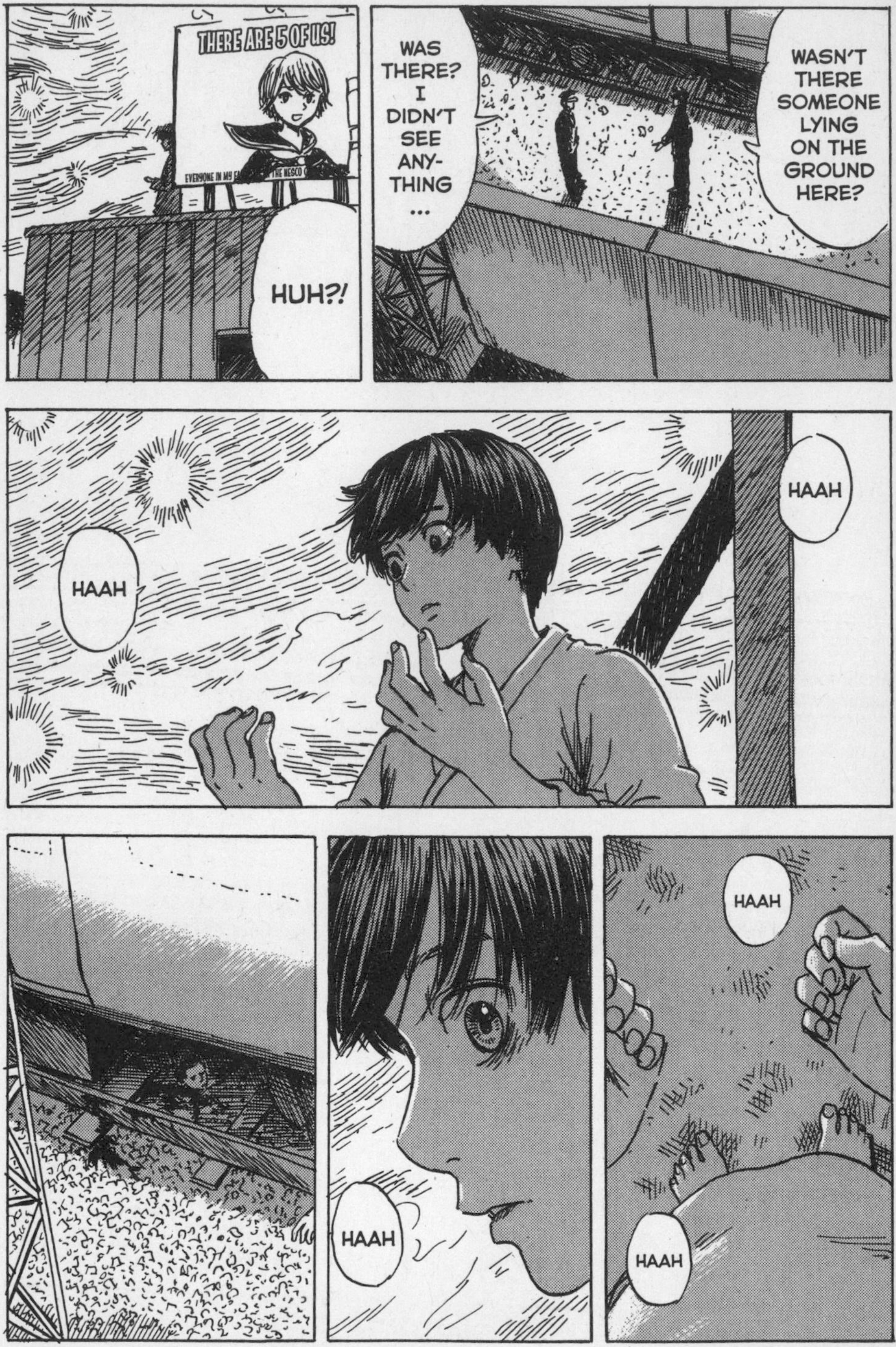
WASN'T THERE SOMEONE LYING ON THE GROUND HERE?
WAS THERE? I DIDN'T SEE ANYTHING...
THERE ARE 5 OF US!
HUH?!
HAAH
HAAH
HAAH
HAAH
HAAH

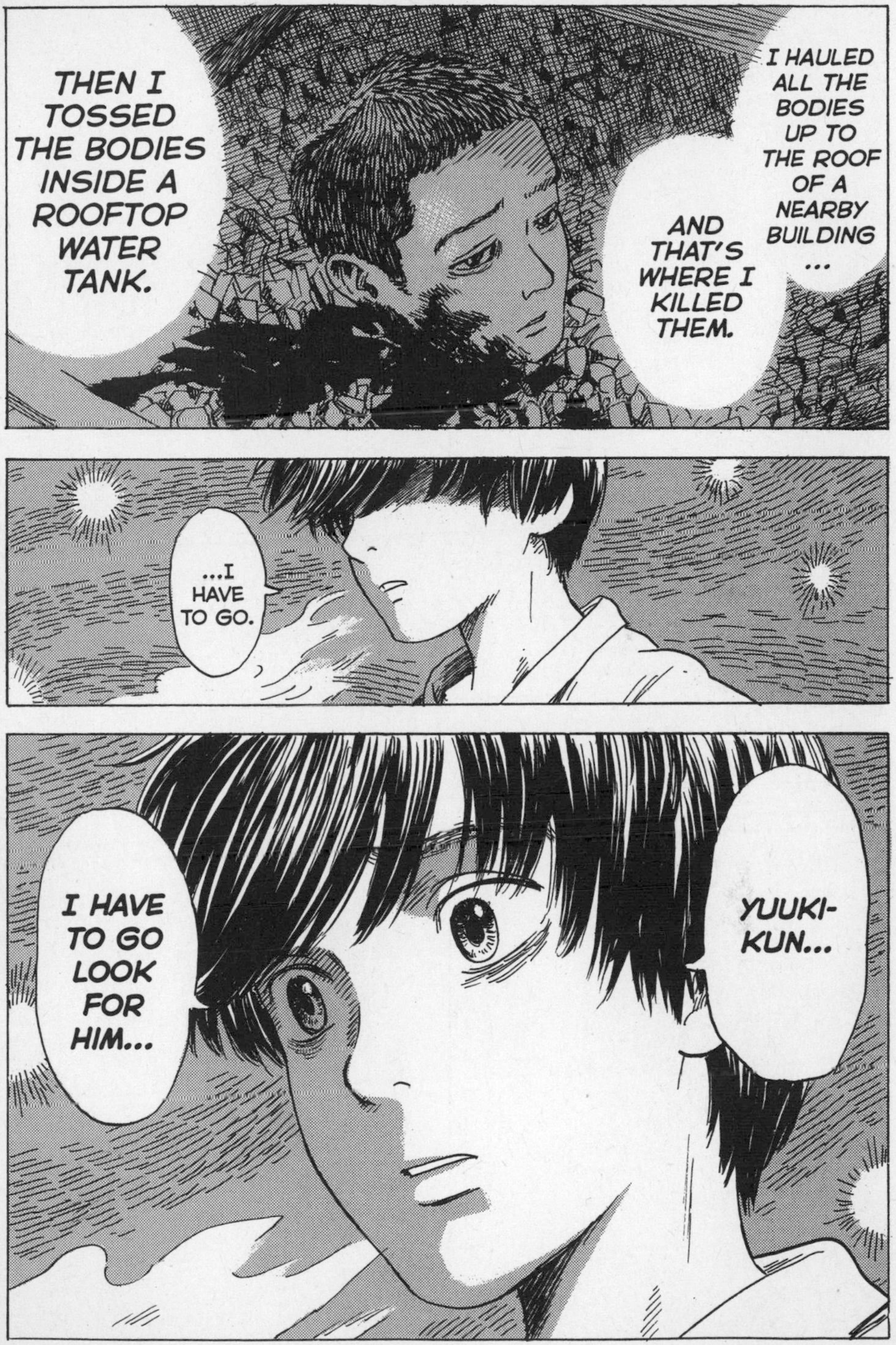
I HAULED ALL THE BODIES UP TO THE ROOF OF A NEARBY BUILDING ...
AND THAT'S WHERE I KILLED THEM.
THEN I TOSSED THE BODIES INSIDE A ROOFTOP WATER TANK.
...I HAVE TO GO.
YUUKI-KUN...
I HAVE TO GO LOOK FOR HIM...

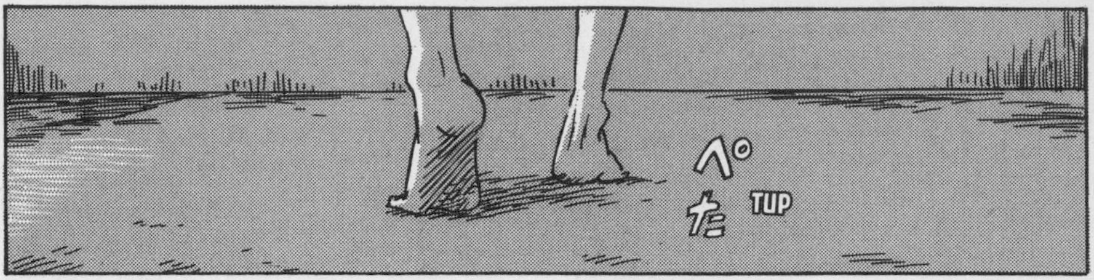
ぺた
TUP
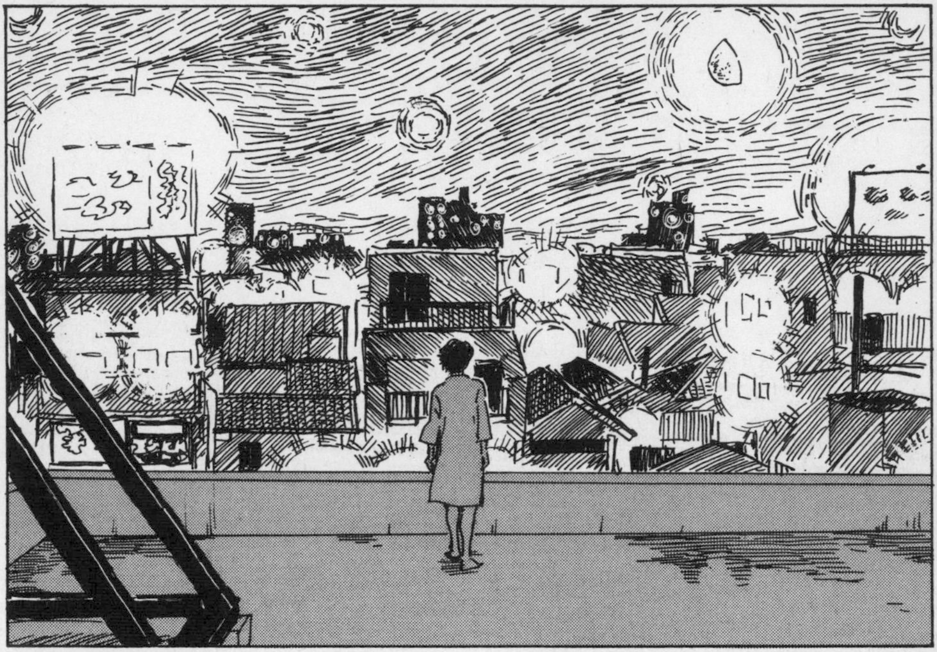
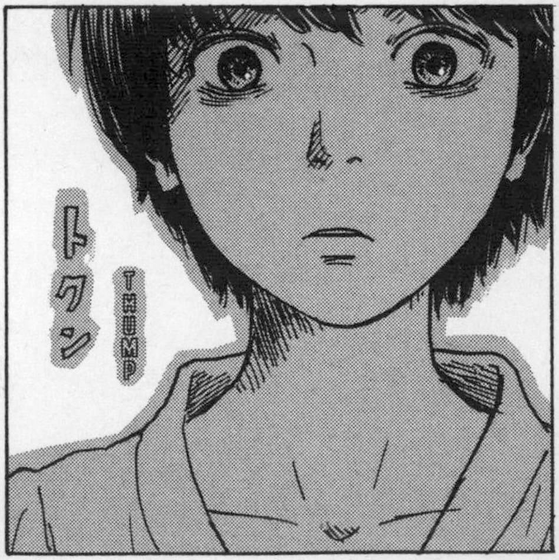
トクン
THUMP
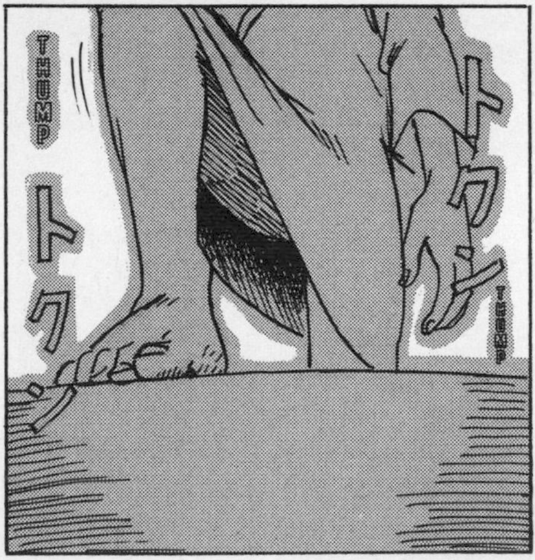
トクン
THUMP
トクン
THUMP

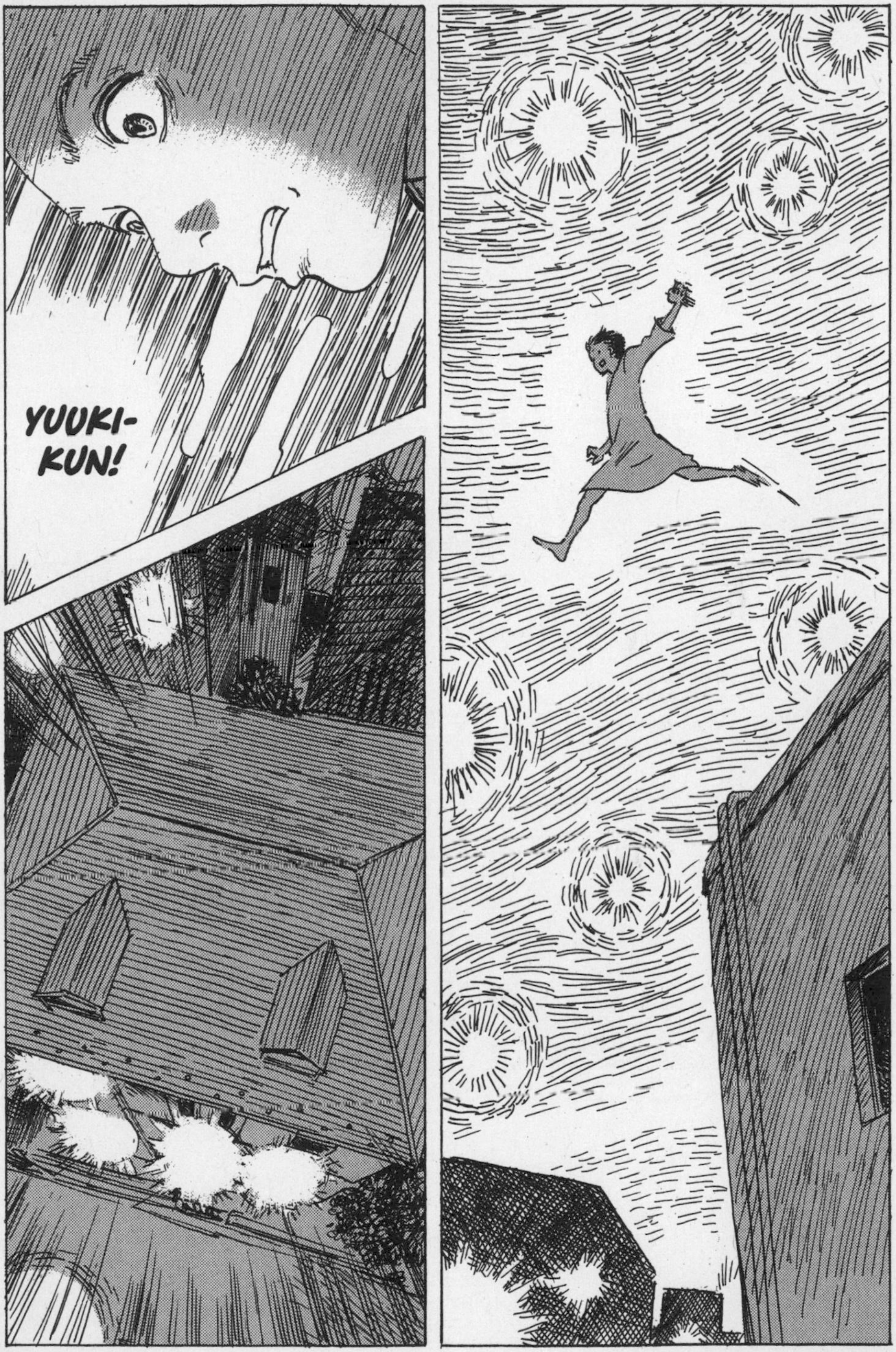
YUUKI-
KUN!

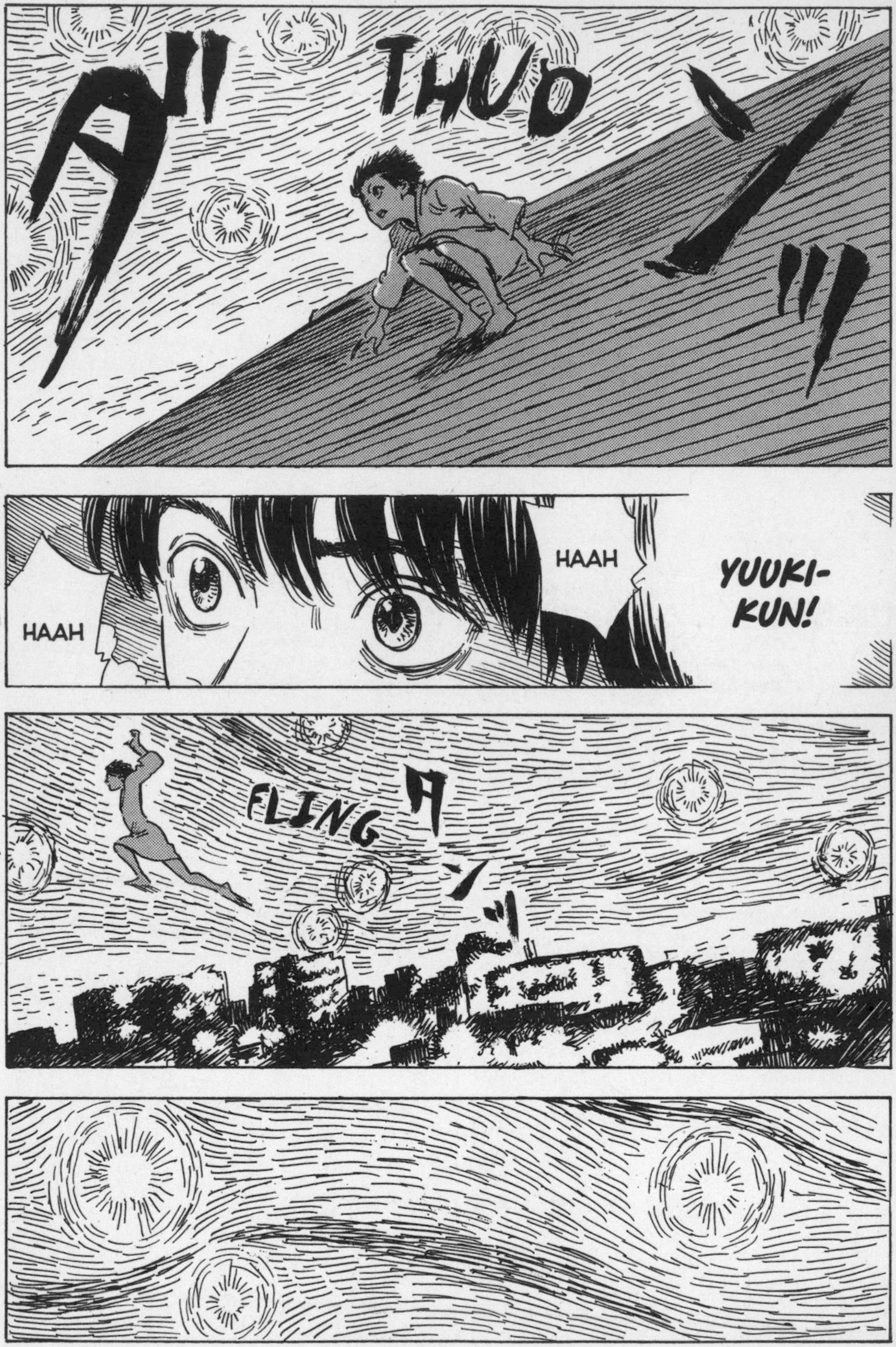
THUD
YUUKI-KUN!
HAAH
HAAH
FLING

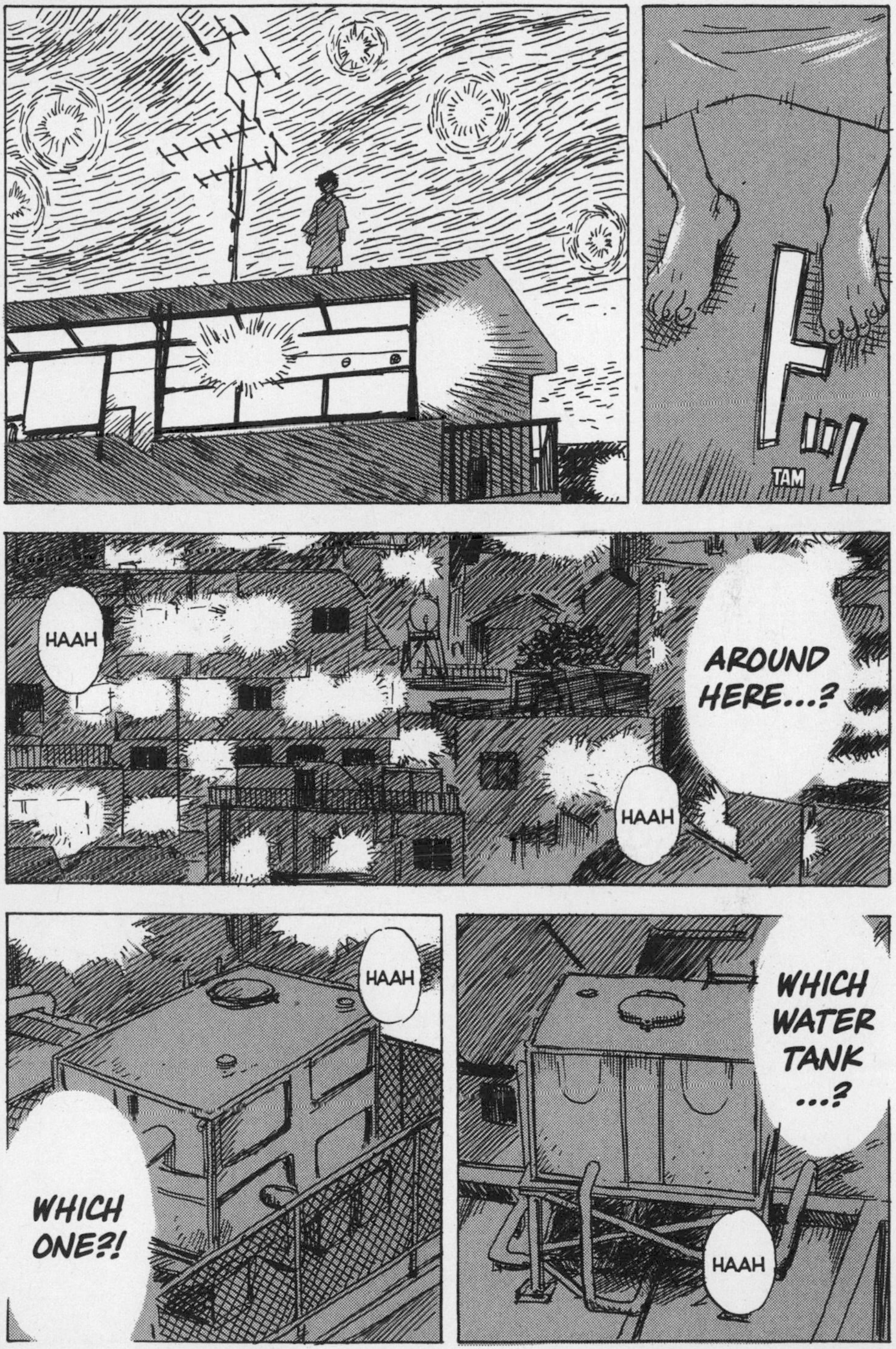
TAM
AROUND HERE...?
HAAH
HAAH
WHICH WATER TANK ...?
HAAH
HAAH
WHICH ONE?!

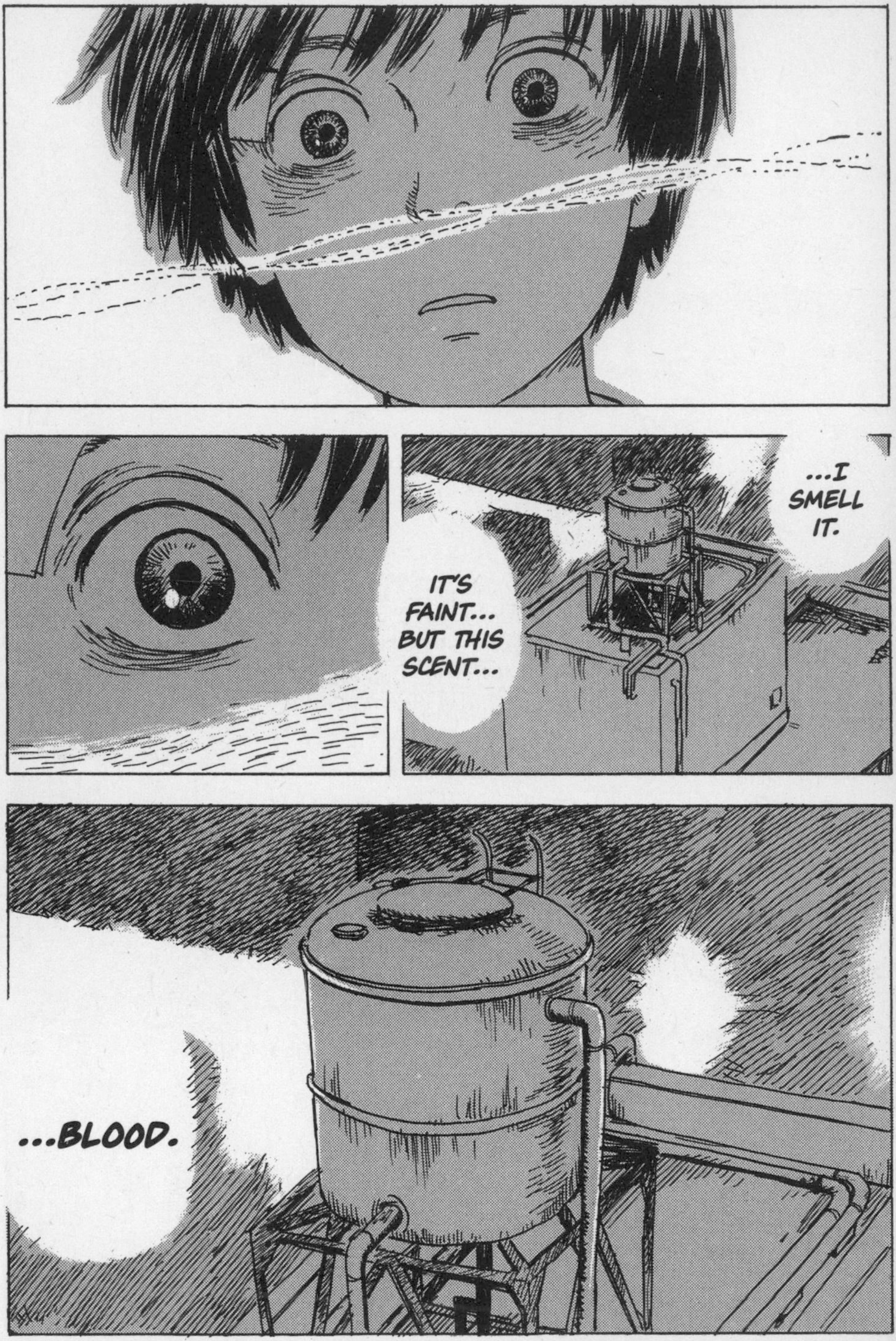
...I SMELL IT.
IT'S FAINT... BUT THIS SCENT...
...BLOOD.

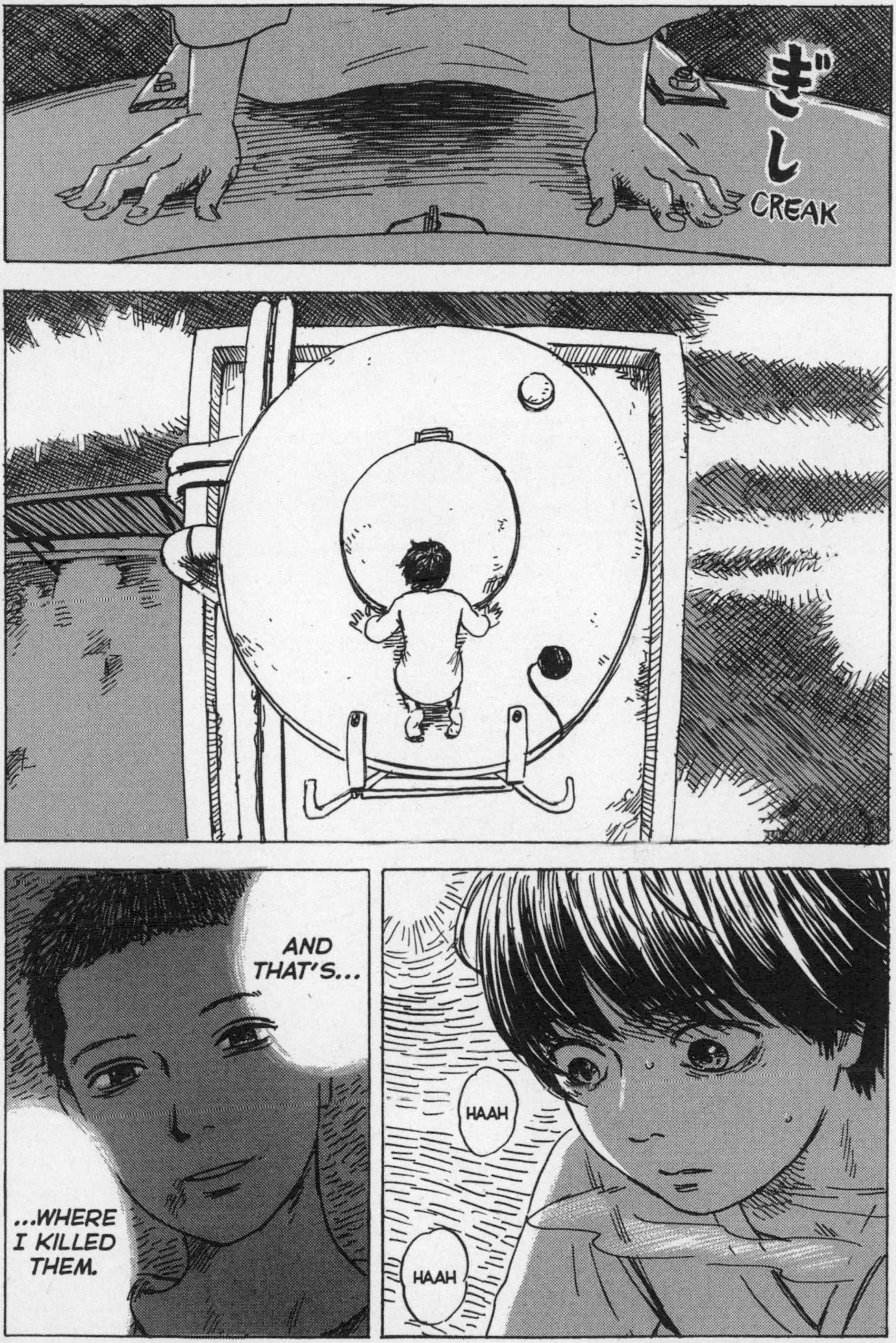
ぎし
CREAK
HAAH
HAAH
AND THAT'S...
...WHERE I KILLED THEM.

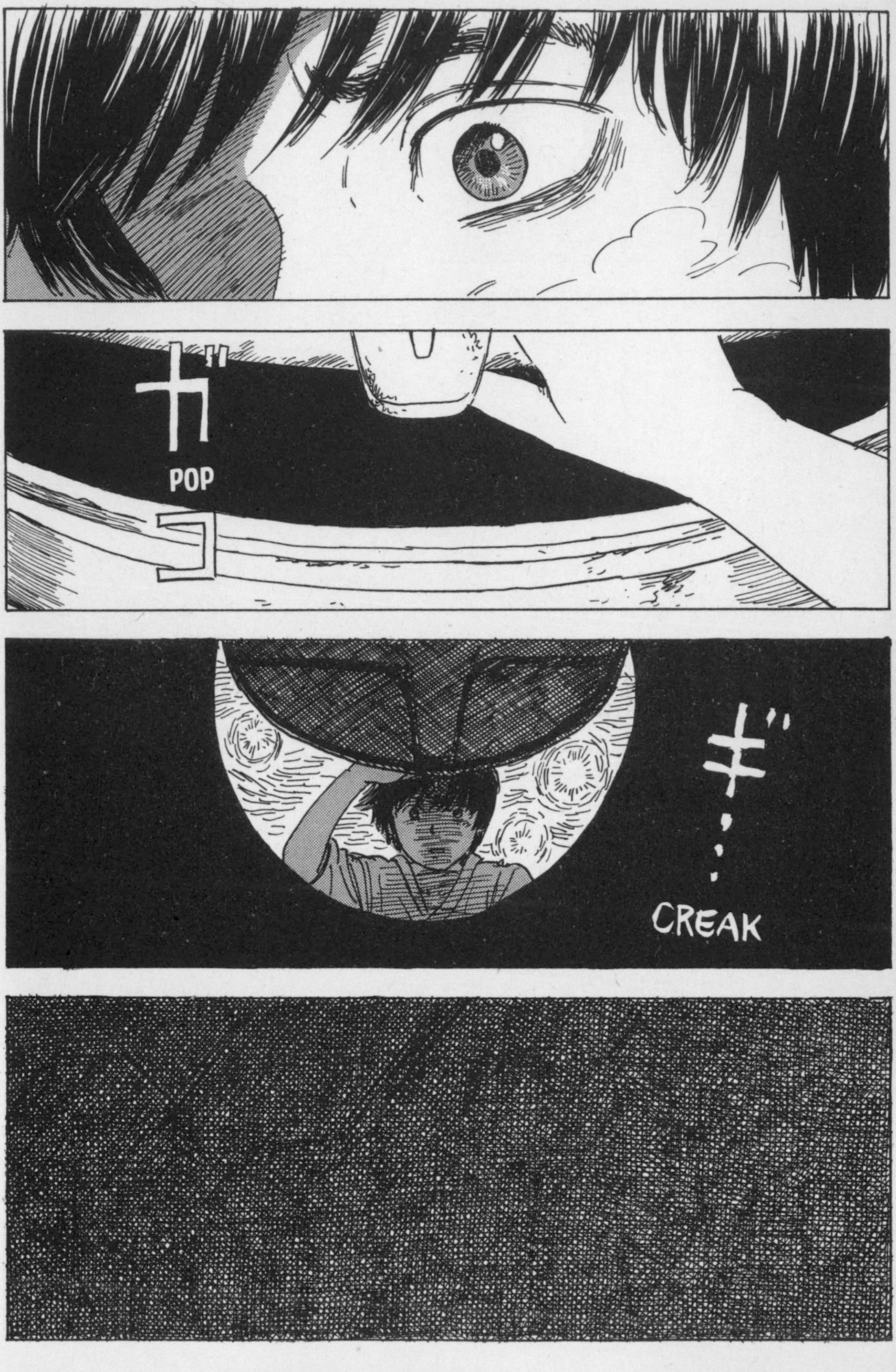
ガ
POP
ゴ
ギ…
CREAK

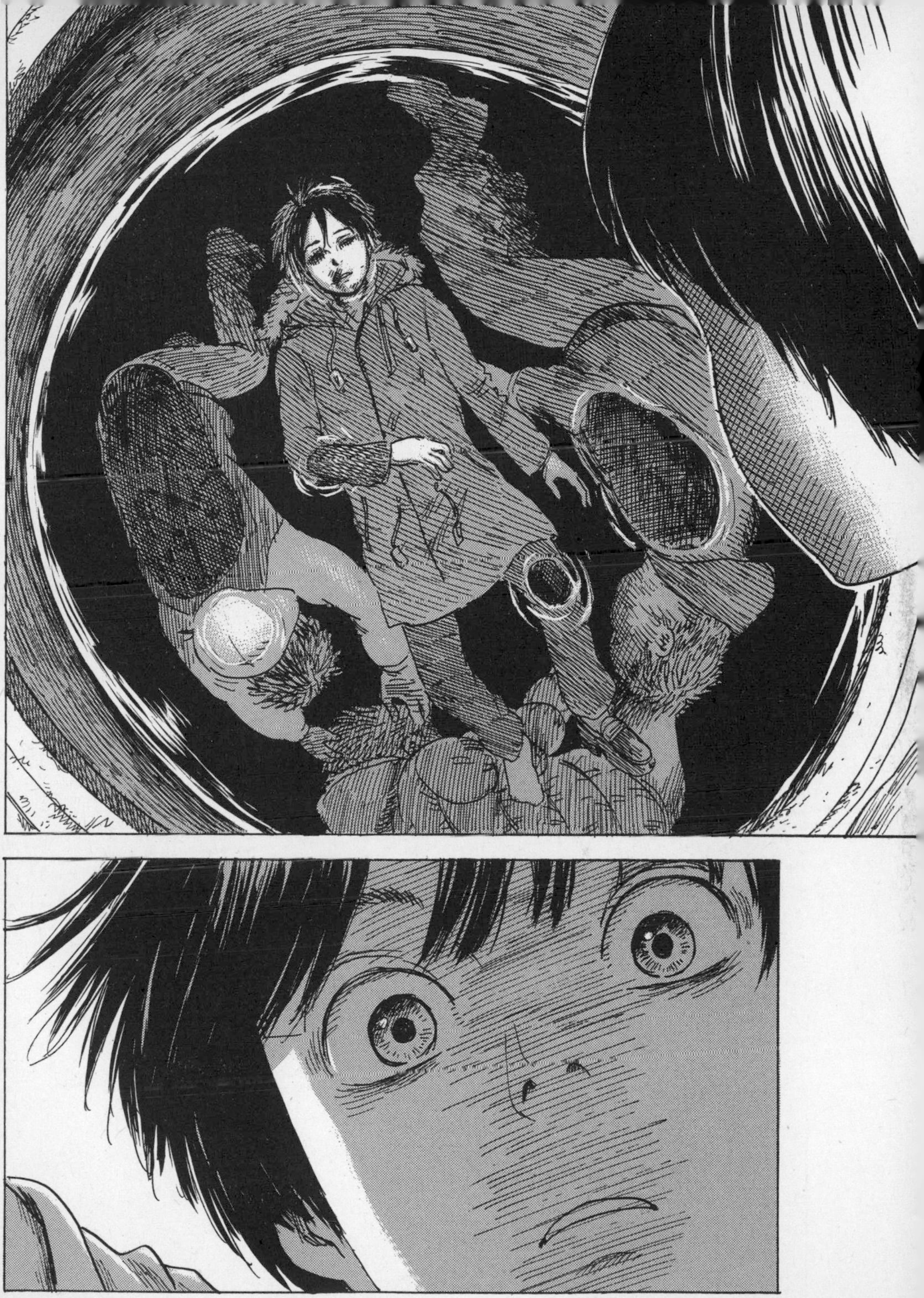

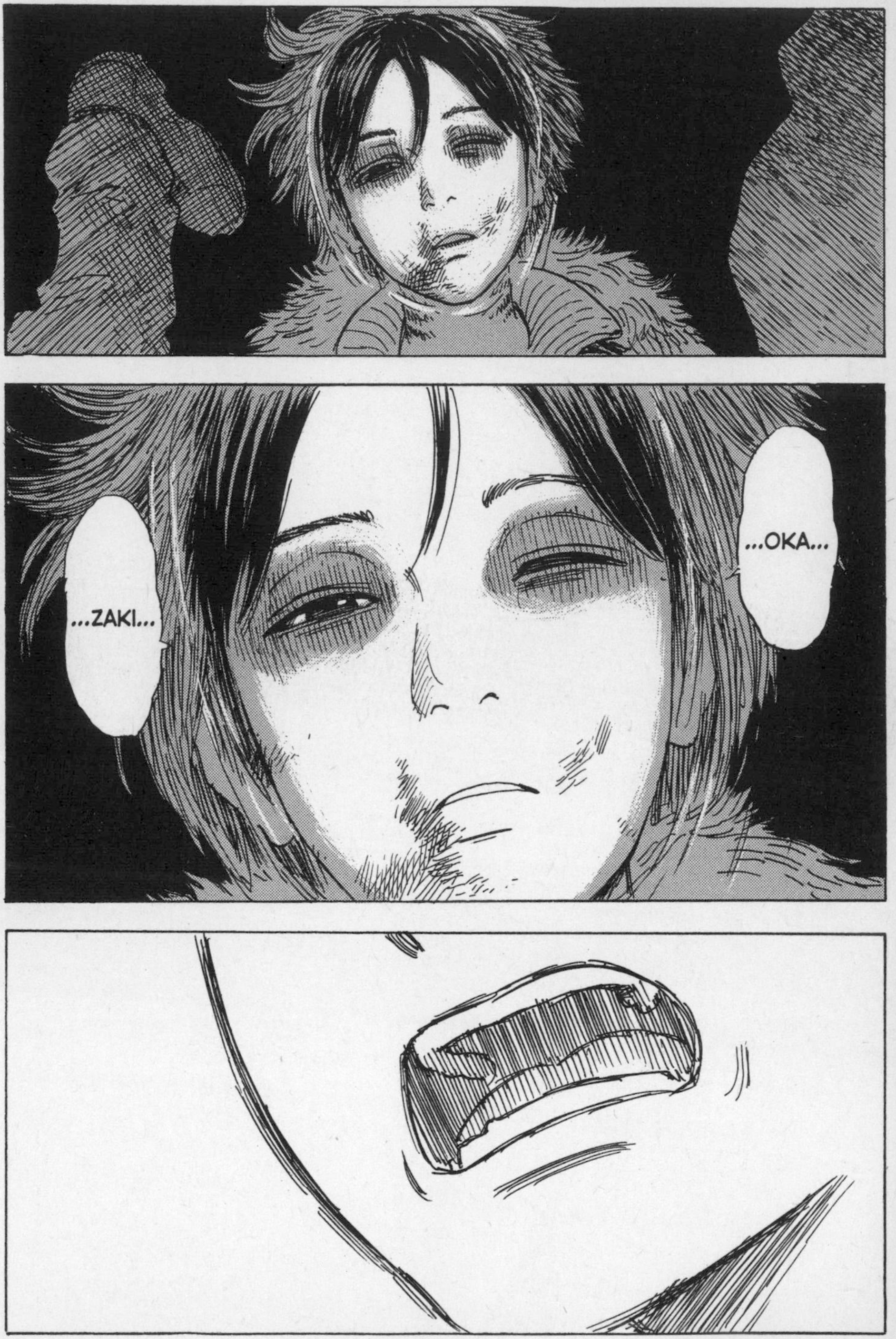
...OKA...
...ZAKI...

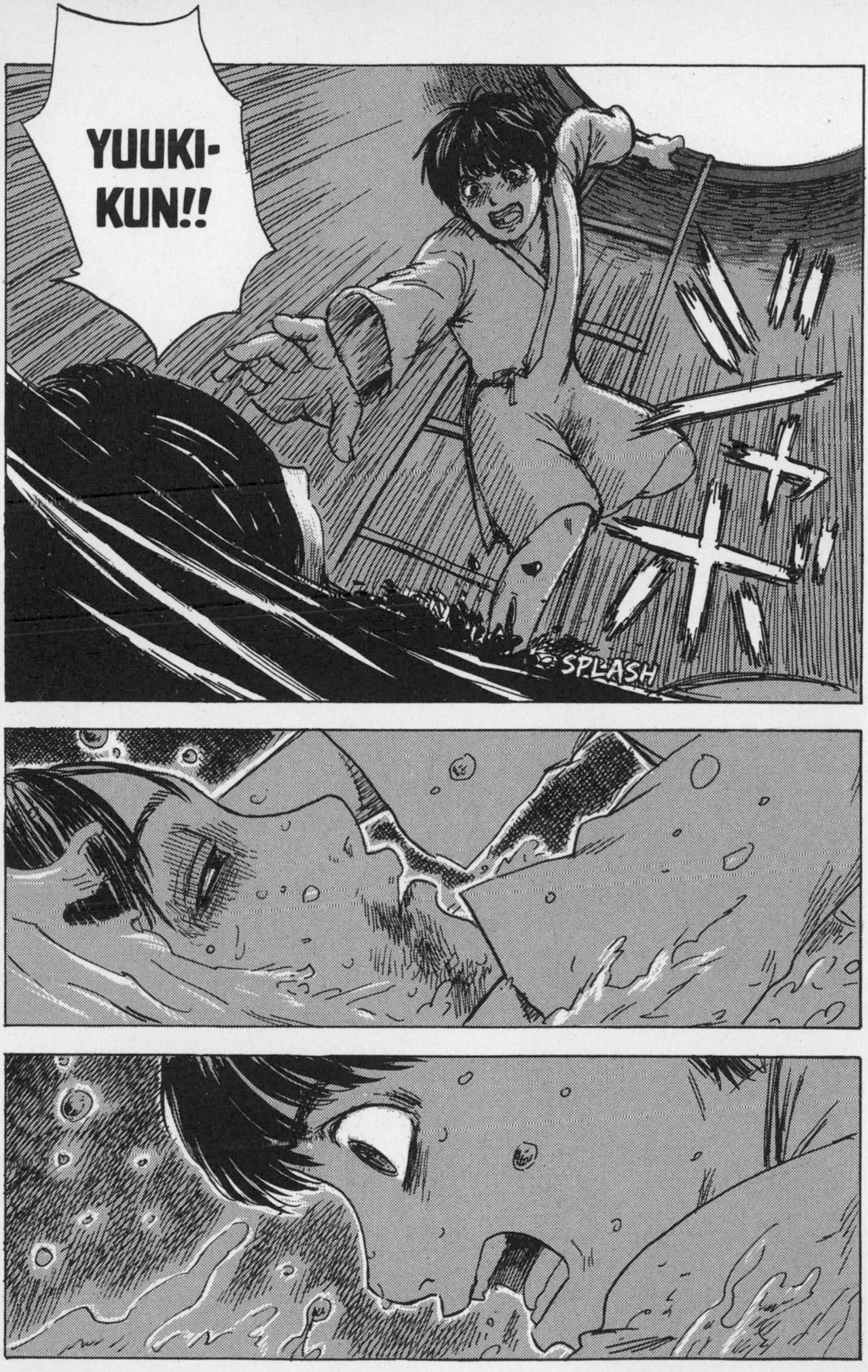
YUUKI-
KUN!!
SPLASH

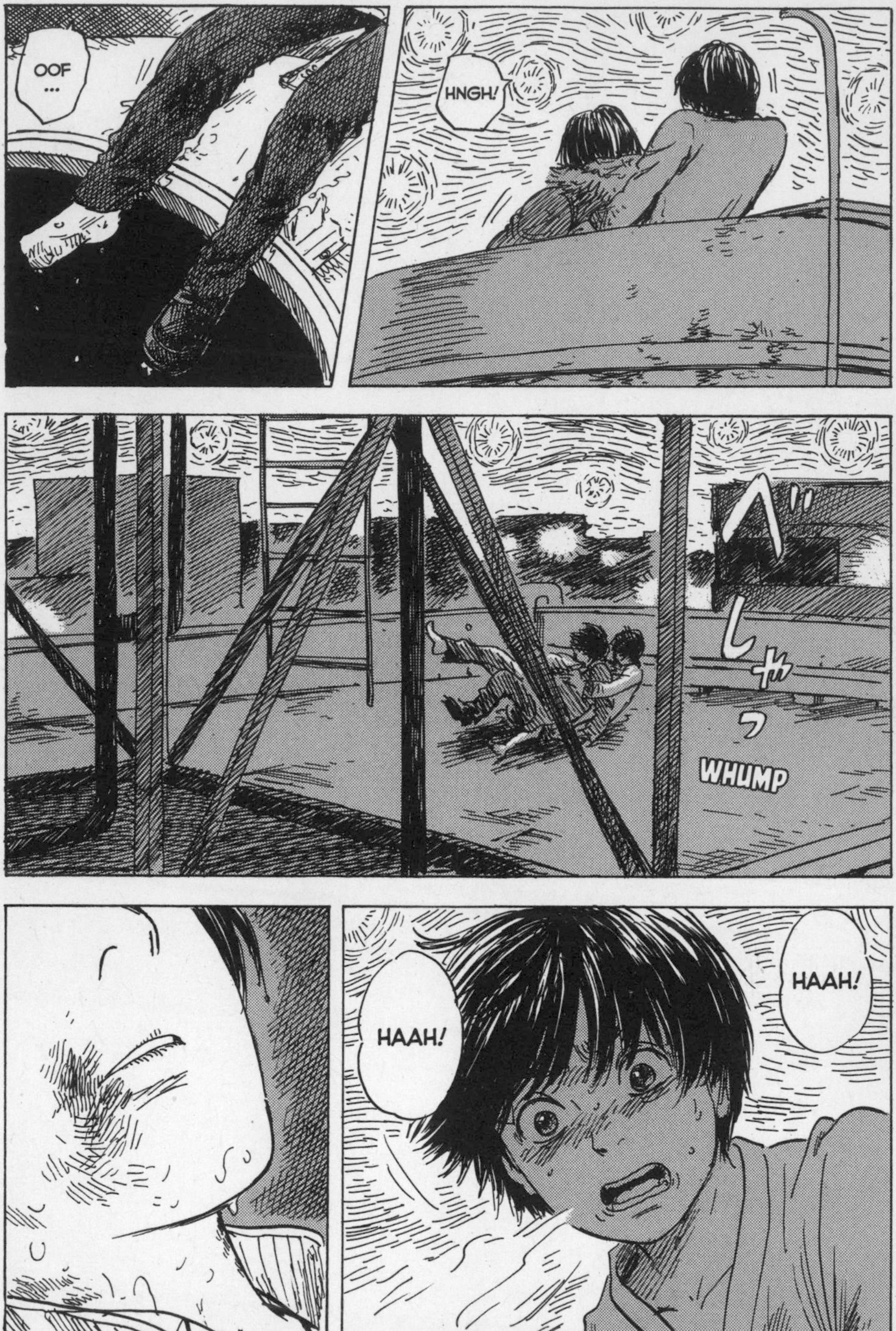
HNGH!
OOF ...
べしゃっ
WHUMP
HAAH!
HAAH!

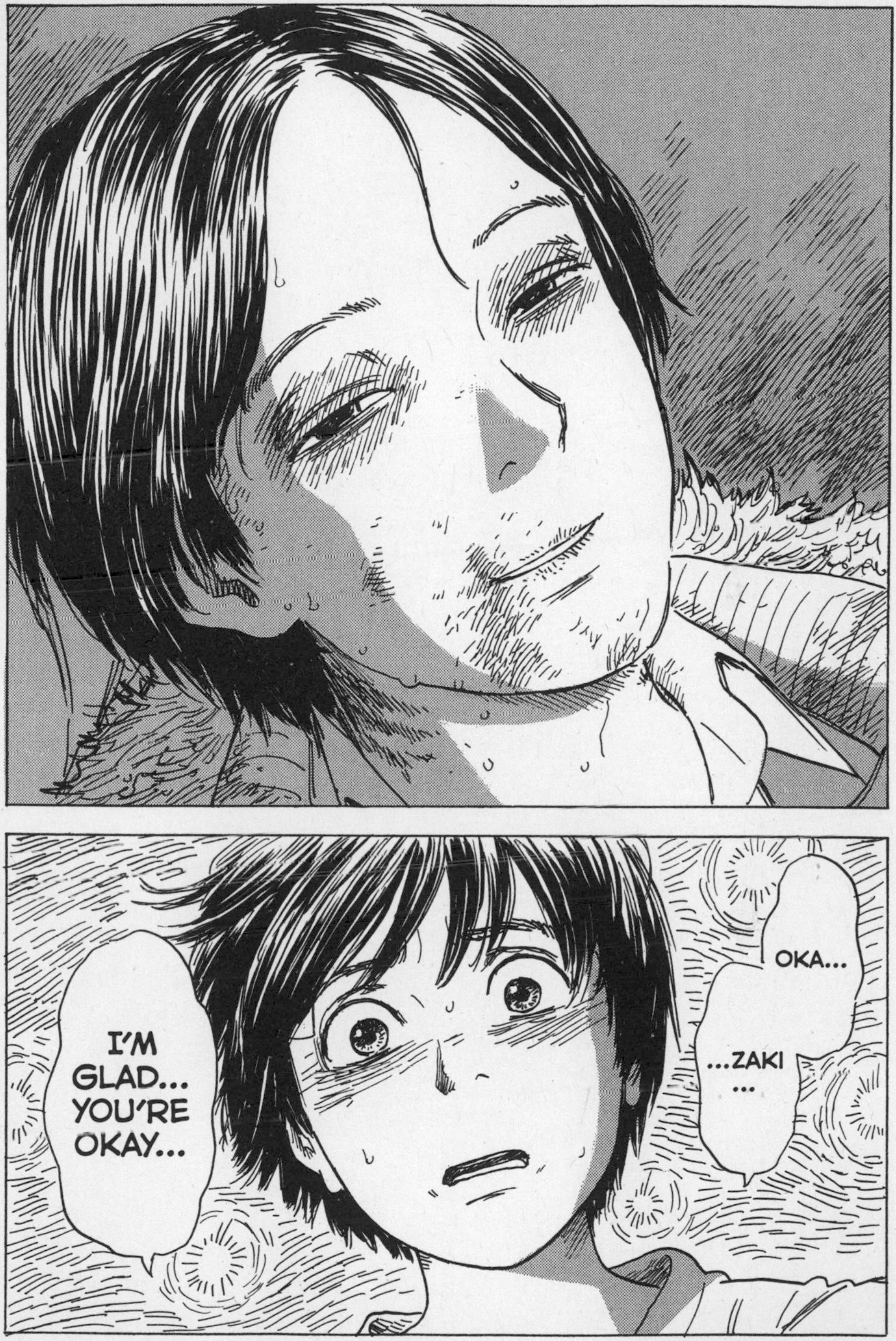
OKA...
...ZAKI ...
I'M GLAD... YOU'RE OKAY...

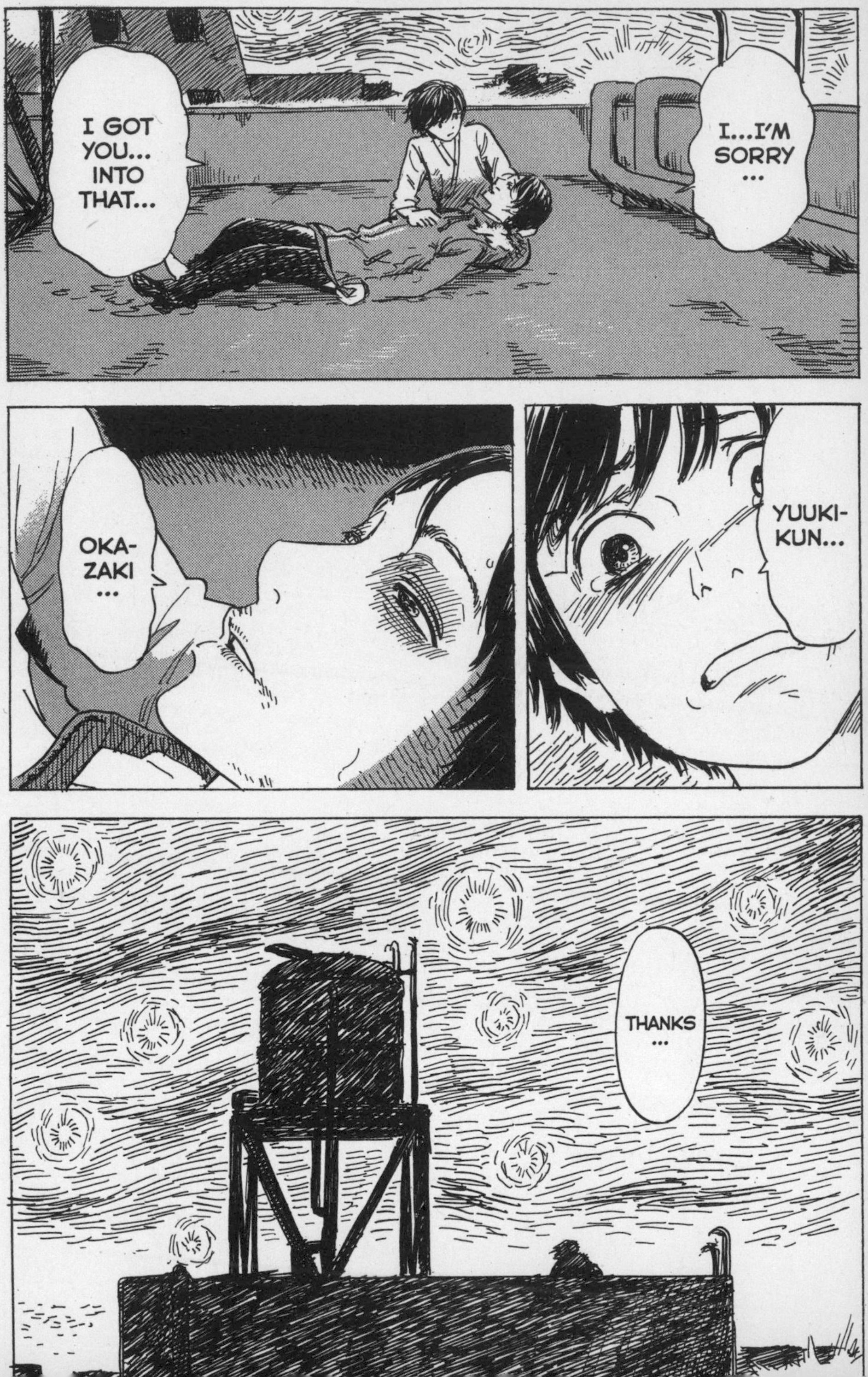
I...I'M SORRY...
I GOT YOU... INTO THAT...
YUUKI-KUN...
OKA-ZAKI...
THANKS...

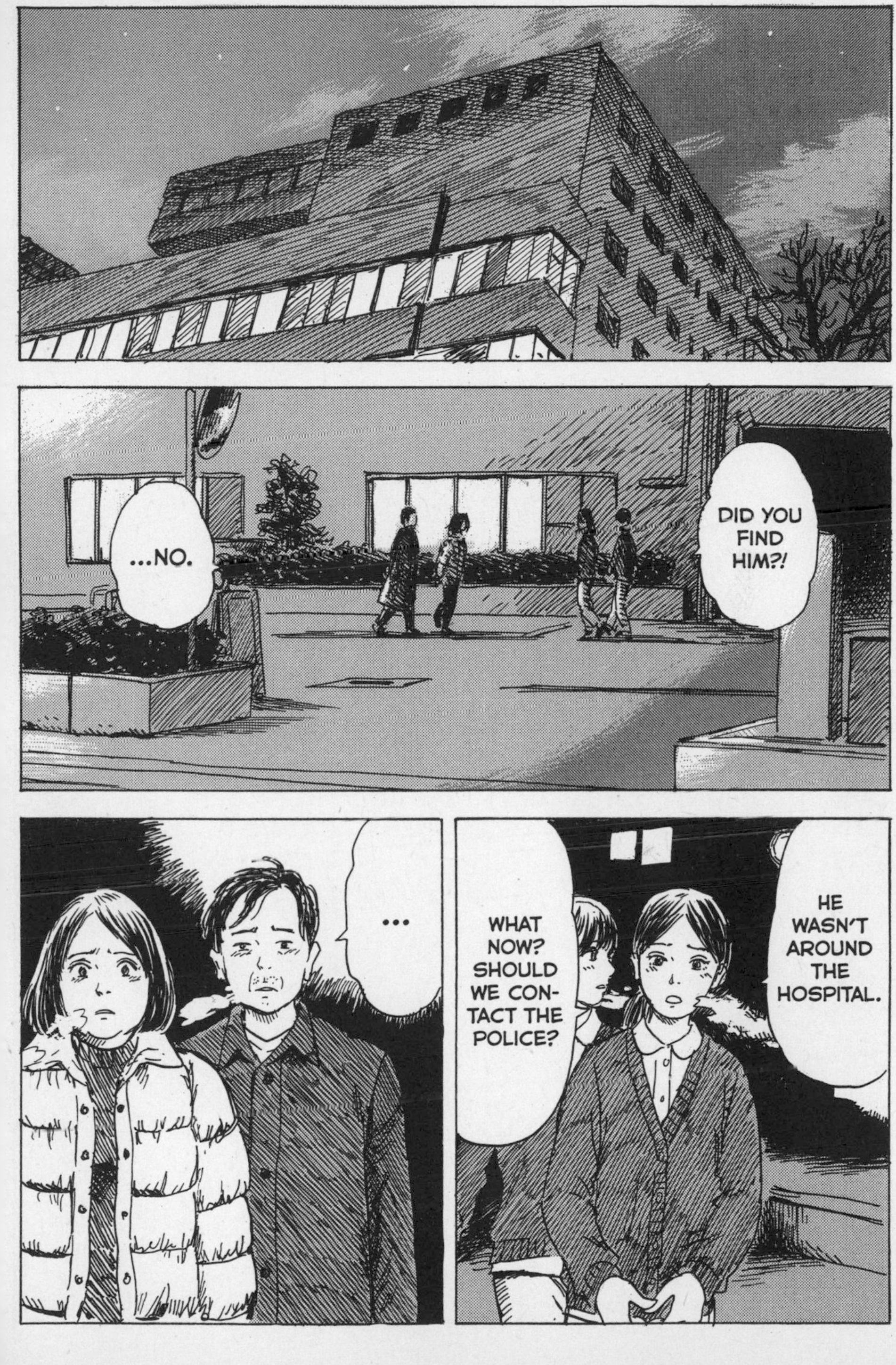
DID YOU FIND HIM?!
...NO.
HE WASN'T AROUND THE HOSPITAL.
WHAT NOW? SHOULD WE CON-TACT THE POLICE?
...

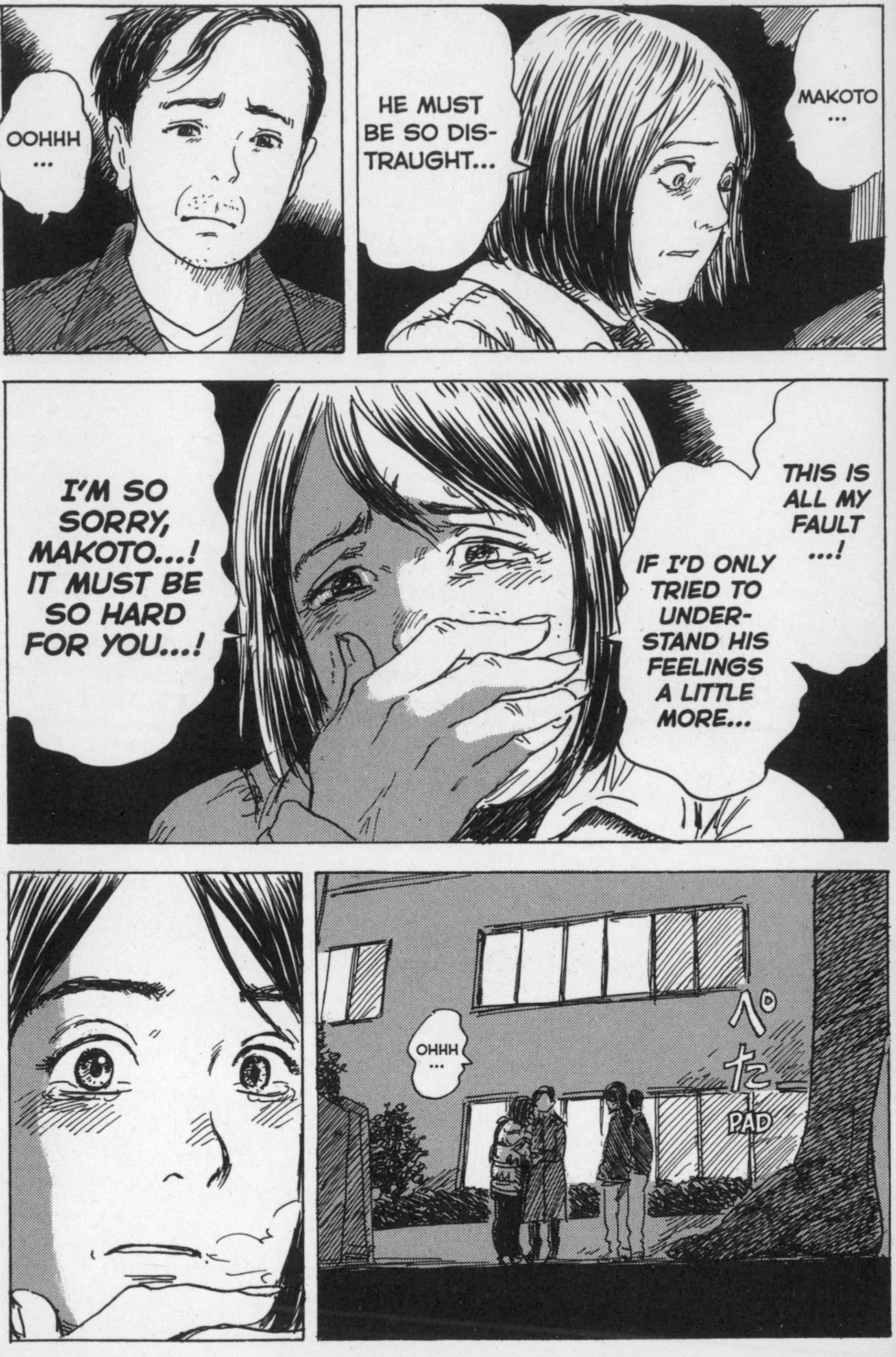
MAKOTO ...
HE MUST BE SO DIS- TRAUGHT...
OOHHH ...
THIS IS ALL MY FAULT ...!
IF I'D ONLY TRIED TO UNDER- STAND HIS FEELINGS A LITTLE MORE...
I'M SO SORRY, MAKOTO...! IT MUST BE SO HARD FOR YOU...!
OHHH ...
ペた
PAD

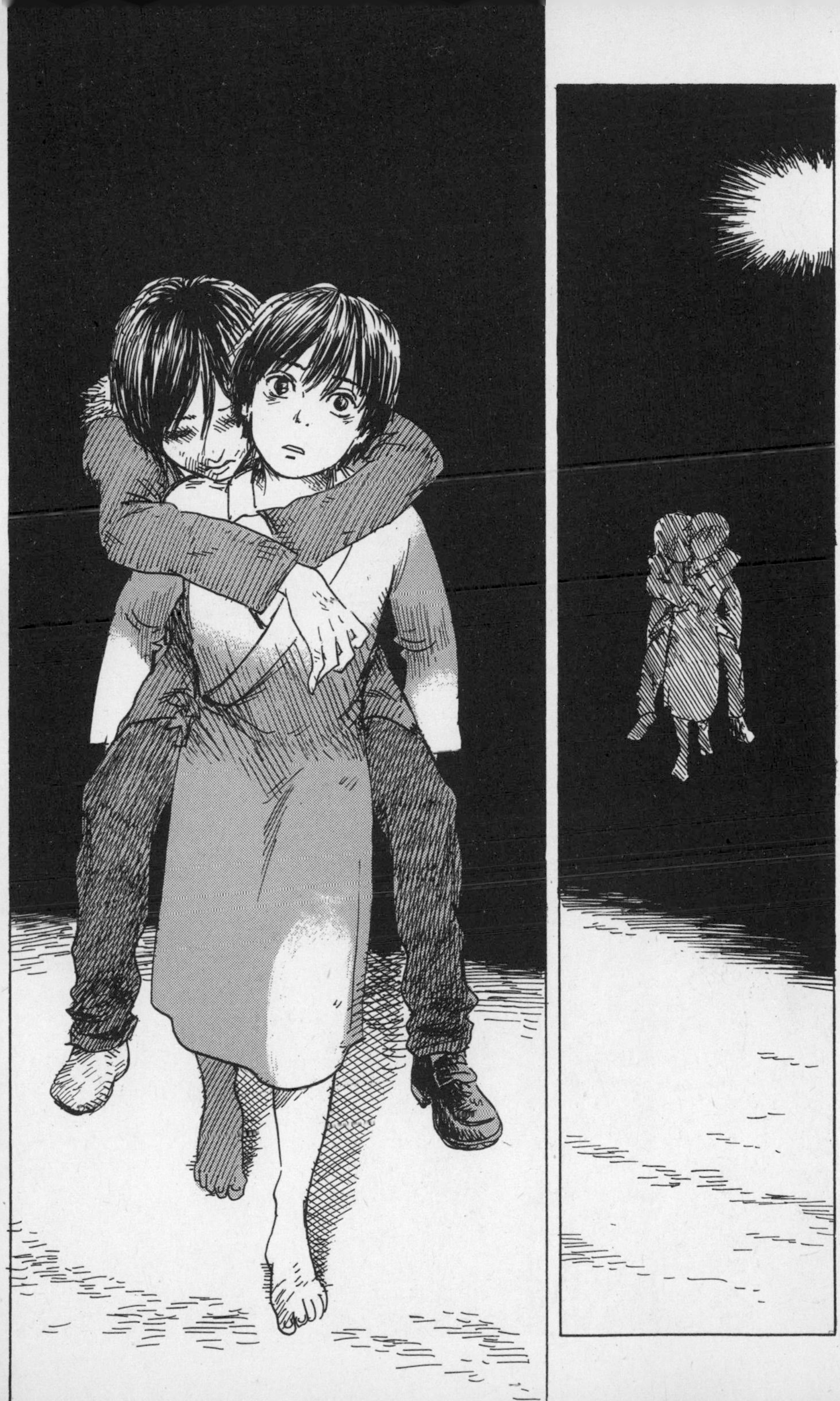

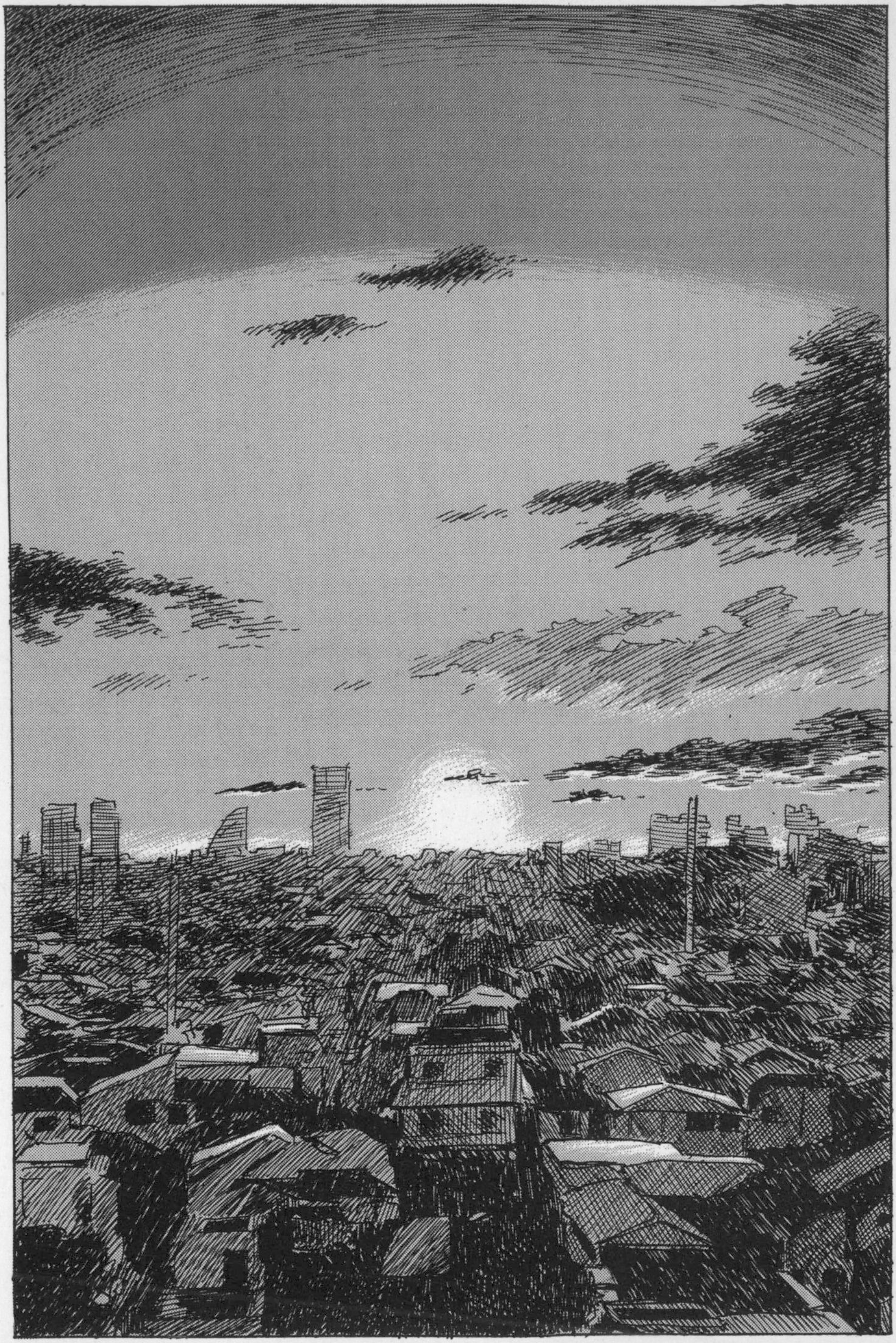

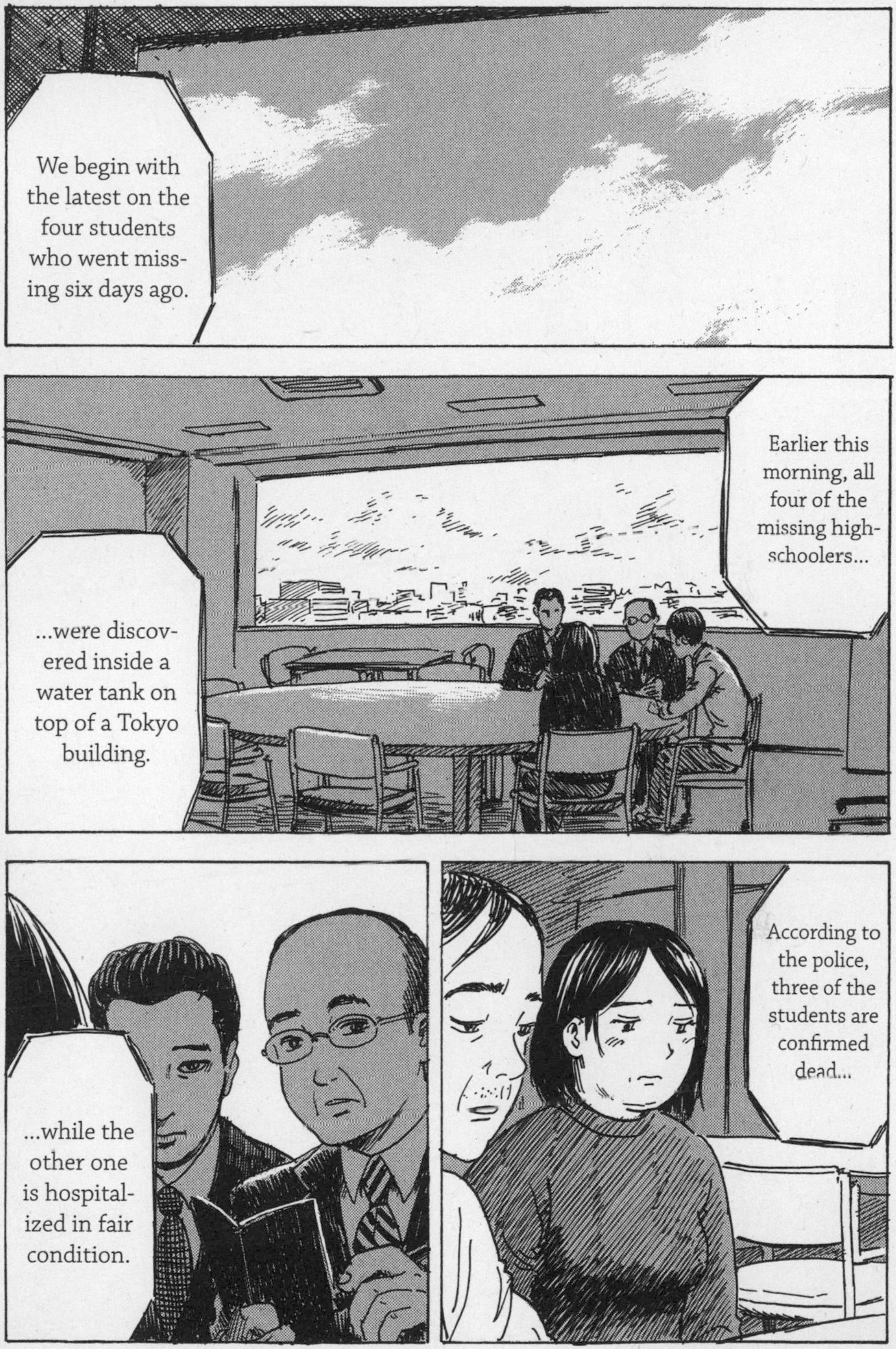
We begin with the latest on the four students who went miss-ing six days ago.
Earlier this morning, all four of the missing high-schoolers...
...were discov-ered inside a water tank on top of a Tokyo building.
According to the police, three of the students are confirmed dead...
...while the other one is hospital-ized in fair condition.

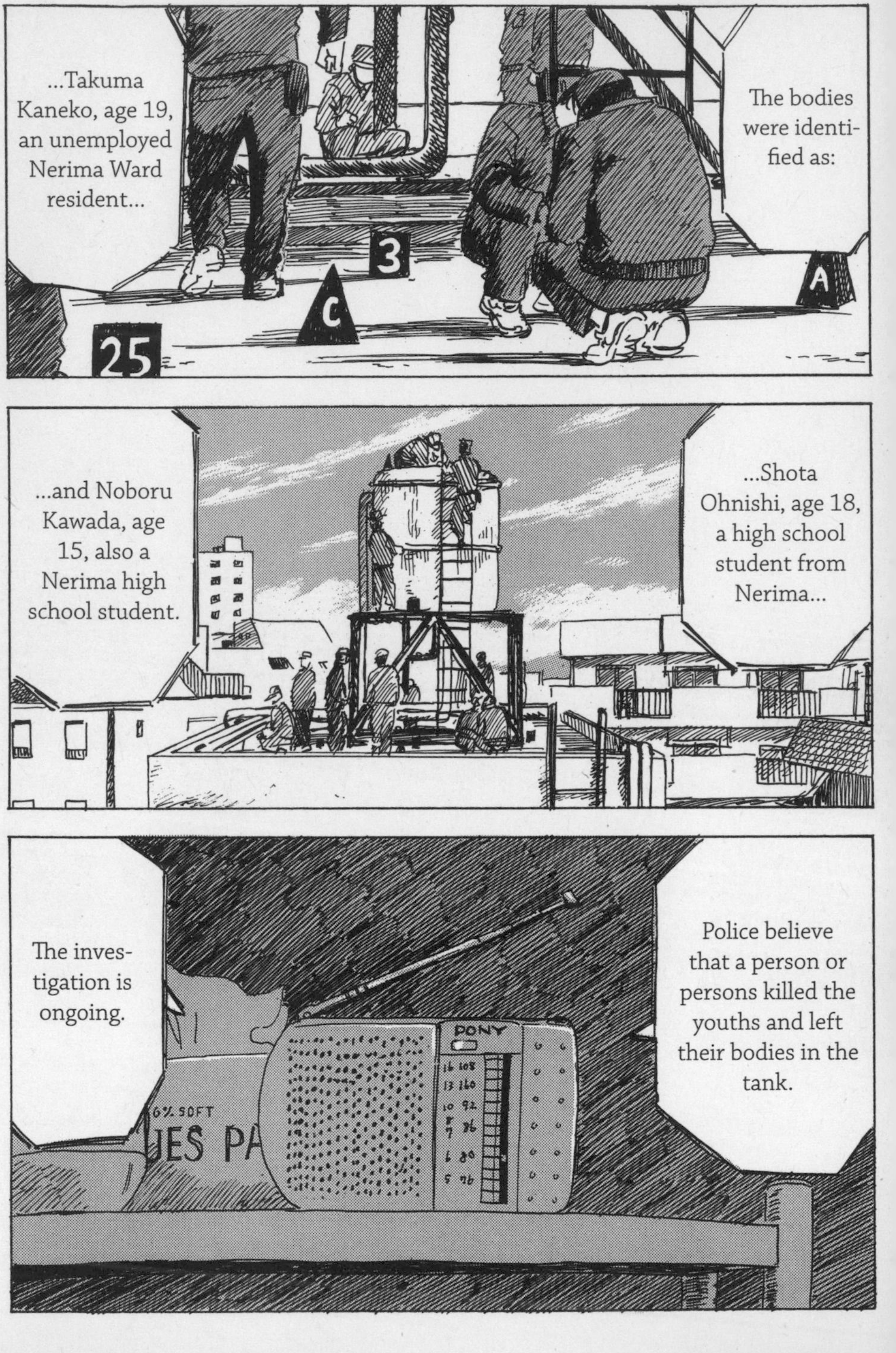
The bodies were identi-fied as:
...Takuma Kaneko, age 19, an unemployed Nerima Ward resident...
3
C
A
25
...Shota Ohnishi, age 18, a high school student from Nerima...
...and Noboru Kawada, age 15, also a Nerima high school student.
Police believe that a person or persons killed the youths and left their bodies in the tank.
PONY
The inves-tigation is ongoing.

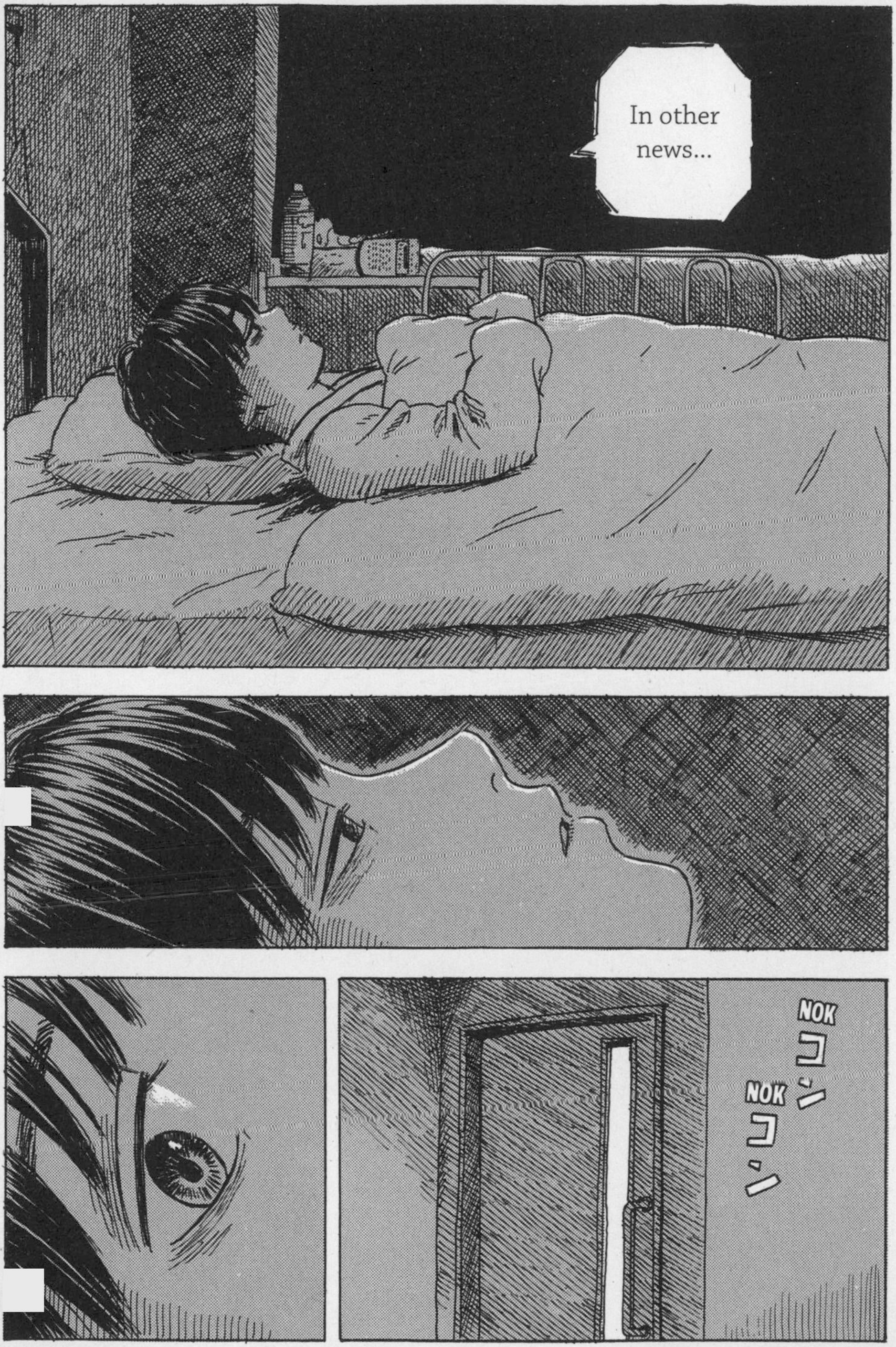
In other news...
NOK
コン
NOK
コン

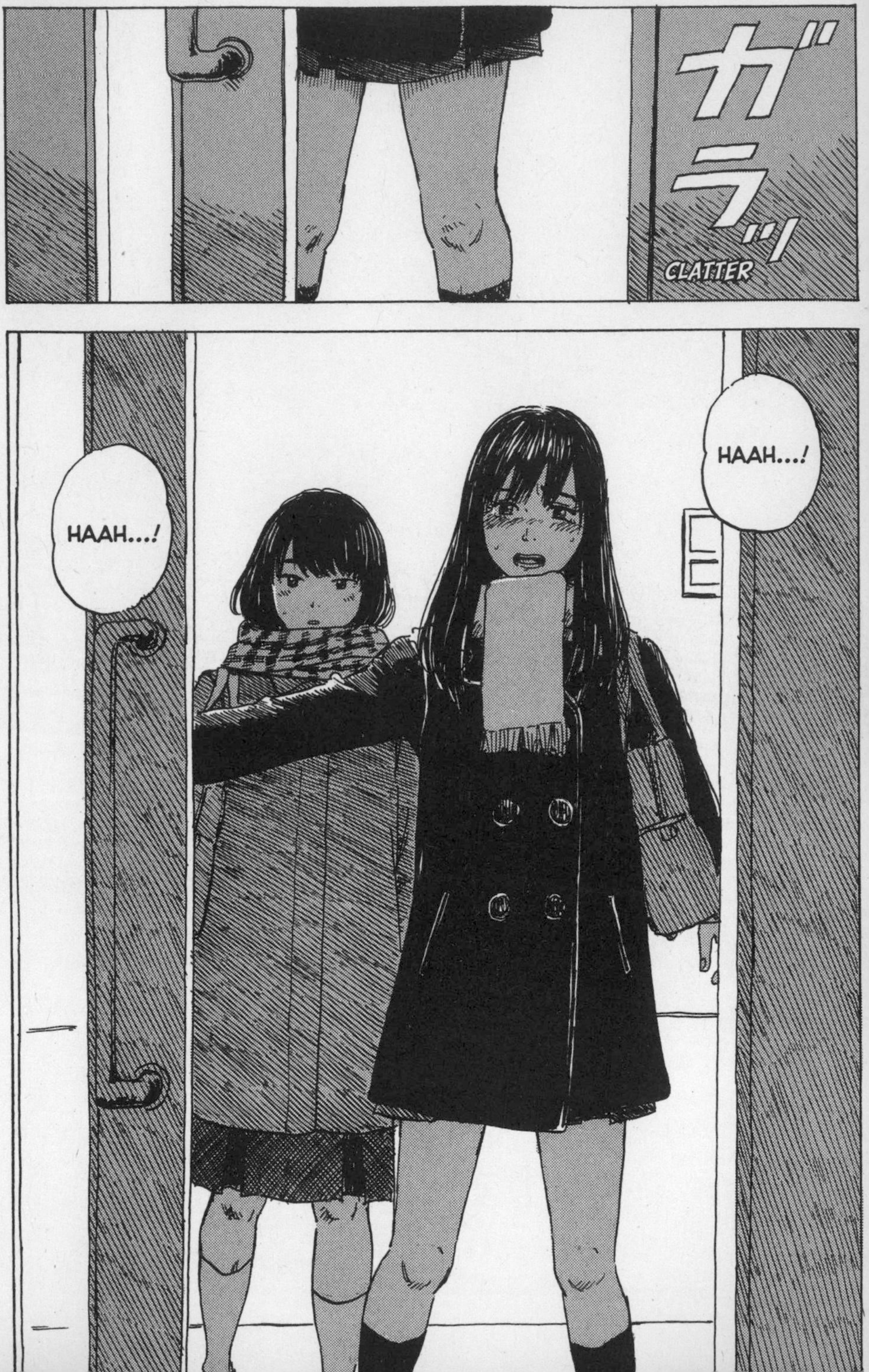
ガラッ
CLATTER
HAAH...!
HAAH...!

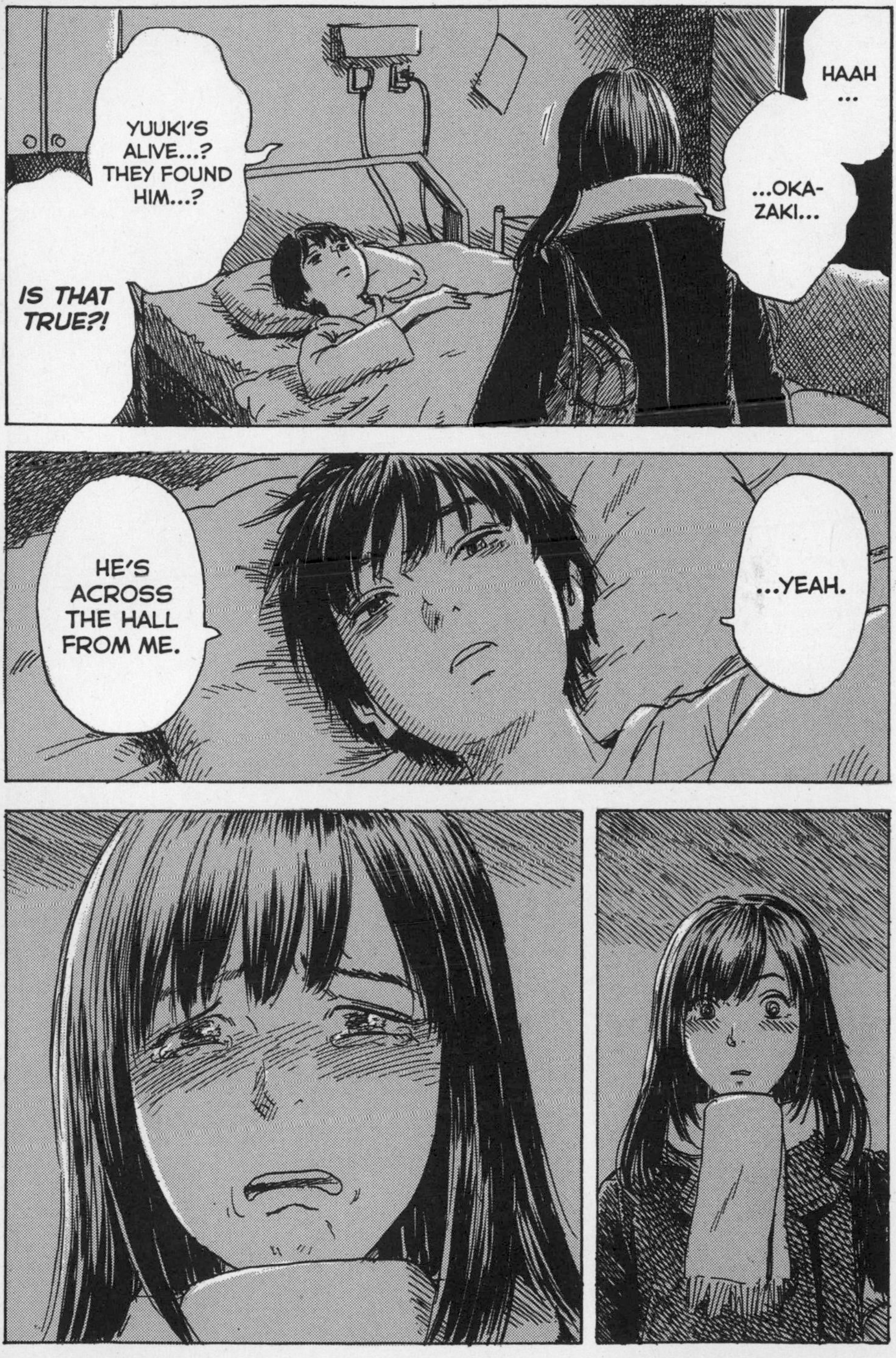
HAAH ...
...OKA-ZAKI...
YUUKI'S ALIVE...? THEY FOUND HIM...?
IS THAT TRUE?!
...YEAH.
HE'S ACROSS THE HALL FROM ME.

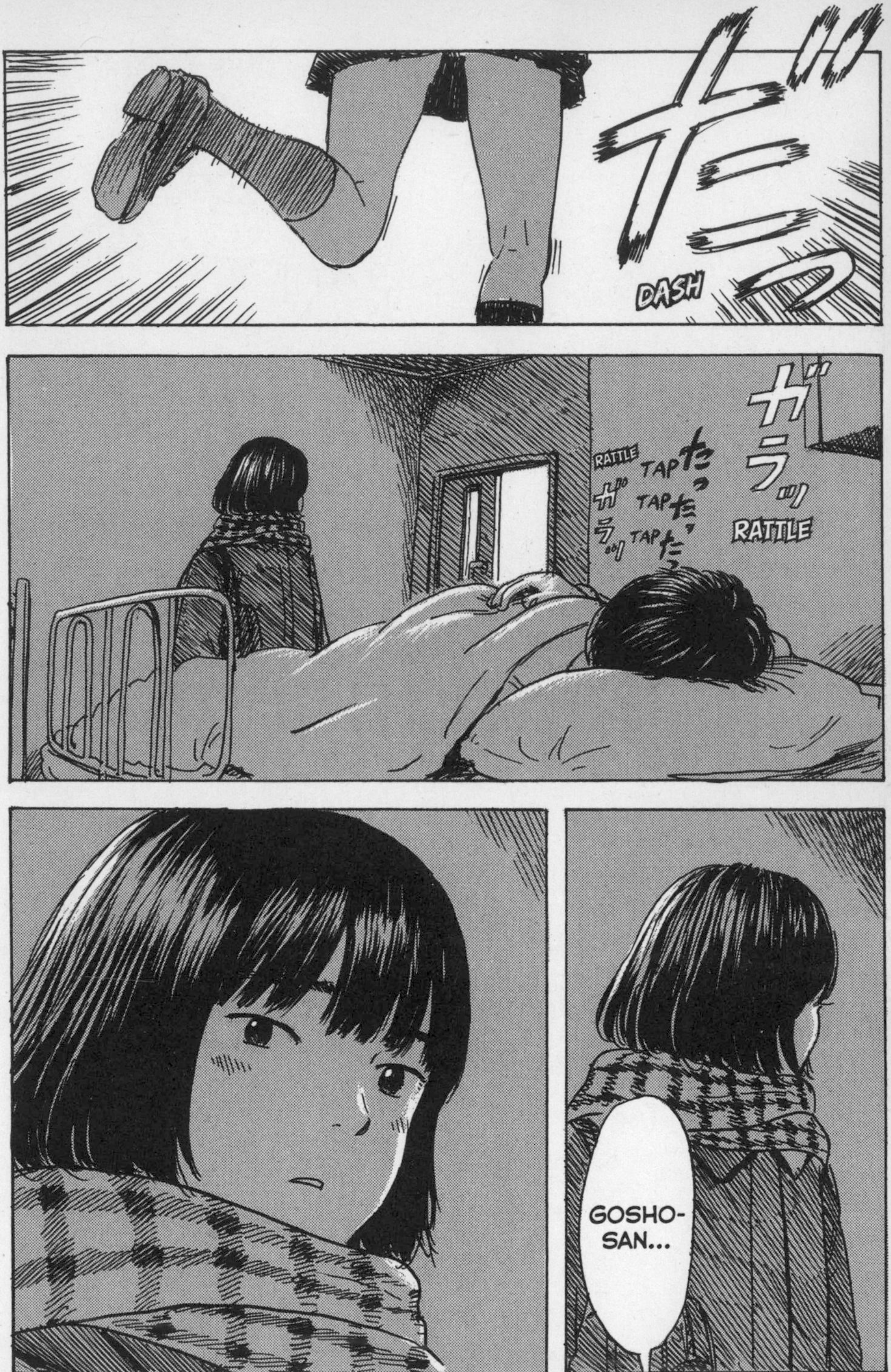
だーっ
DASH
ガラッ
RATTLE
たっ たっ たっ
TAP TAP TAP
ガラッ
RATTLE
GOSHO-SAN...

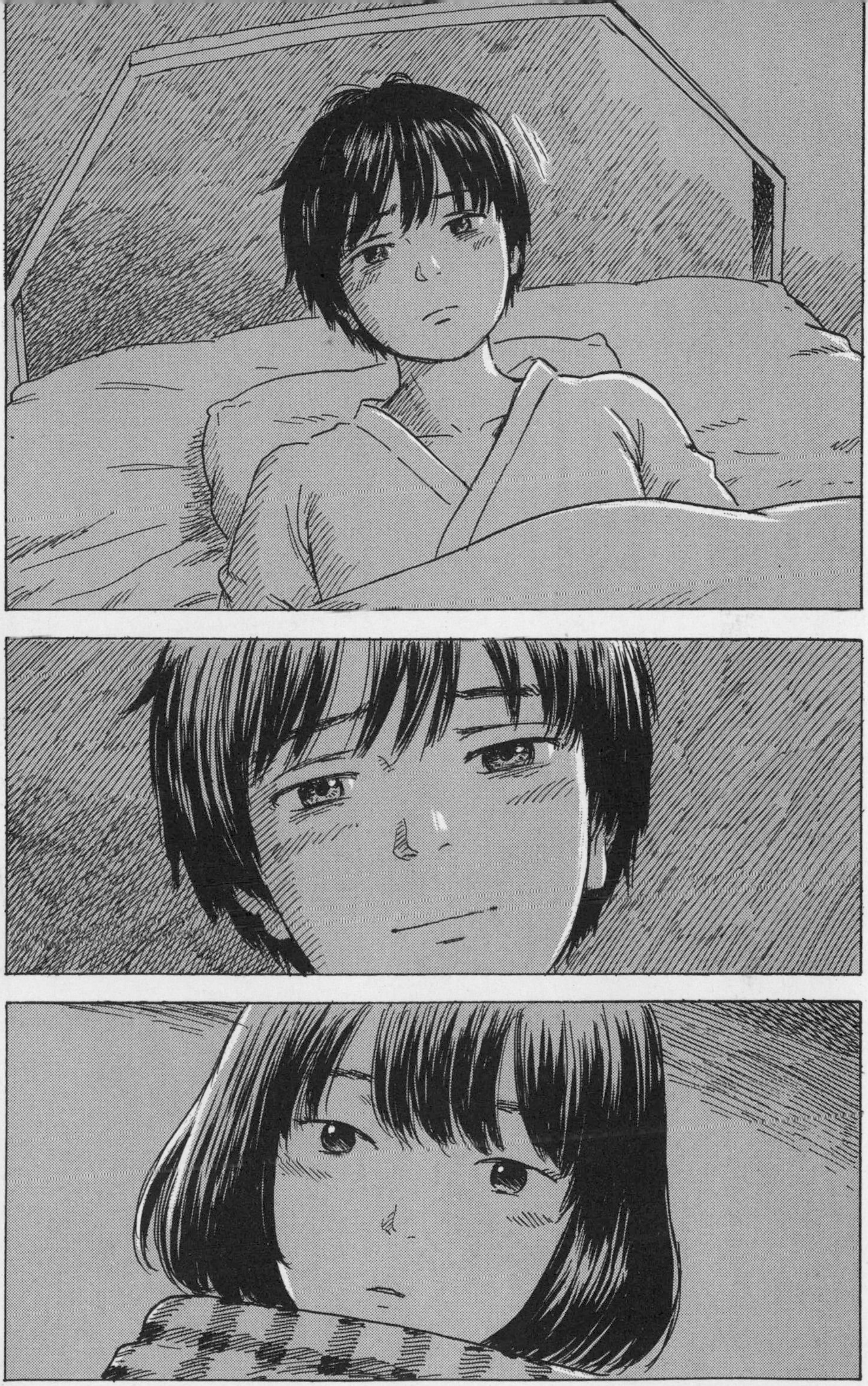

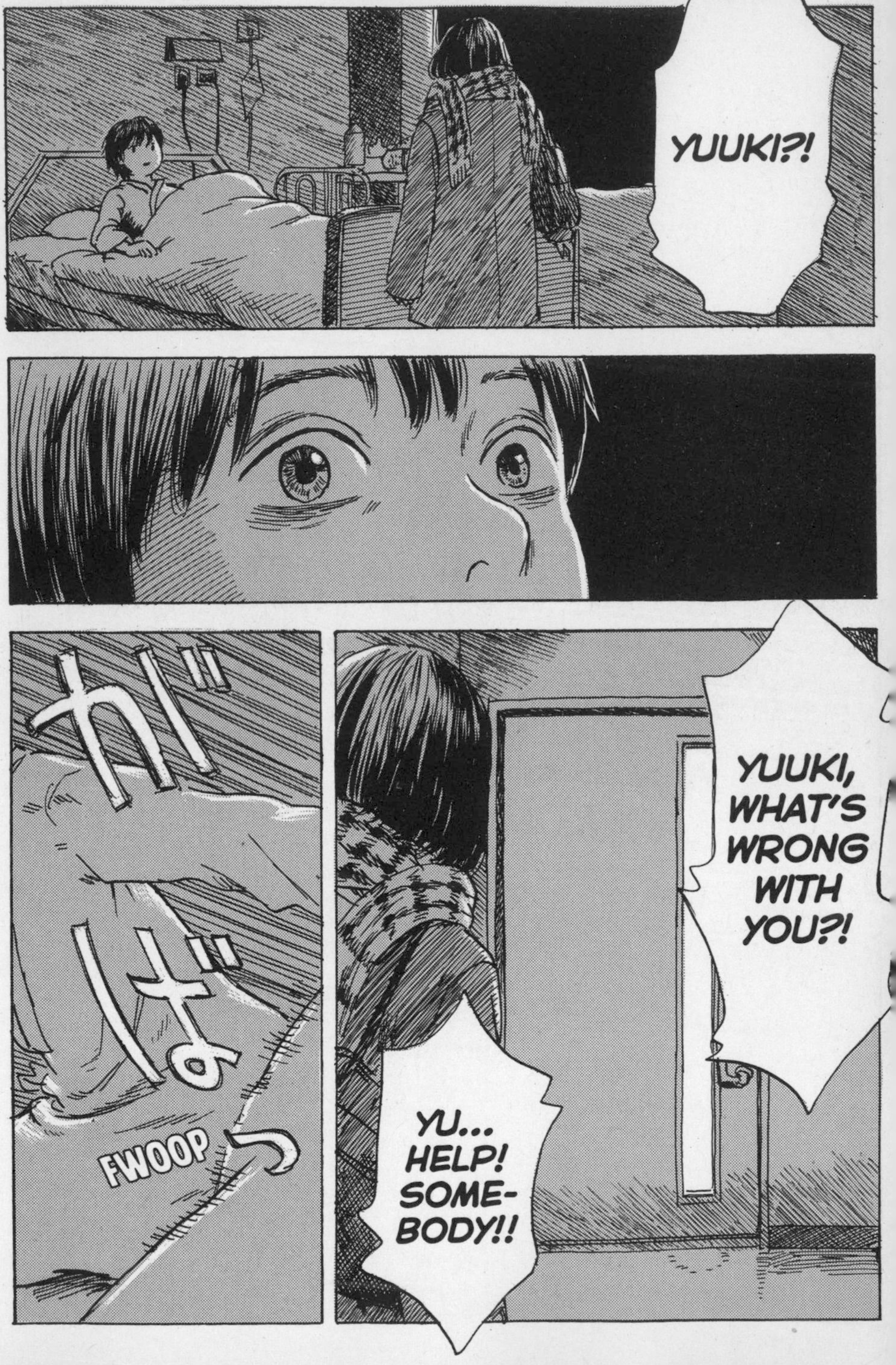
YUUKI?!
YUUKI, WHAT'S WRONG WITH YOU?!
YU... HELP! SOMEBODY!!
がば
FWOOP

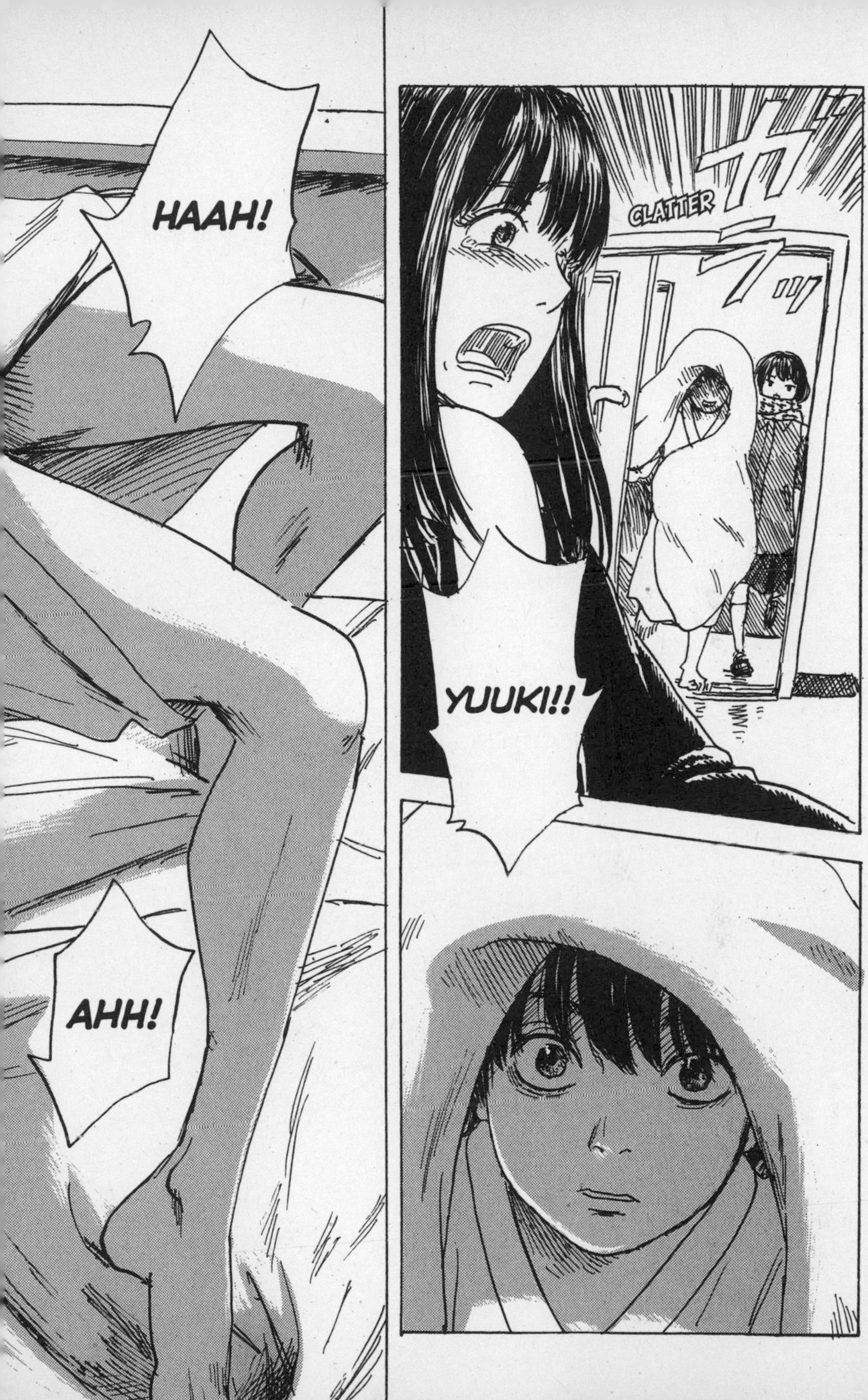
ガラッ
CLATTER
YUUKI!!
HAAH!
AHH!

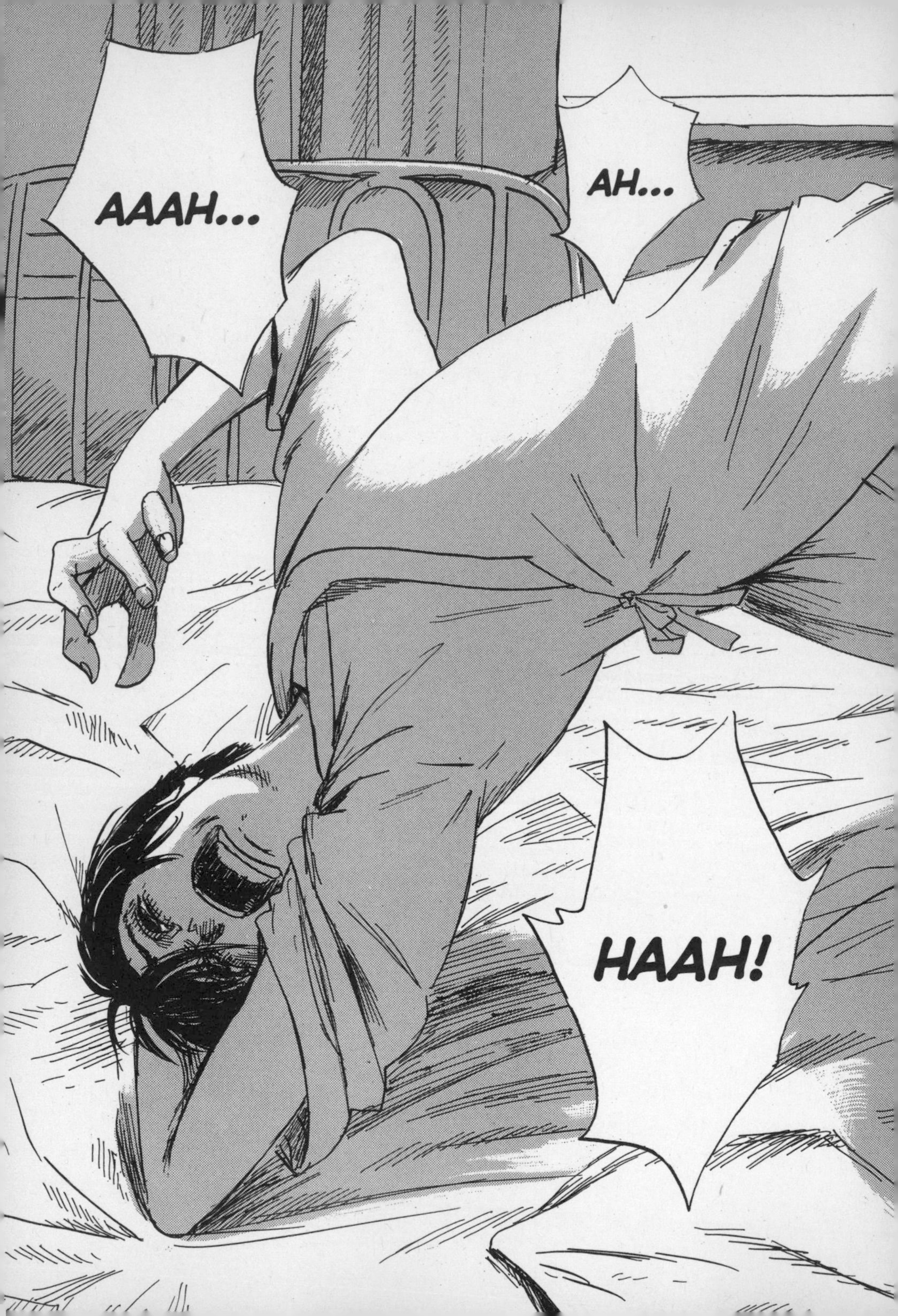
AH...
AAAH...
HAAH!

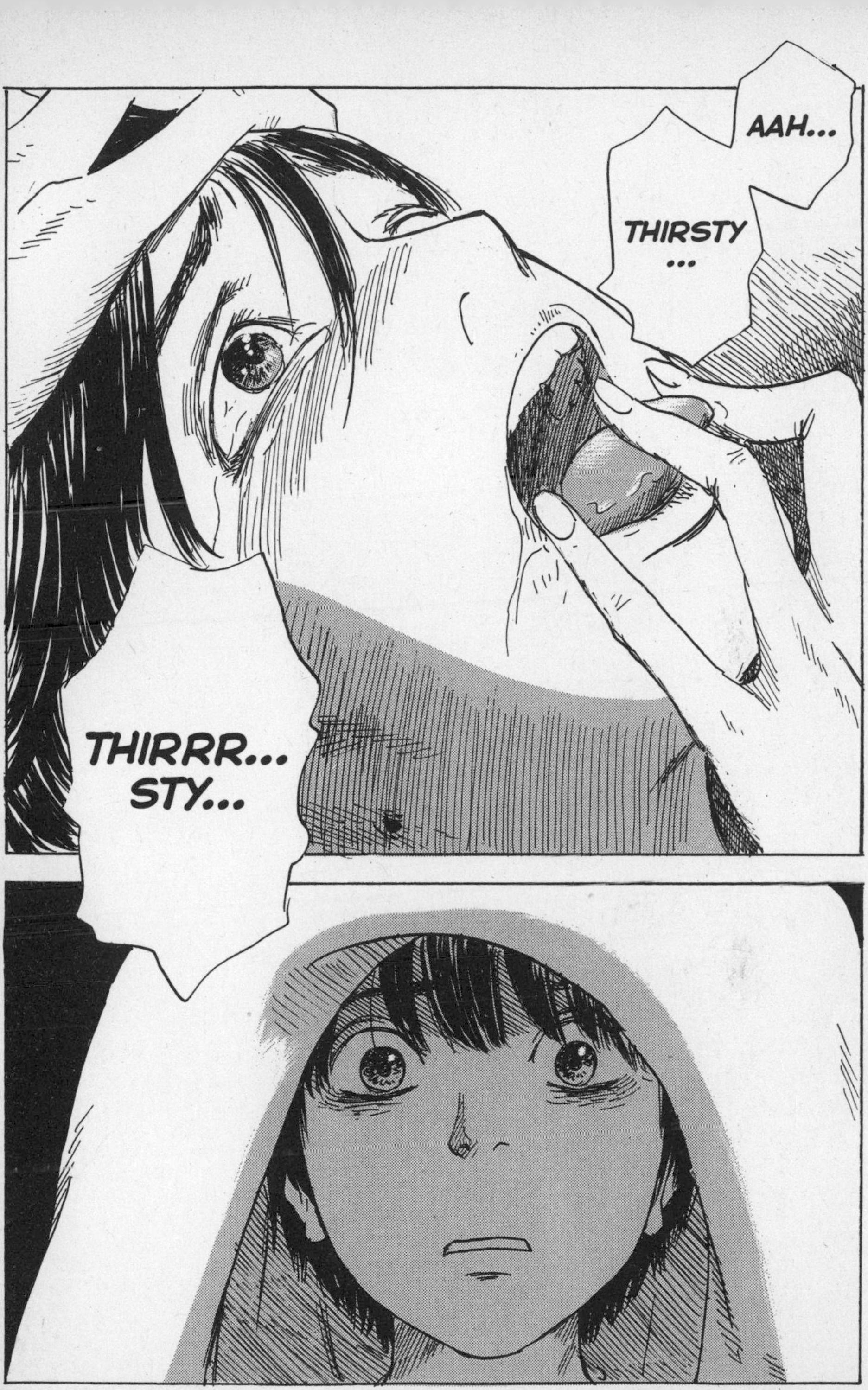
AAH...
THIRSTY ...
THIRRR... STY...

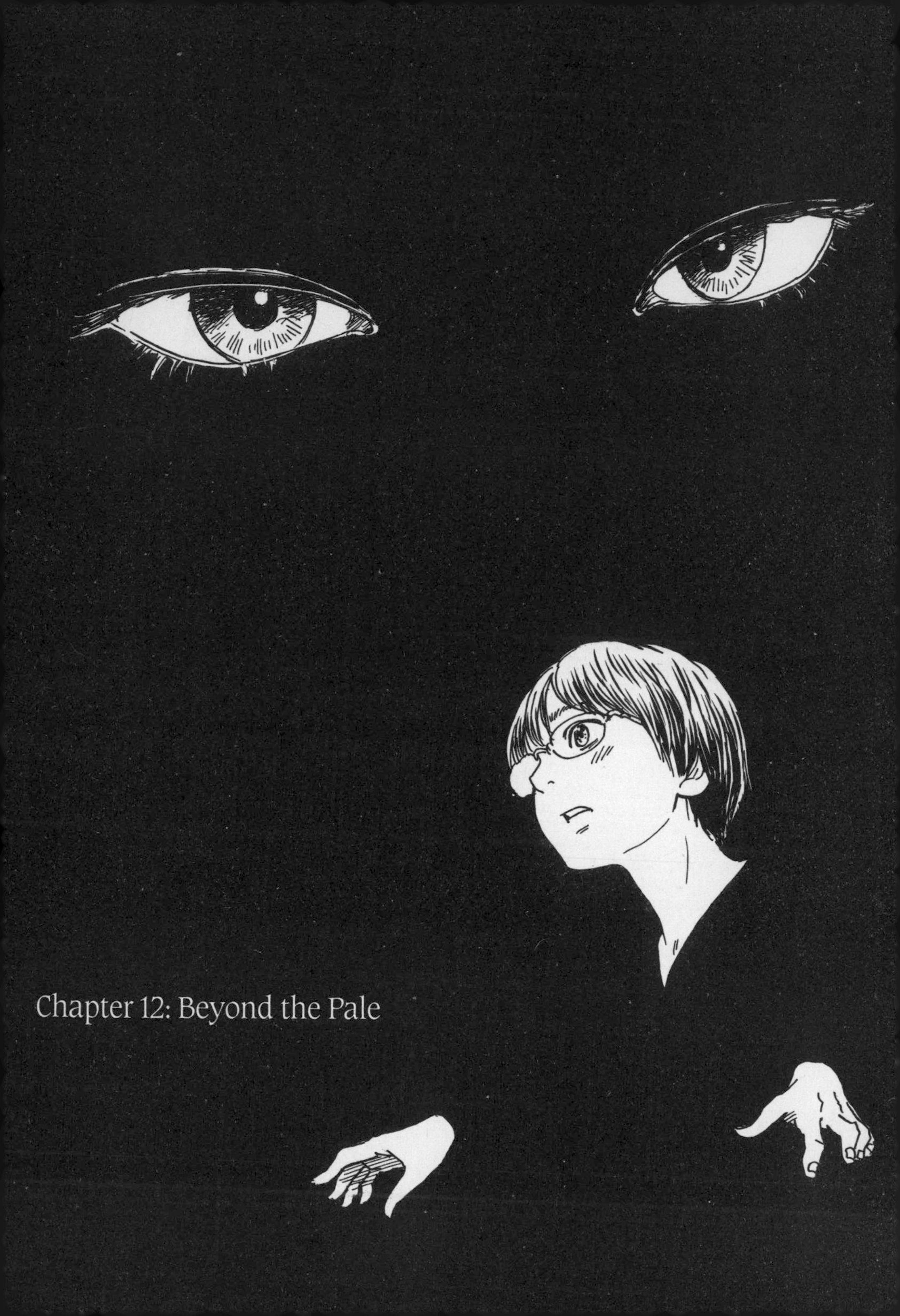

Chapter 12: Beyond the Pale

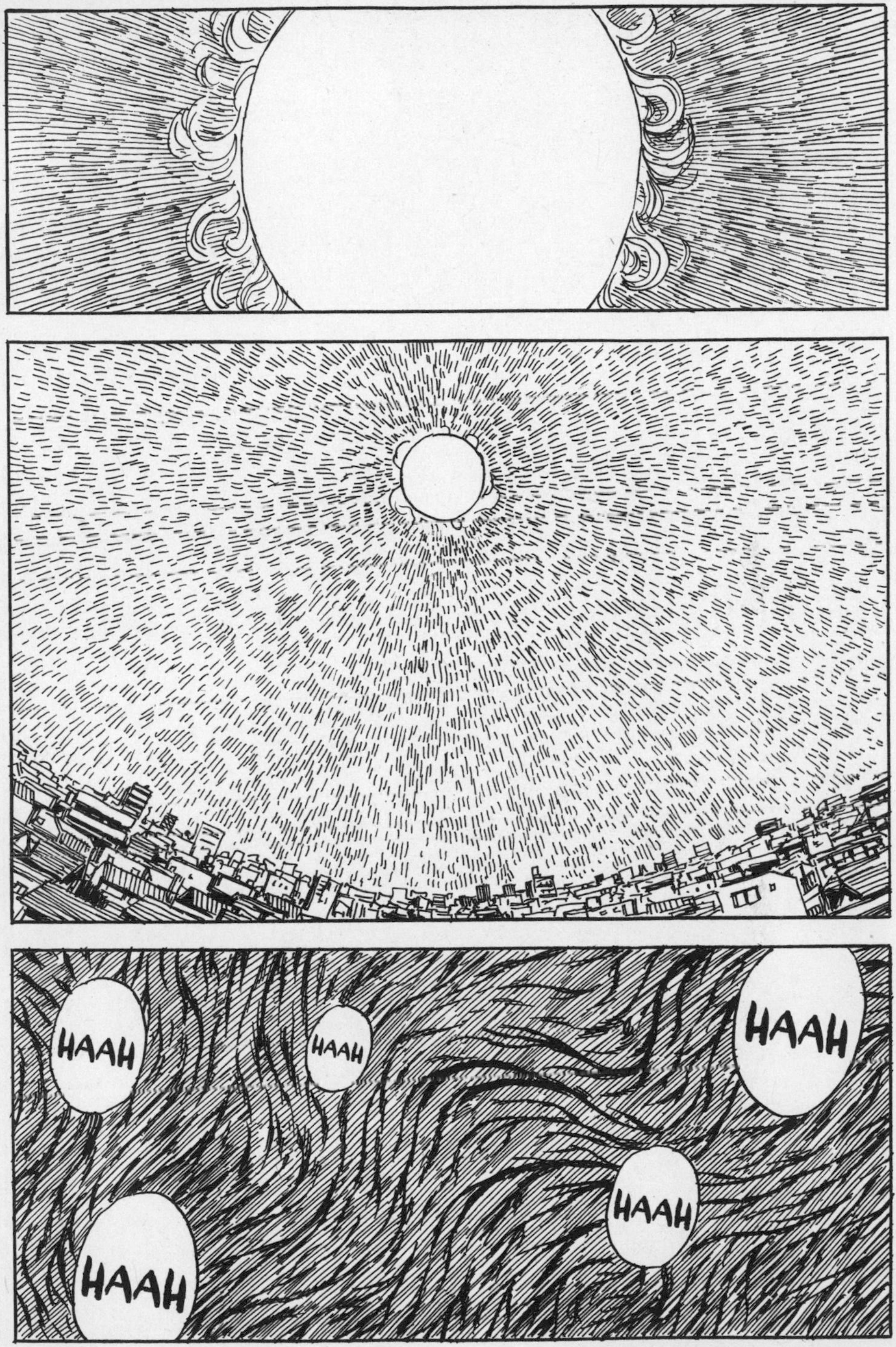
HAAH
HAAH
HAAH
HAAH
HAAH

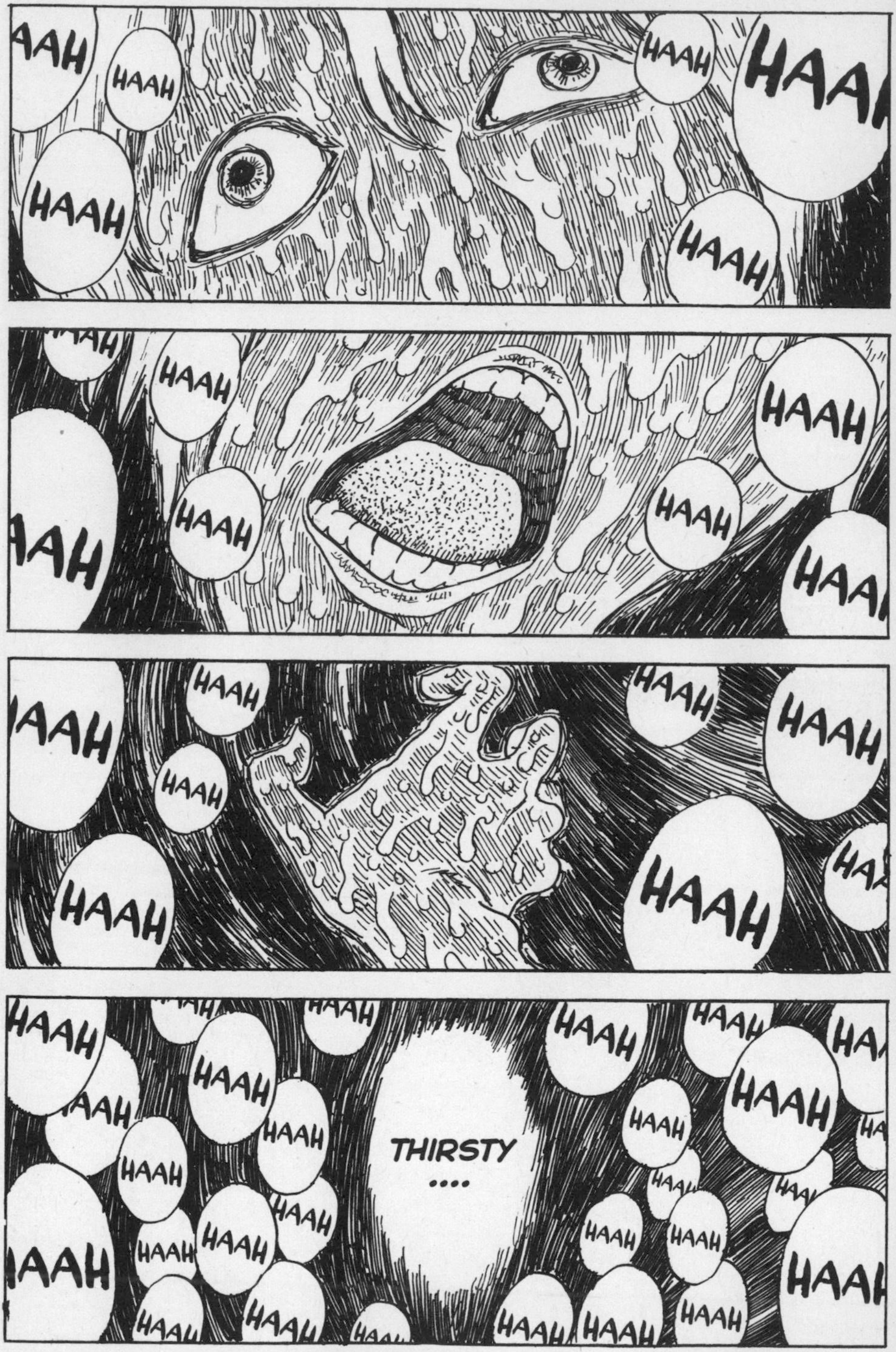
HAAH
HAAH
HAAH
HAAH
HAAH
HAAH
HAAH
HAAH
HAAH
HAAH
HAAH
HAAH
HAAH
HAAH
HAAH
HAAH
HAAH
HAAH
HAAH
HAAH
THIRSTY ....
HAAH
HAAH
HAAH
HAAH
HAAH
HAAH
HAAH
HAAH
HAAH

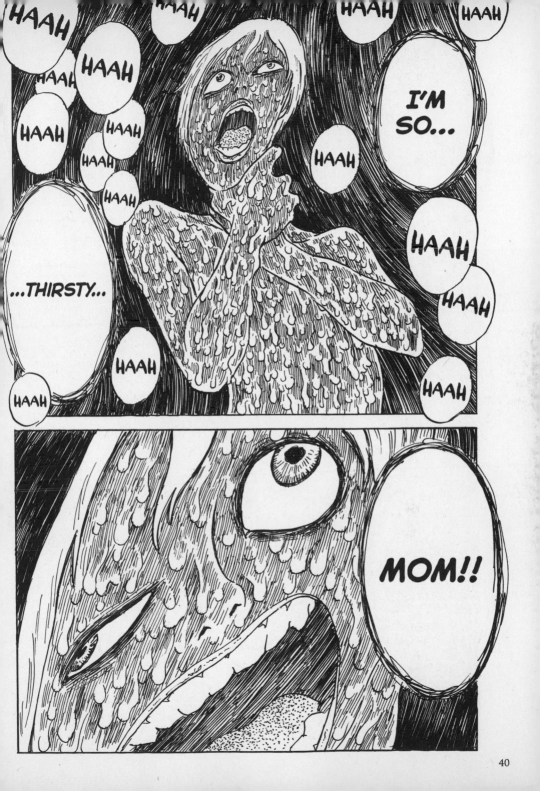

40

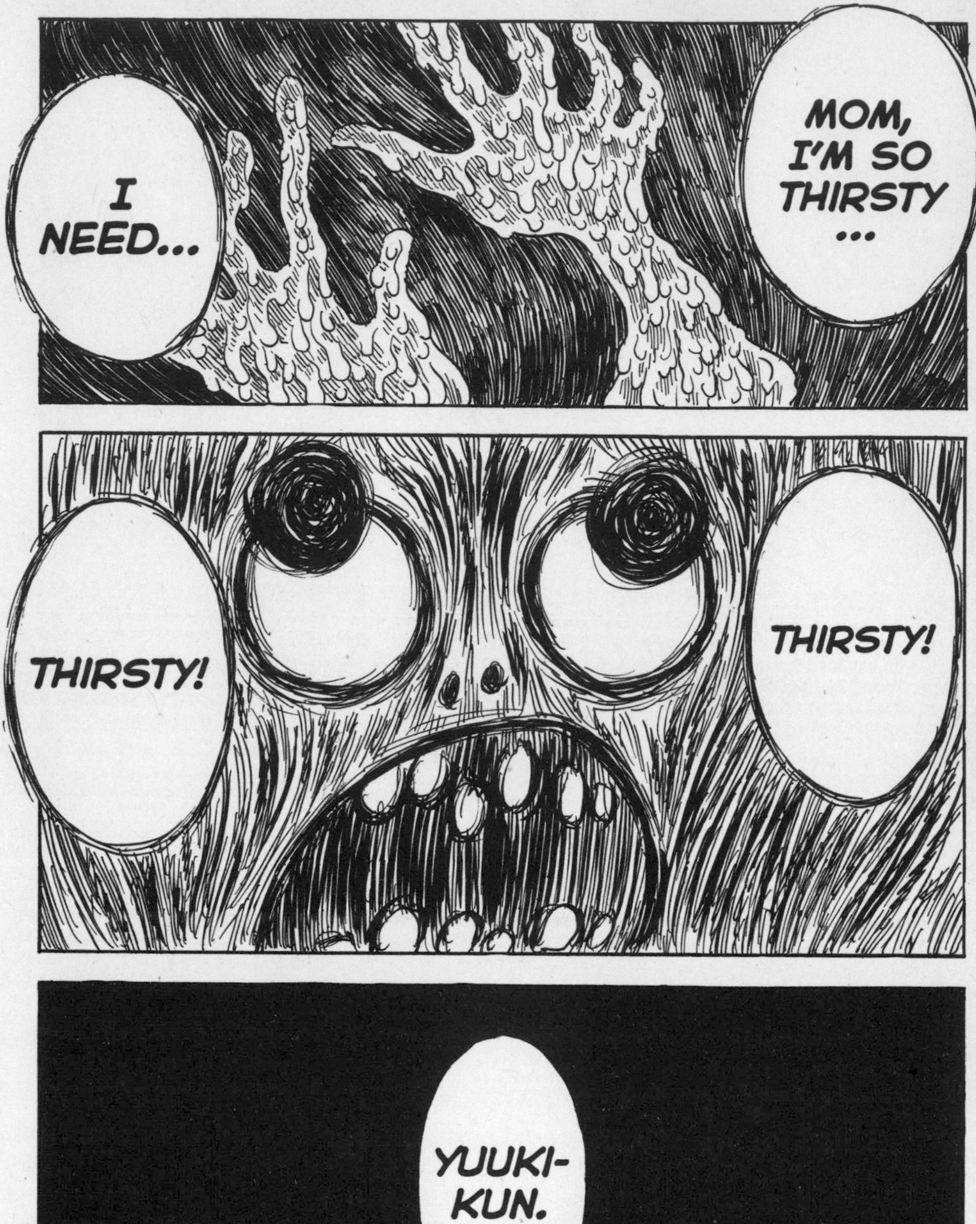
MOM, I'M SO THIRSTY ...
I NEED...
THIRSTY!
THIRSTY!
YUUKI-KUN.

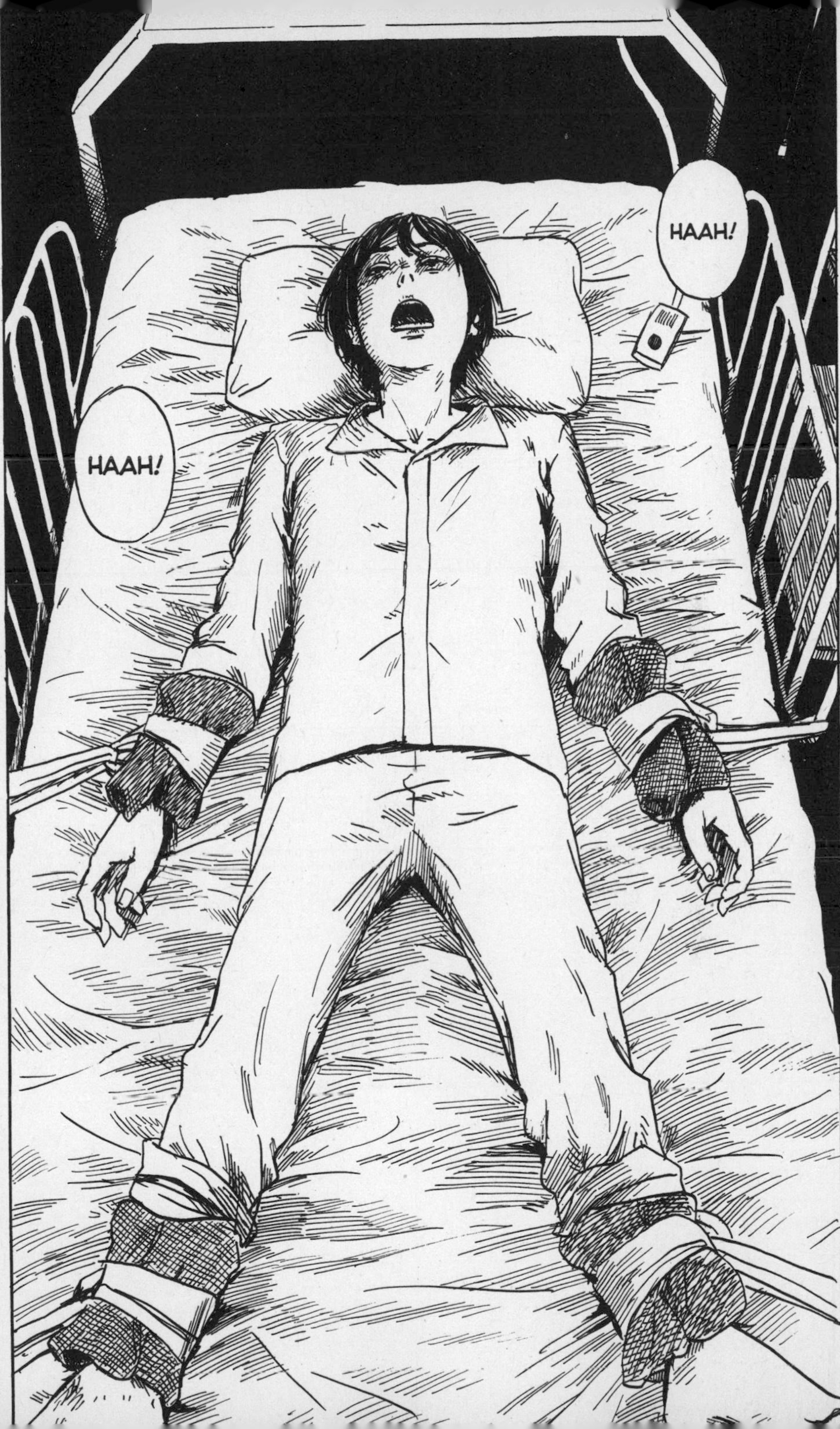
HAAH!
HAAH!

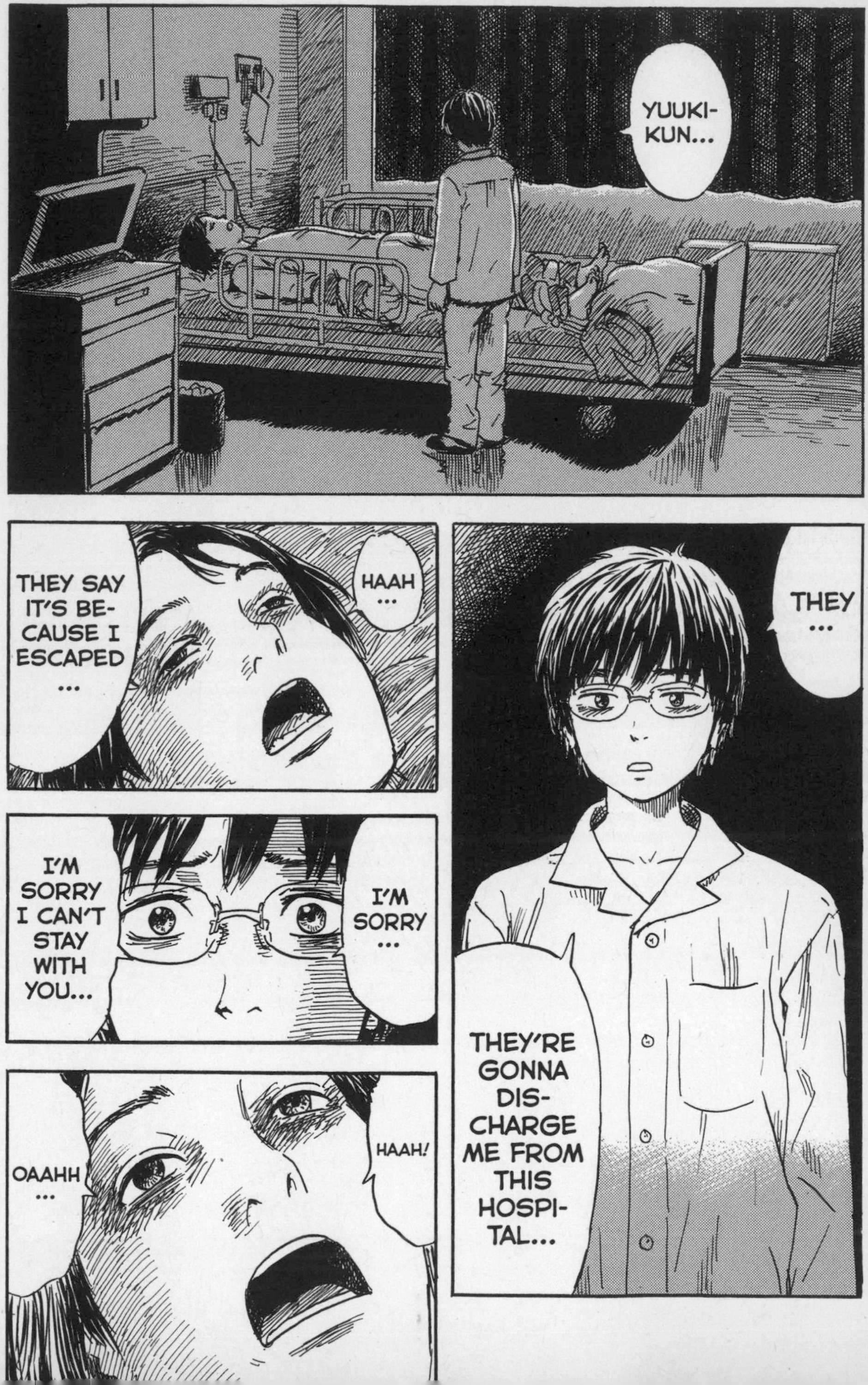
YUUKI-KUN...
THEY...
THEY'RE GONNA DIS-CHARGE ME FROM THIS HOSPI-TAL...
HAAH...
THEY SAY IT'S BE-CAUSE I ESCAPED...
I'M SORRY...
I'M SORRY I CAN'T STAY WITH YOU...
HAAH!
OAAHH...

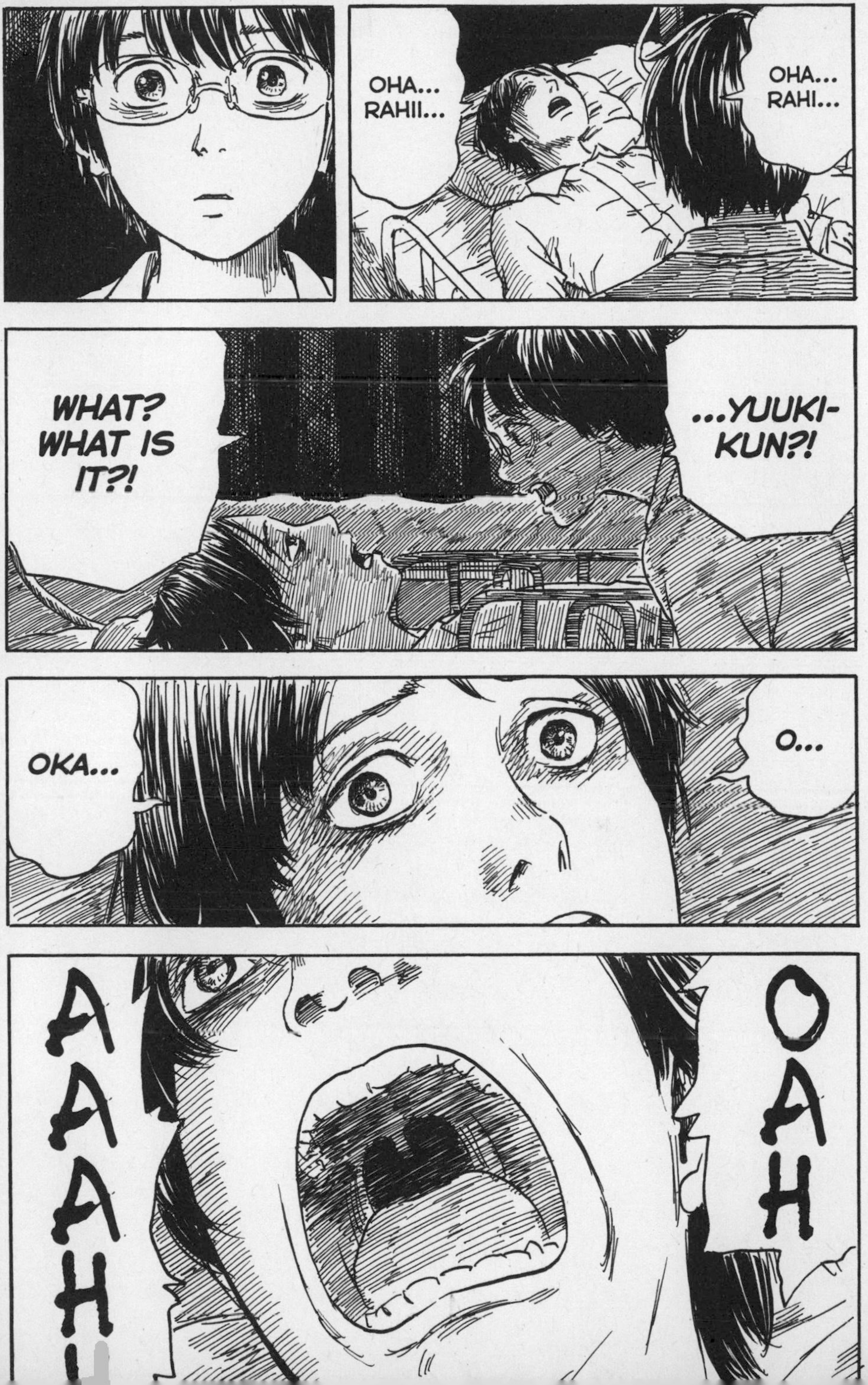
OHA... RAHI...
OHA... RAHII...
...YUUKI-KUN?!
WHAT? WHAT IS IT?!
O...
OKA...
OAH
AAAH

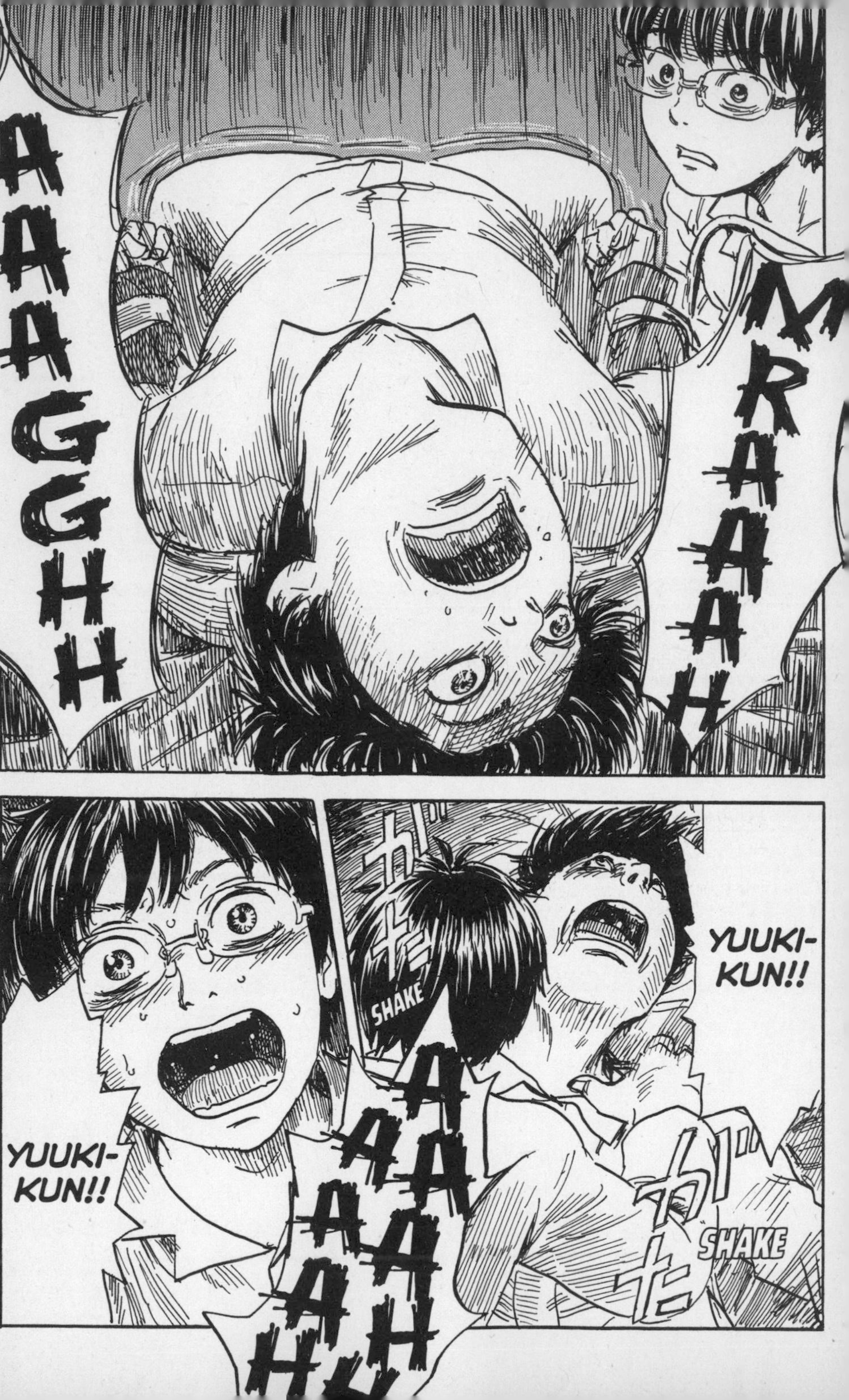
MRAAAAH
AAAGGHH
YUUKI-KUN!!
SHAKE
AAAAAAH
SHAKE
YUUKI-KUN!!

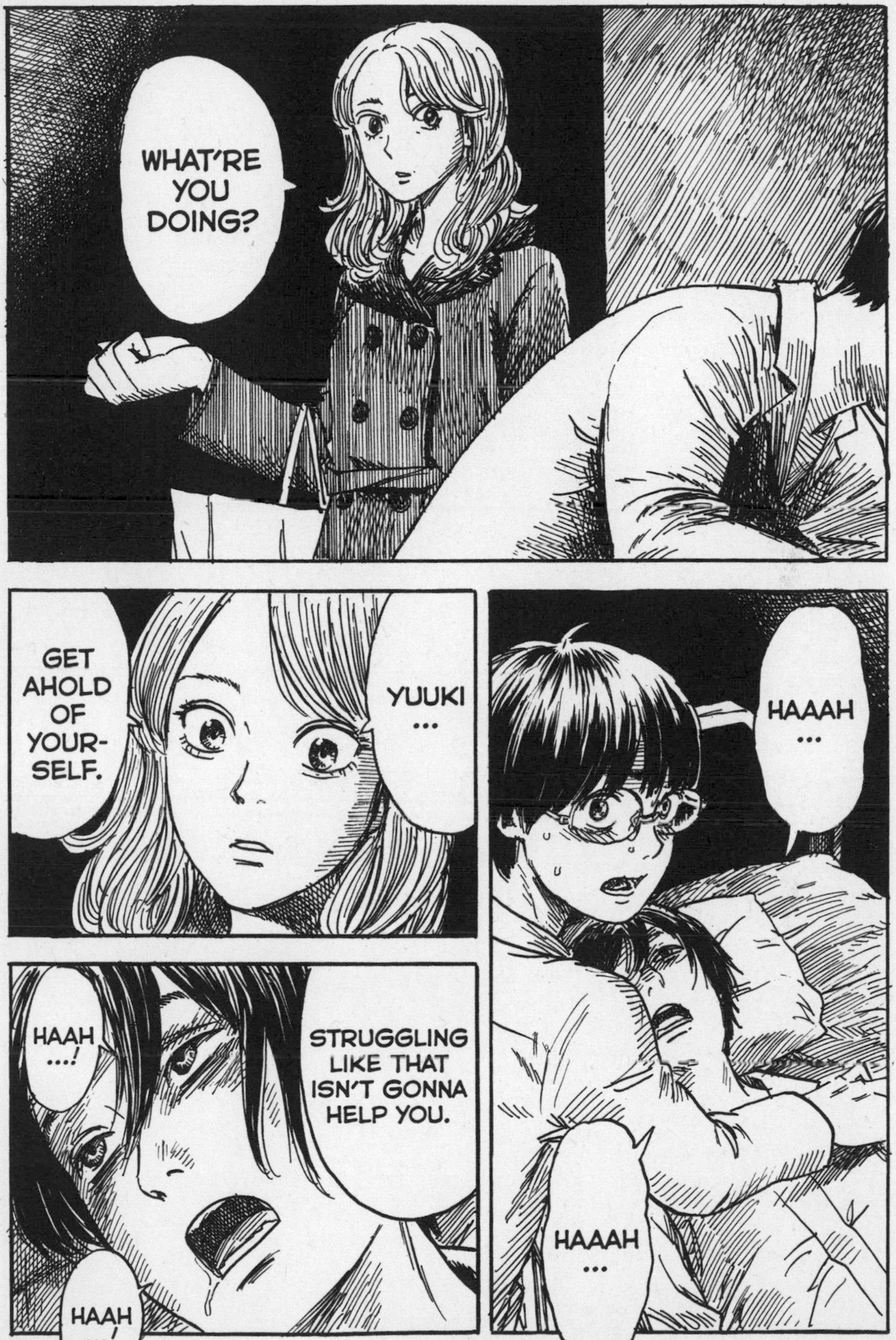
WHAT'RE YOU DOING?
HAAAH ...
HAAAH ...
YUUKI ...
GET AHOLD OF YOUR-SELF.
STRUGGLING LIKE THAT ISN'T GONNA HELP YOU.
HAAH ...!
HAAH ...!

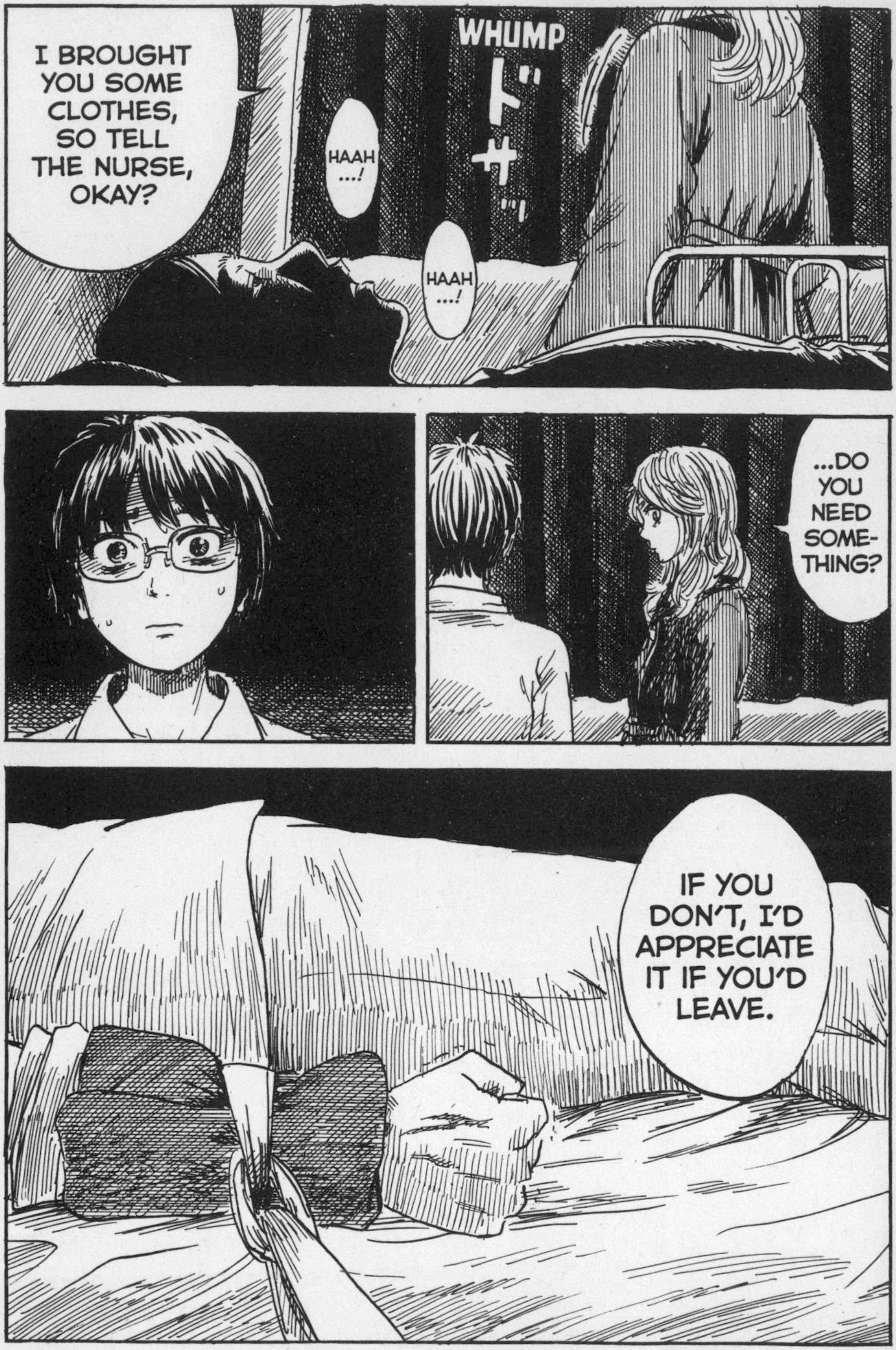
WHUMP
ドサッ
I BROUGHT YOU SOME CLOTHES, SO TELL THE NURSE, OKAY?
HAAH ...!
HAAH ...!
...DO YOU NEED SOME-THING?
IF YOU DON'T, I'D APPRECIATE IT IF YOU'D LEAVE.

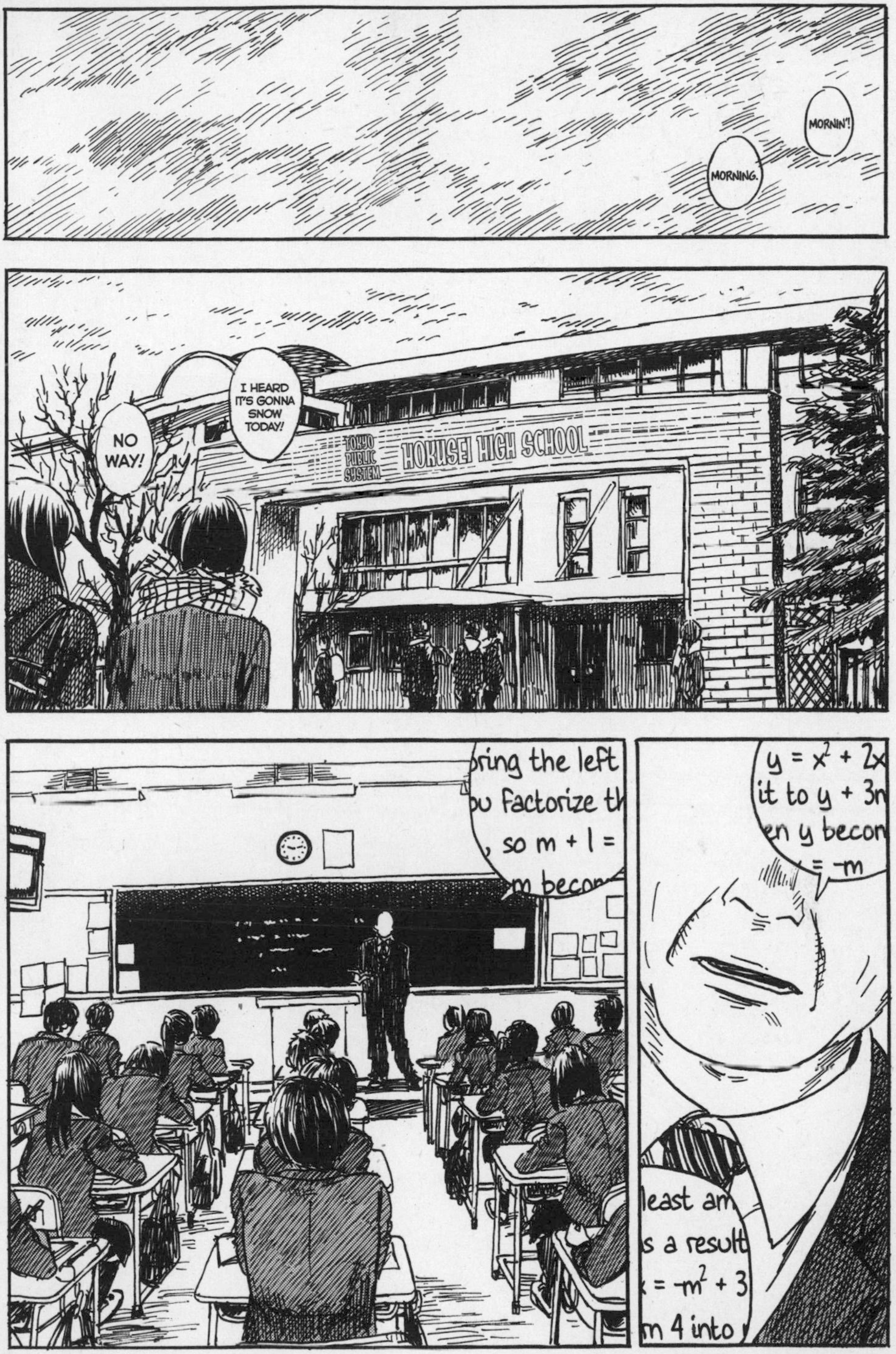
MORNIN'!
MORNING.
I HEARD IT'S GONNA SNOW TODAY!
NO WAY!
TOKYO PUBLIC SYSTEM
HOKUSEI HIGH SCHOOL
y = x² + 2x
it to y + 3
en y becon
= -m
least an
s a result
= -m² + 3
m 4 into
ring the left
u factorize th
, so m + l =
m becon

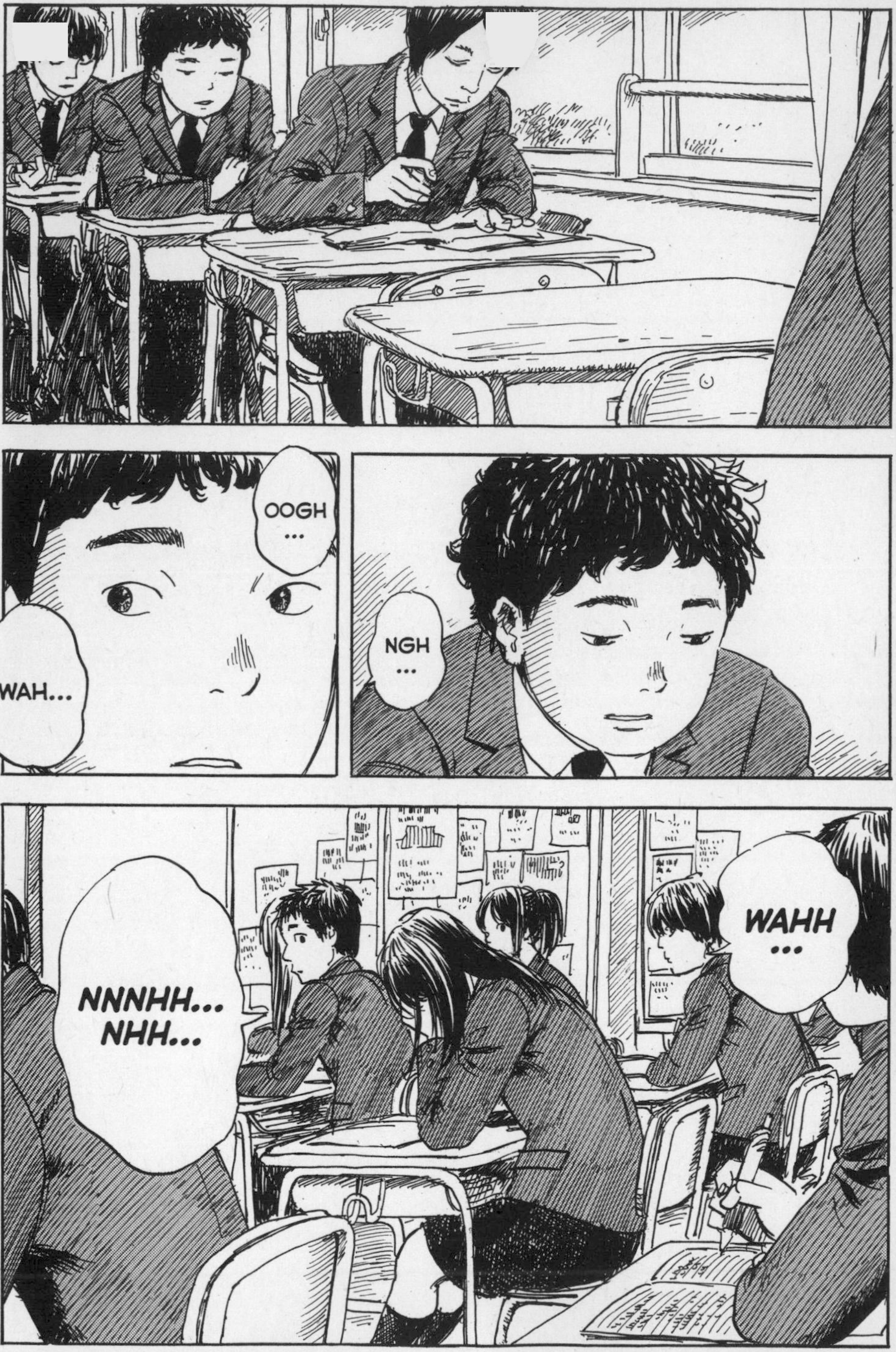
NGH ...
OOGH ...
WAH...
WAHH ...
NNNHH... NHH...

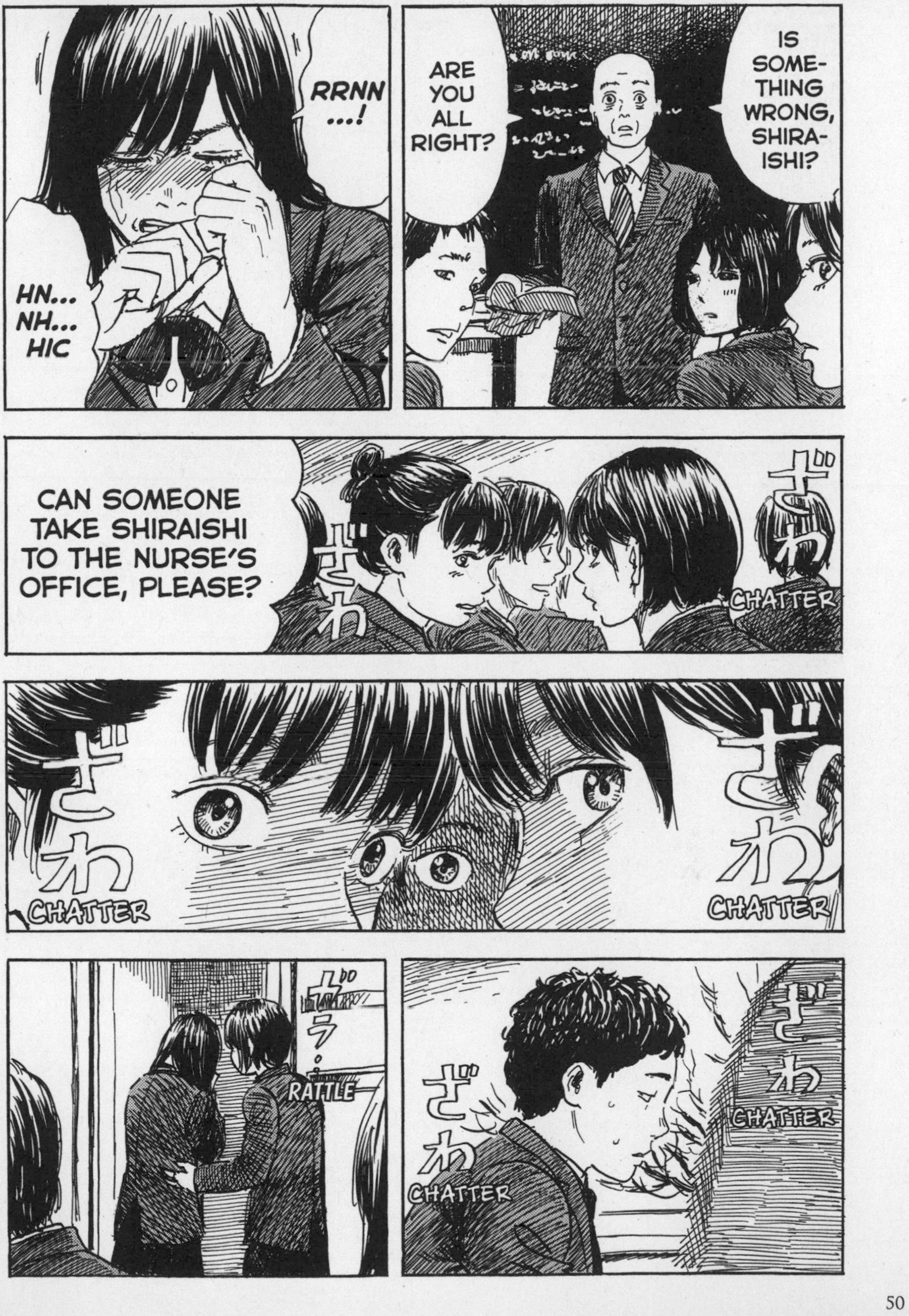
IS SOMETHING WRONG, SHIRAISHI?
ARE YOU ALL RIGHT?
RRNN ...!
HN... NH... HIC
ざわ
CHATTER
CAN SOMEONE TAKE SHIRAISHI TO THE NURSE'S OFFICE, PLEASE?
ざわ
ざわ
CHATTER
ざわ
CHATTER
ざわ
CHATTER
ざわ
CHATTER
カラ…
RATTLE

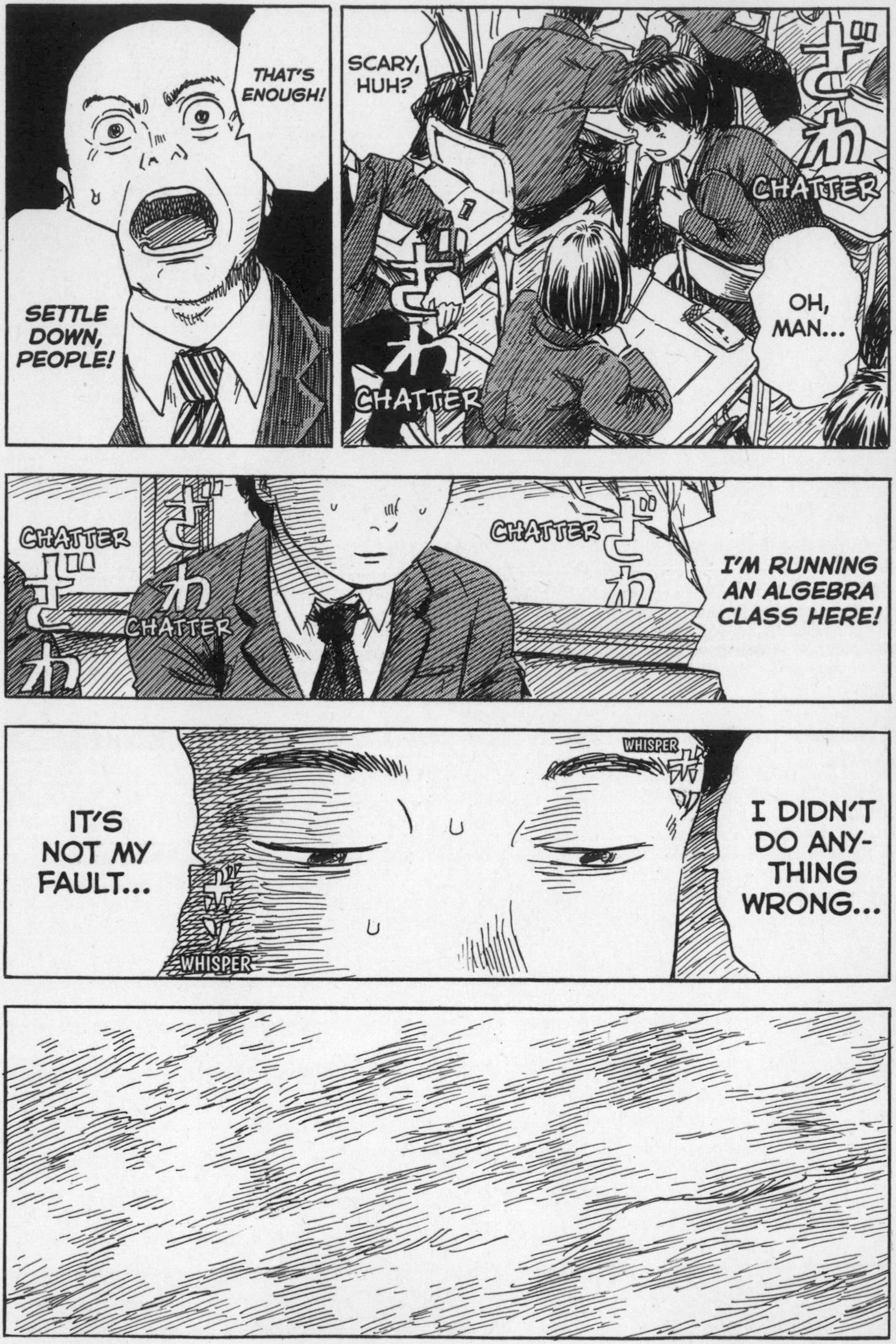
SCARY, HUH?
ざわ
CHATTER
ざわ
CHATTER
OH, MAN...
THAT'S ENOUGH!
SETTLE DOWN, PEOPLE!
I'M RUNNING AN ALGEBRA CLASS HERE!
ざわ
CHATTER
ざわ
CHATTER
ざわ
CHATTER
WHISPER
I DIDN'T DO ANYTHING WRONG...
IT'S NOT MY FAULT...
WHISPER

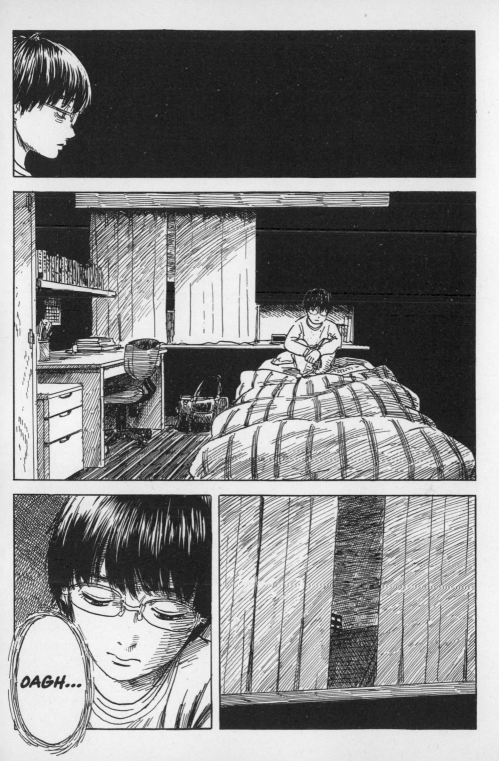

OAGH...

52

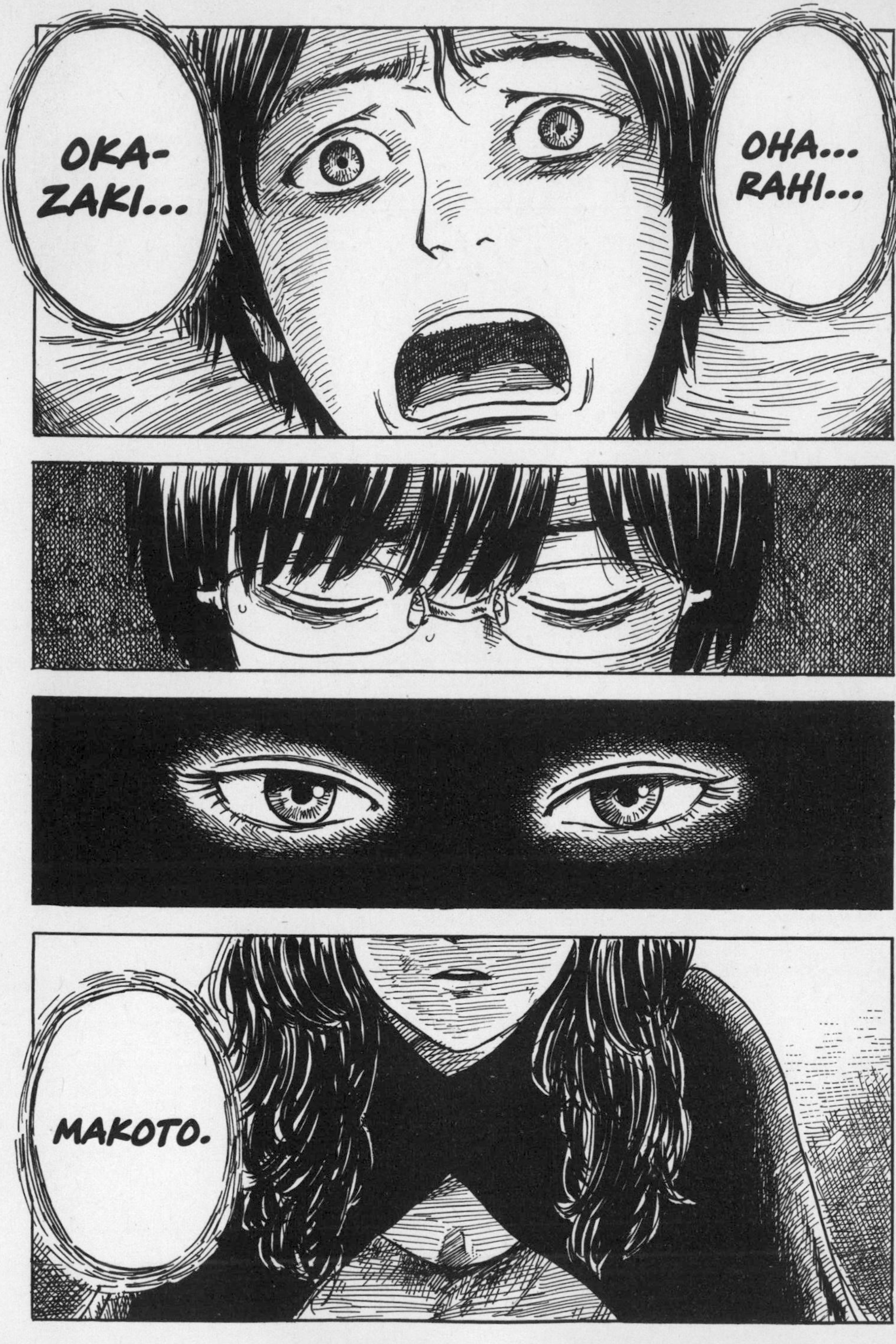
OHA... RAHI...
OKA-ZAKI...
MAKOTO.

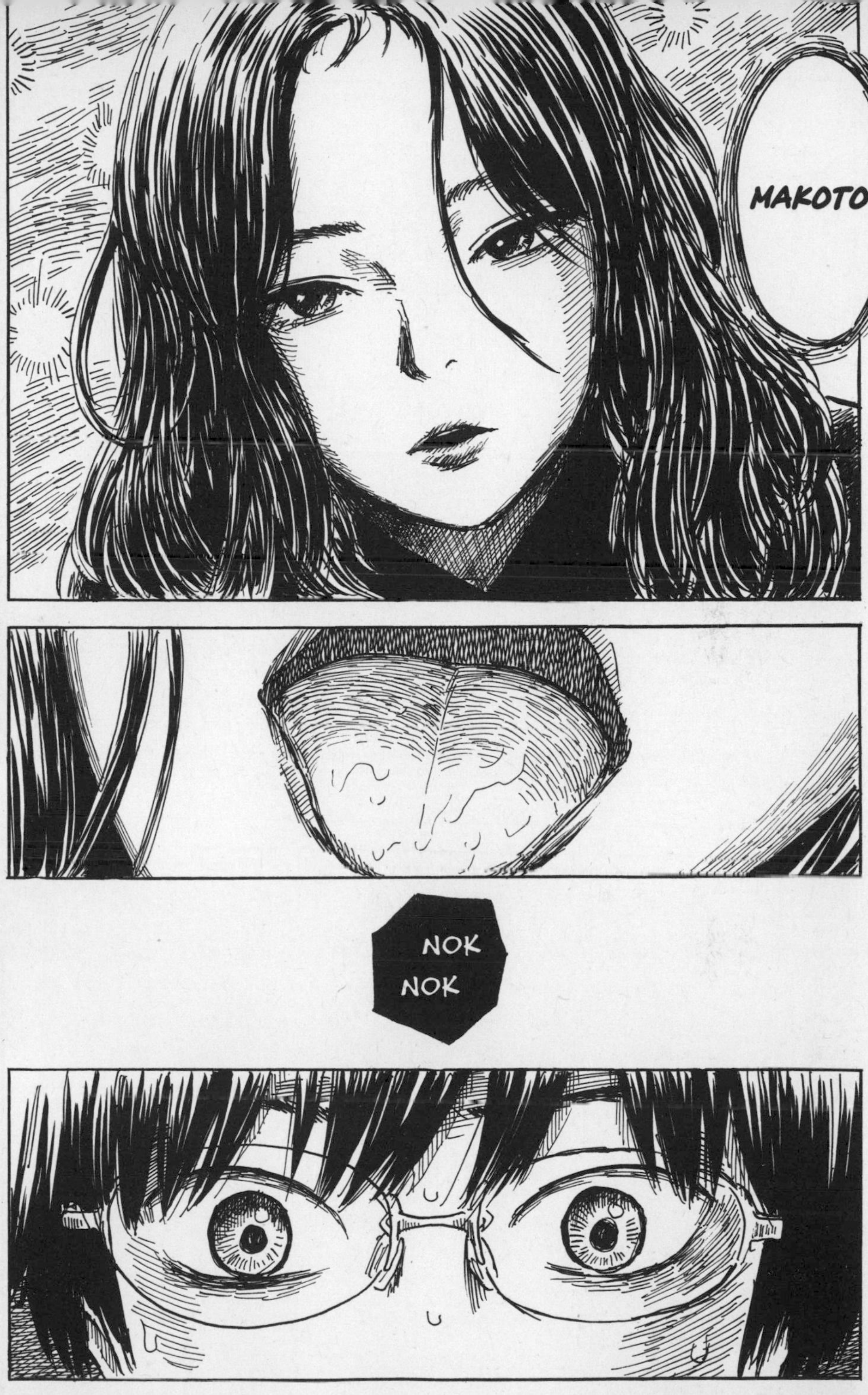
MAKOTO.
NOK
NOK

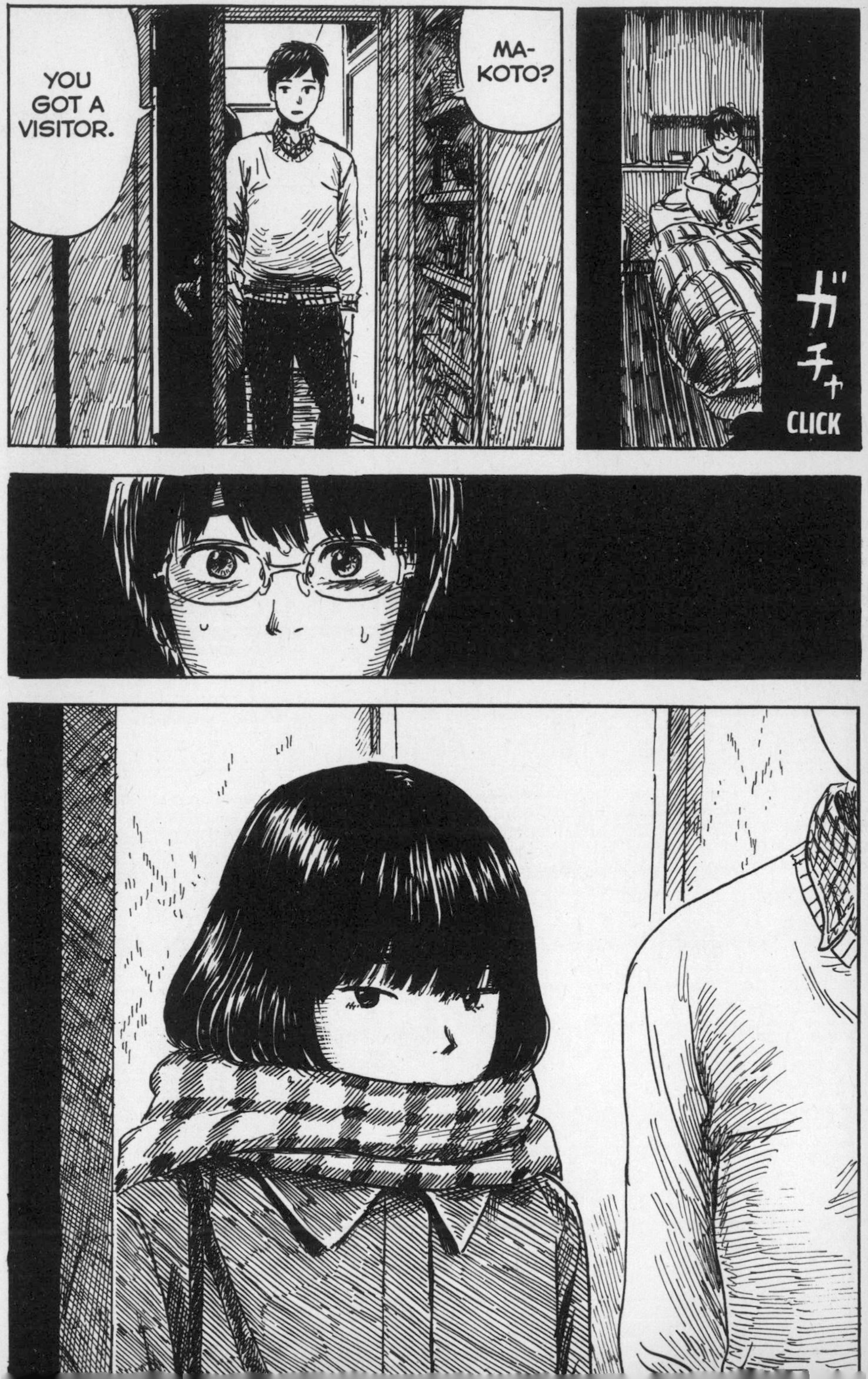
ガチャ
CLICK
MA-KOTO?
YOU GOT A VISITOR.

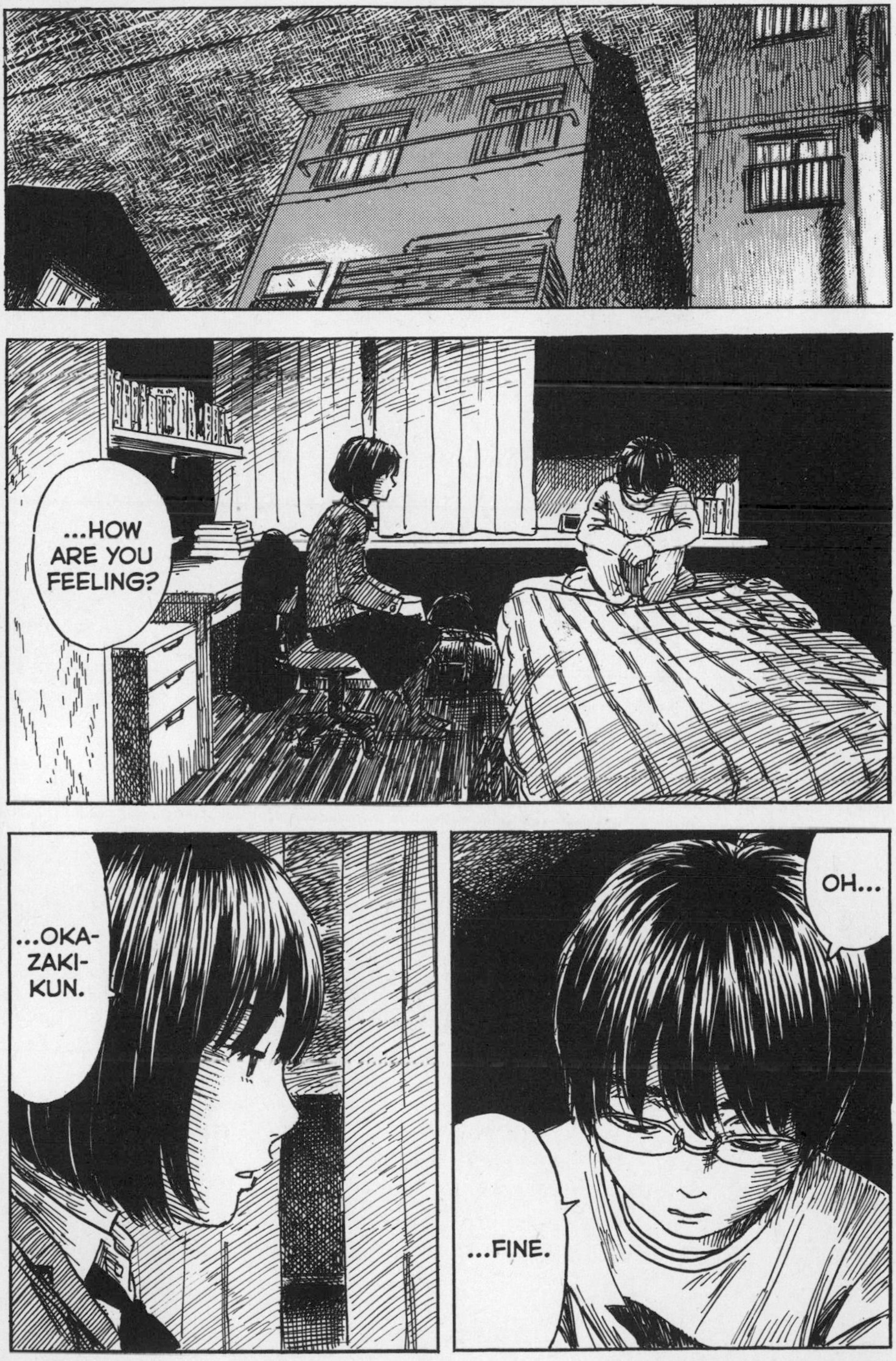
...HOW ARE YOU FEELING?
OH...
...FINE.
...OKA-ZAKI-KUN.

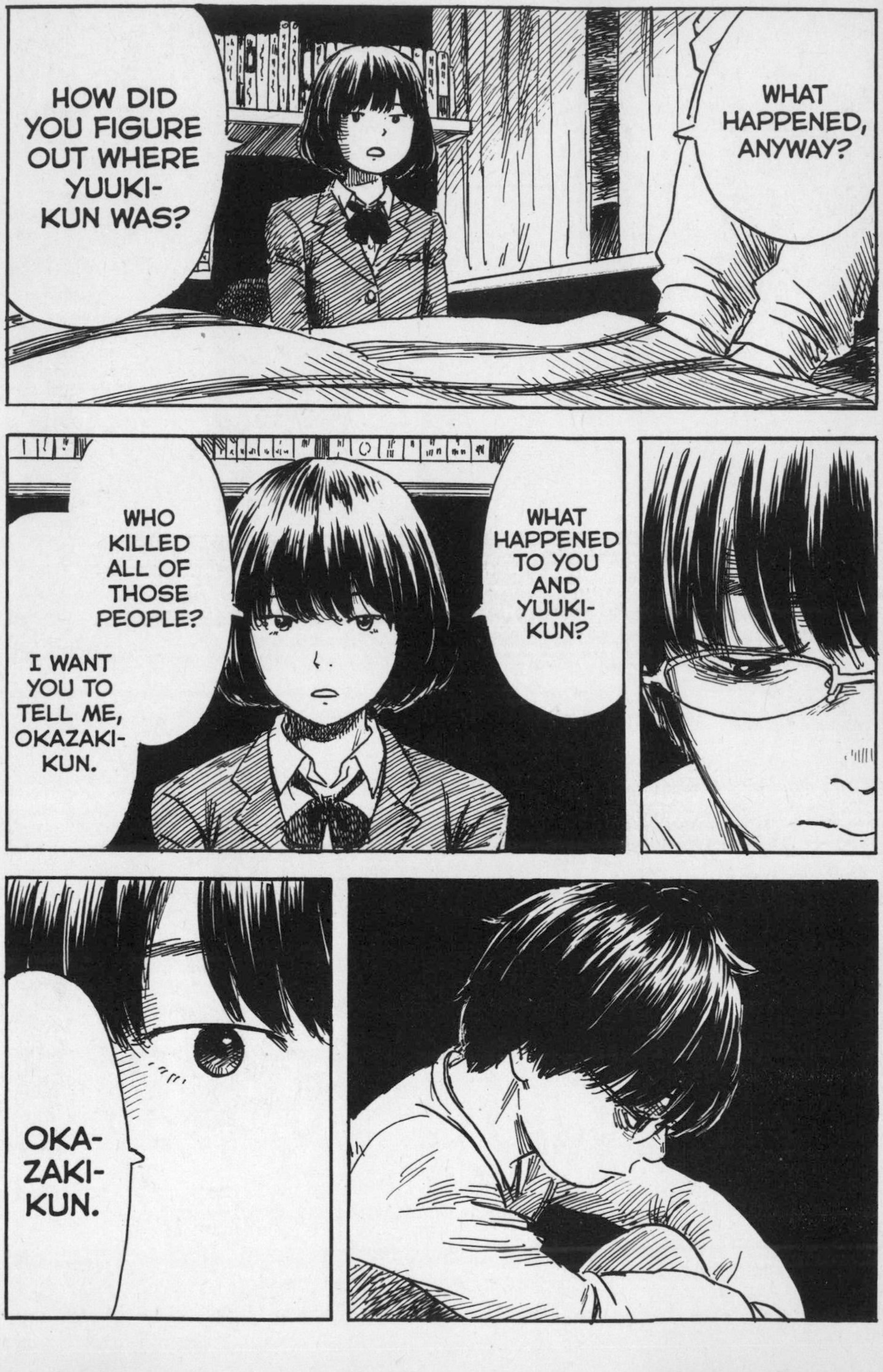
WHAT HAPPENED, ANYWAY?
HOW DID YOU FIGURE OUT WHERE YUUKI-KUN WAS?
WHAT HAPPENED TO YOU AND YUUKI-KUN?
WHO KILLED ALL OF THOSE PEOPLE?
I WANT YOU TO TELL ME, OKAZAKI-KUN.
OKAZAKI-KUN.

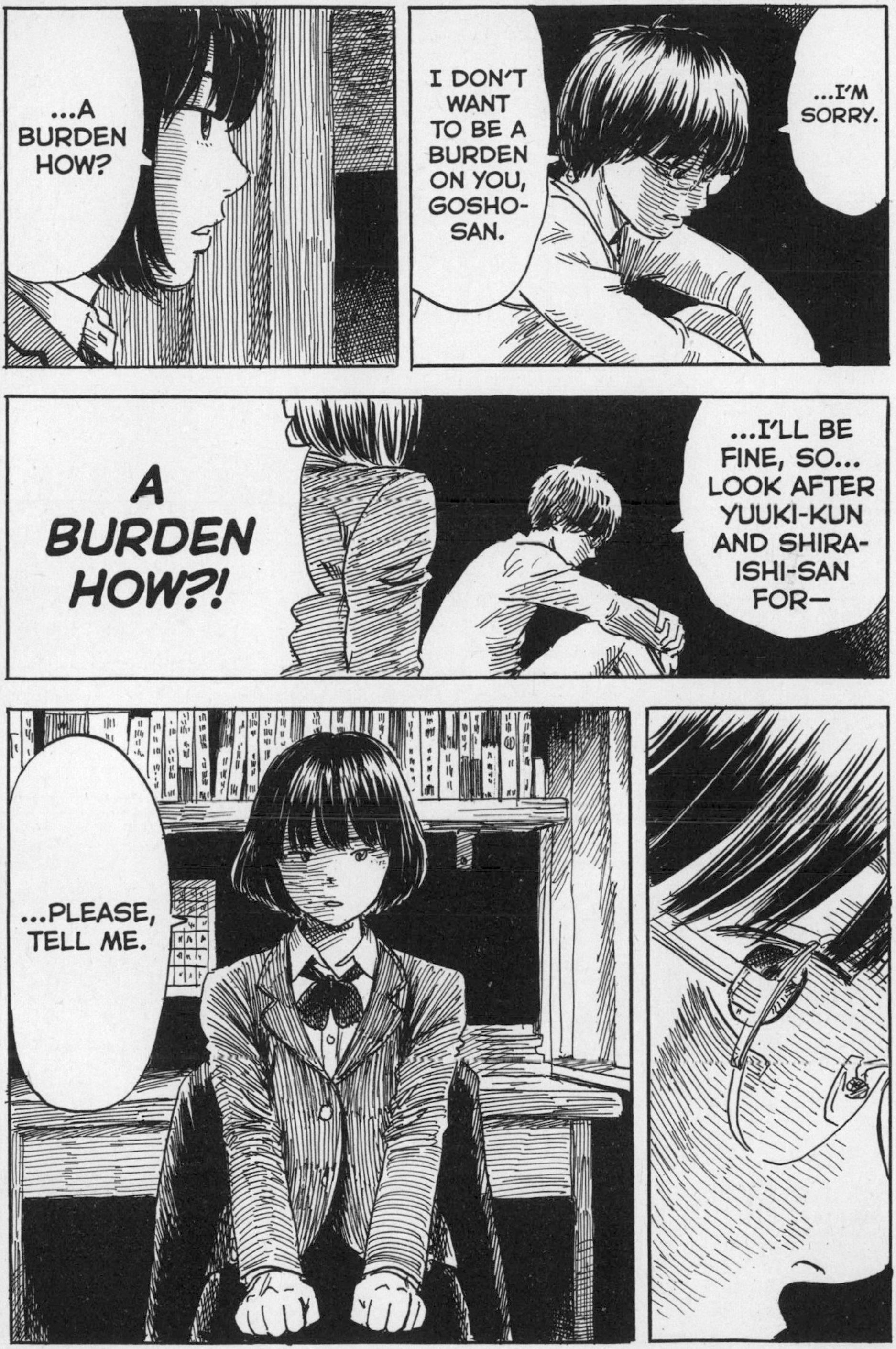
...I'M SORRY.
I DON'T WANT TO BE A BURDEN ON YOU, GOSHO-SAN.
...A BURDEN HOW?
...I'LL BE FINE, SO... LOOK AFTER YUUKI-KUN AND SHIRA-ISHI-SAN FOR—
A BURDEN HOW?!
...PLEASE, TELL ME.

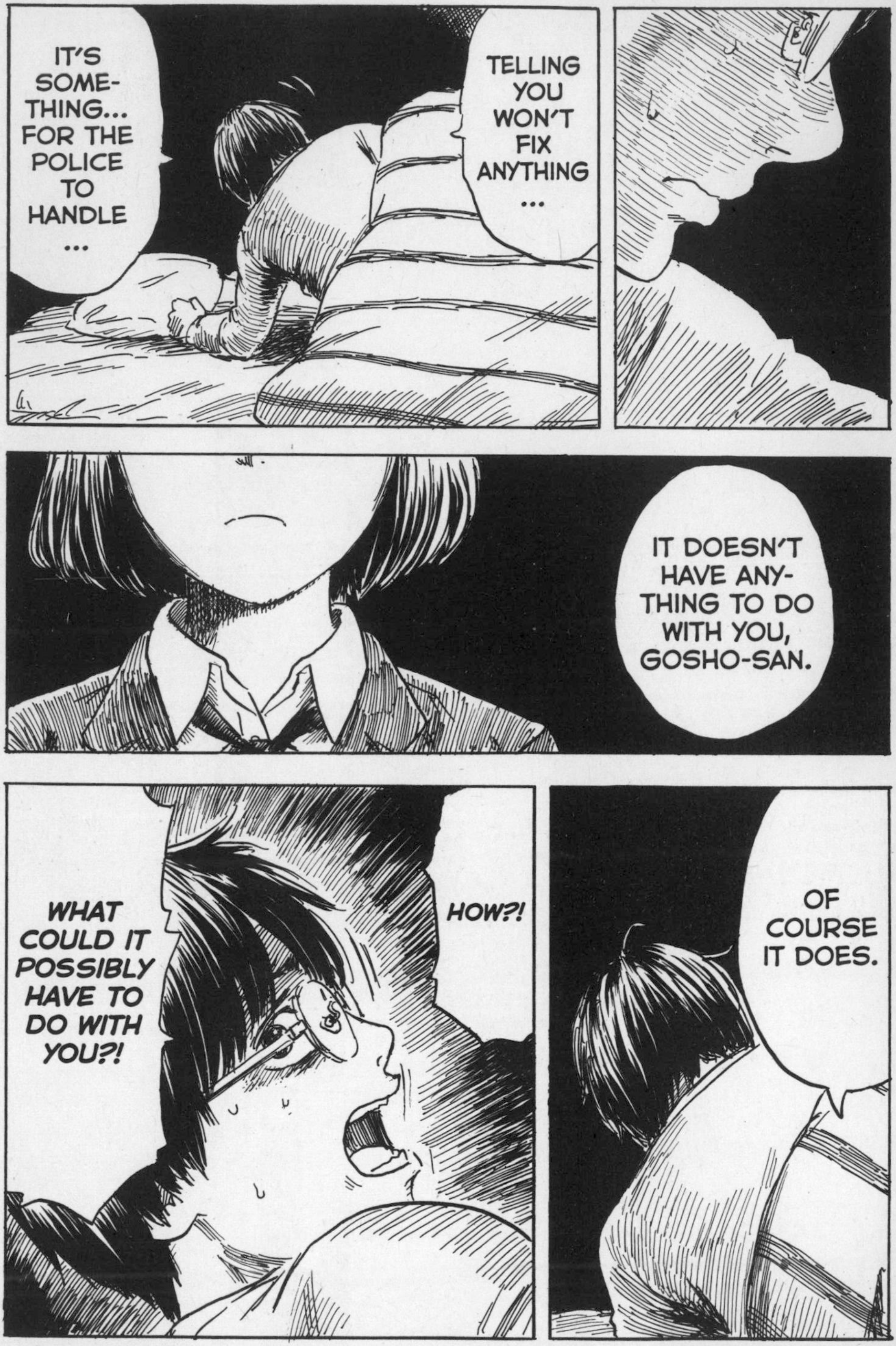
TELLING YOU WON'T FIX ANYTHING...
IT'S SOME-THING... FOR THE POLICE TO HANDLE...
IT DOESN'T HAVE ANY-THING TO DO WITH YOU, GOSHO-SAN.
OF COURSE IT DOES.
HOW?!
WHAT COULD IT POSSIBLY HAVE TO DO WITH YOU?!

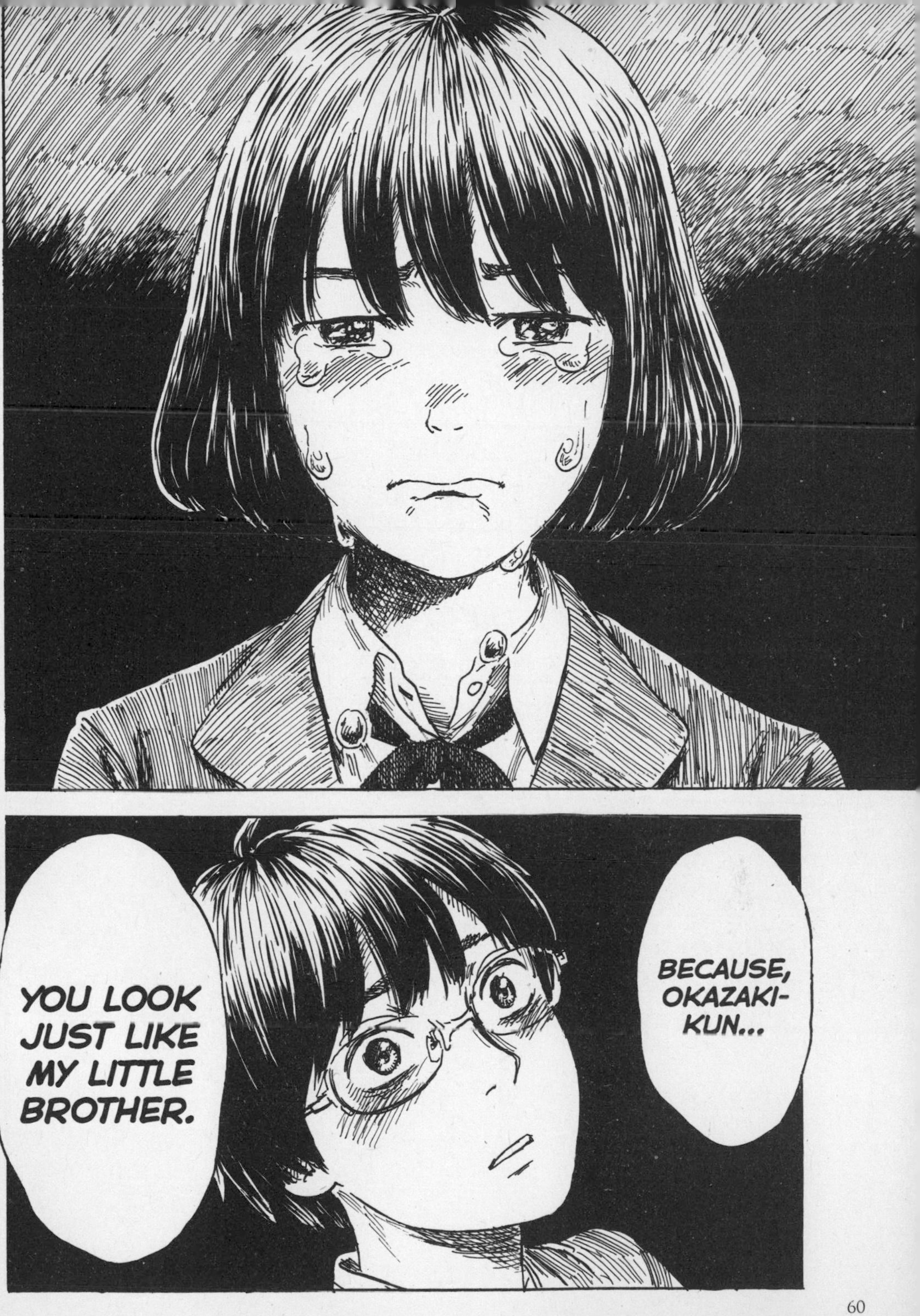
BECAUSE, OKAZAKI-KUN...
YOU LOOK JUST LIKE MY LITTLE BROTHER.

MY BROTHER...
...MY BROTHER DIED.
HE GOT SICK FIVE YEARS AGO...AND HE DIED.
I COULDN'T DO A SINGLE THING FOR HIM...
SO...SO IT DOES HAVE TO DO WITH ME.

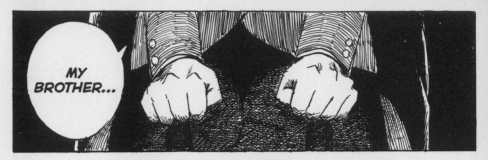

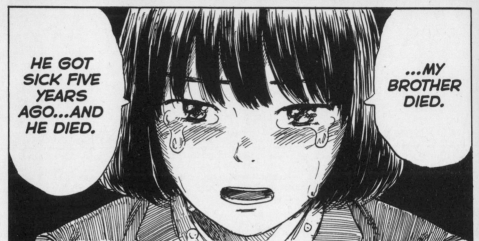

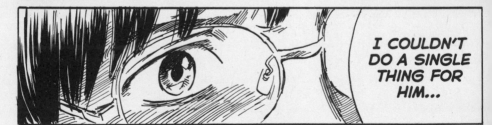

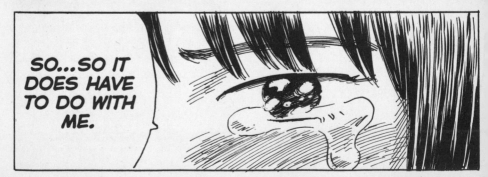

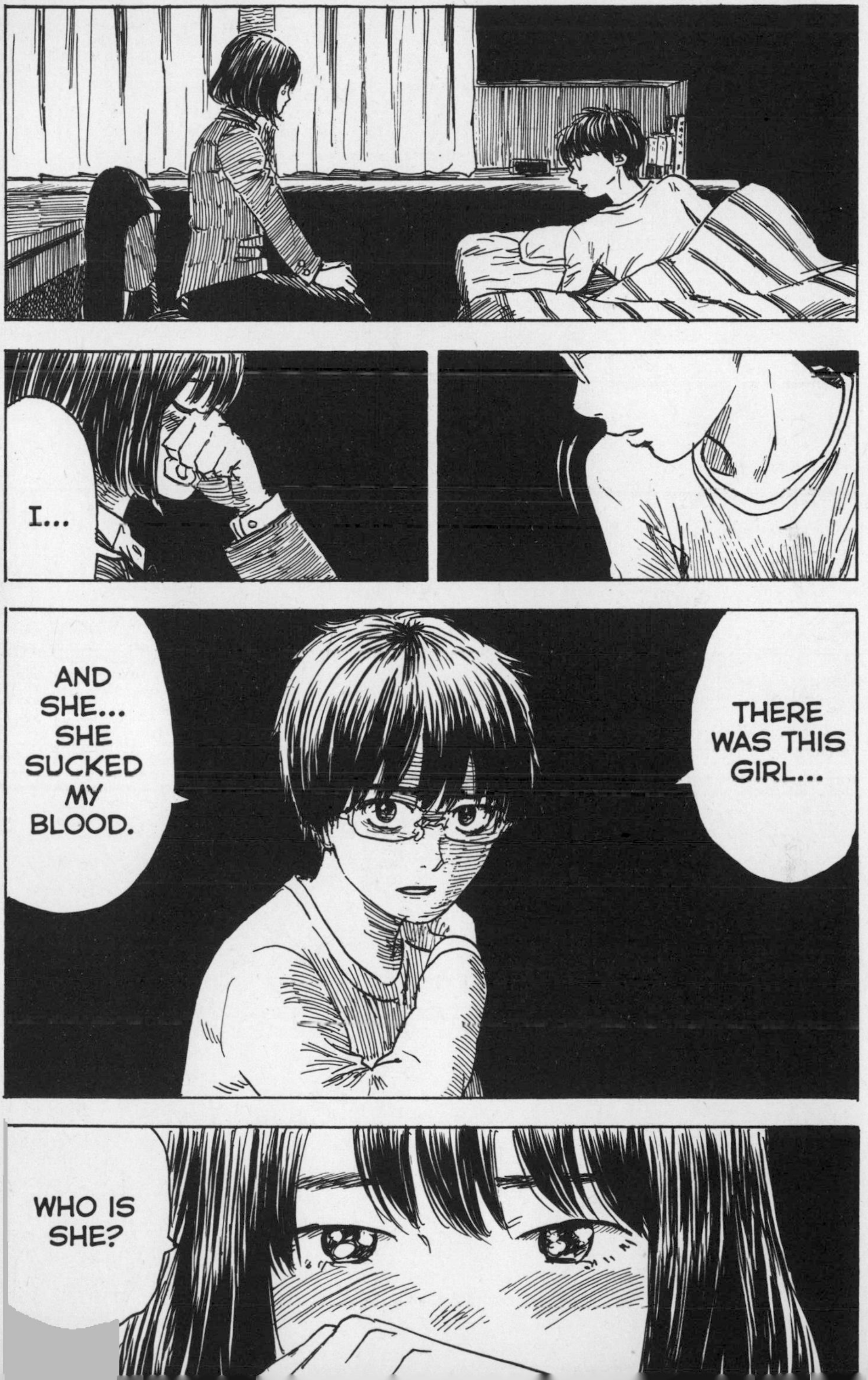
I...
THERE WAS THIS GIRL...
AND SHE... SHE SUCKED MY BLOOD.
WHO IS SHE?

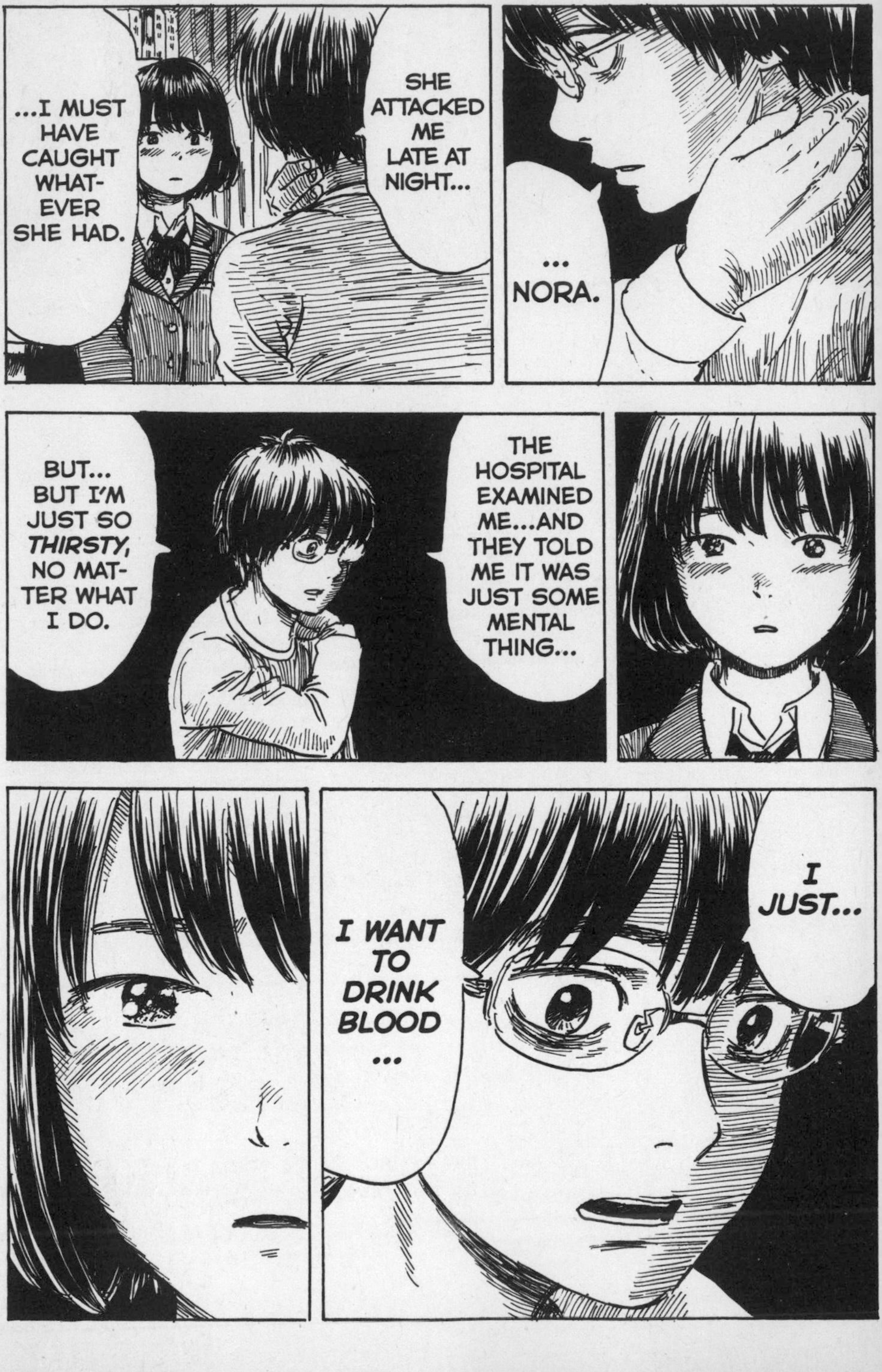
... NORA.
SHE ATTACKED ME LATE AT NIGHT...
...I MUST HAVE CAUGHT WHAT-EVER SHE HAD.
THE HOSPITAL EXAMINED ME...AND THEY TOLD ME IT WAS JUST SOME MENTAL THING...
BUT... BUT I'M JUST SO *THIRSTY*, NO MAT-TER WHAT I DO.
I JUST...
I WANT TO DRINK BLOOD ...

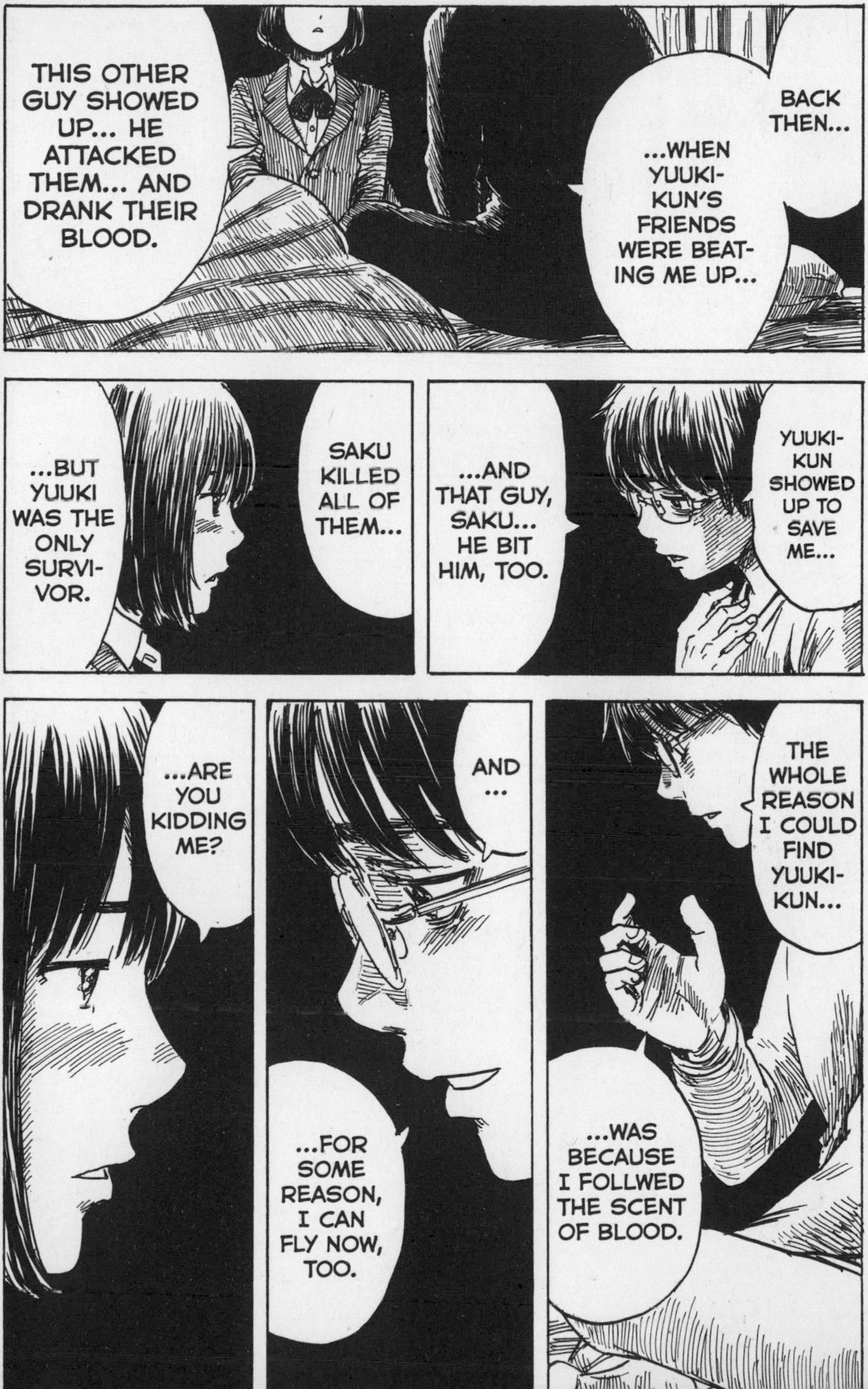
BACK THEN...
...WHEN YUUKI-KUN'S FRIENDS WERE BEATING ME UP...
THIS OTHER GUY SHOWED UP... HE ATTACKED THEM... AND DRANK THEIR BLOOD.
YUUKI-KUN SHOWED UP TO SAVE ME...
...AND THAT GUY, SAKU... HE BIT HIM, TOO.
SAKU KILLED ALL OF THEM...
...BUT YUUKI WAS THE ONLY SURVIVOR.
THE WHOLE REASON I COULD FIND YUUKI-KUN...
...WAS BECAUSE I FOLLWED THE SCENT OF BLOOD.
AND ...
...FOR SOME REASON, I CAN FLY NOW, TOO.
...ARE YOU KIDDING ME?

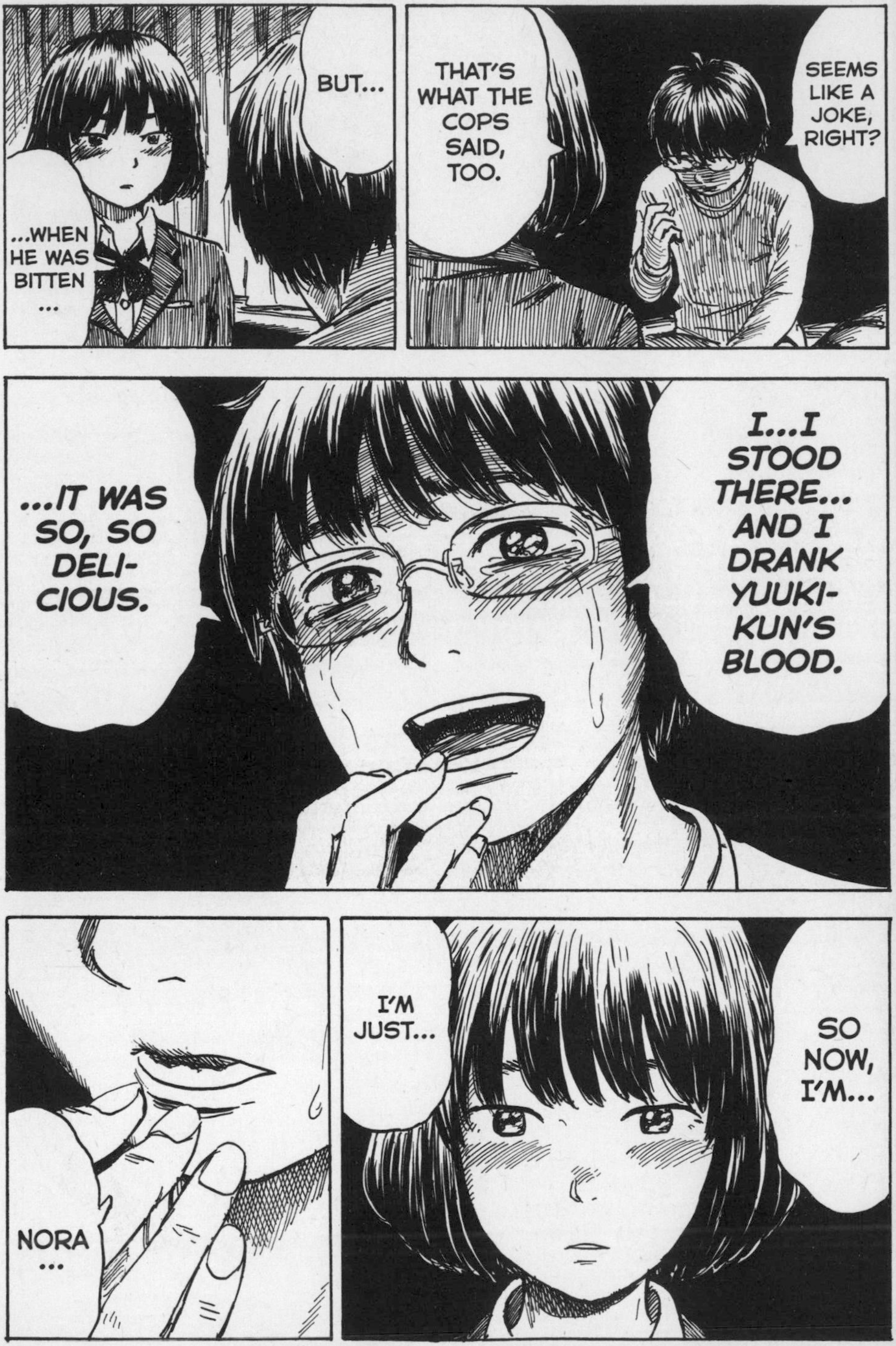
SEEMS LIKE A JOKE, RIGHT?
THAT'S WHAT THE COPS SAID, TOO.
BUT...
...WHEN HE WAS BITTEN ...
I...I STOOD THERE... AND I DRANK YUUKI-KUN'S BLOOD.
...IT WAS SO, SO DELI-CIOUS.
SO NOW, I'M...
I'M JUST...
NORA ...

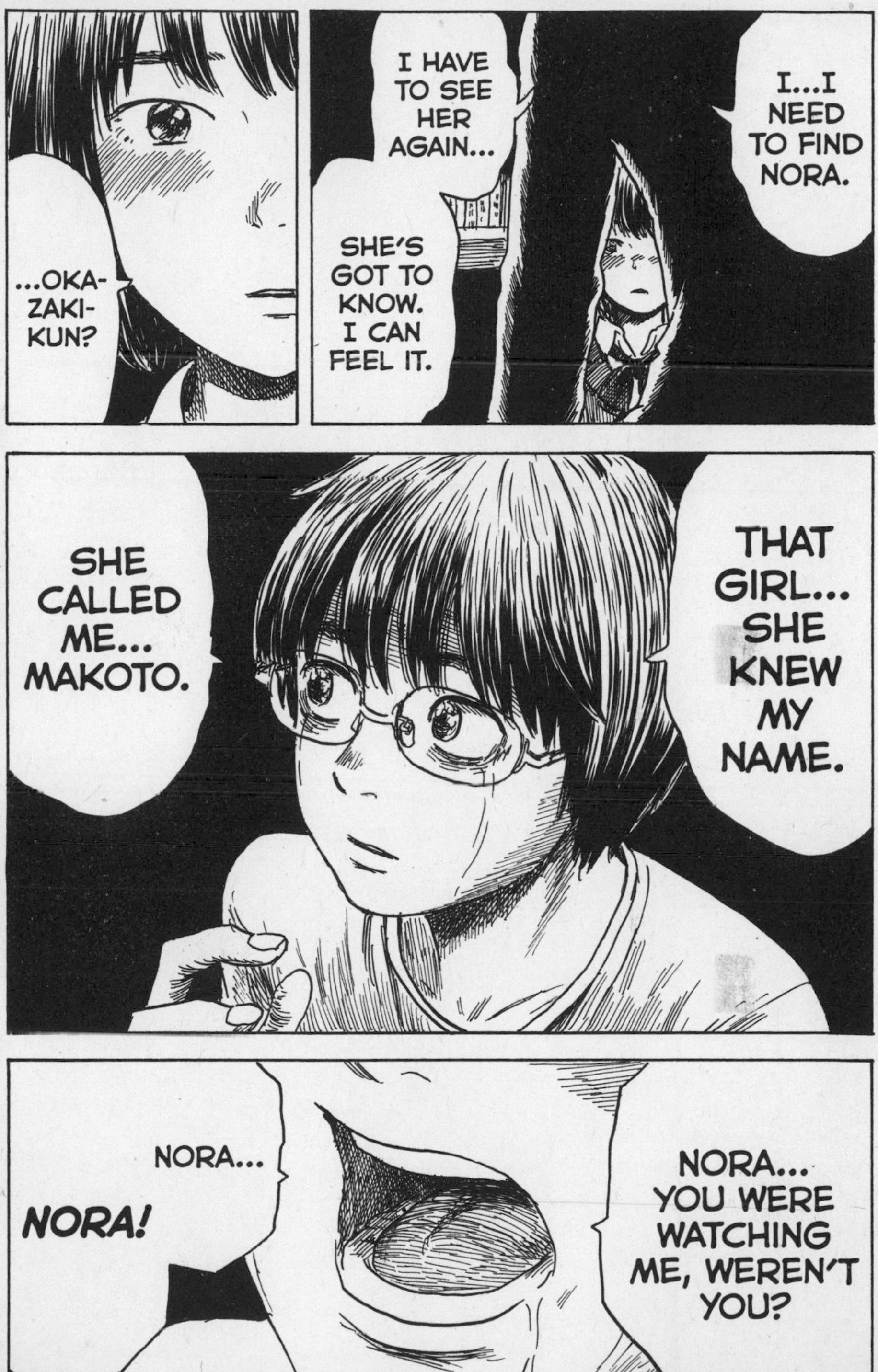
I...I NEED TO FIND NORA.
I HAVE TO SEE HER AGAIN...
SHE'S GOT TO KNOW. I CAN FEEL IT.
...OKA-ZAKI-KUN?
THAT GIRL... SHE KNEW MY NAME.
SHE CALLED ME... MAKOTO.
NORA... YOU WERE WATCHING ME, WEREN'T YOU?
NORA...
NORA!

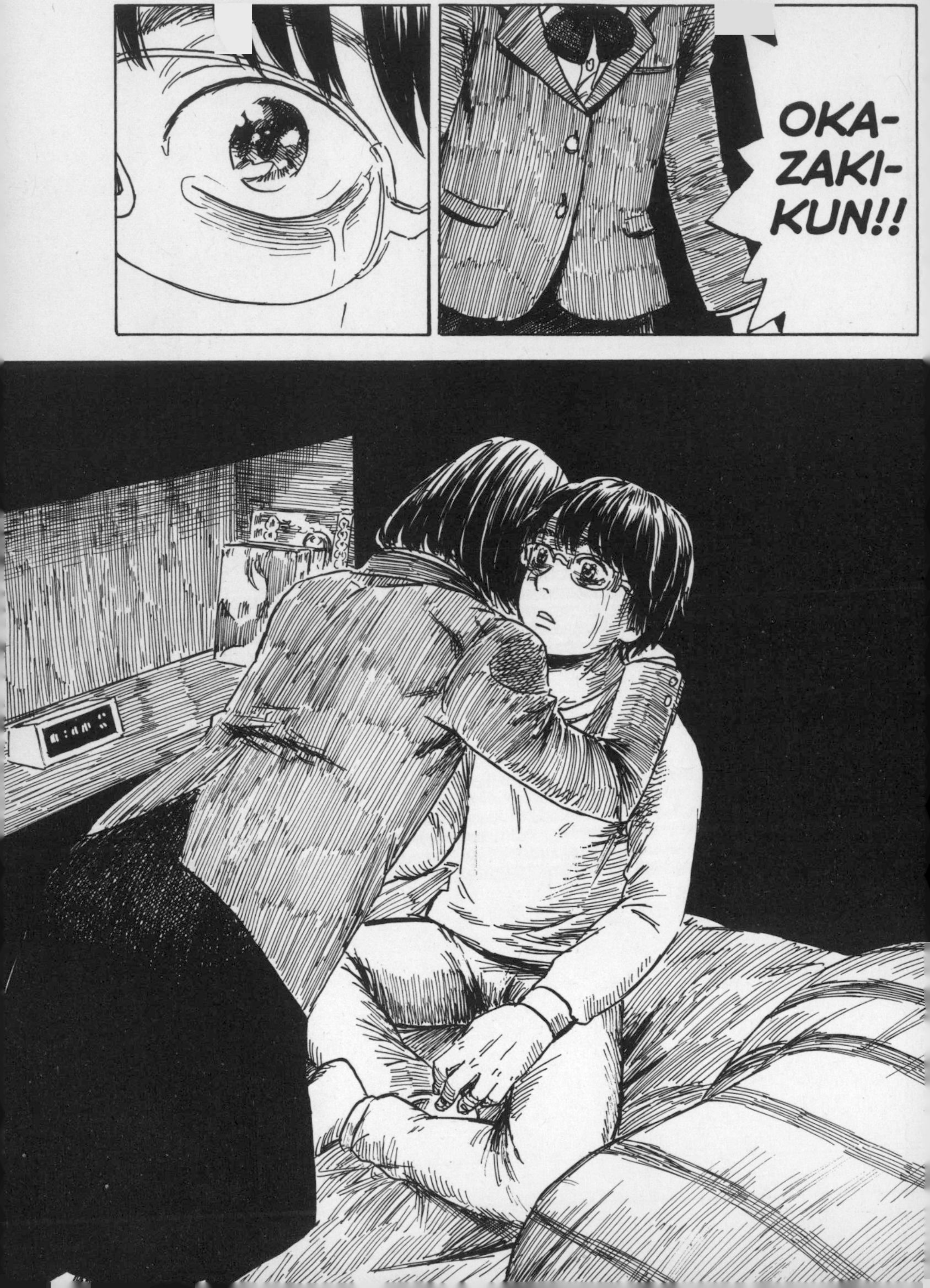
OKA-ZAKI-KUN!!

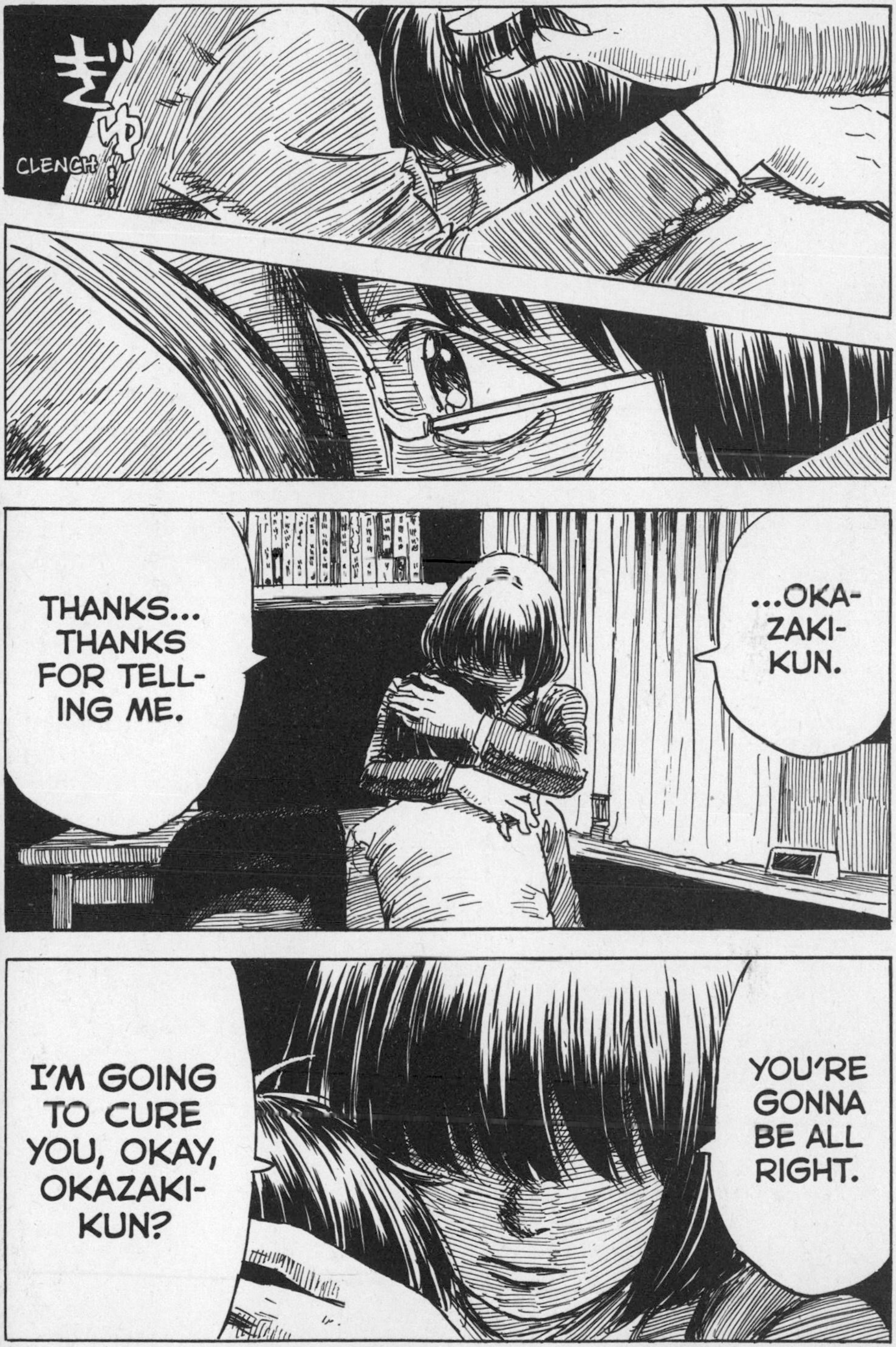
ぎゅ…
CLENCH
...OKAZAKI-KUN.
THANKS... THANKS FOR TELLING ME.
YOU'RE GONNA BE ALL RIGHT.
I'M GOING TO CURE YOU, OKAY, OKAZAKI-KUN?

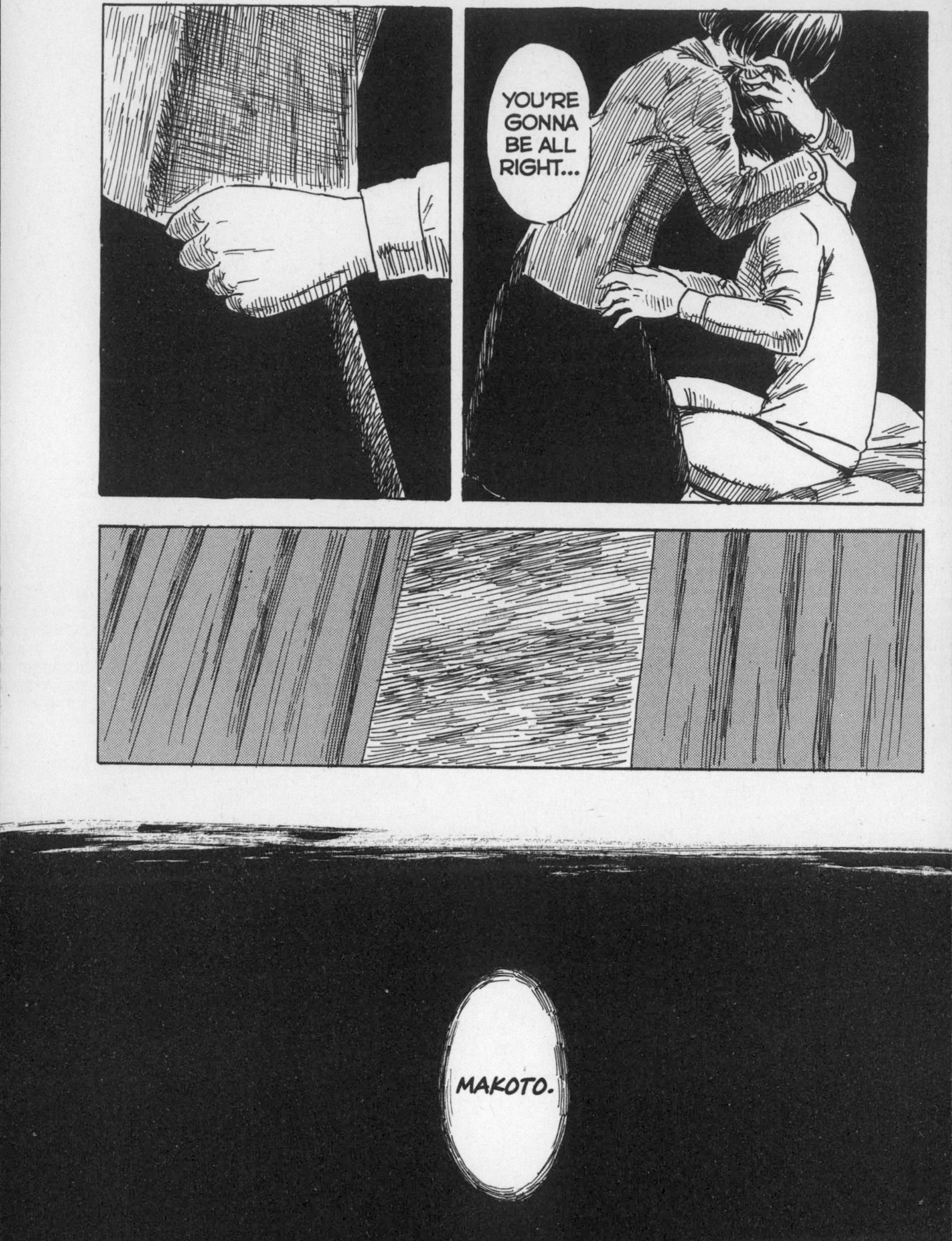
YOU'RE GONNA BE ALL RIGHT...
MAKOTO.

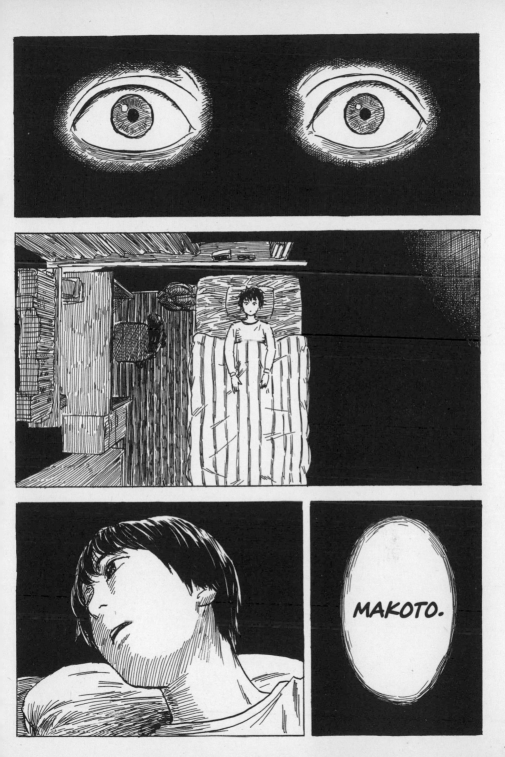

MAKOTO.

70

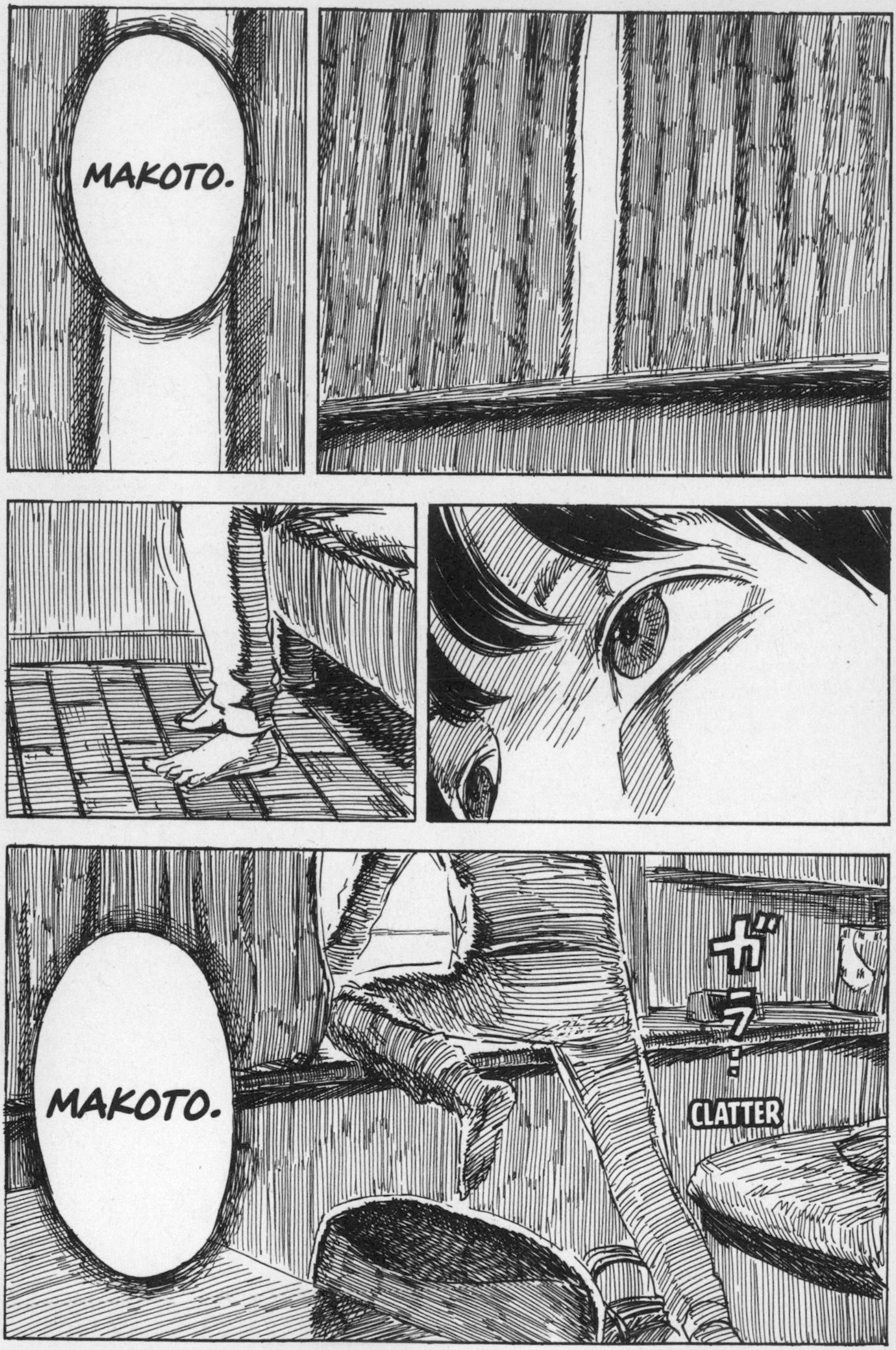
MAKOTO.
ガラッ!
CLATTER
MAKOTO.

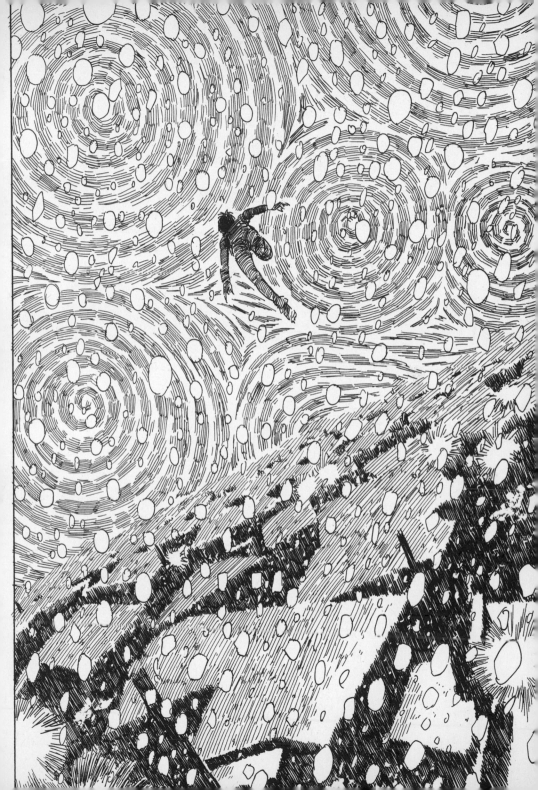

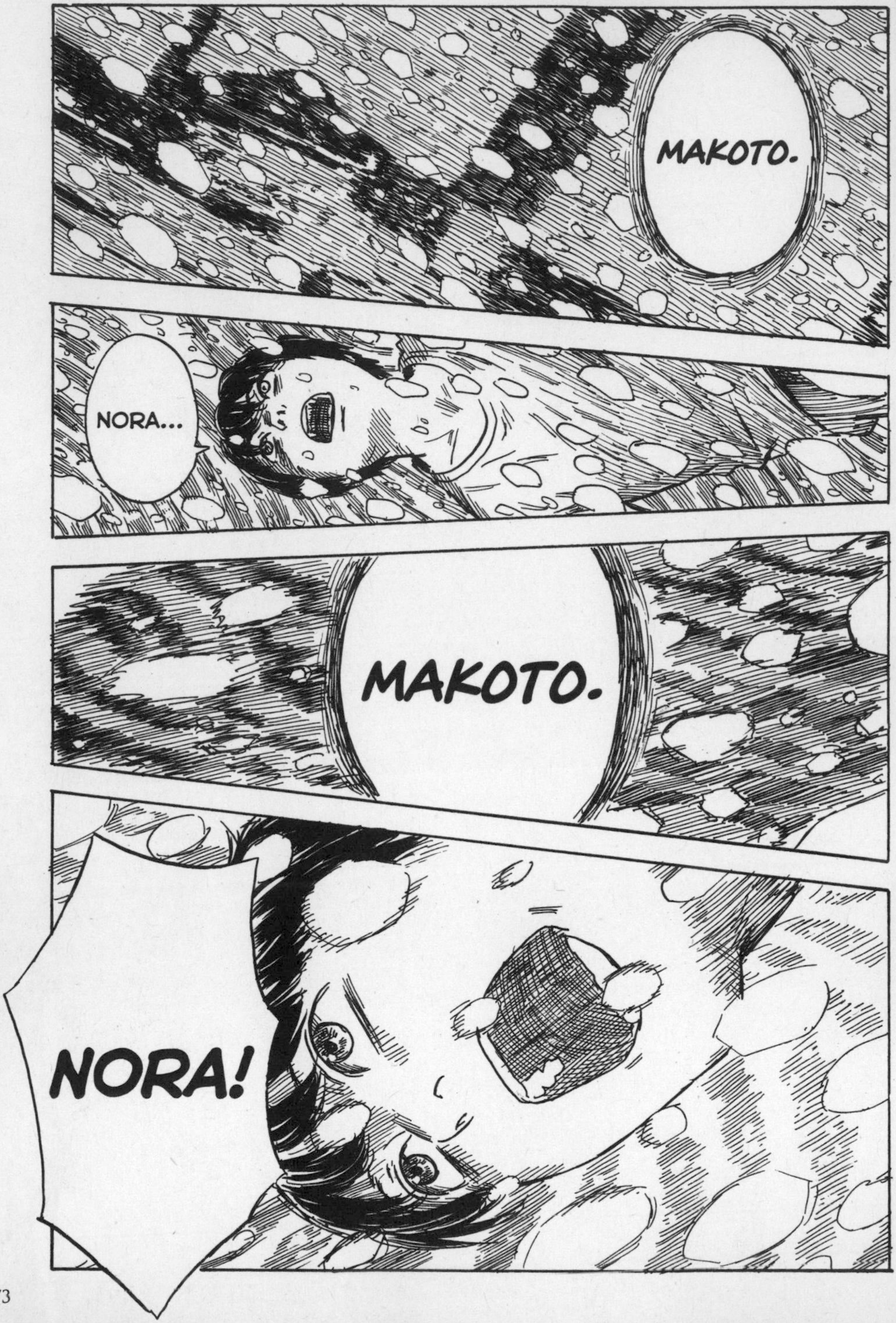
MAKOTO.
NORA...
MAKOTO.
NORA!

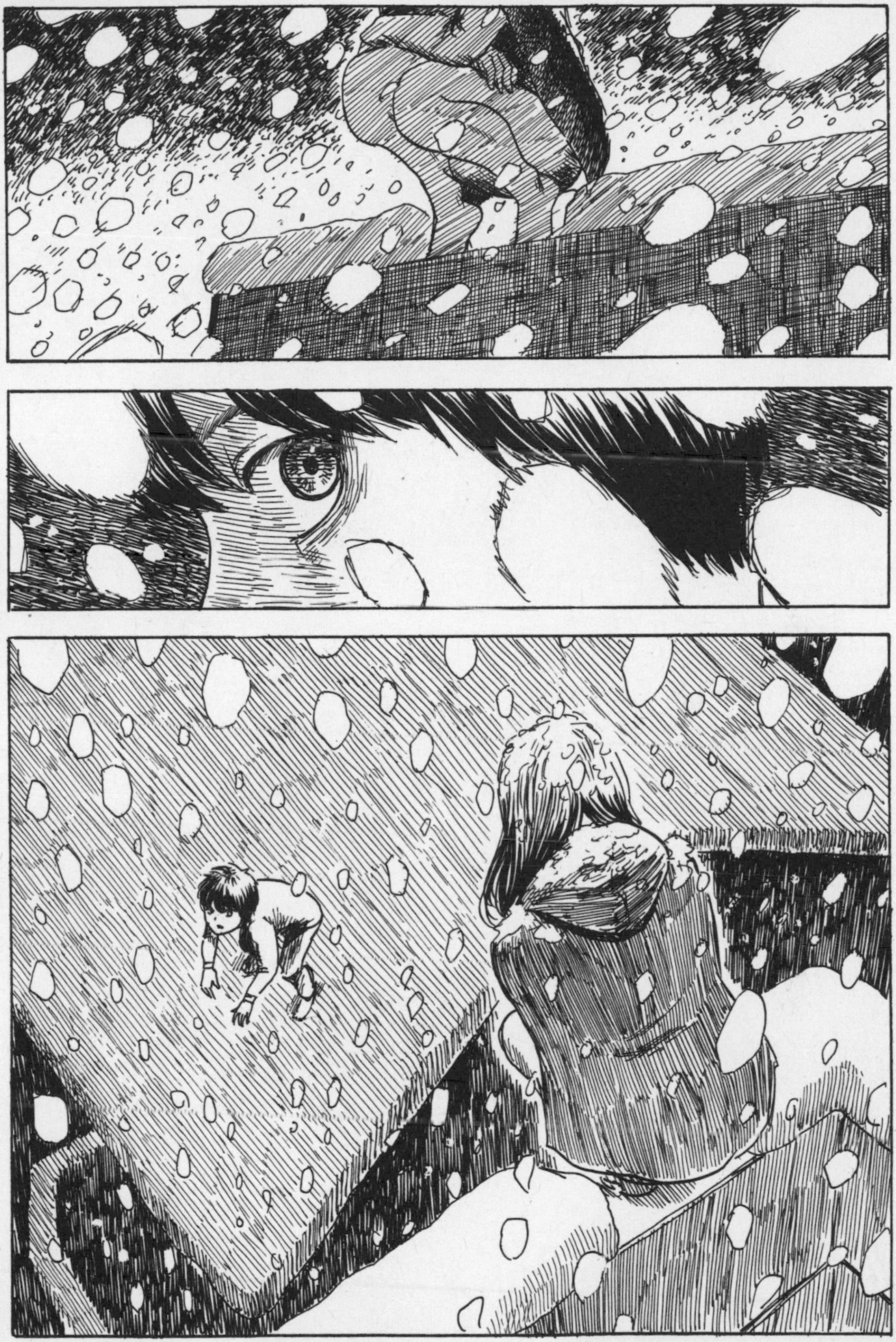

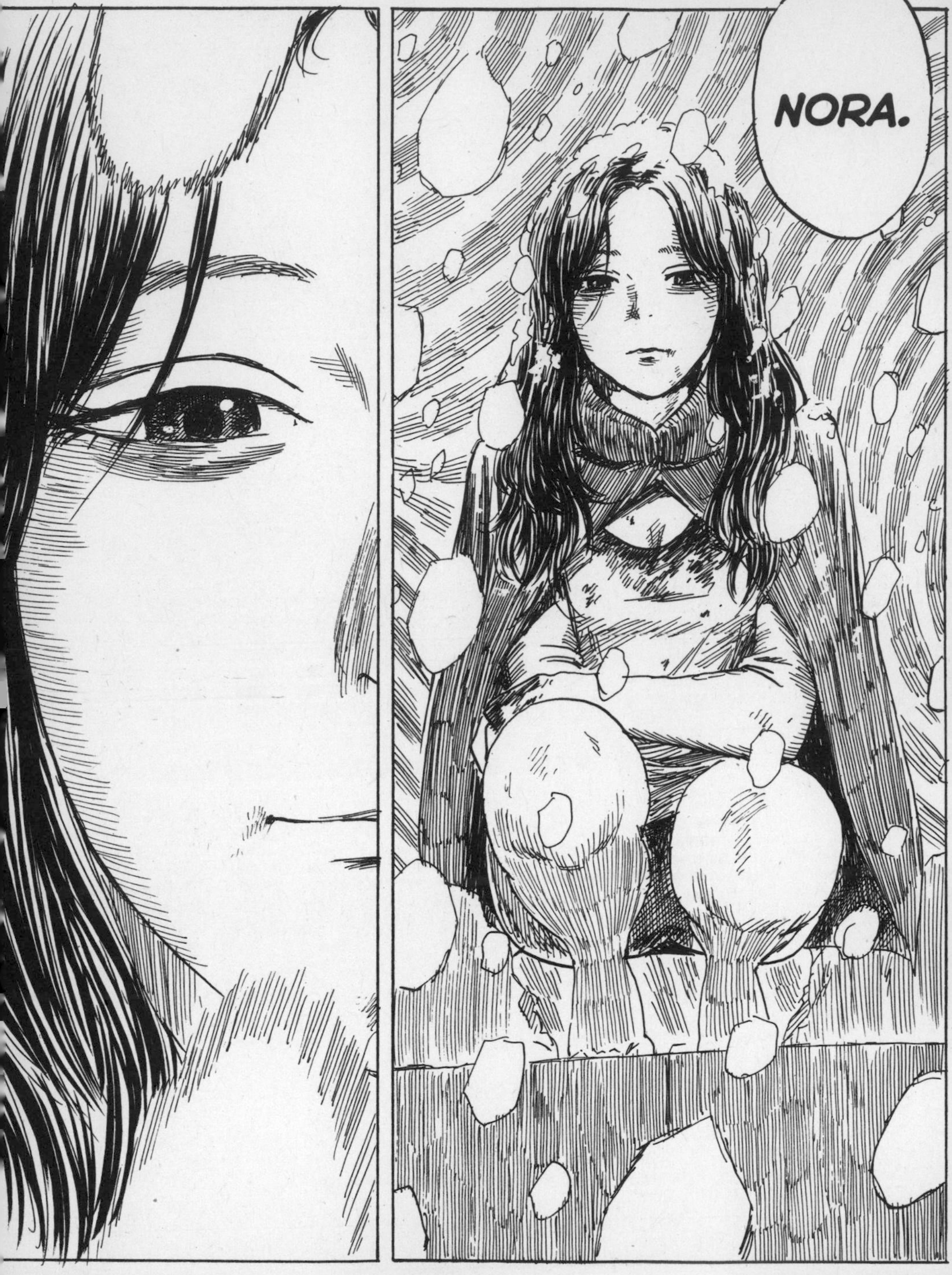
NORA.

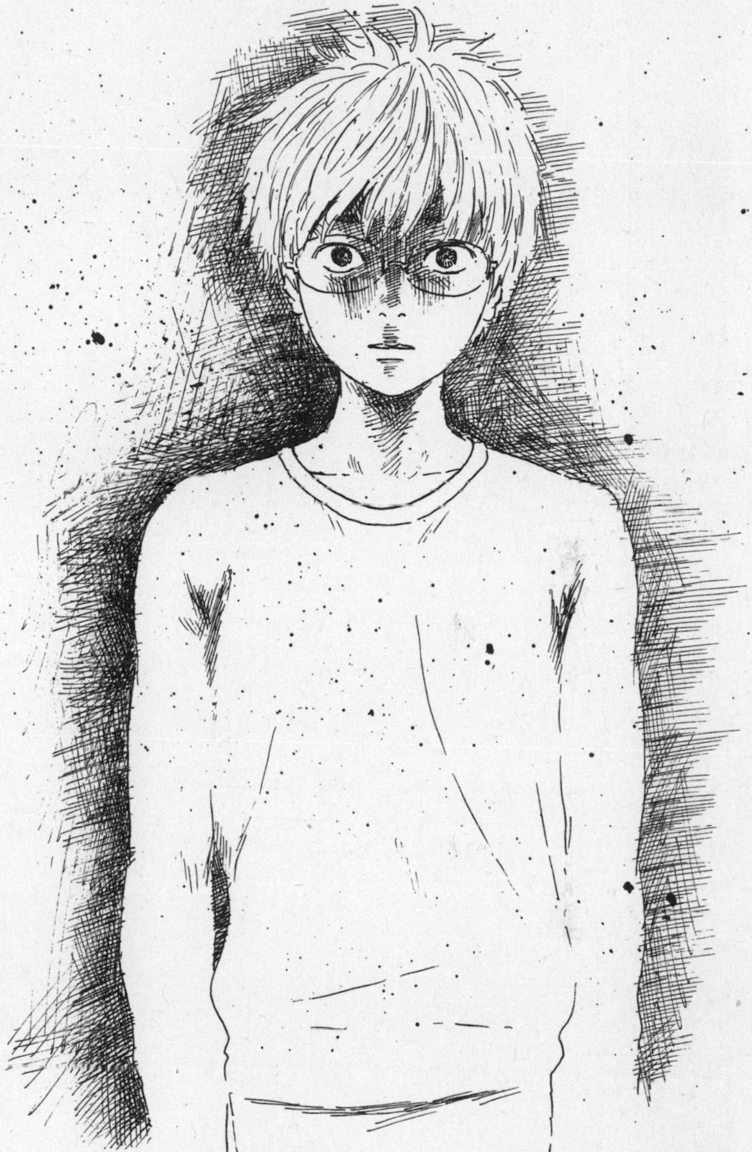

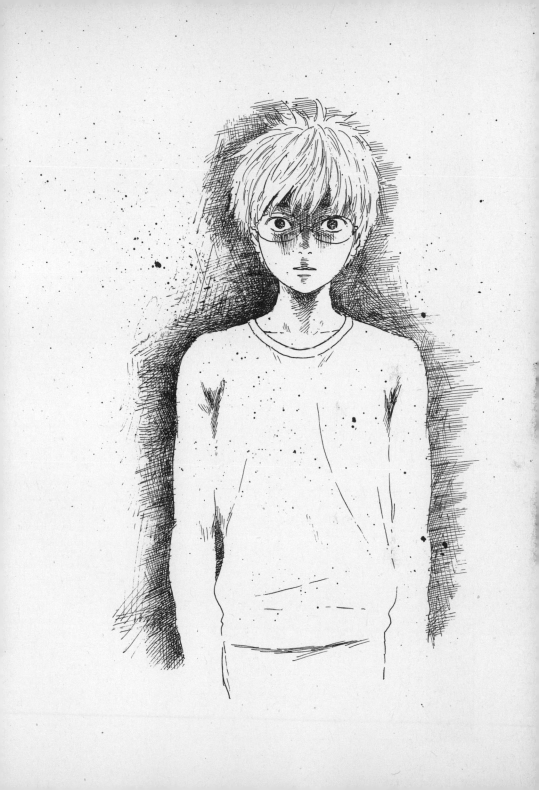

Chapter 13: The Bedroom

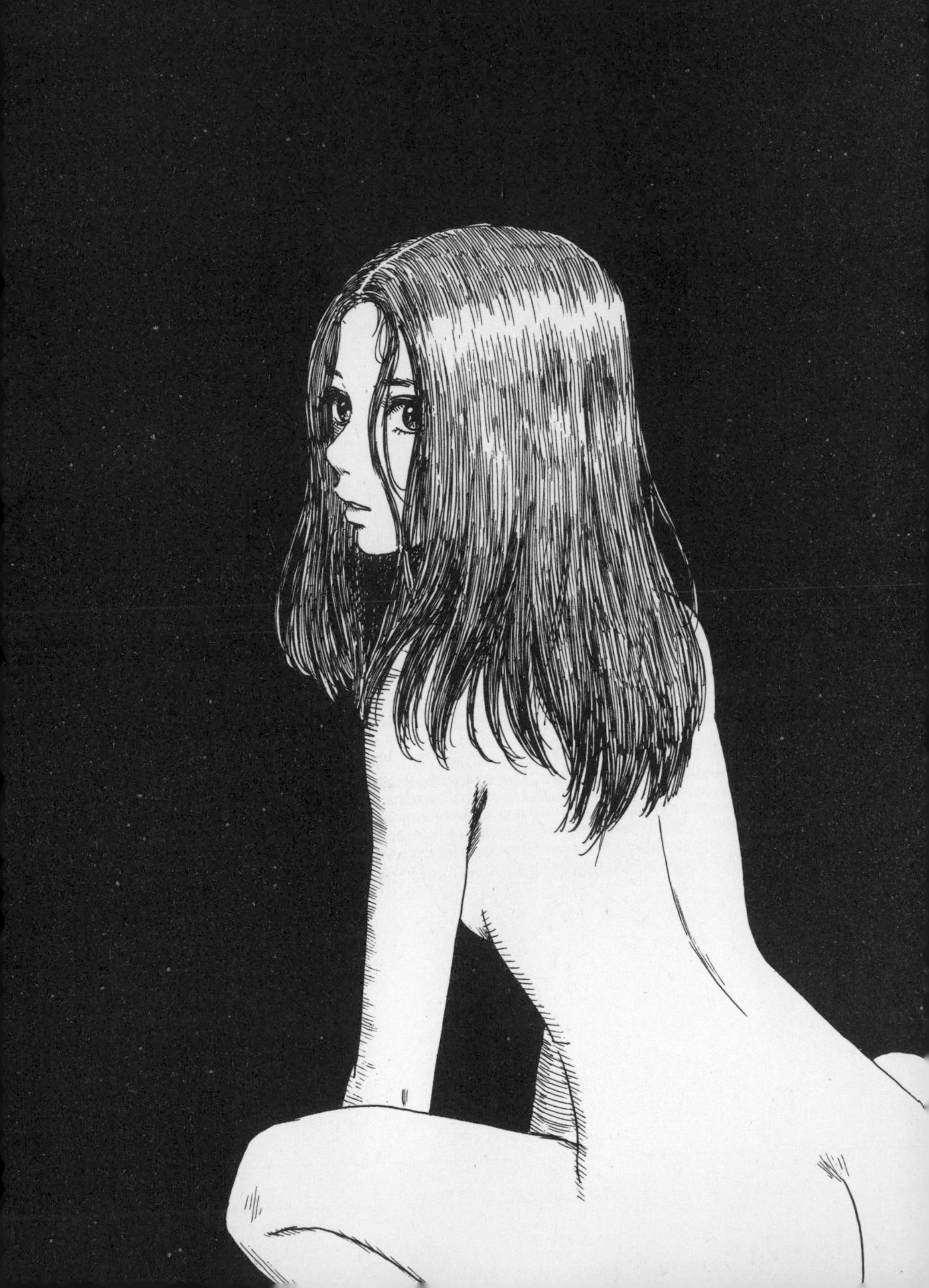

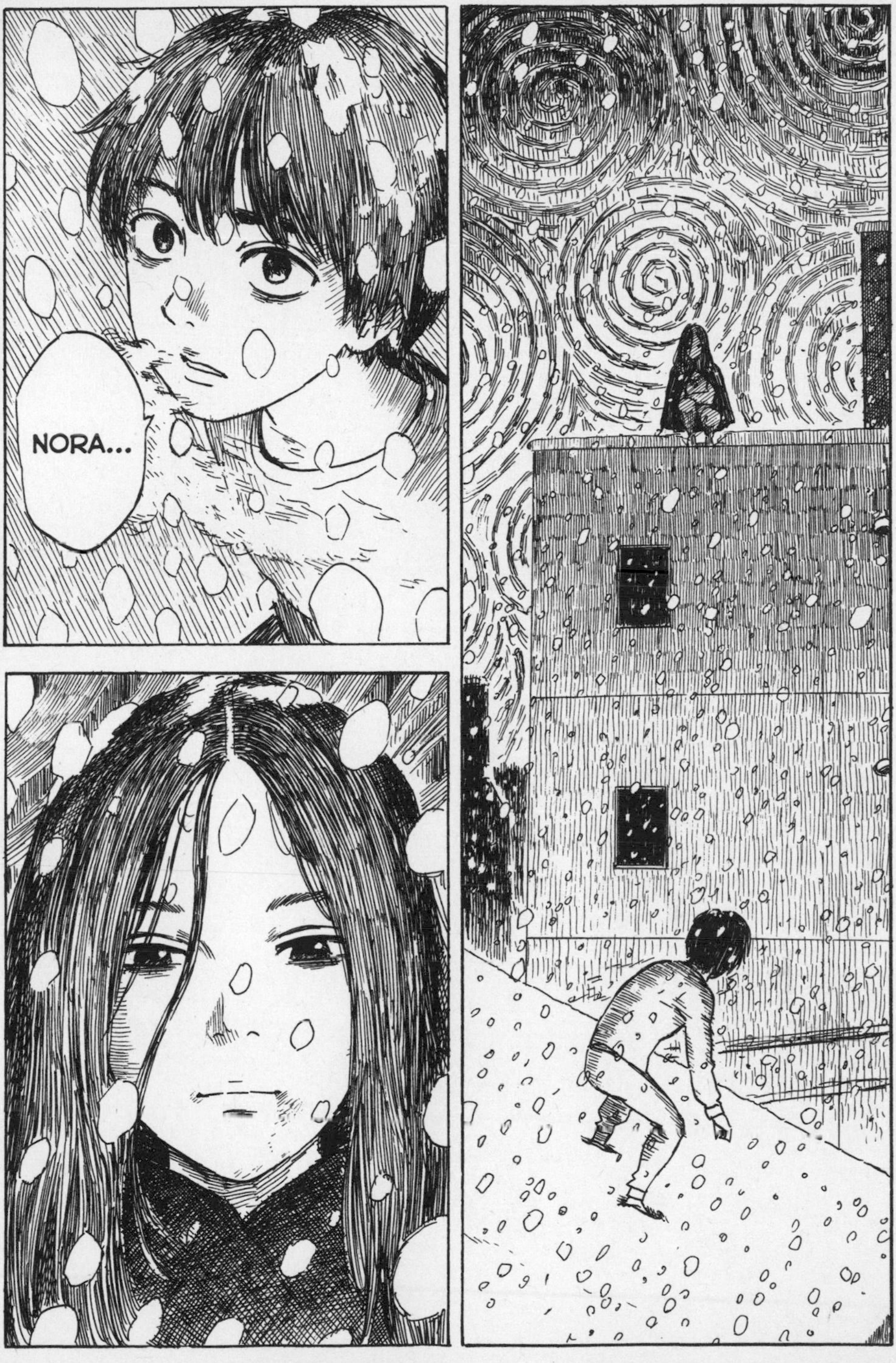
NORA...

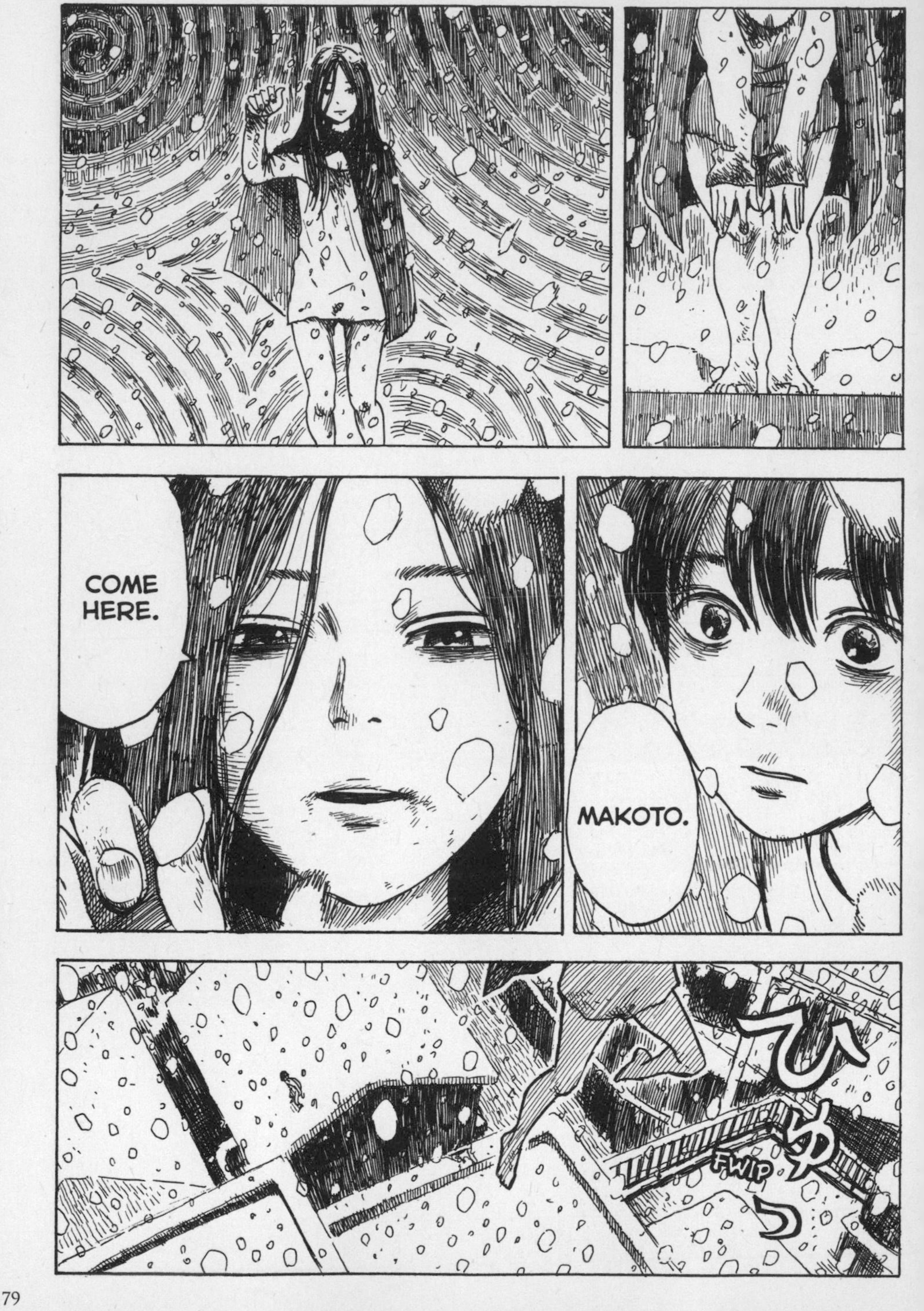
MAKOTO.
COME HERE.
ひゅっ
FWIP

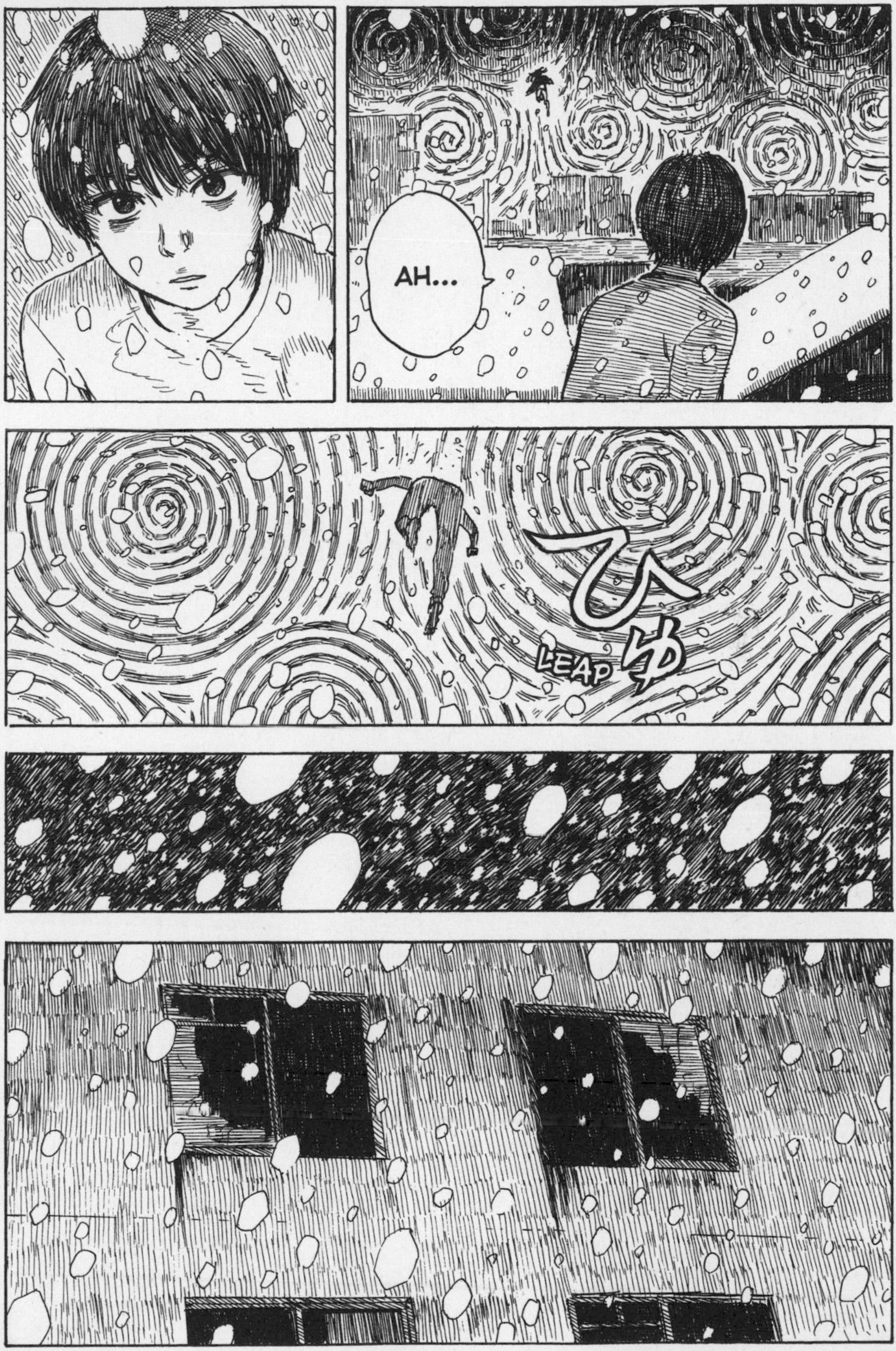
AH...
ひゅ
LEAP

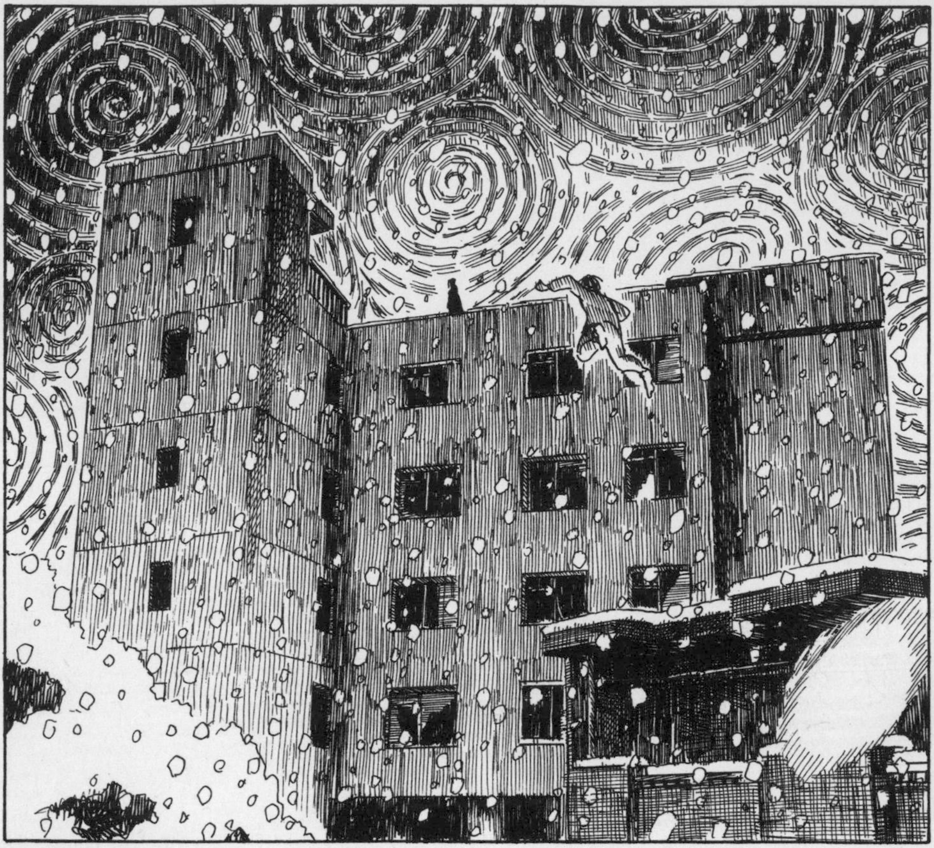

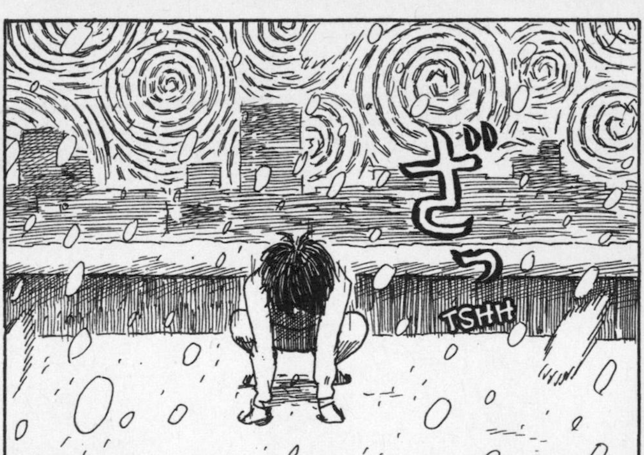
どっ
DD
TSHH

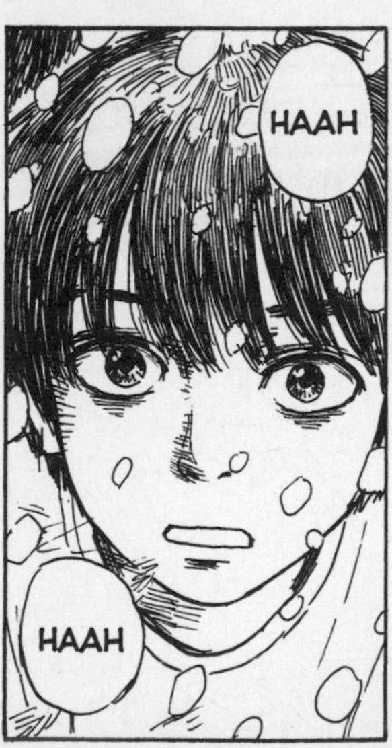
HAAH
HAAH

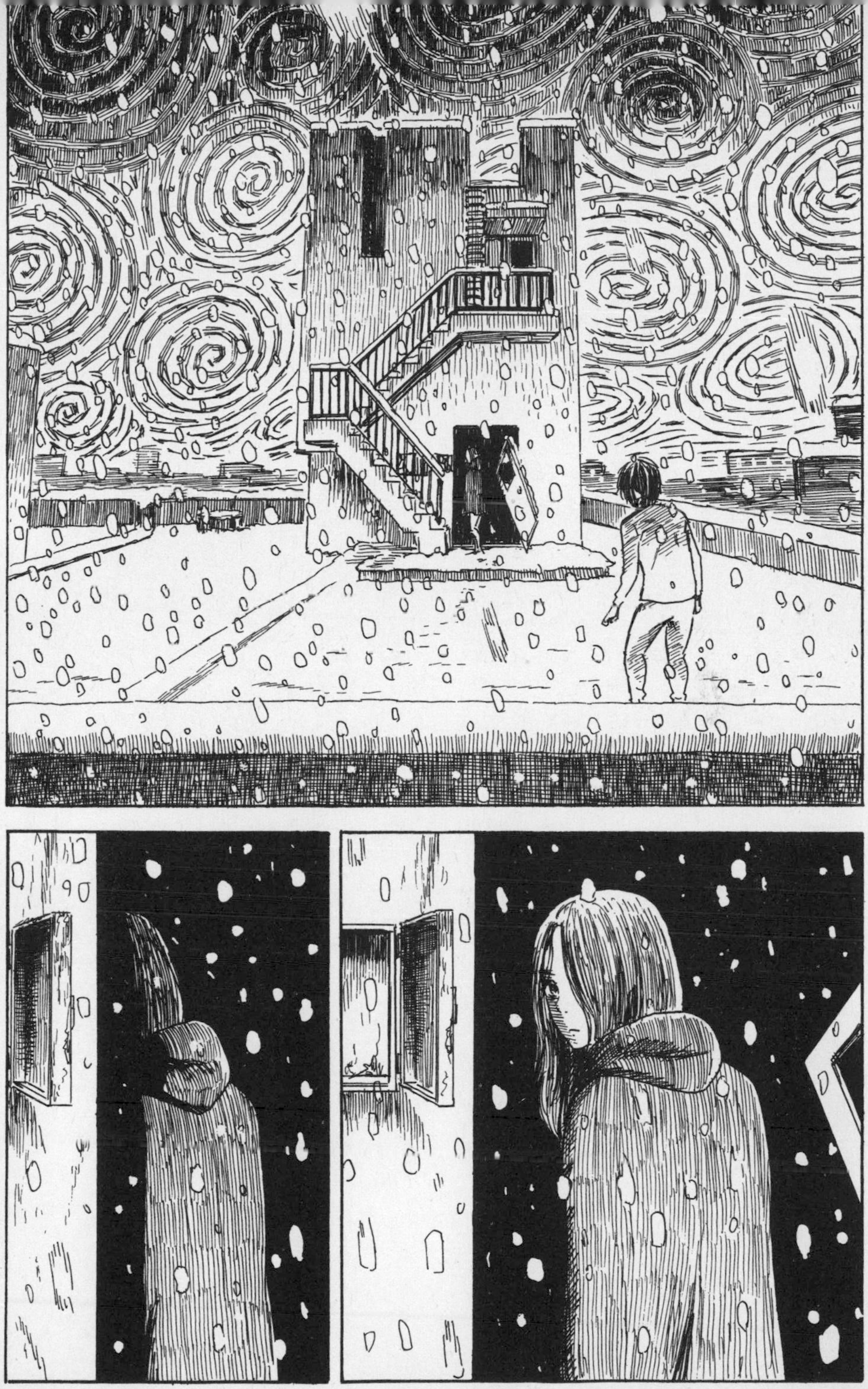

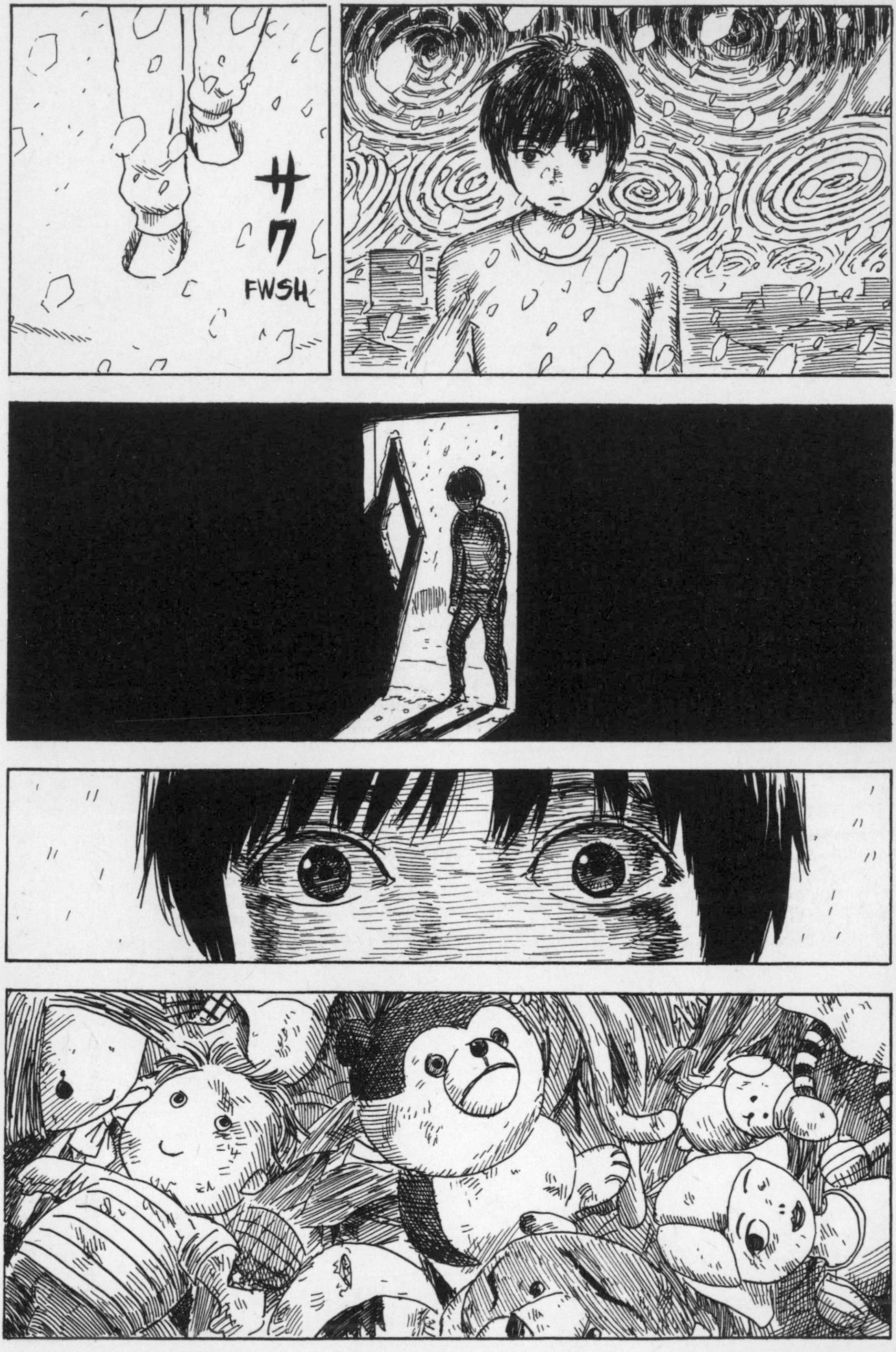
サク
FWSH

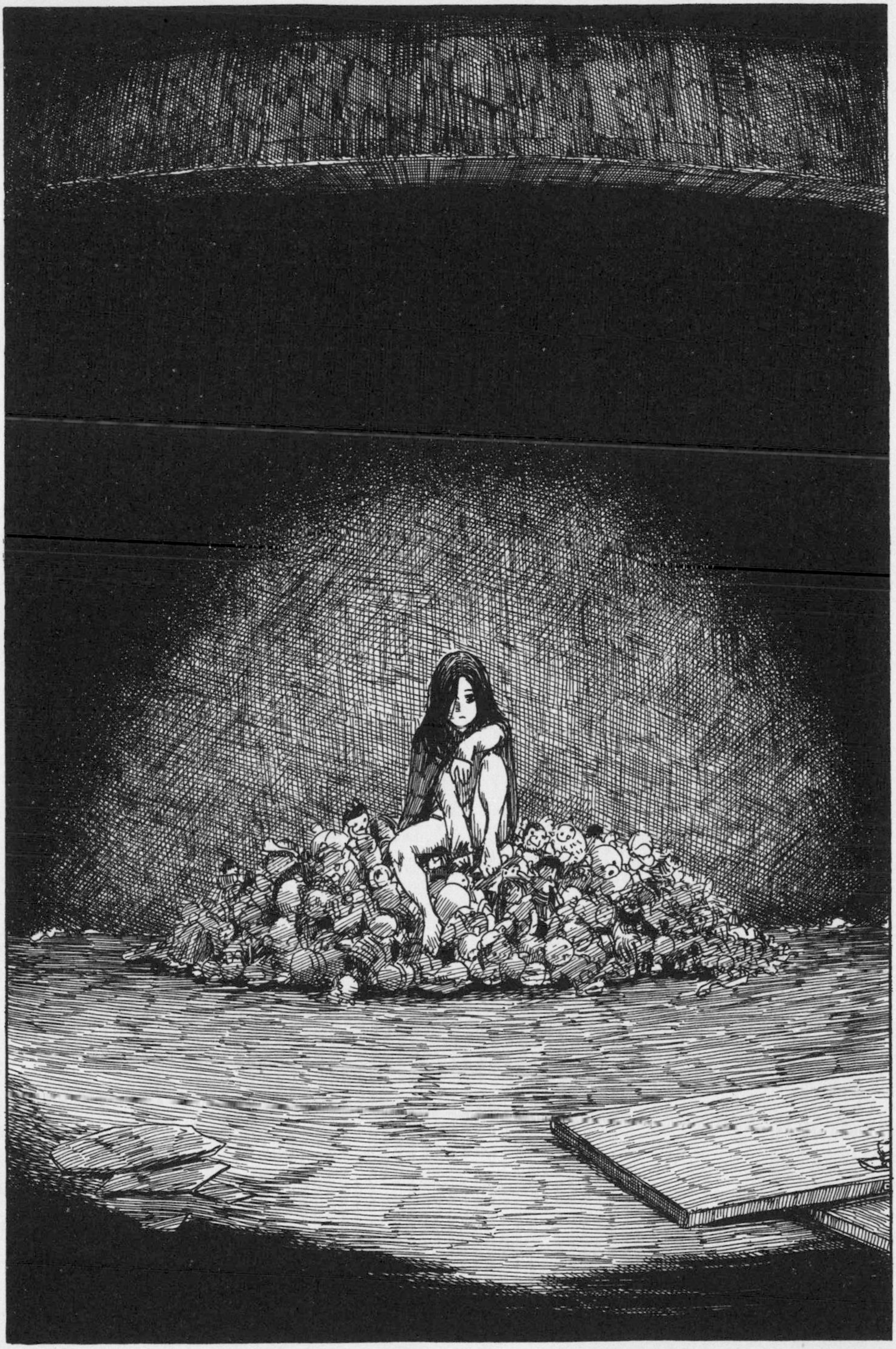

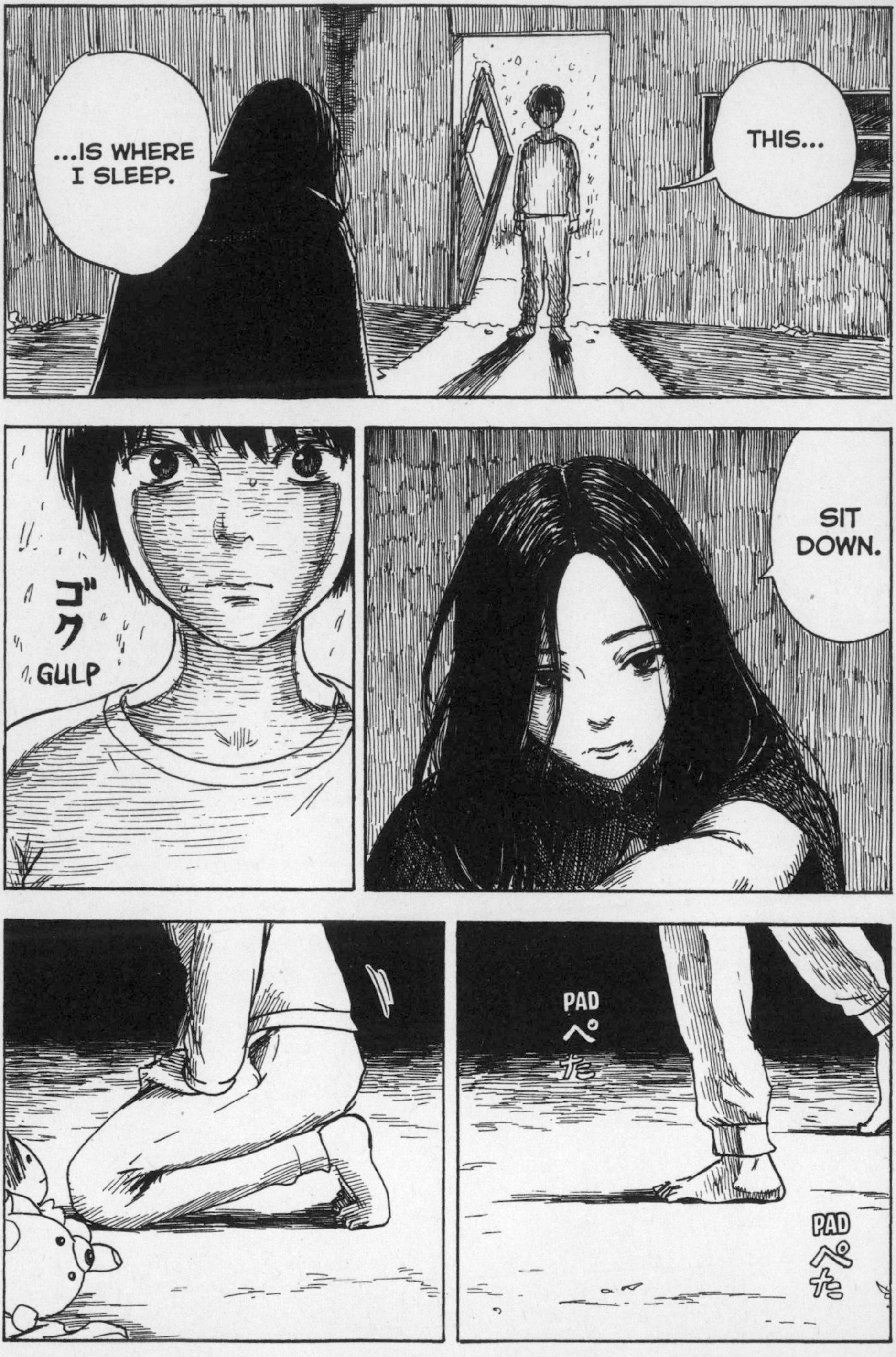
THIS...
...IS WHERE I SLEEP.
SIT DOWN.
ゴク
GULP
PAD
ぺた
PAD
ぺた

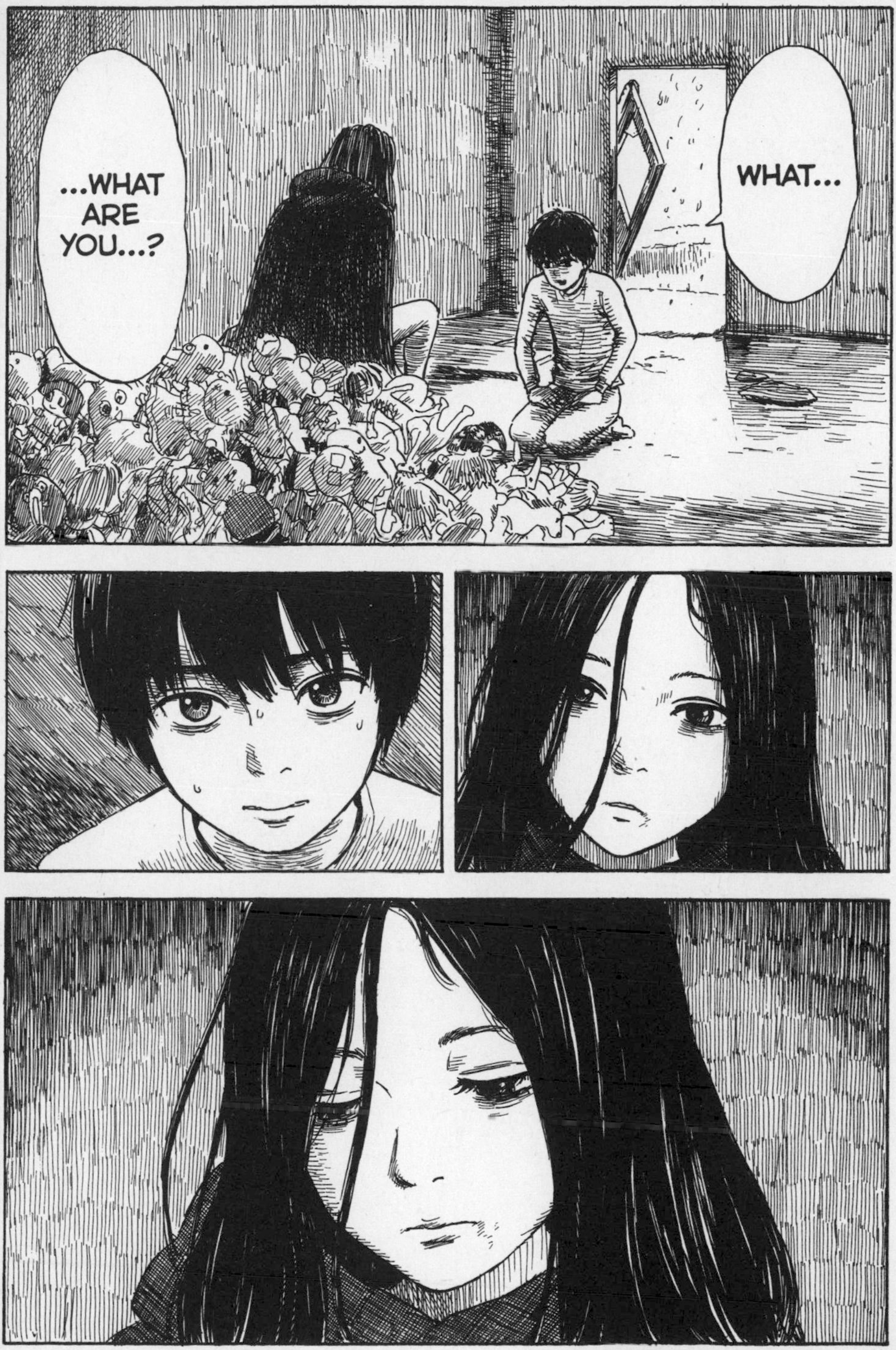
WHAT...
...WHAT ARE YOU...?

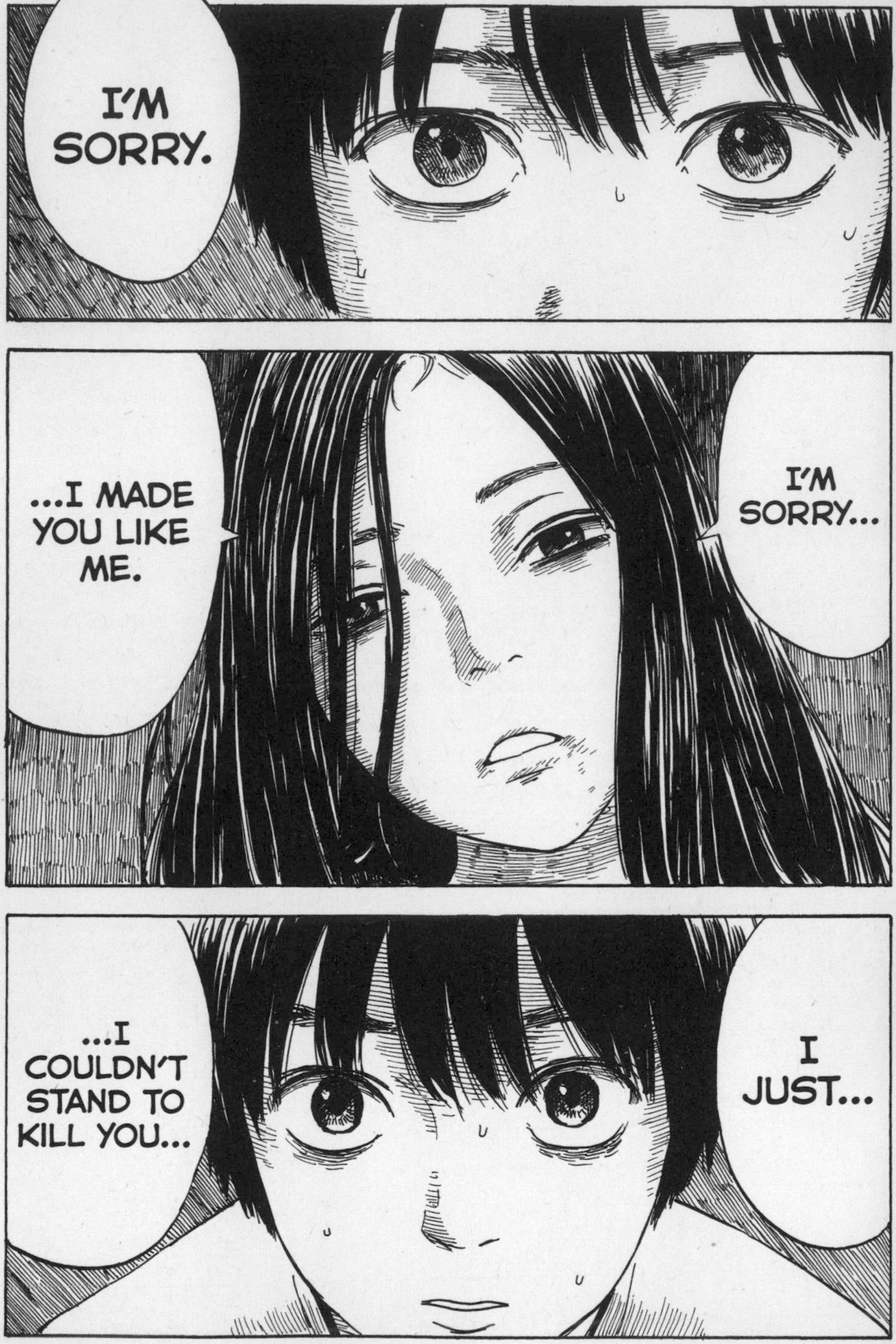
I'M SORRY.
I'M SORRY...
...I MADE YOU LIKE ME.
I JUST...
...I COULDN'T STAND TO KILL YOU...

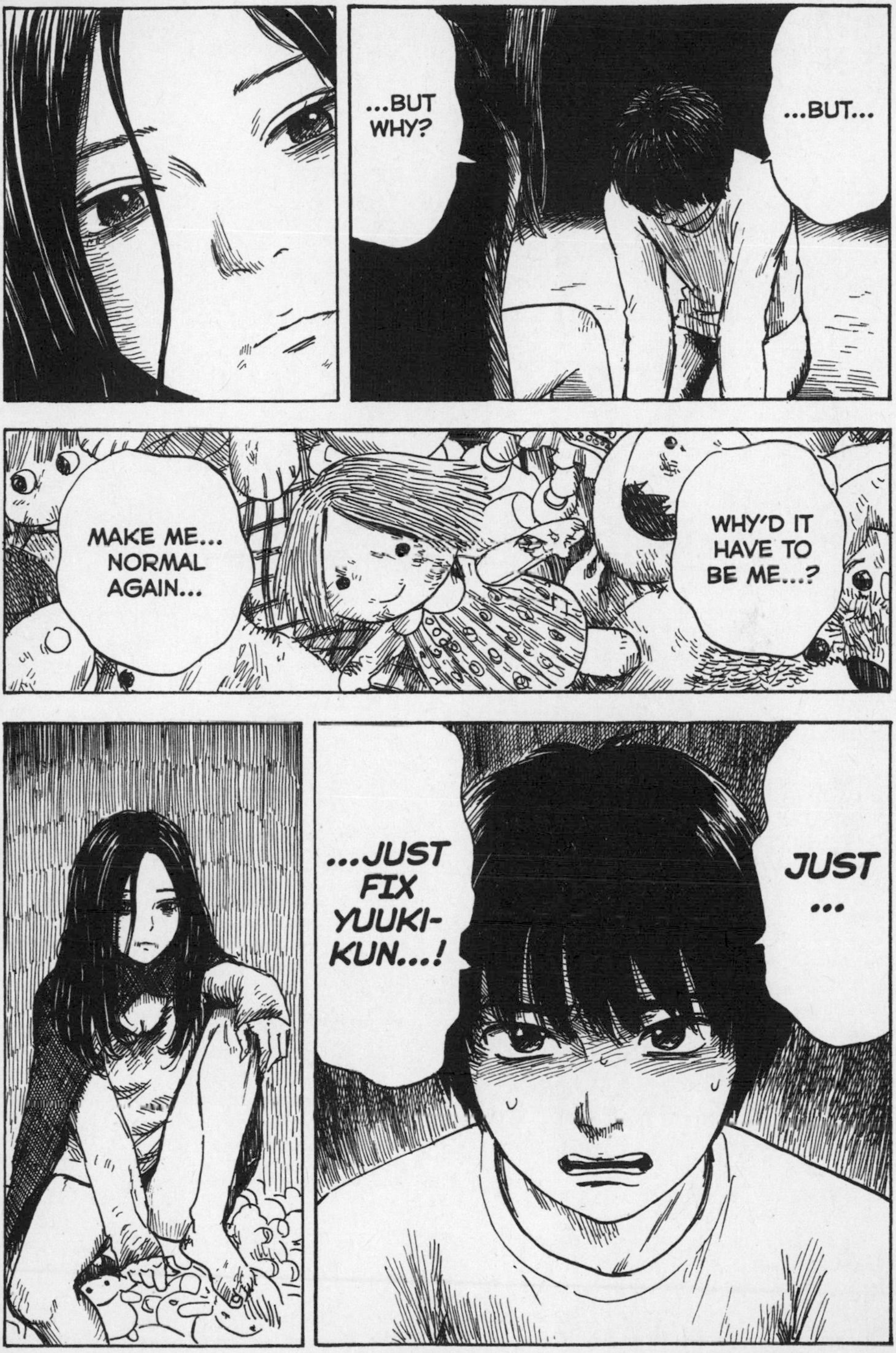
...BUT...
...BUT WHY?
WHY'D IT HAVE TO BE ME...?
MAKE ME... NORMAL AGAIN...
JUST ...
...JUST FIX YUUKI-KUN...!

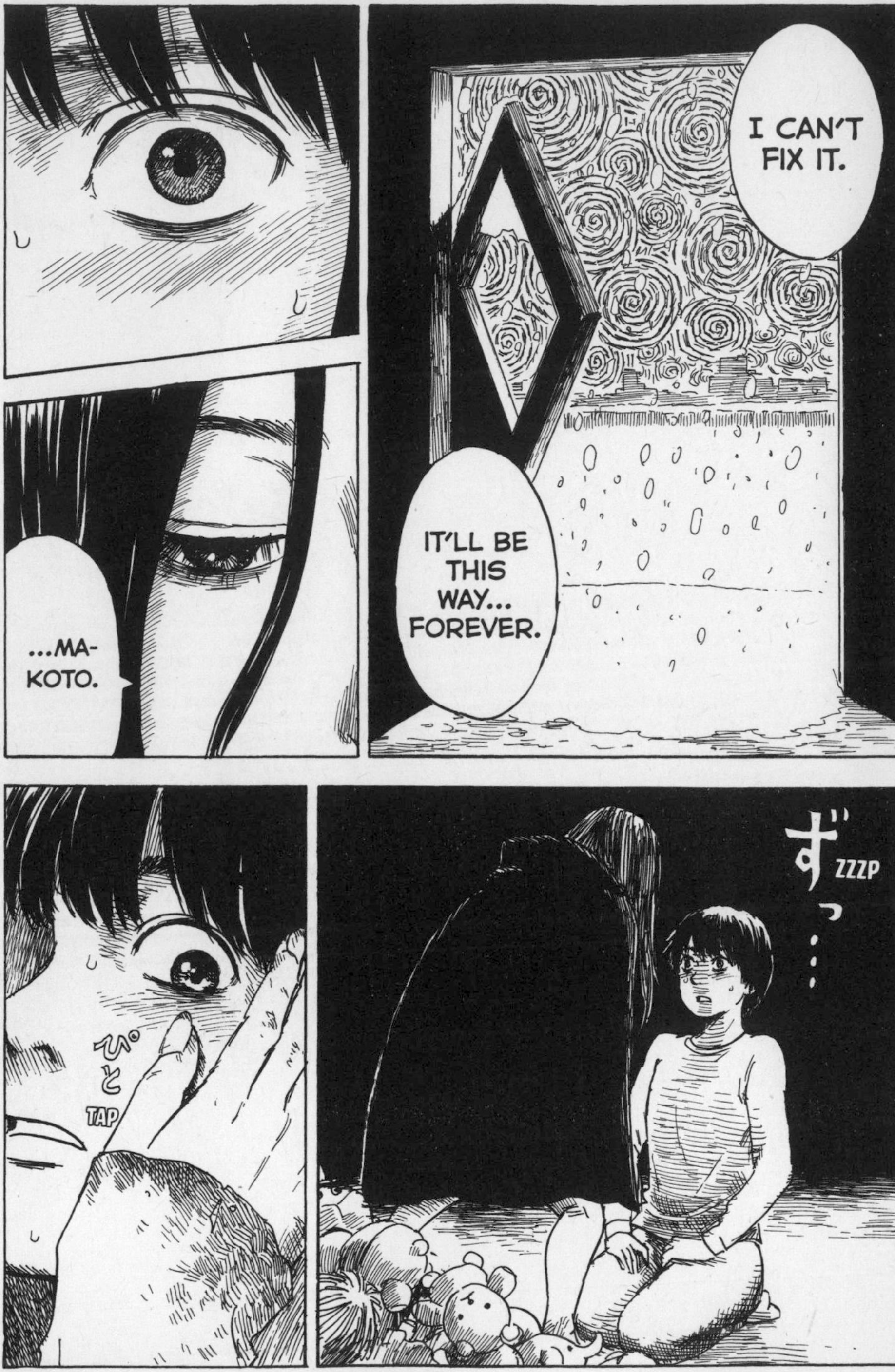
I CAN'T FIX IT.
IT'LL BE THIS WAY... FOREVER.
...MA-KOTO.
ずっ…
ZZZP
ぴと
TAP

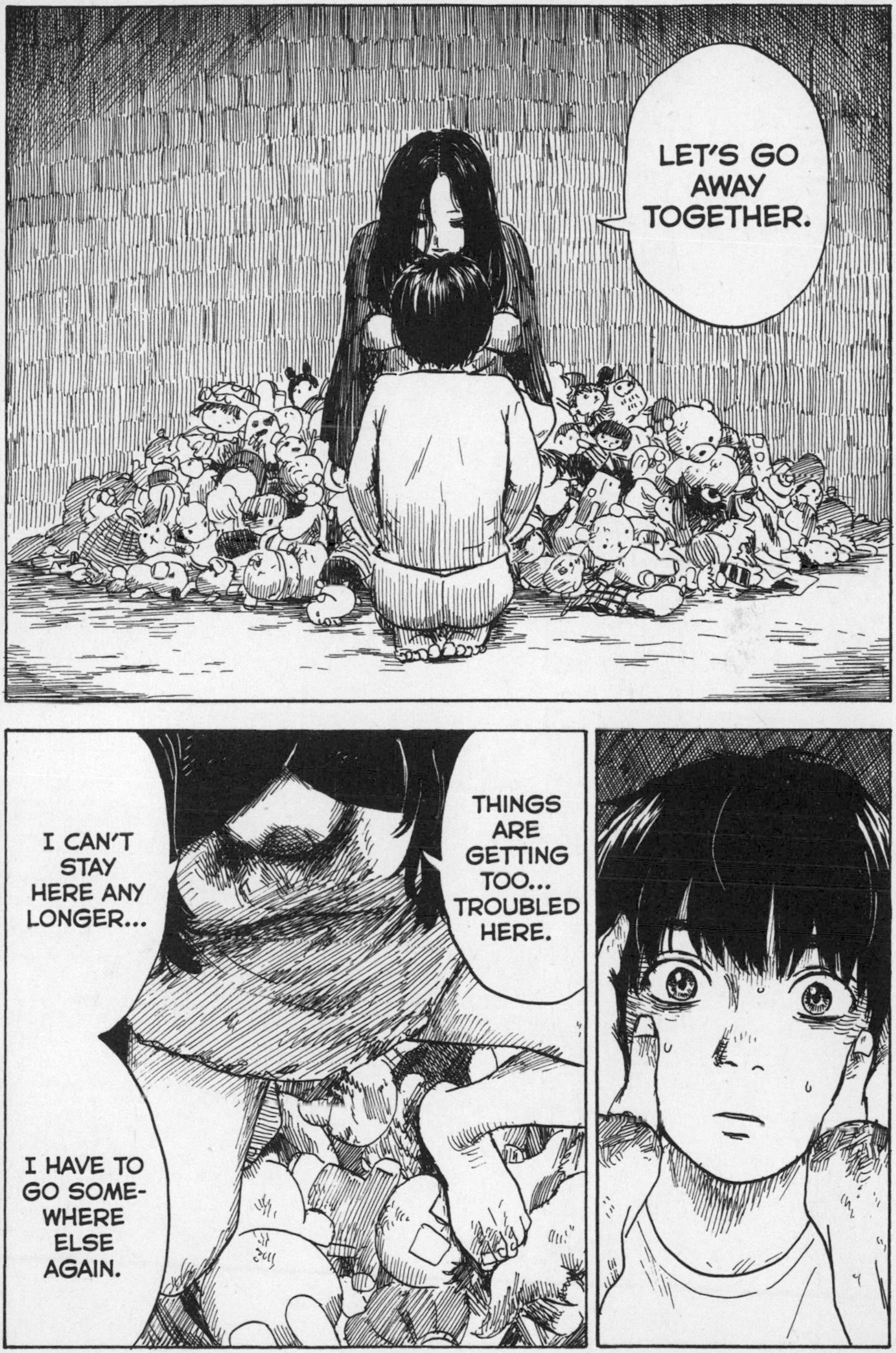
LET'S GO AWAY TOGETHER.
THINGS ARE GETTING TOO... TROUBLED HERE.
I CAN'T STAY HERE ANY LONGER...
I HAVE TO GO SOME-WHERE ELSE AGAIN.

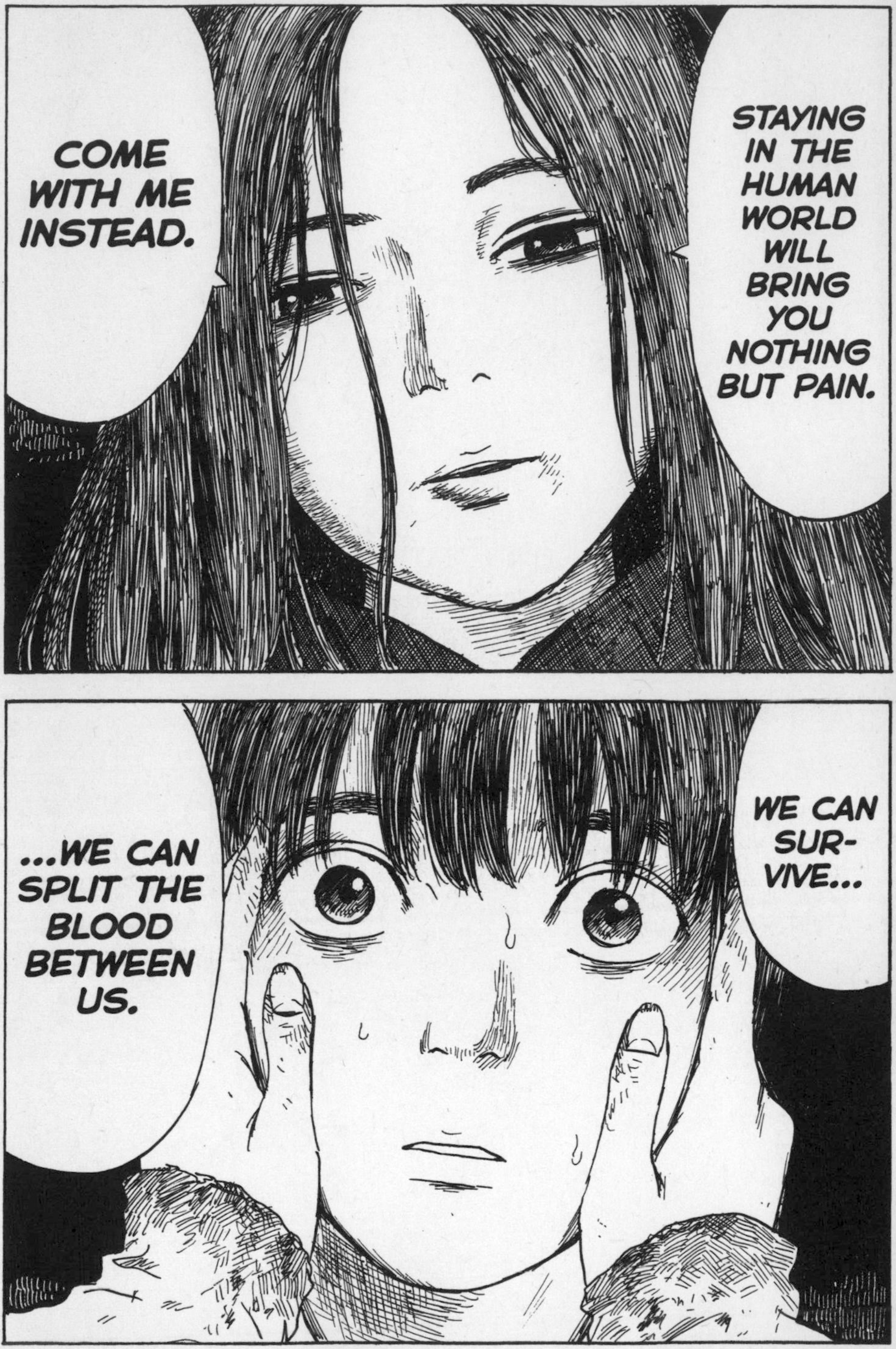
STAYING IN THE HUMAN WORLD WILL BRING YOU NOTHING BUT PAIN.
COME WITH ME INSTEAD.
WE CAN SUR-VIVE...
...WE CAN SPLIT THE BLOOD BETWEEN US.

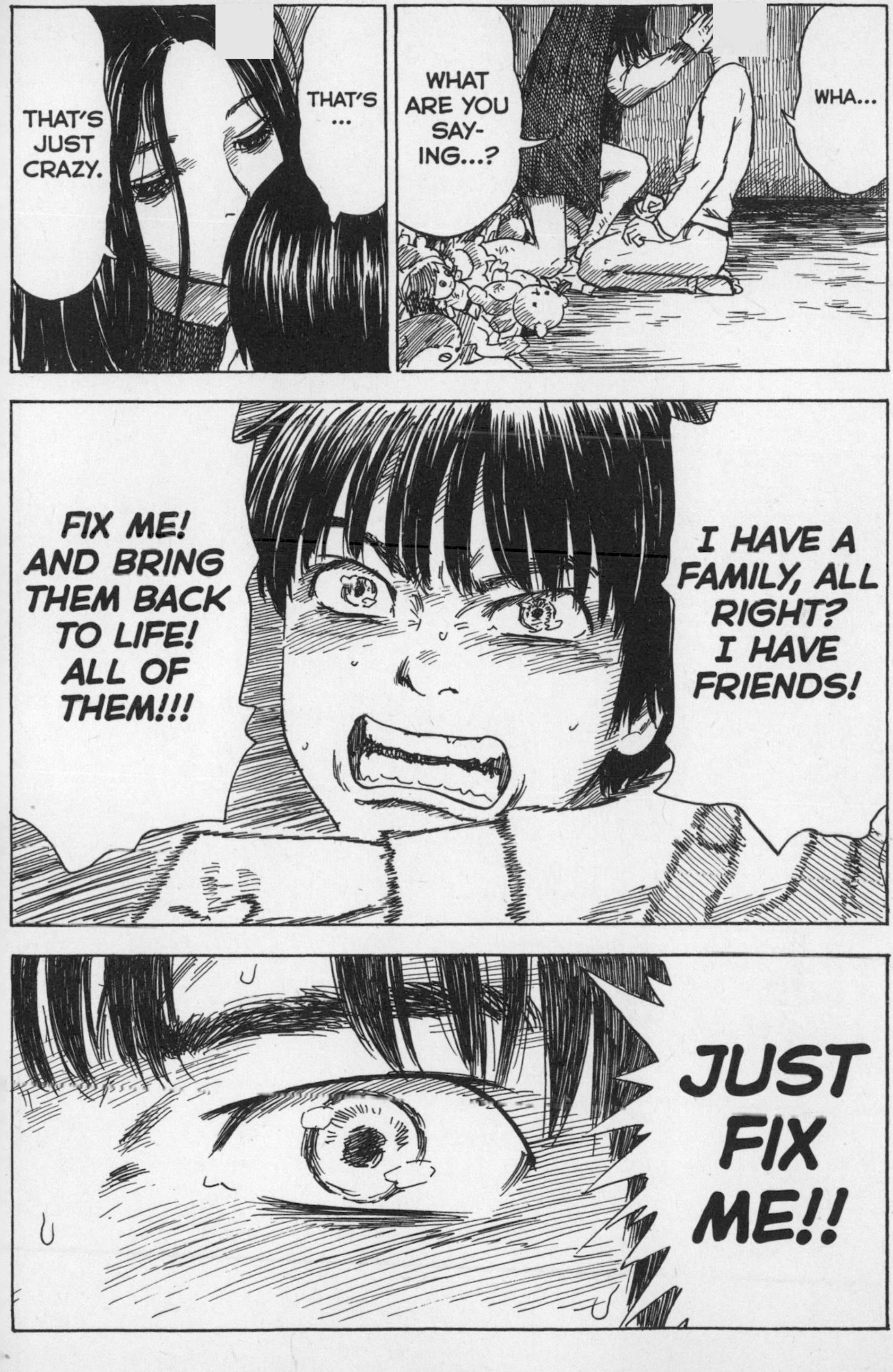
WHA...
WHAT ARE YOU SAY-ING...?
THAT'S ...
THAT'S JUST CRAZY.
I HAVE A FAMILY, ALL RIGHT? I HAVE FRIENDS!
FIX ME! AND BRING THEM BACK TO LIFE! ALL OF THEM!!!
JUST FIX ME!!

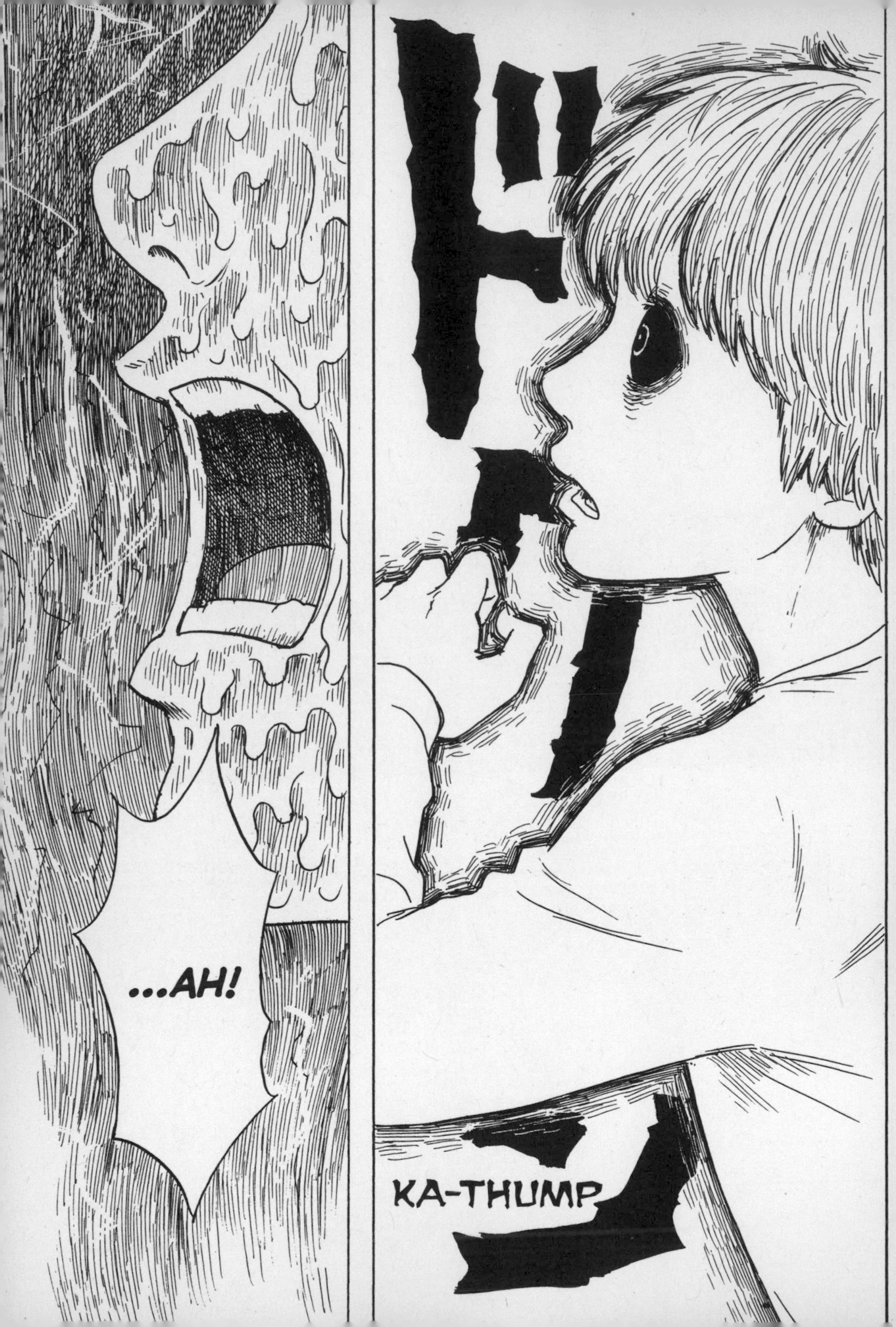
KA-THUMP
...AH!

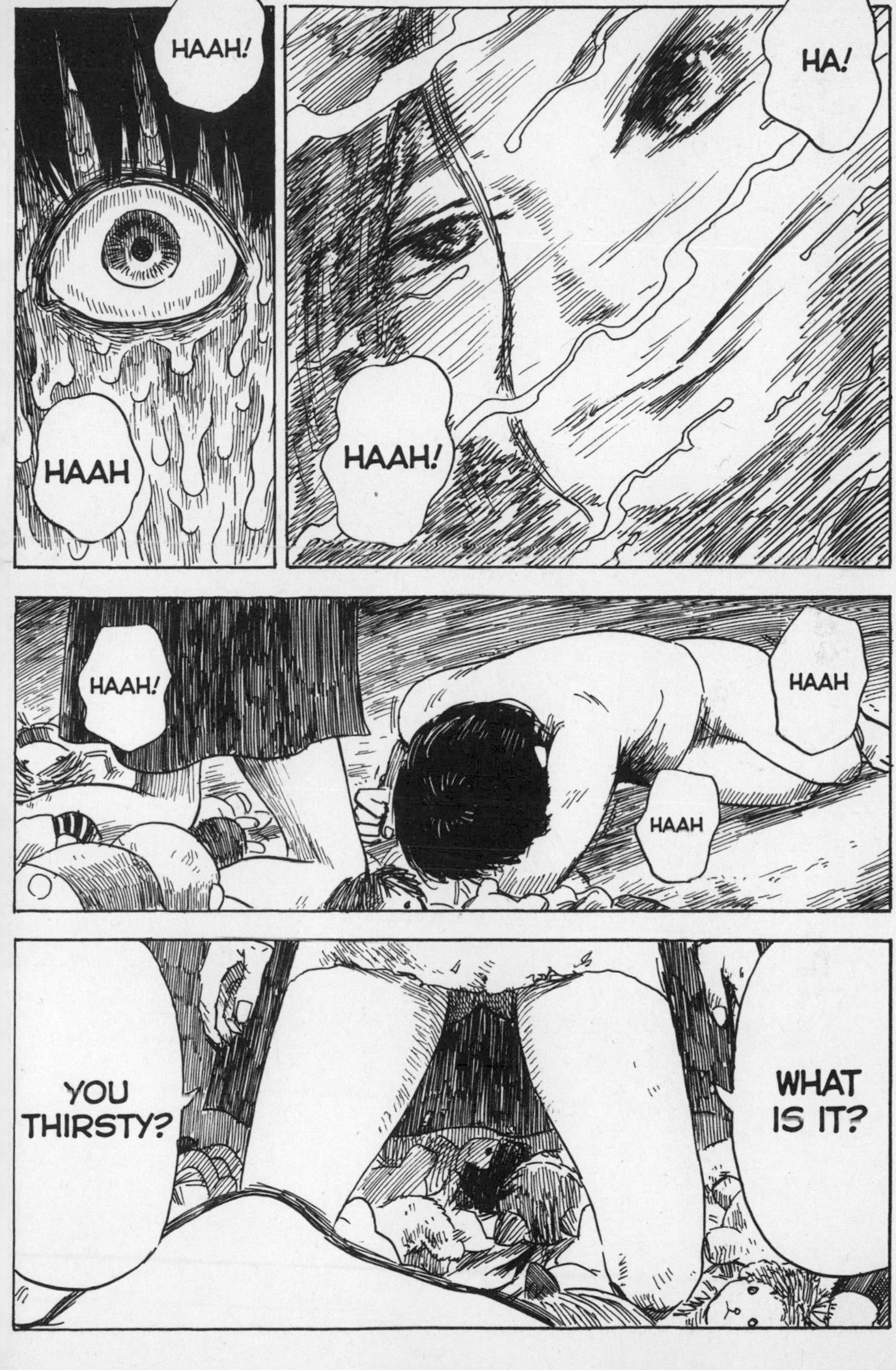
HA!
HAAH!
HAAH!
HAAH
HAAH
HAAH
HAAH!
WHAT IS IT?
YOU THIRSTY?

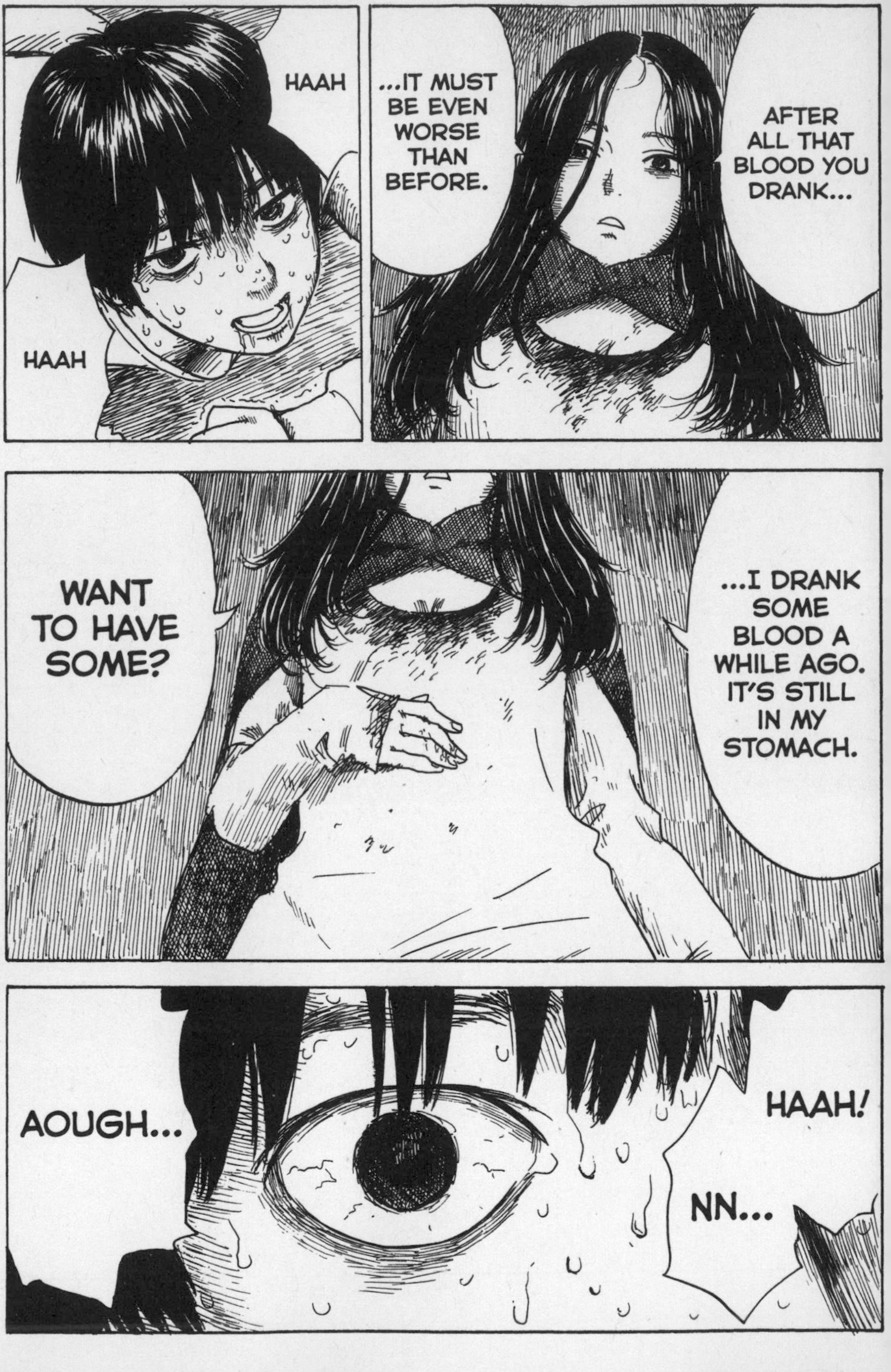
AFTER ALL THAT BLOOD YOU DRANK...
...IT MUST BE EVEN WORSE THAN BEFORE.
HAAH
HAAH
...I DRANK SOME BLOOD A WHILE AGO. IT'S STILL IN MY STOMACH.
WANT TO HAVE SOME?
HAAH!
NN...
AOUGH...

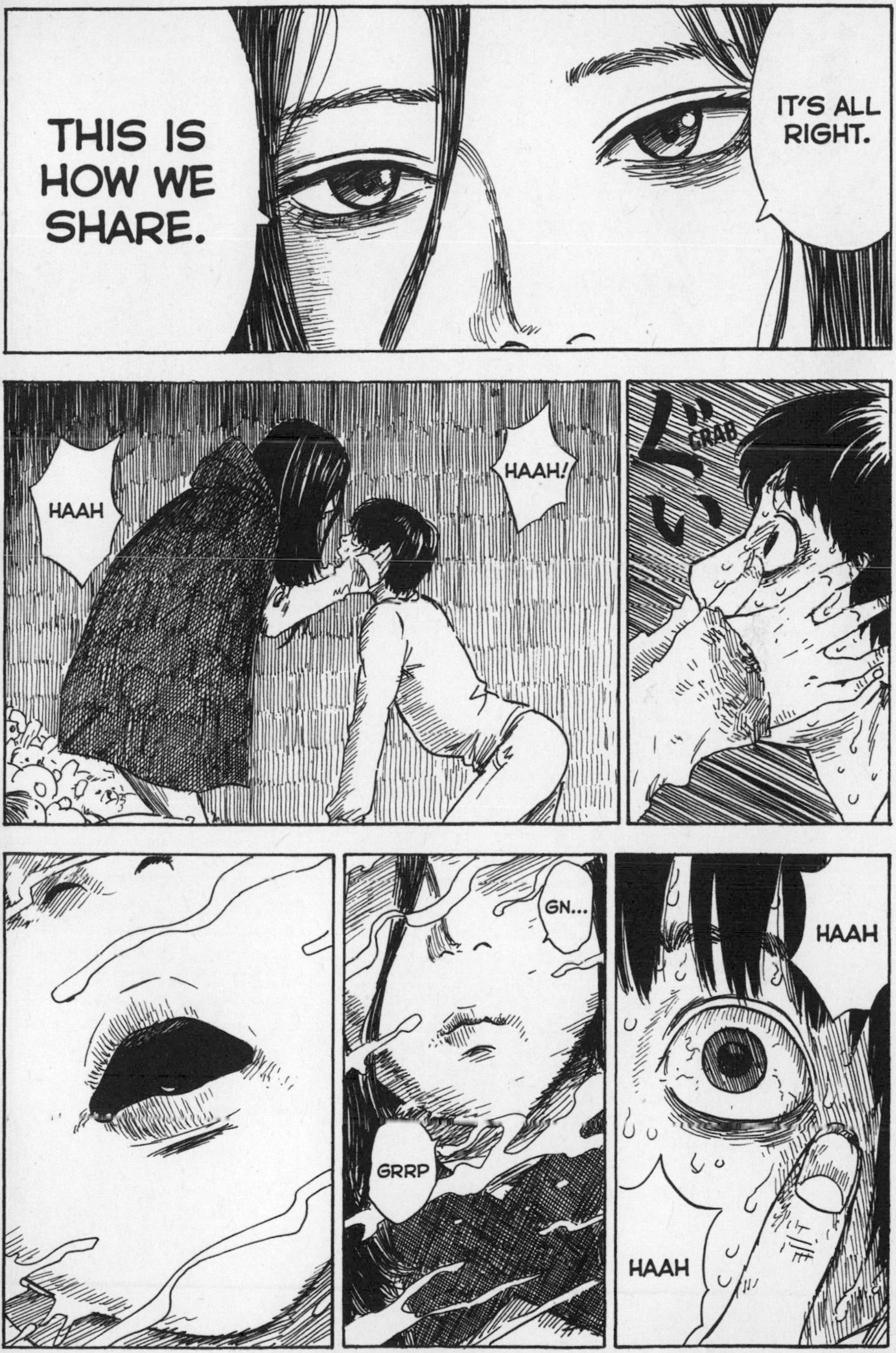
IT'S ALL RIGHT.
THIS IS HOW WE SHARE.
GRAB
ぐい
HAAH!
HAAH
HAAH
HAAH
GN...
GRRP

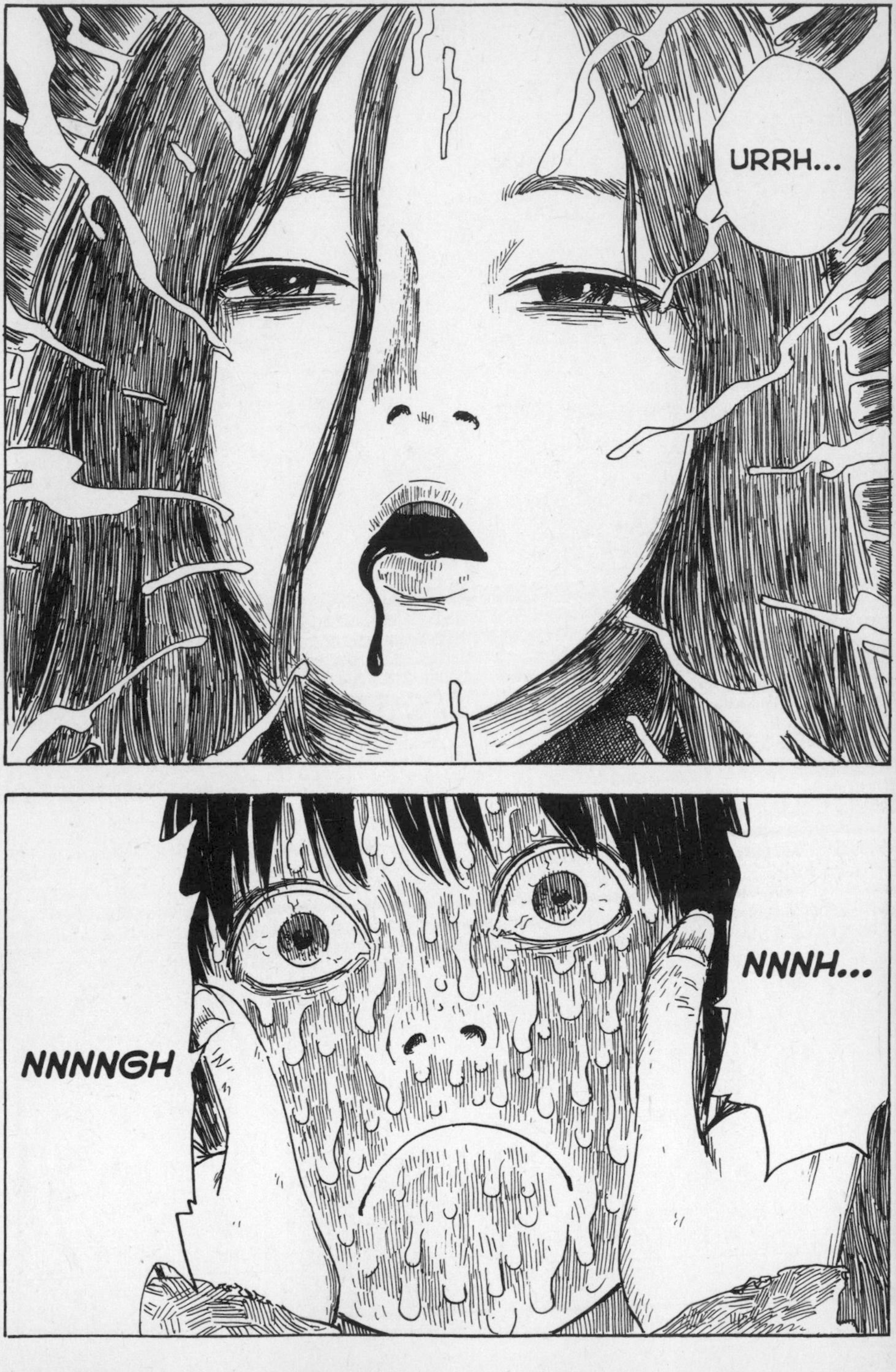
URRH...
NNNH...
NNNNGH

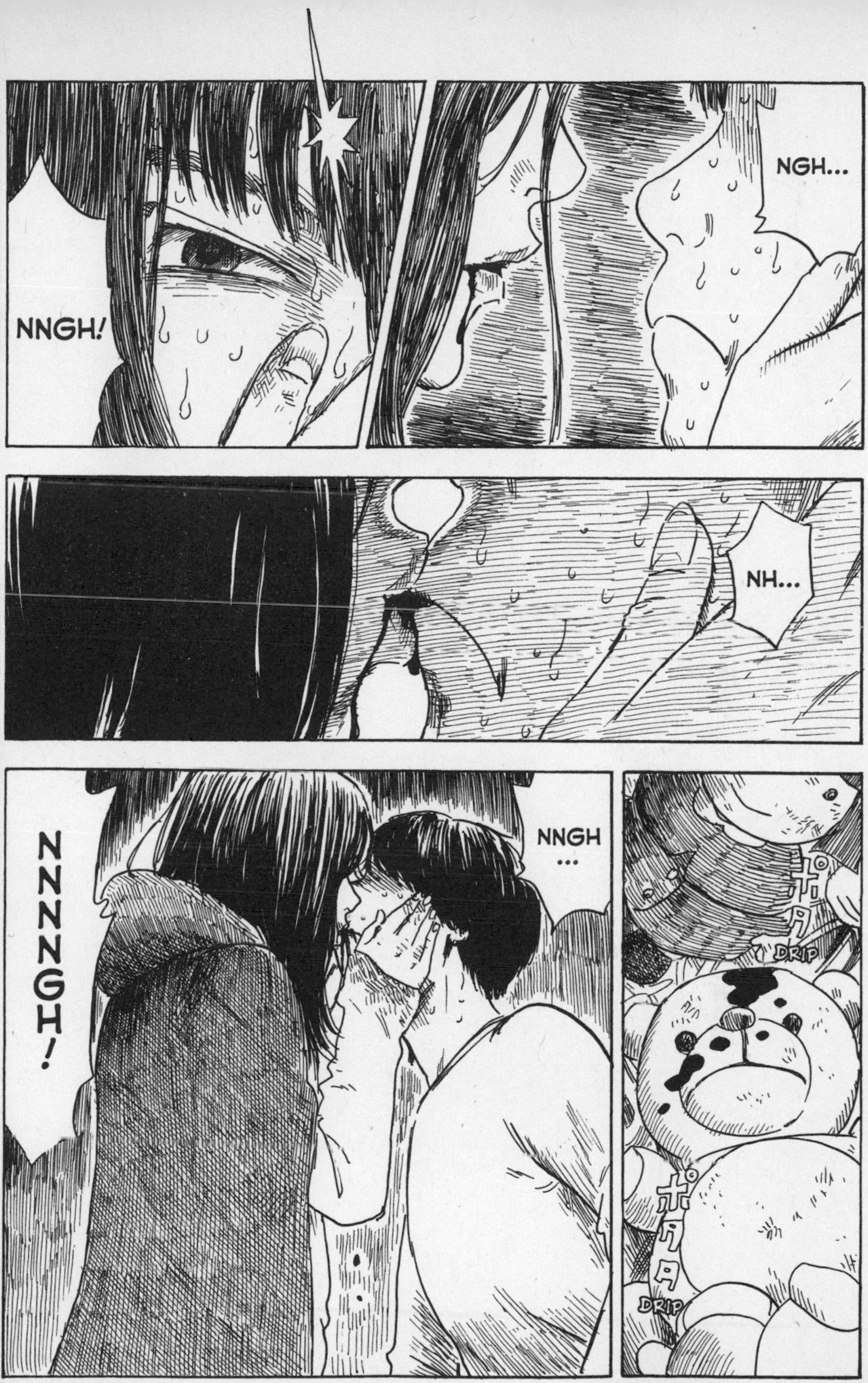
NGH...
NNGH!
NH...
ポタ
DRIP
ポタタ
DRIP
NNGH
...
NNNNGH!

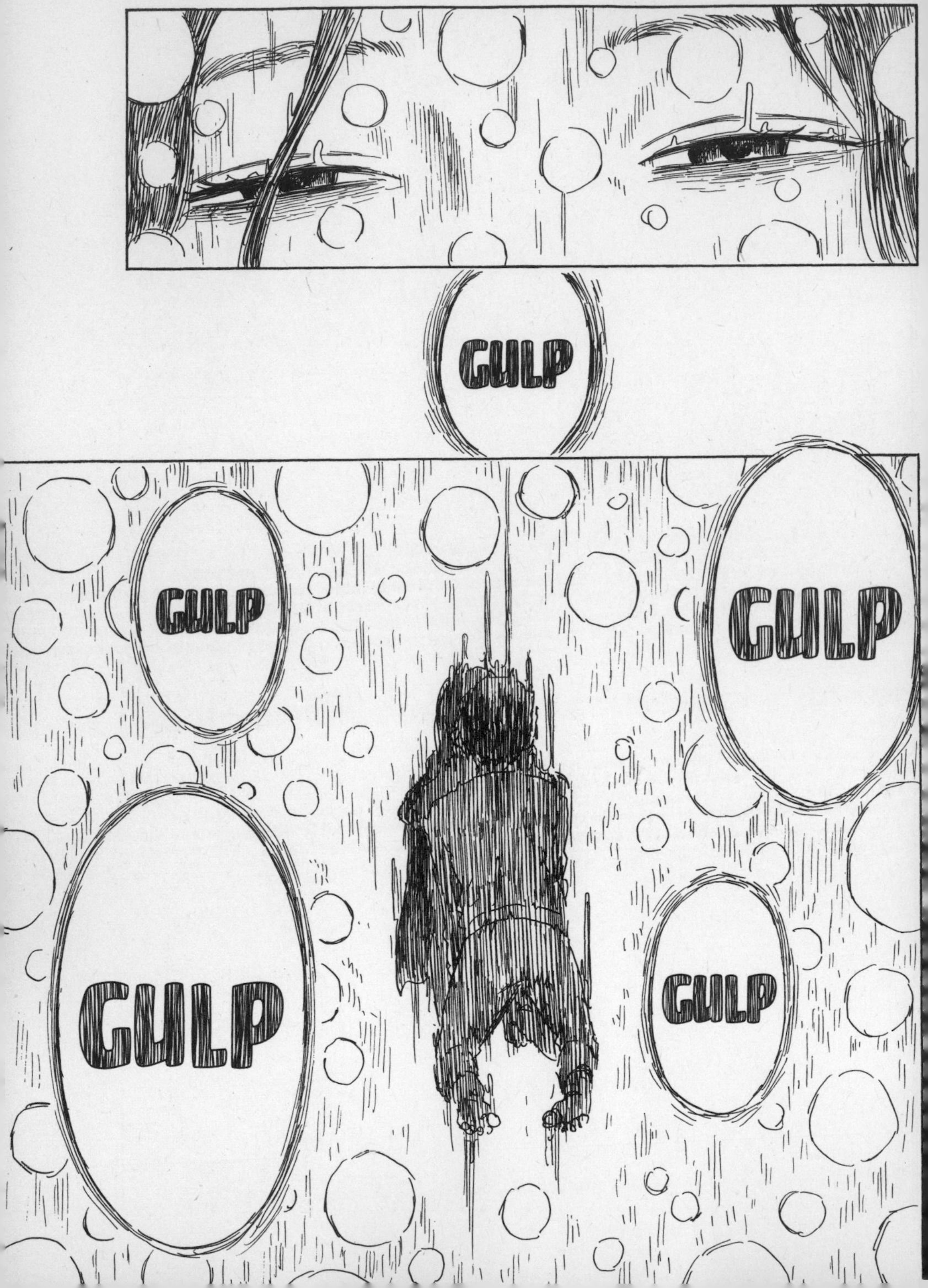
GULP
GULP
GULP
GULP
GULP

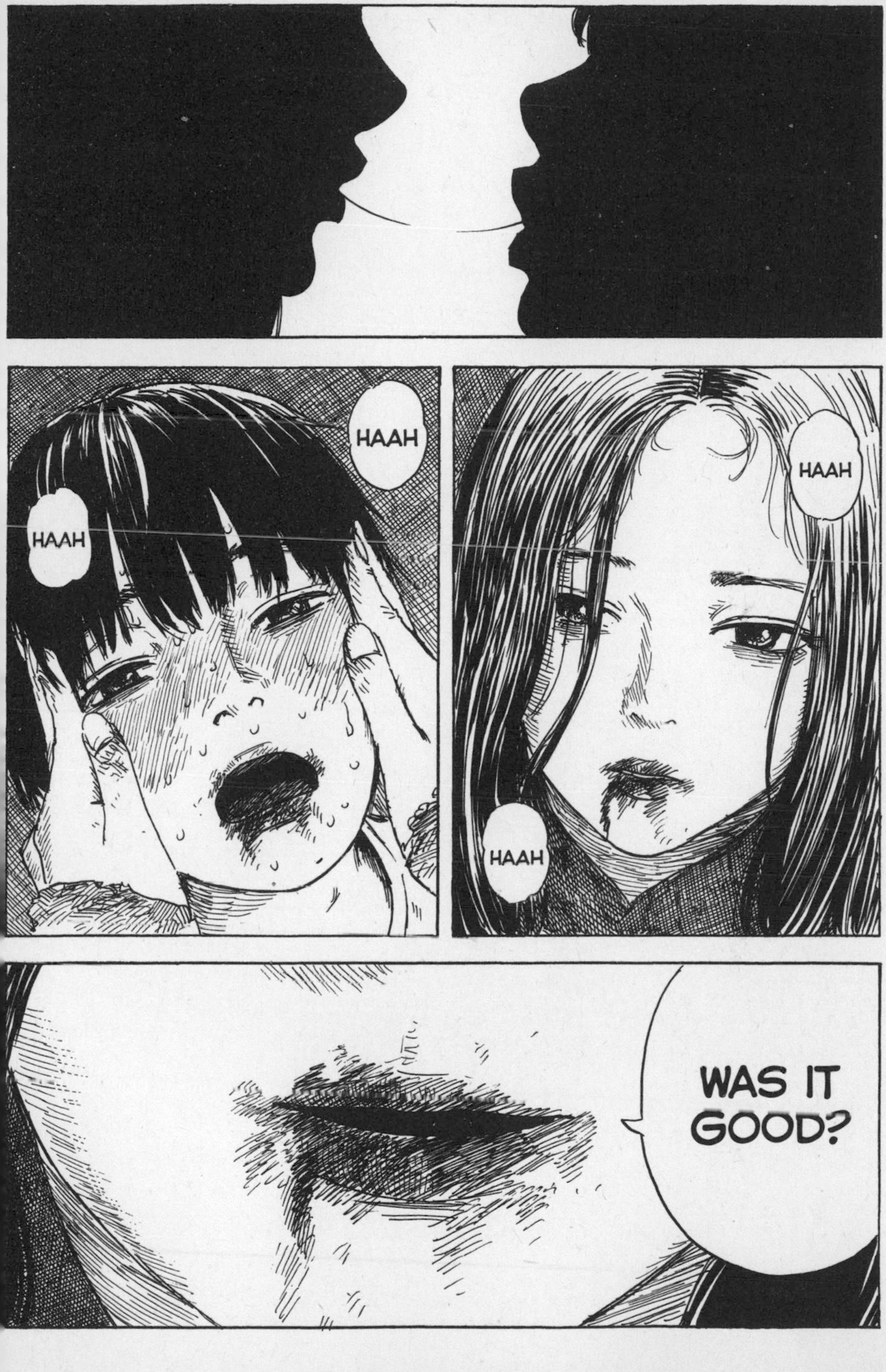
HAAH
HAAH
HAAH
HAAH
WAS IT GOOD?

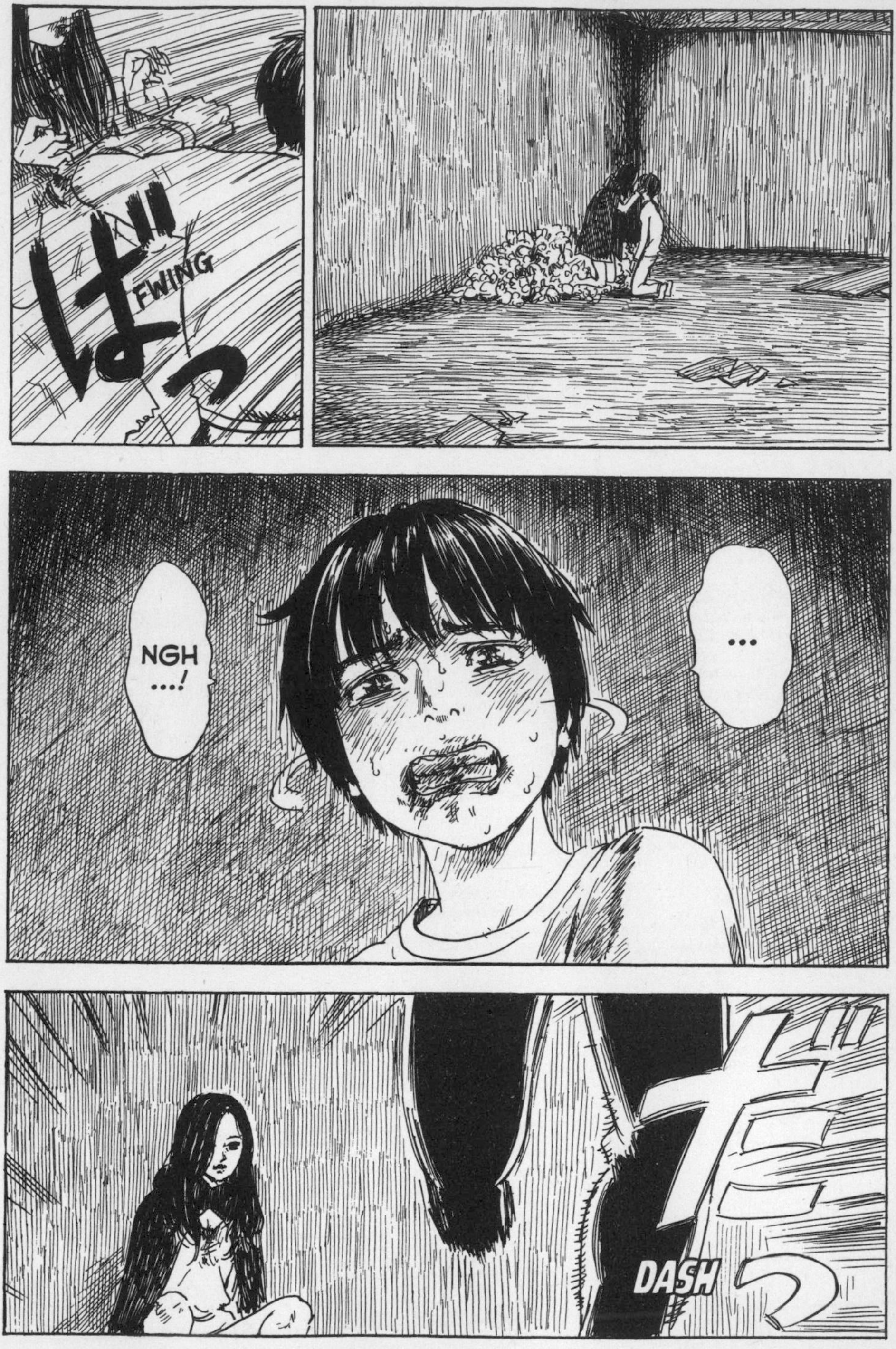
ばっ
FWING
...
NGH
....!
だっ
DASH

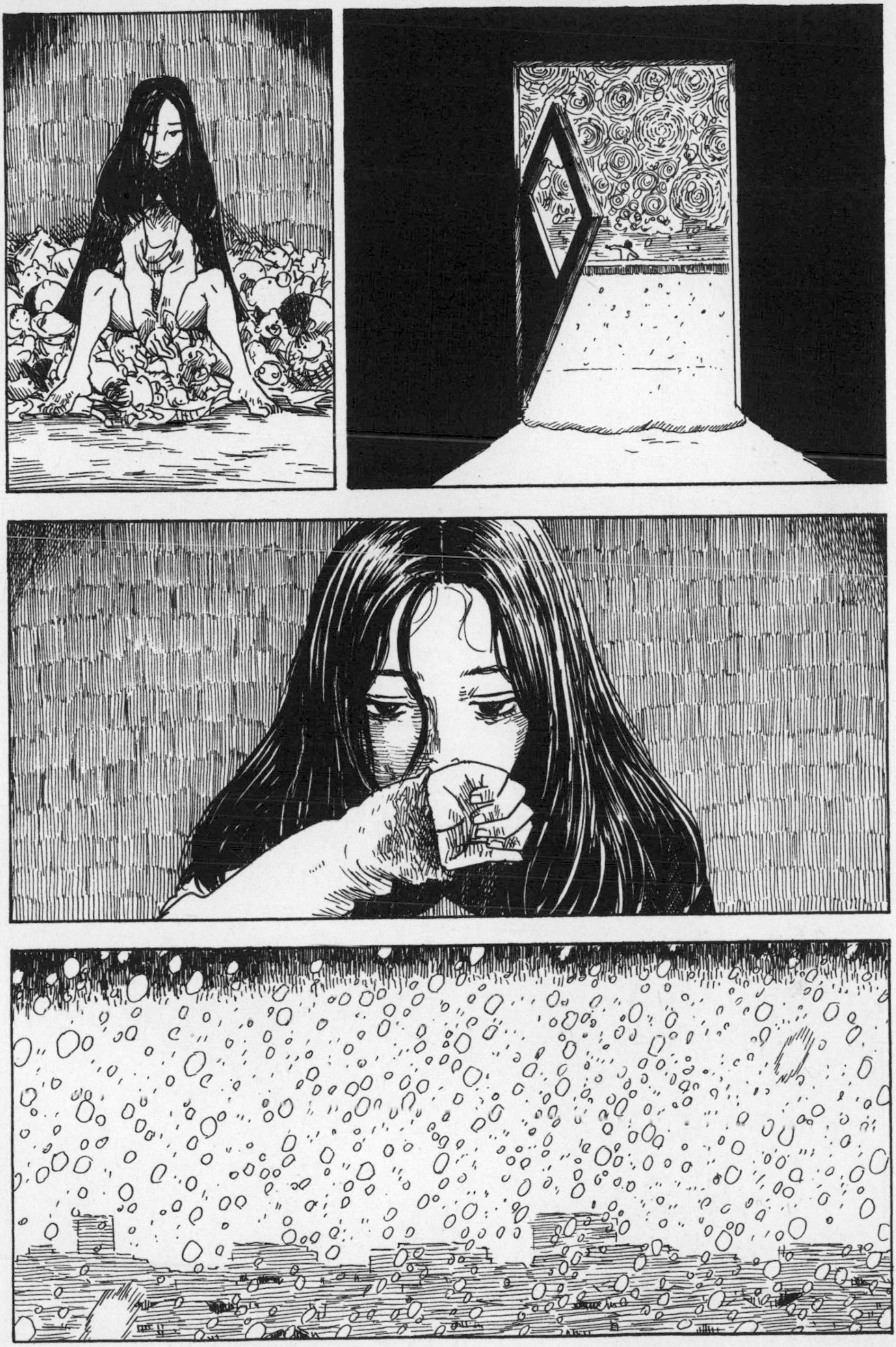

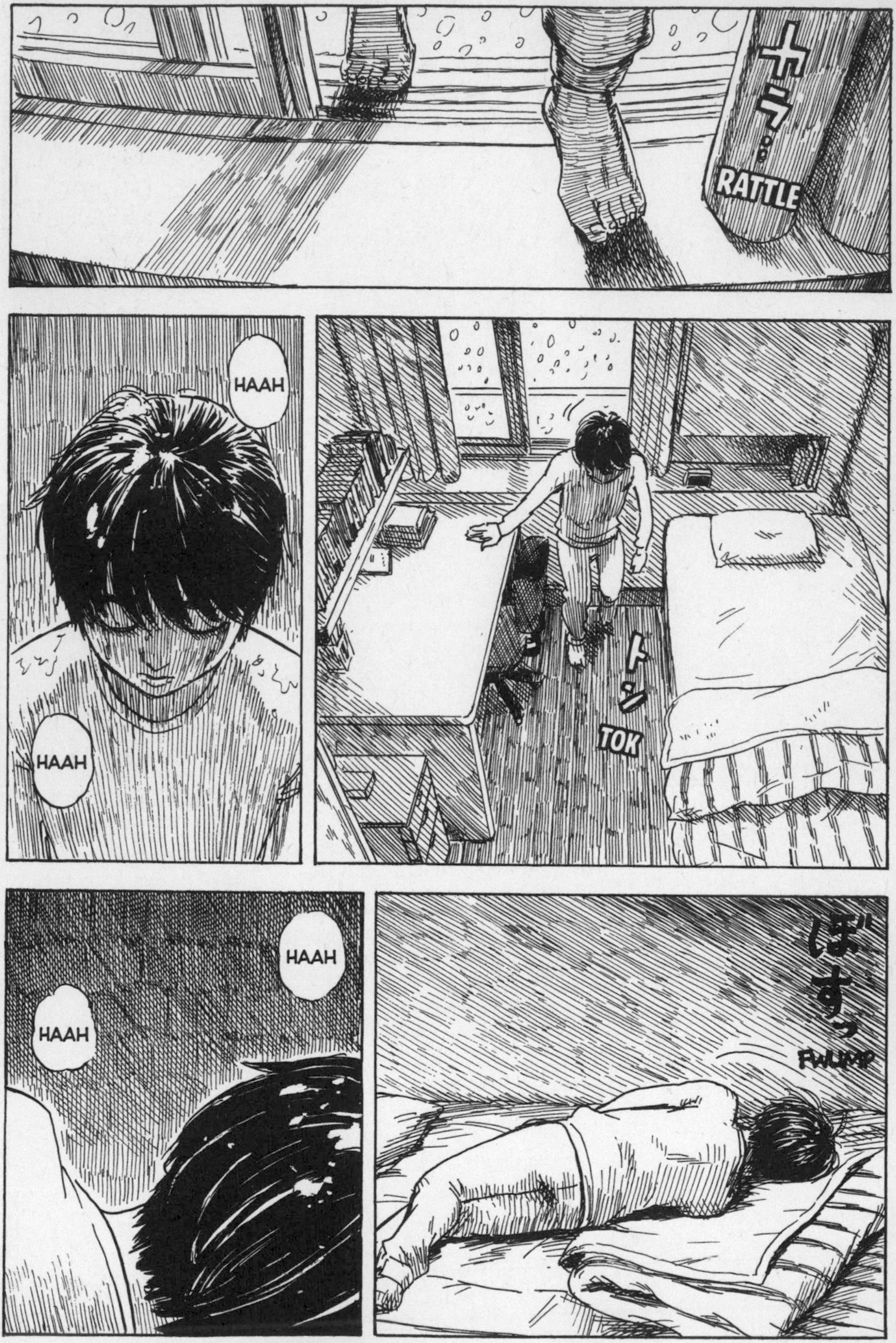
RATTLE
トン
TOK
HAAH
HAAH
ぼすっ
FWUMP
HAAH
HAAH

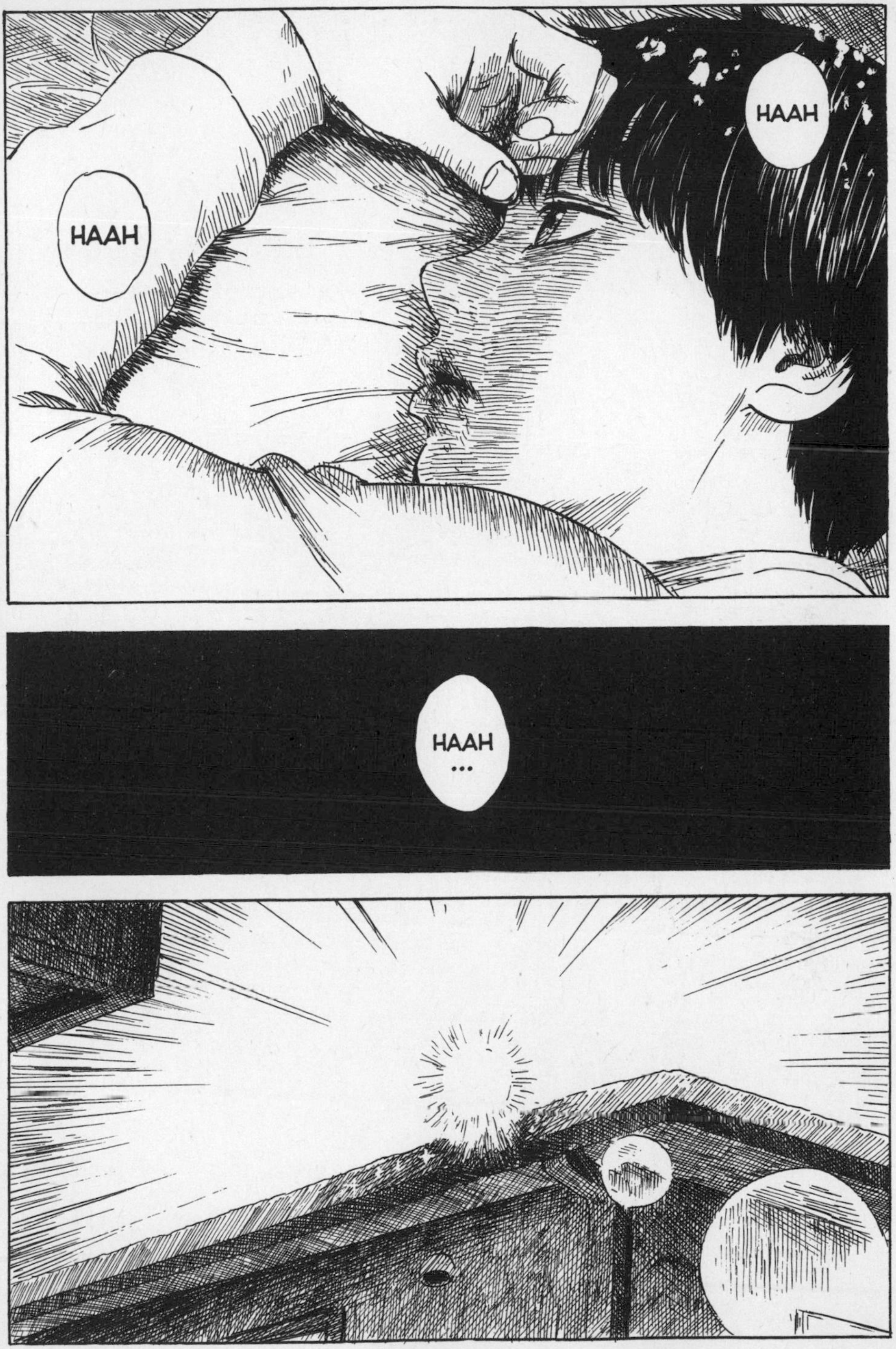
HAAH
HAAH
HAAH
...

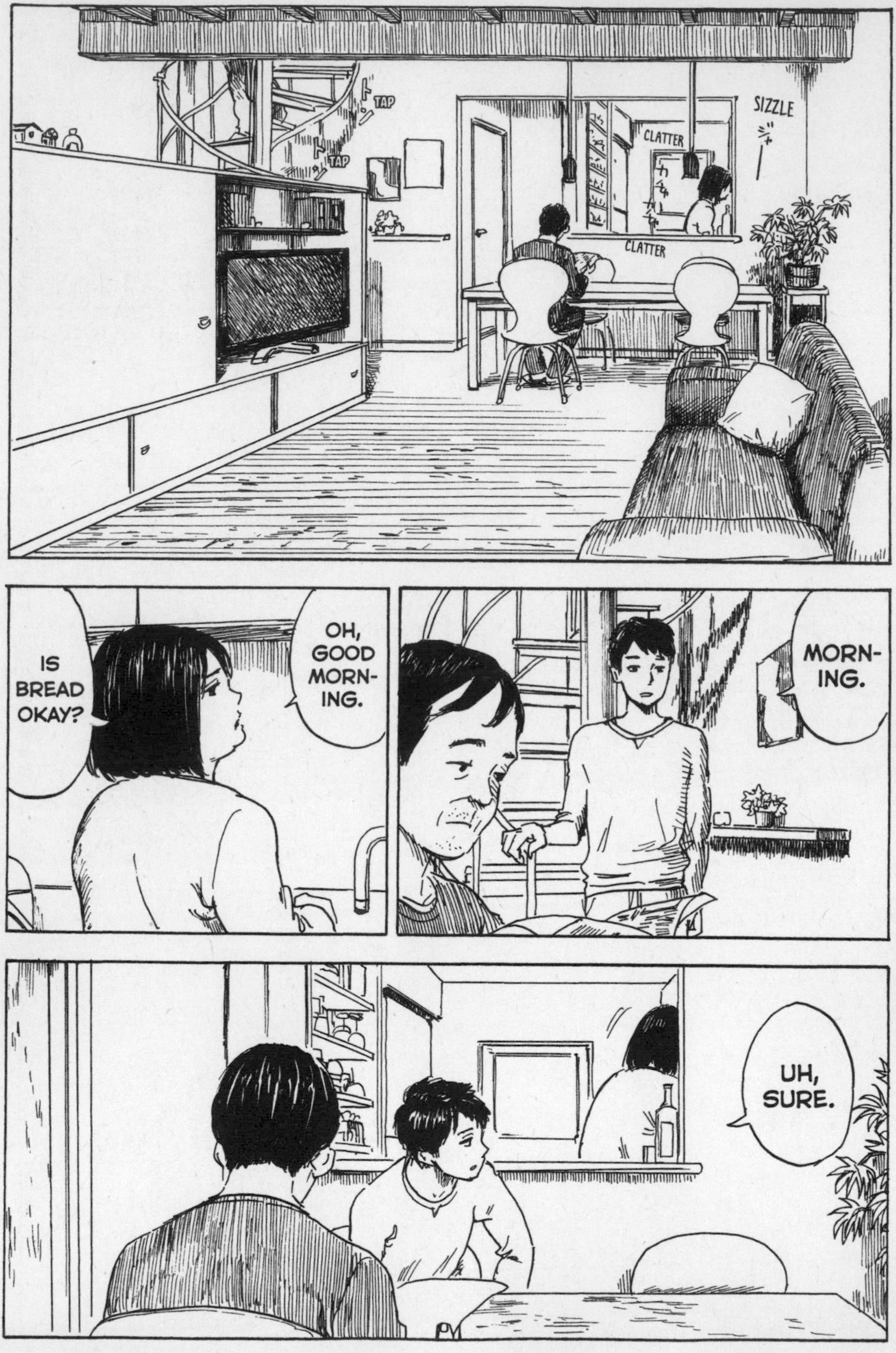
SIZZLE
CLATTER
TAP
TAP
CLATTER
MORN-ING.
OH, GOOD MORN-ING.
IS BREAD OKAY?
UH, SURE.

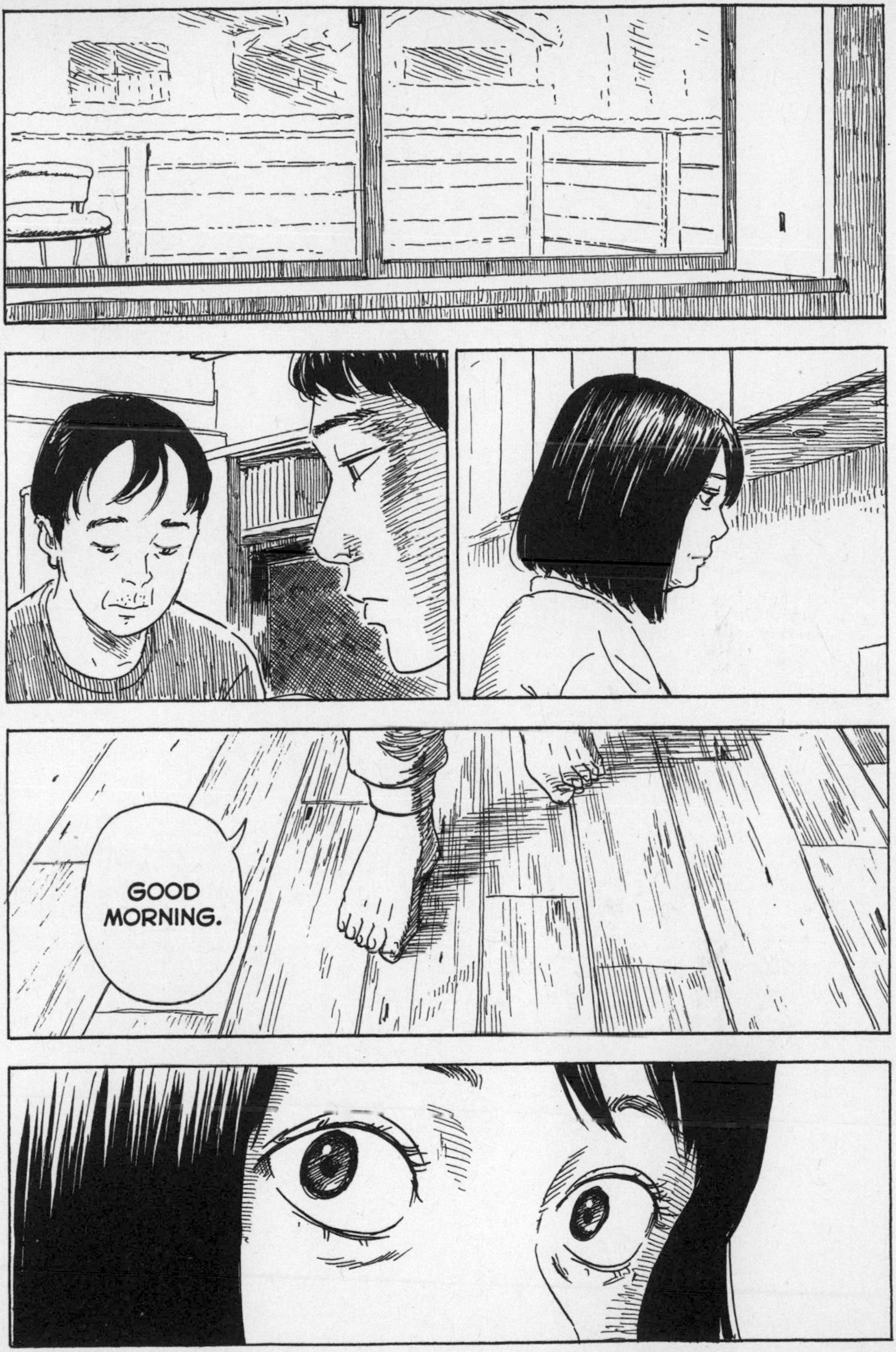
GOOD MORNING.

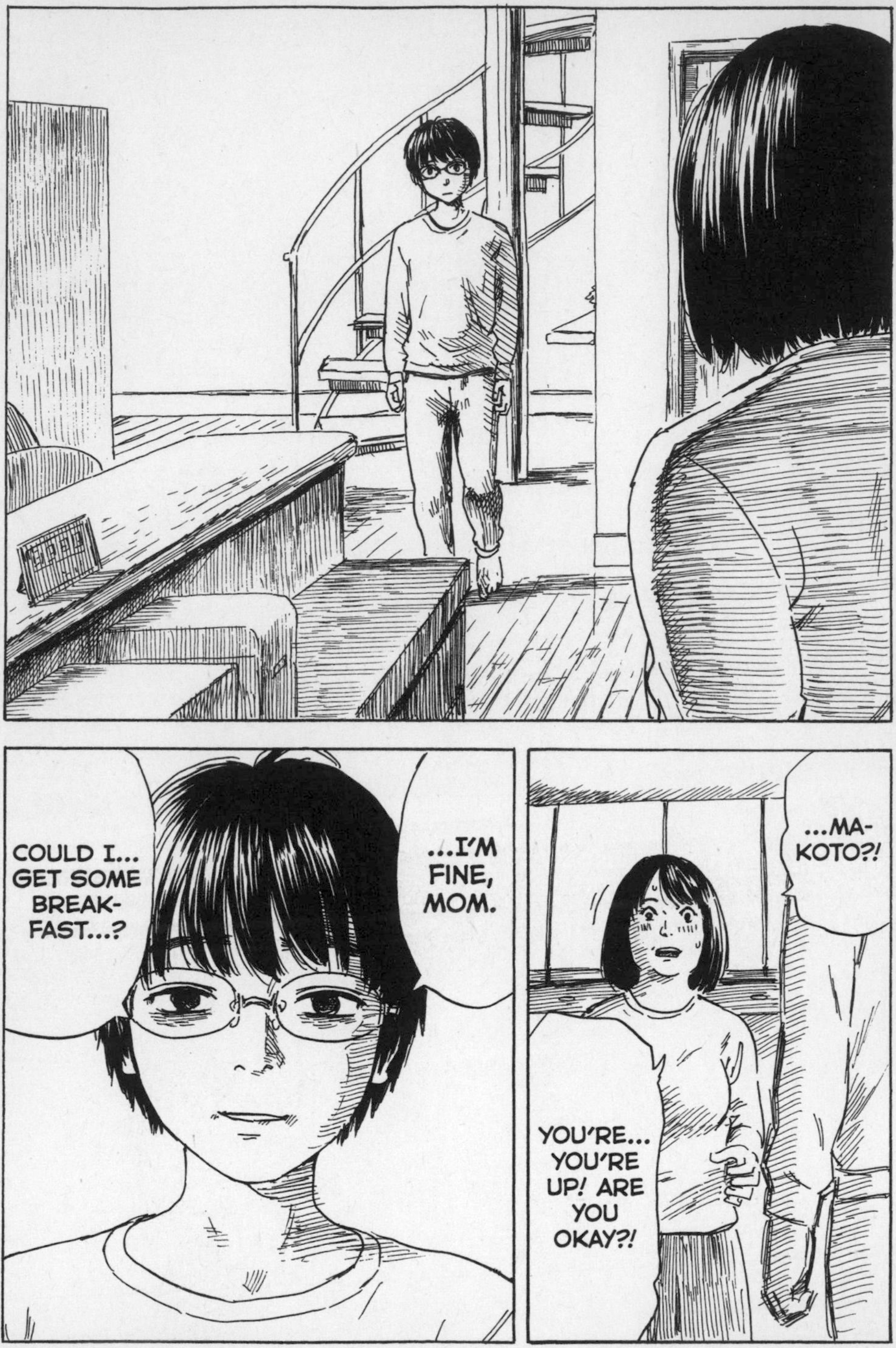
...MA-KOTO?!
YOU'RE... YOU'RE UP! ARE YOU OKAY?!
...I'M FINE, MOM.
COULD I... GET SOME BREAK-FAST...?

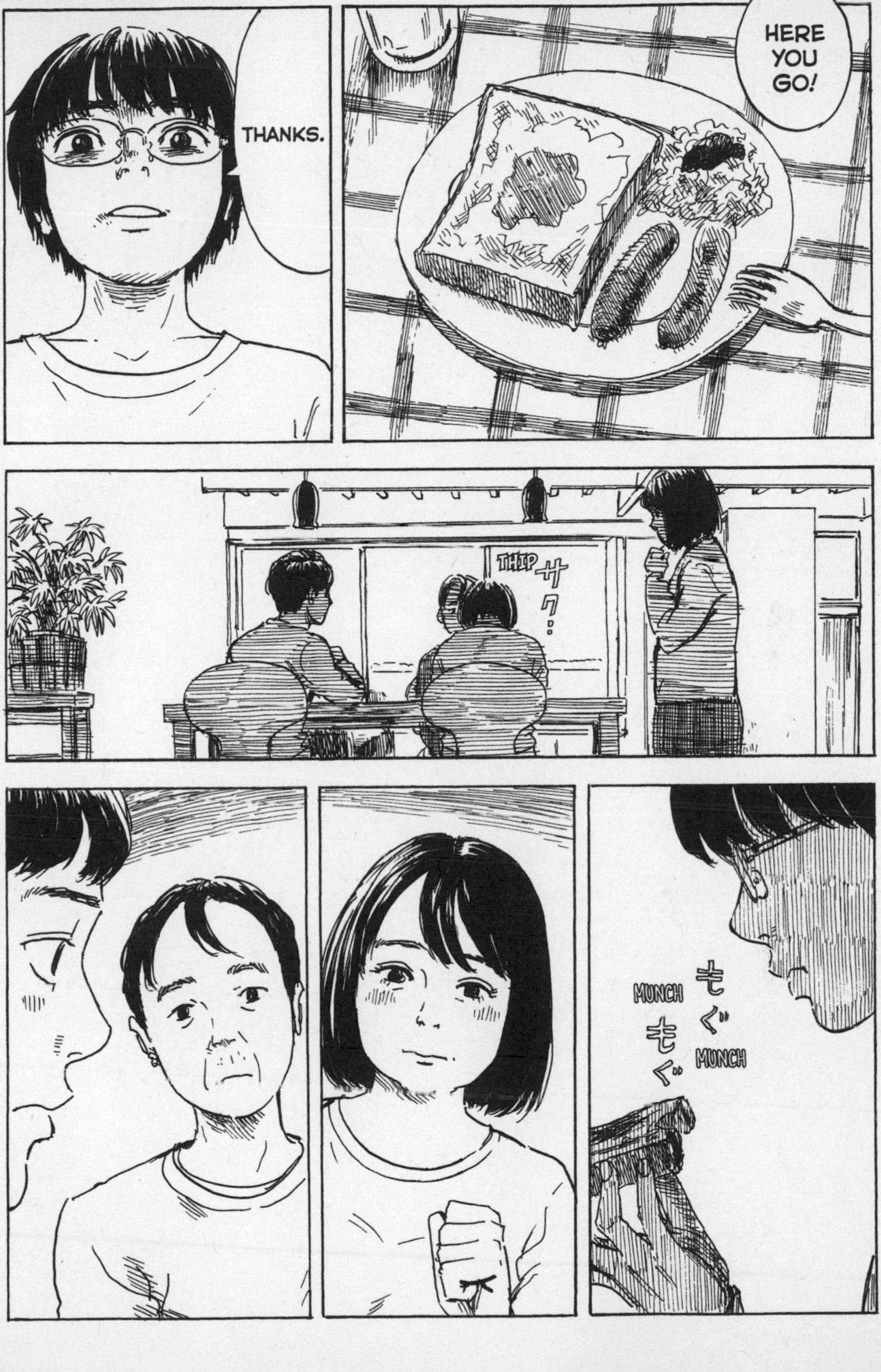
HERE YOU GO!
THANKS.
THIP
サク!!
MUNCH
もぐ
MUNCH
もぐ

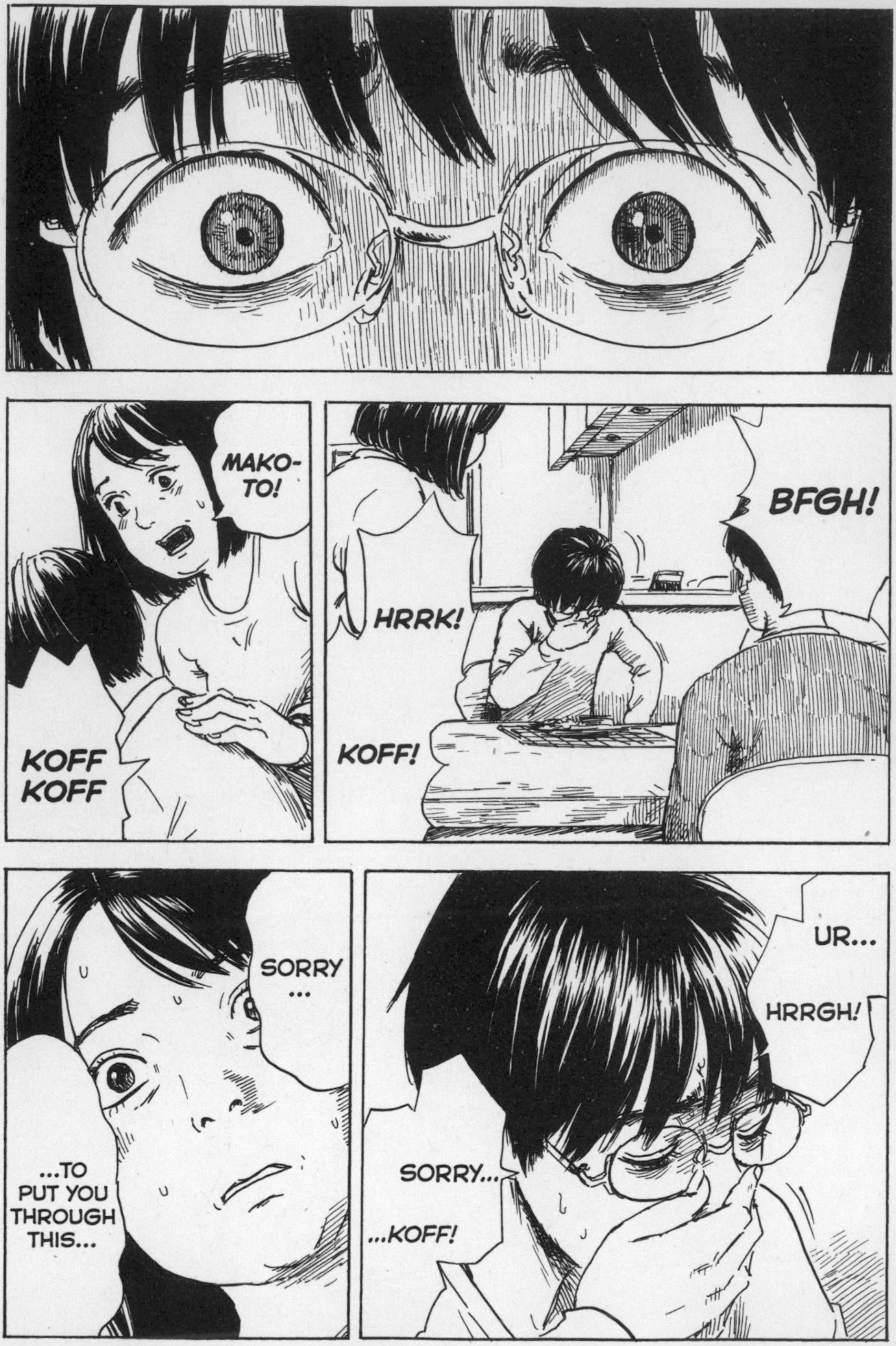
BFGH!
HRRK!
KOFF!
MAKO-TO!
KOFF KOFF
UR...
HRRGH!
SORRY...
...KOFF!
SORRY...
...TO PUT YOU THROUGH THIS...

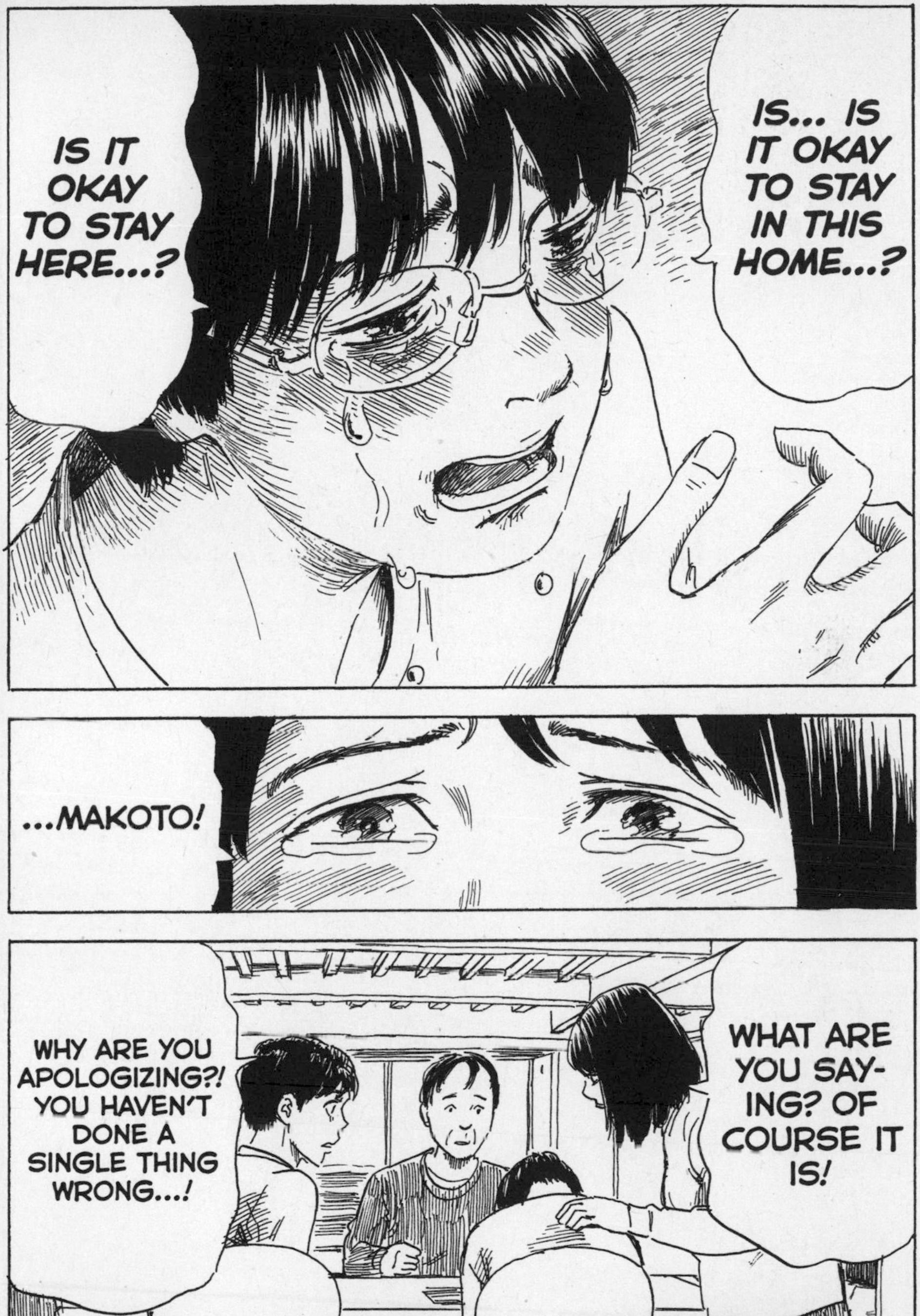
IS... IS IT OKAY TO STAY IN THIS HOME...?
IS IT OKAY TO STAY HERE...?
...MAKOTO!
WHAT ARE YOU SAY-ING? OF COURSE IT IS!
WHY ARE YOU APOLOGIZING?! YOU HAVEN'T DONE A SINGLE THING WRONG...!

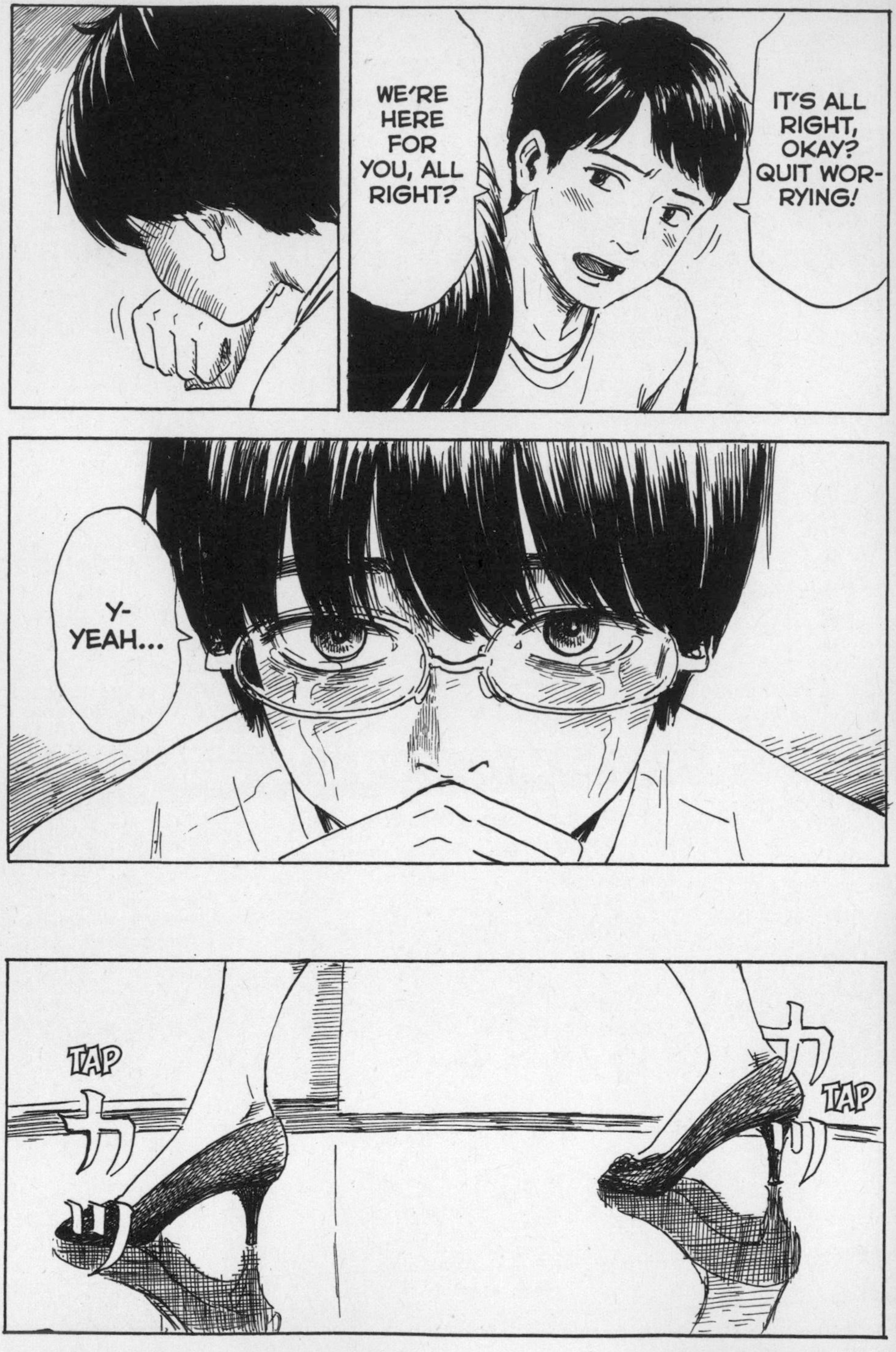
IT'S ALL RIGHT, OKAY? QUIT WOR-RYING!
WE'RE HERE FOR YOU, ALL RIGHT?
Y-YEAH...
TAP
TAP

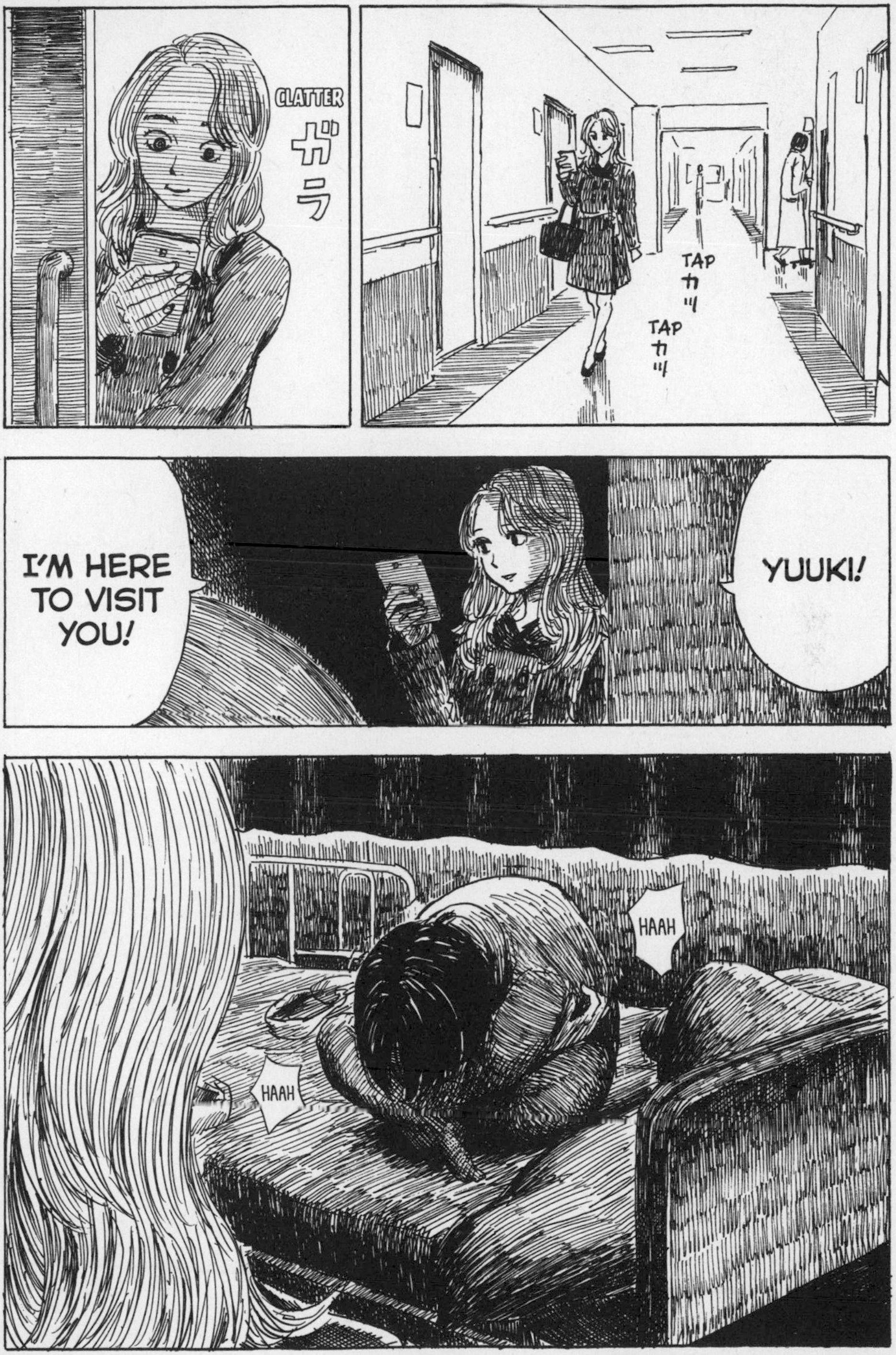
TAP
カツ
TAP
カツ
CLATTER
ガラ
YUUKI!
I'M HERE TO VISIT YOU!
HAAH
HAAH

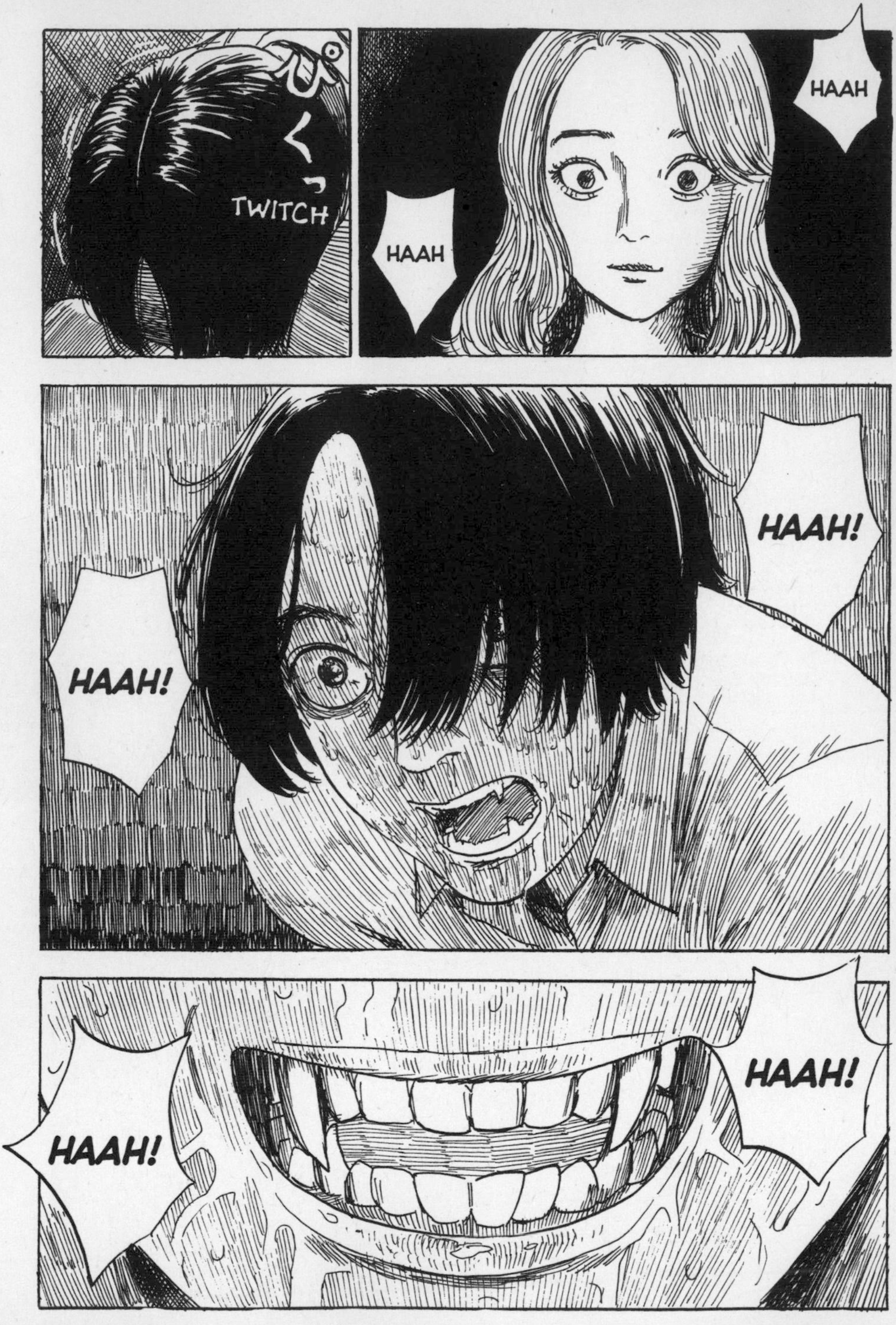
HAAH
HAAH
ぴくっ
TWITCH
HAAH!
HAAH!
HAAH!
HAAH!

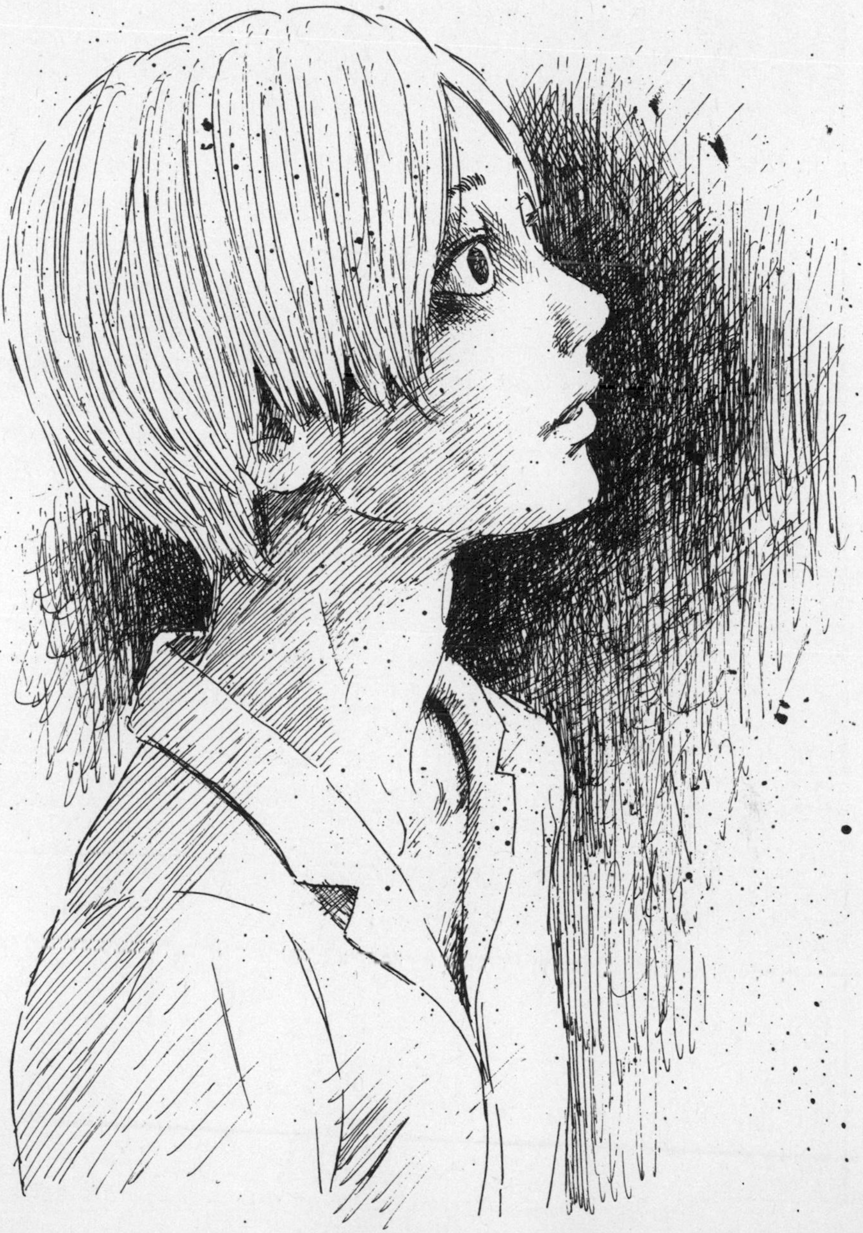

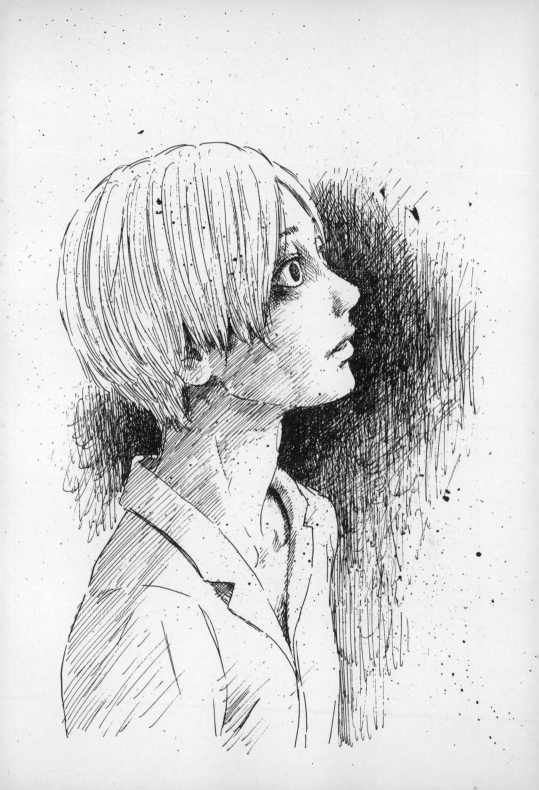

Chapter 14: Detected

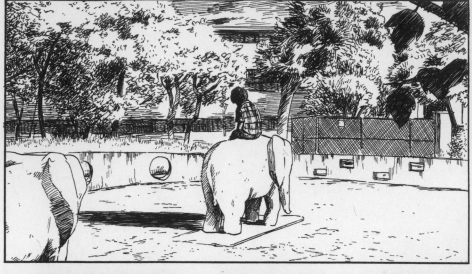

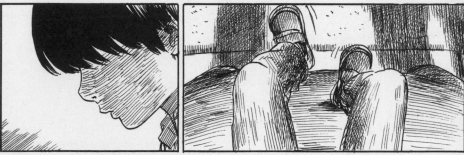

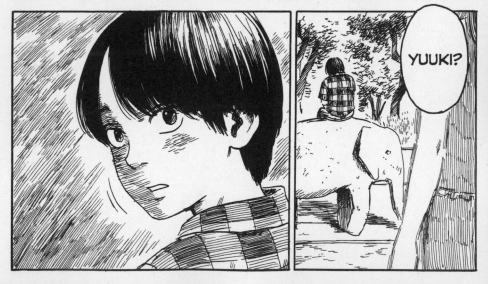

YUUKI?

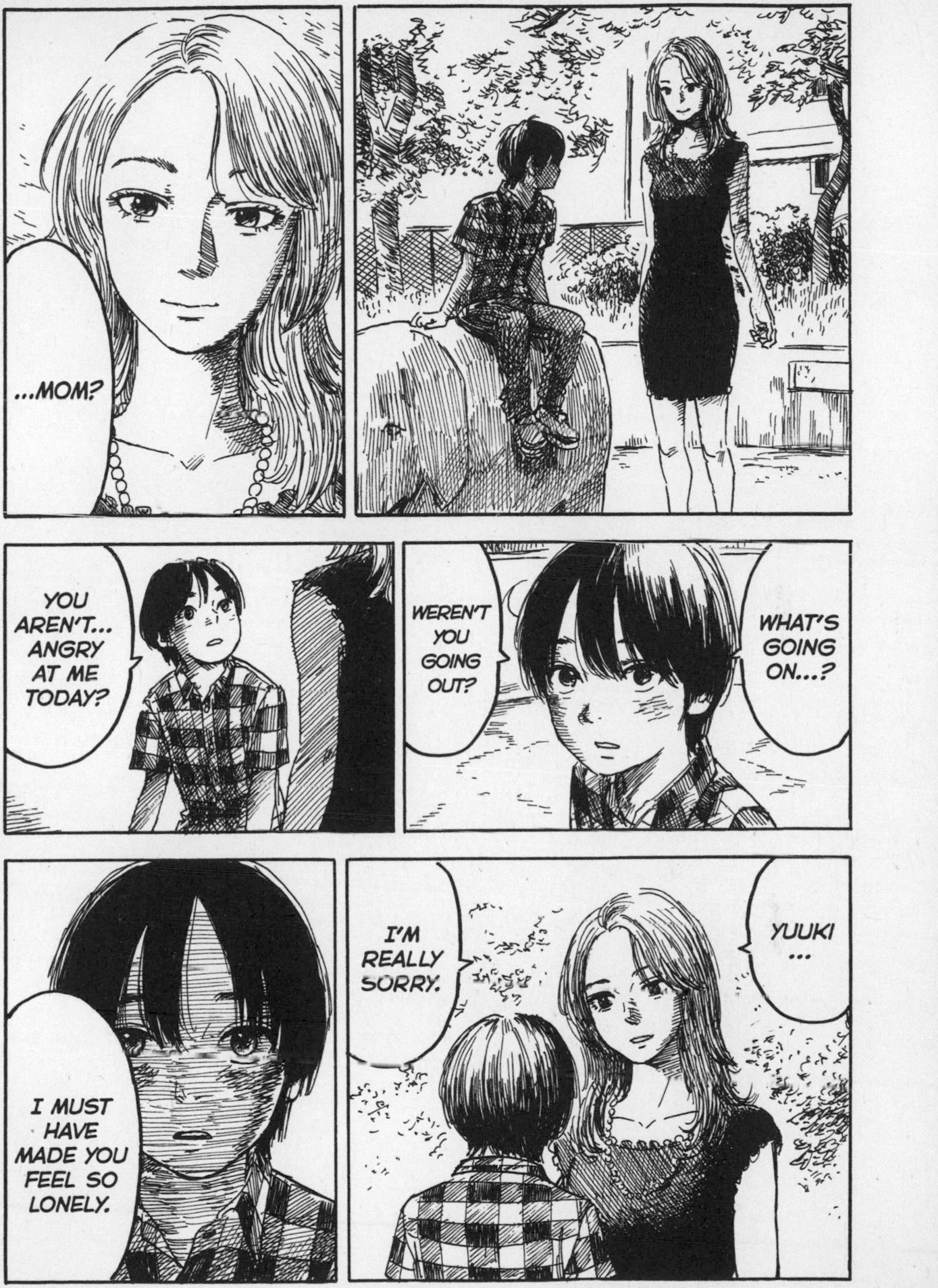
...MOM?
WHAT'S GOING ON...?
WEREN'T YOU GOING OUT?
YOU AREN'T... ANGRY AT ME TODAY?
YUUKI ...
I'M REALLY SORRY.
I MUST HAVE MADE YOU FEEL SO LONELY.

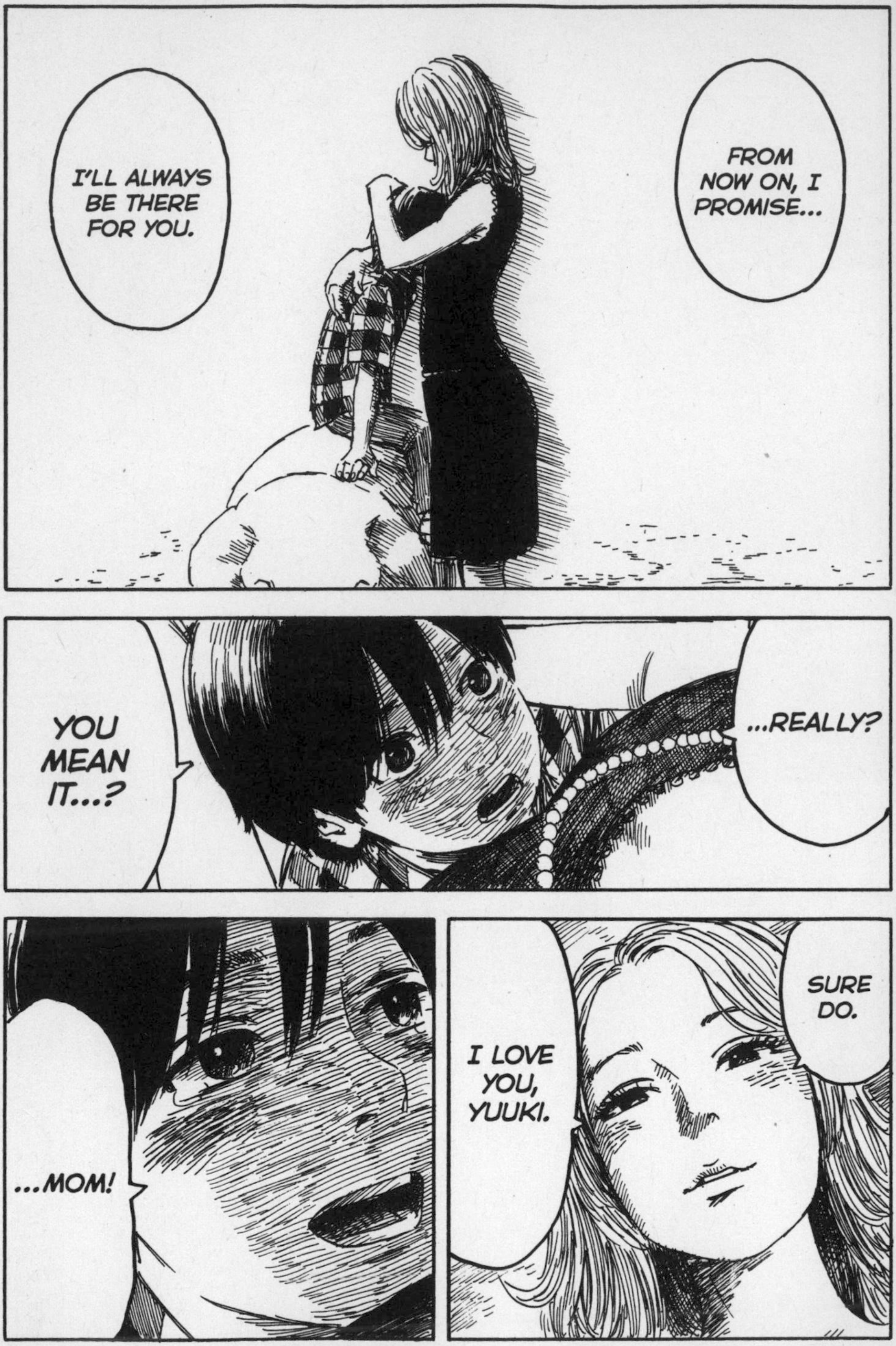
FROM NOW ON, I PROMISE...
I'LL ALWAYS BE THERE FOR YOU.
...REALLY?
YOU MEAN IT...?
SURE DO.
I LOVE YOU, YUUKI.
...MOM!

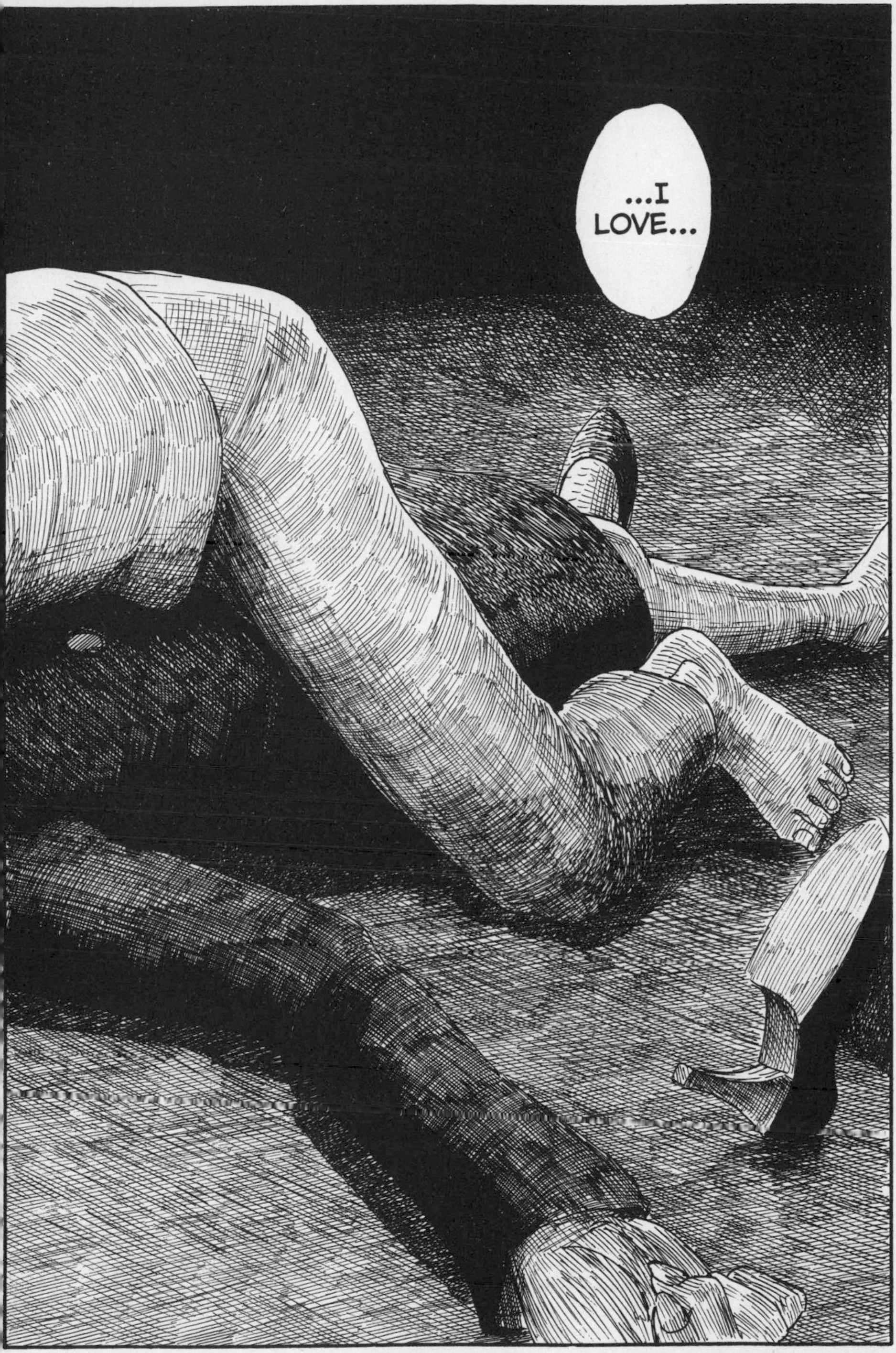
...I LOVE...

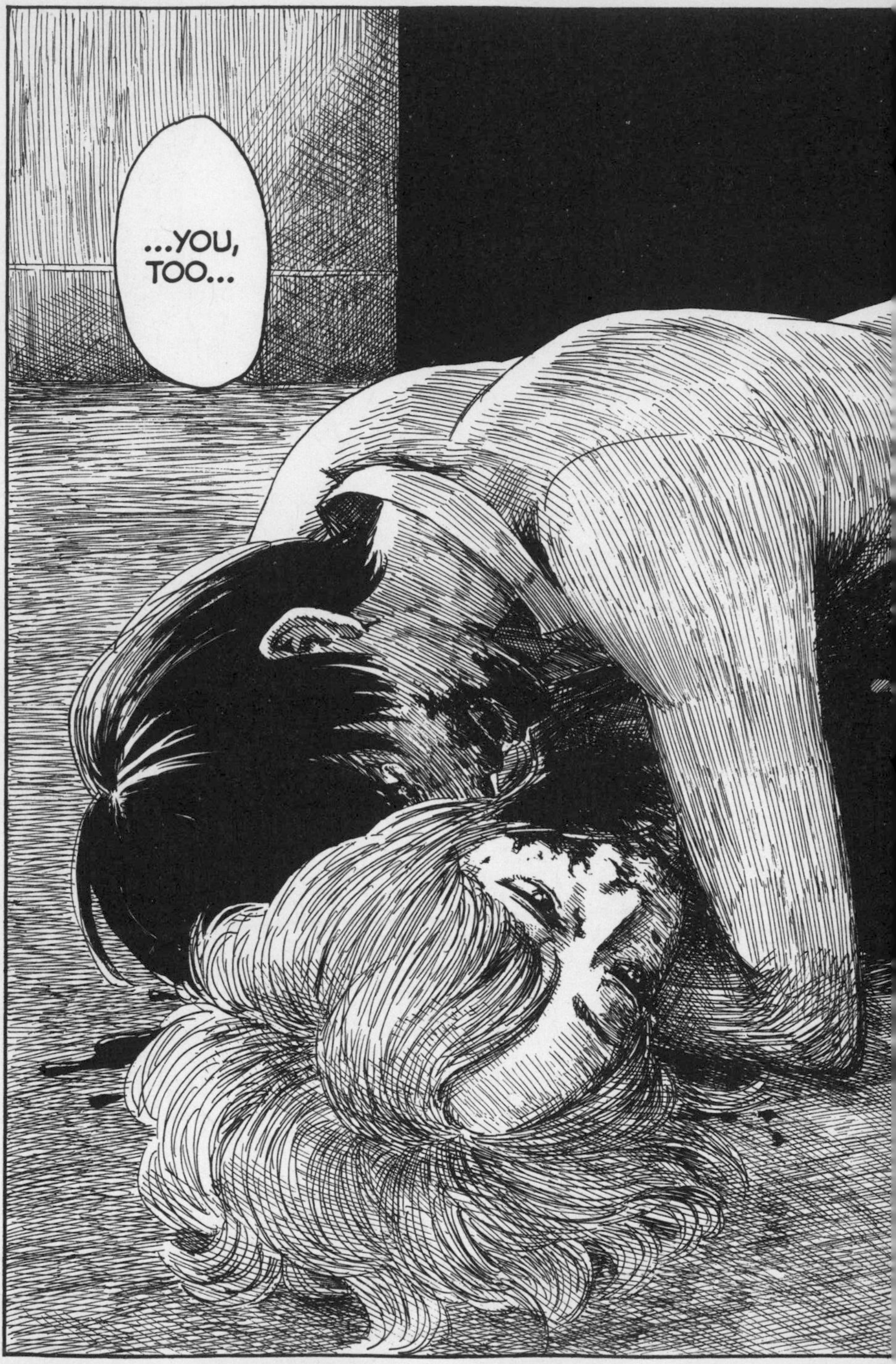
...YOU, TOO...

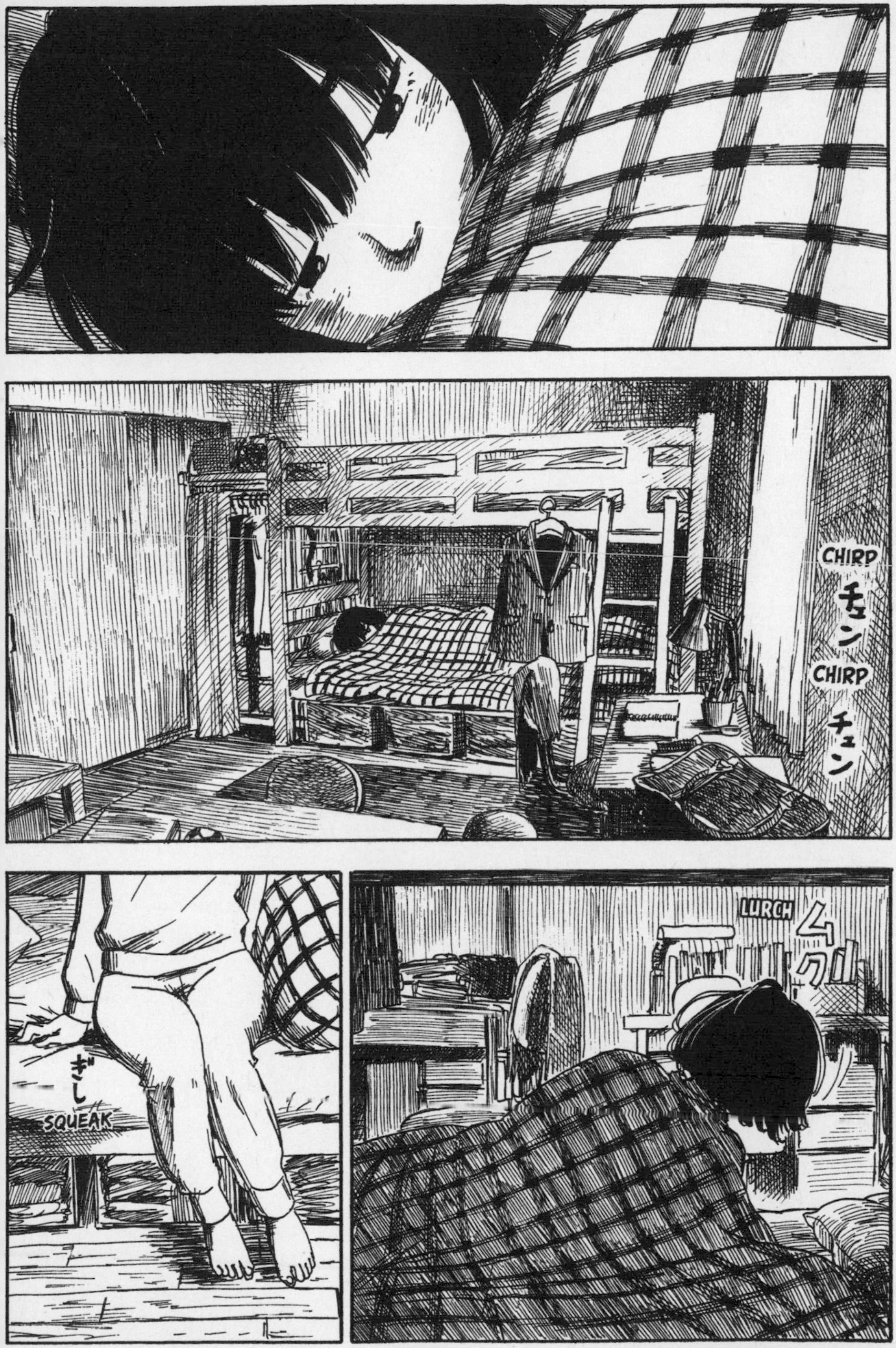
CHIRP
チュン
CHIRP
チュン
LURCH
ムクリ
ぎし
SQUEAK

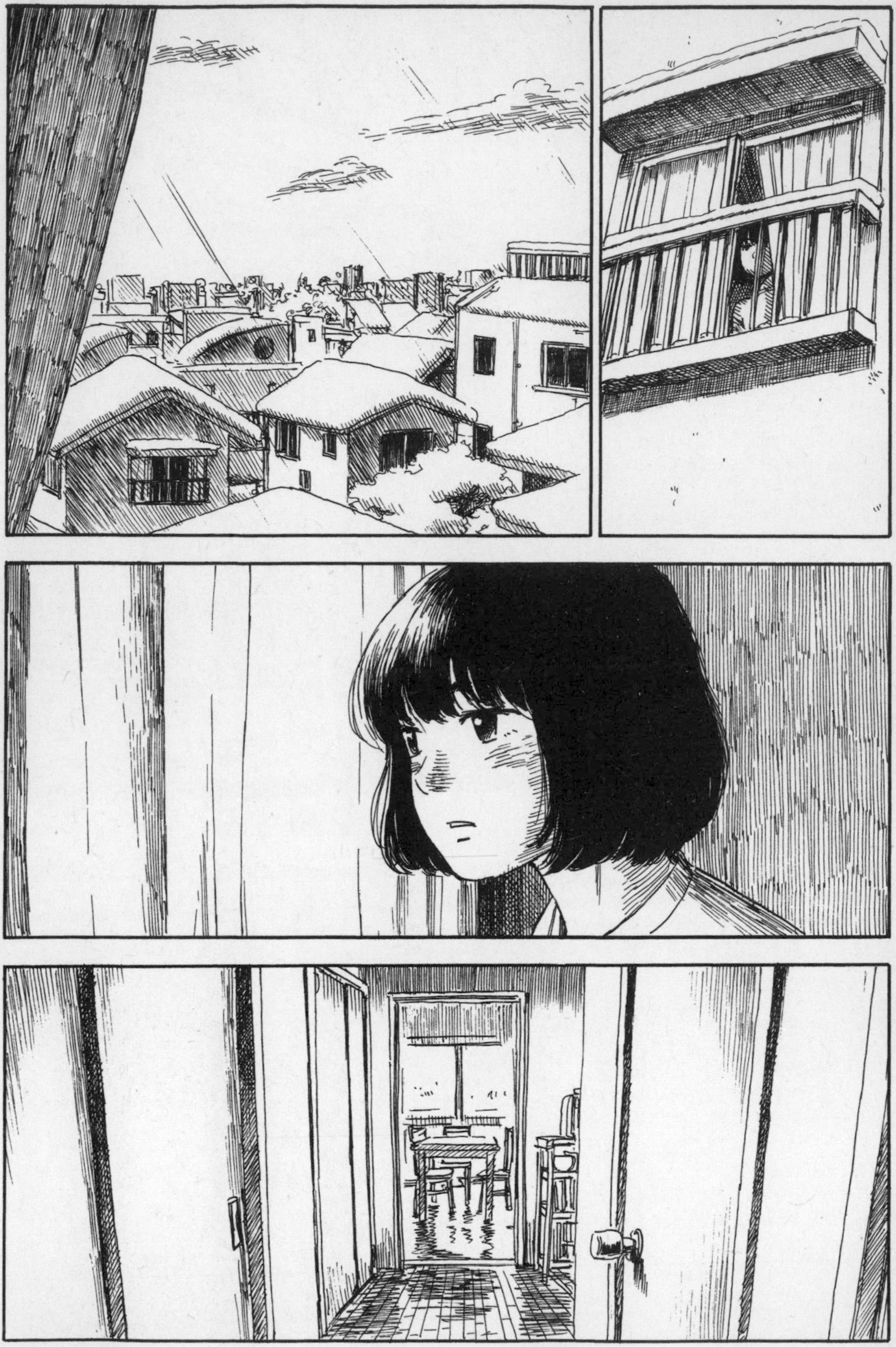

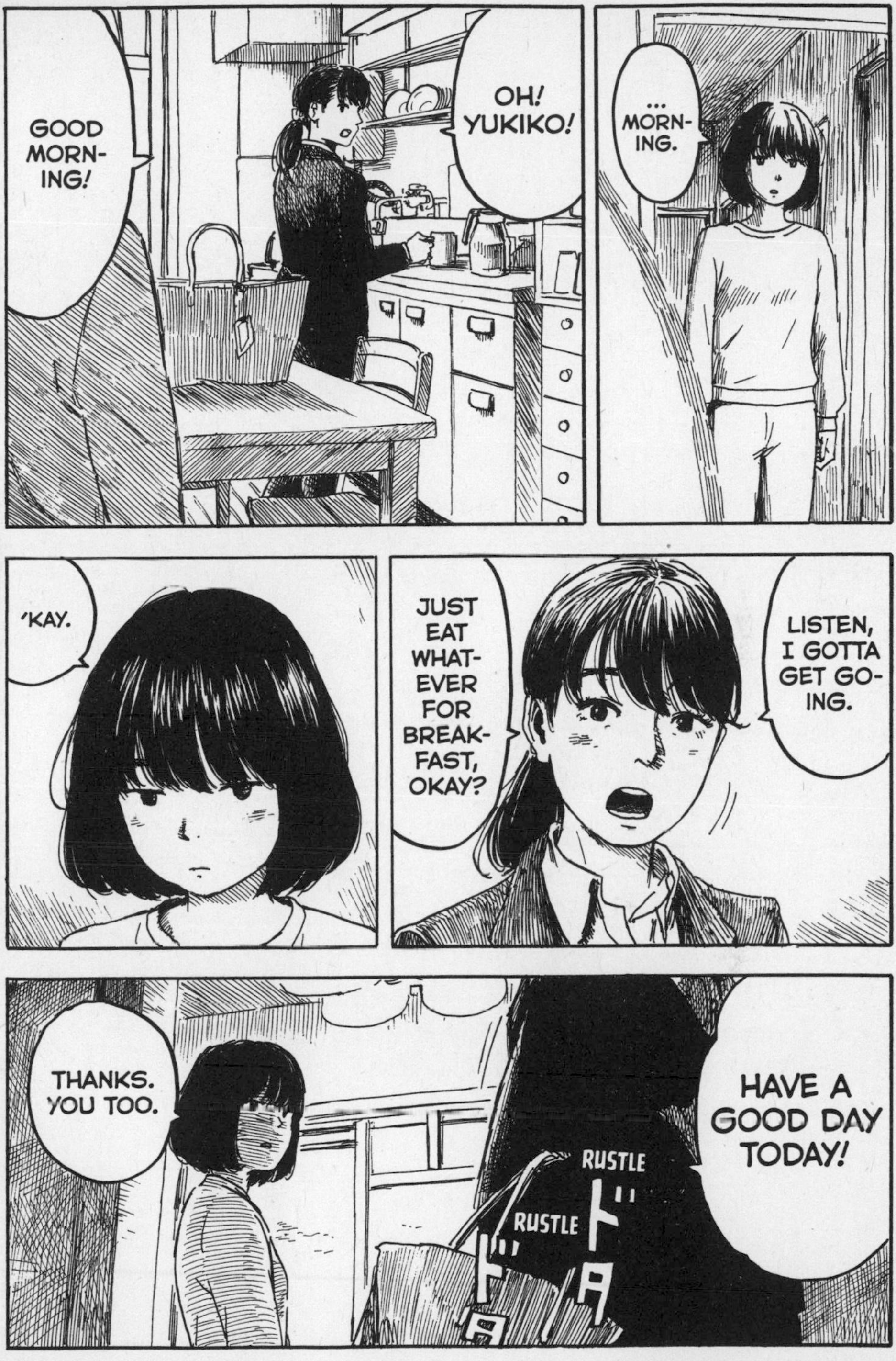
... MORN-ING.
OH! YUKIKO!
GOOD MORN-ING!
LISTEN, I GOTTA GET GO-ING.
JUST EAT WHAT-EVER FOR BREAK-FAST, OKAY?
'KAY.
HAVE A GOOD DAY TODAY!
RUSTLE
ドタ
RUSTLE
ドタ
THANKS. YOU TOO.

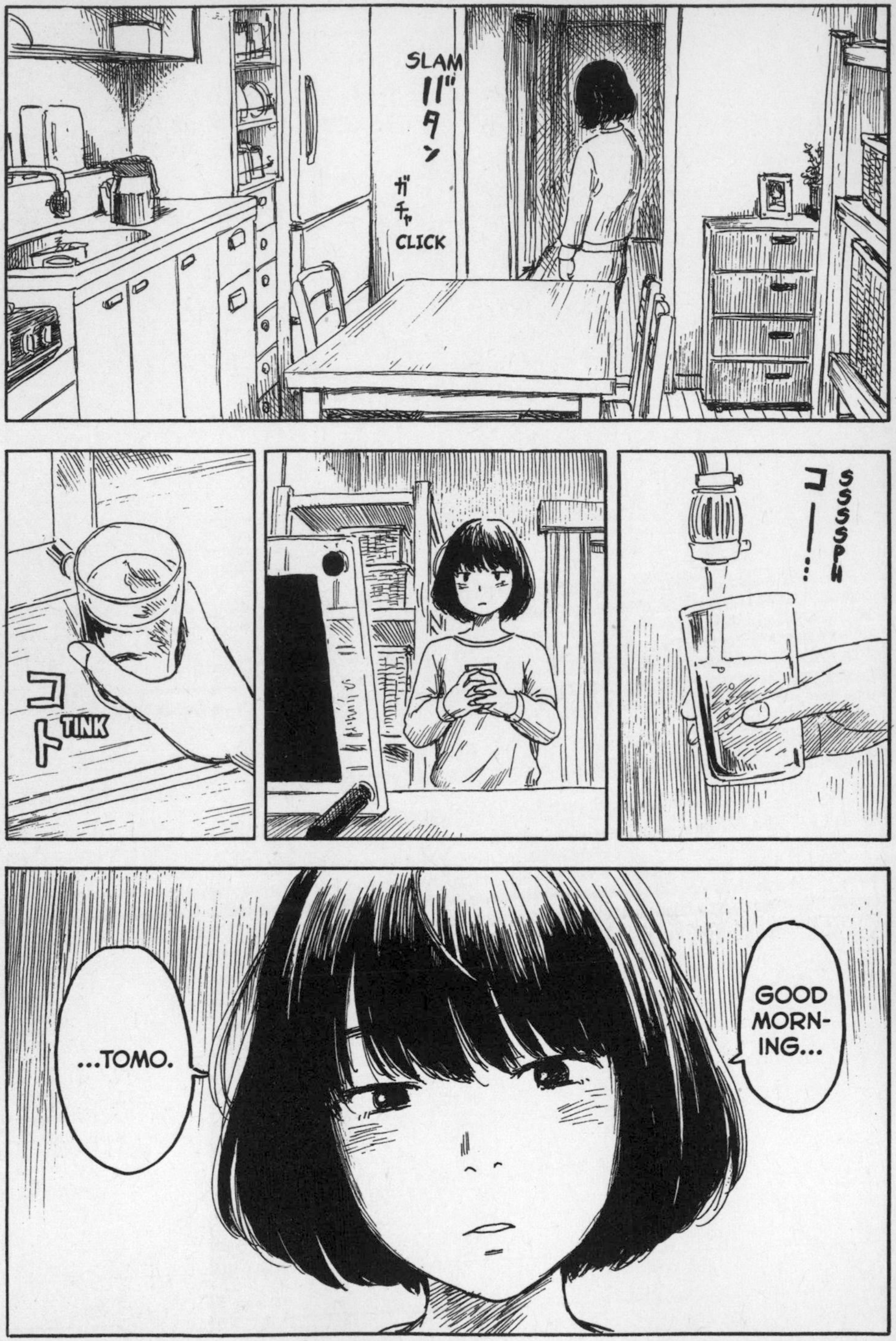
SLAM
バタン
ガチャ
CLICK
コー…
SSSSPH
コト
TINK
GOOD MORN-ING...
...TOMO.

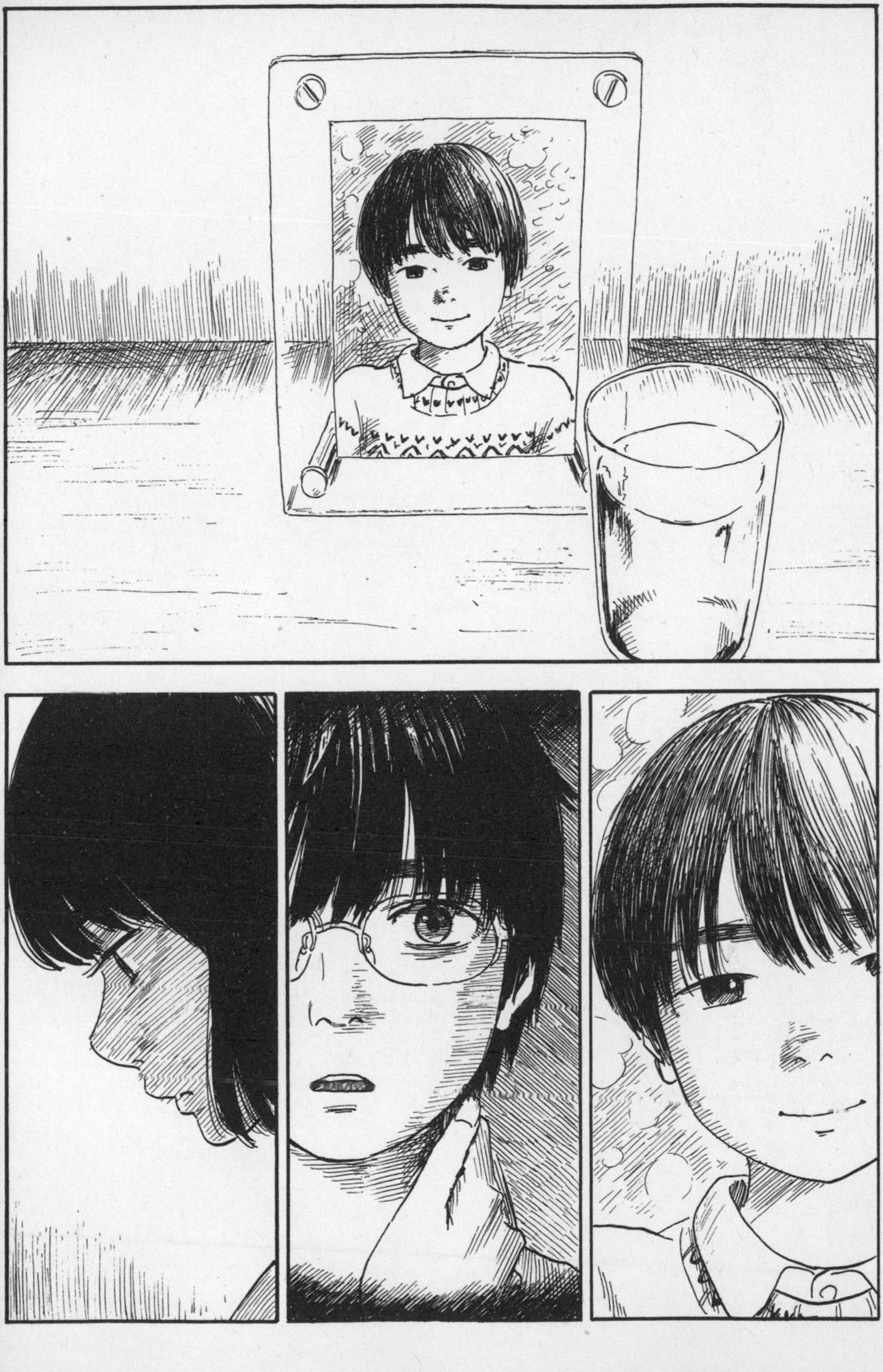

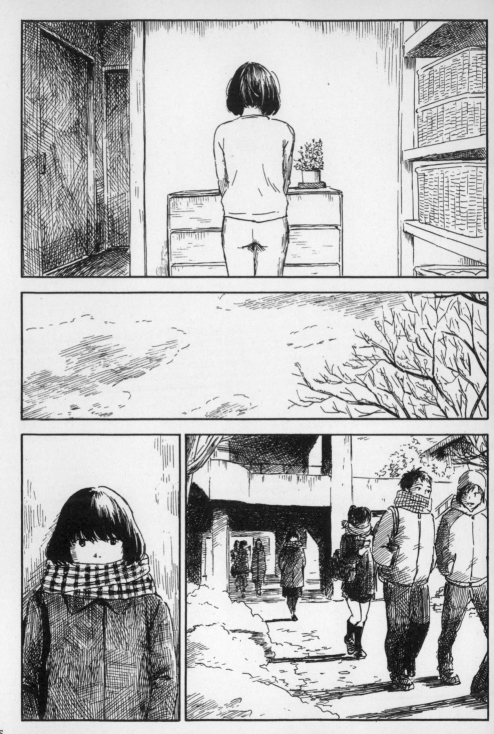

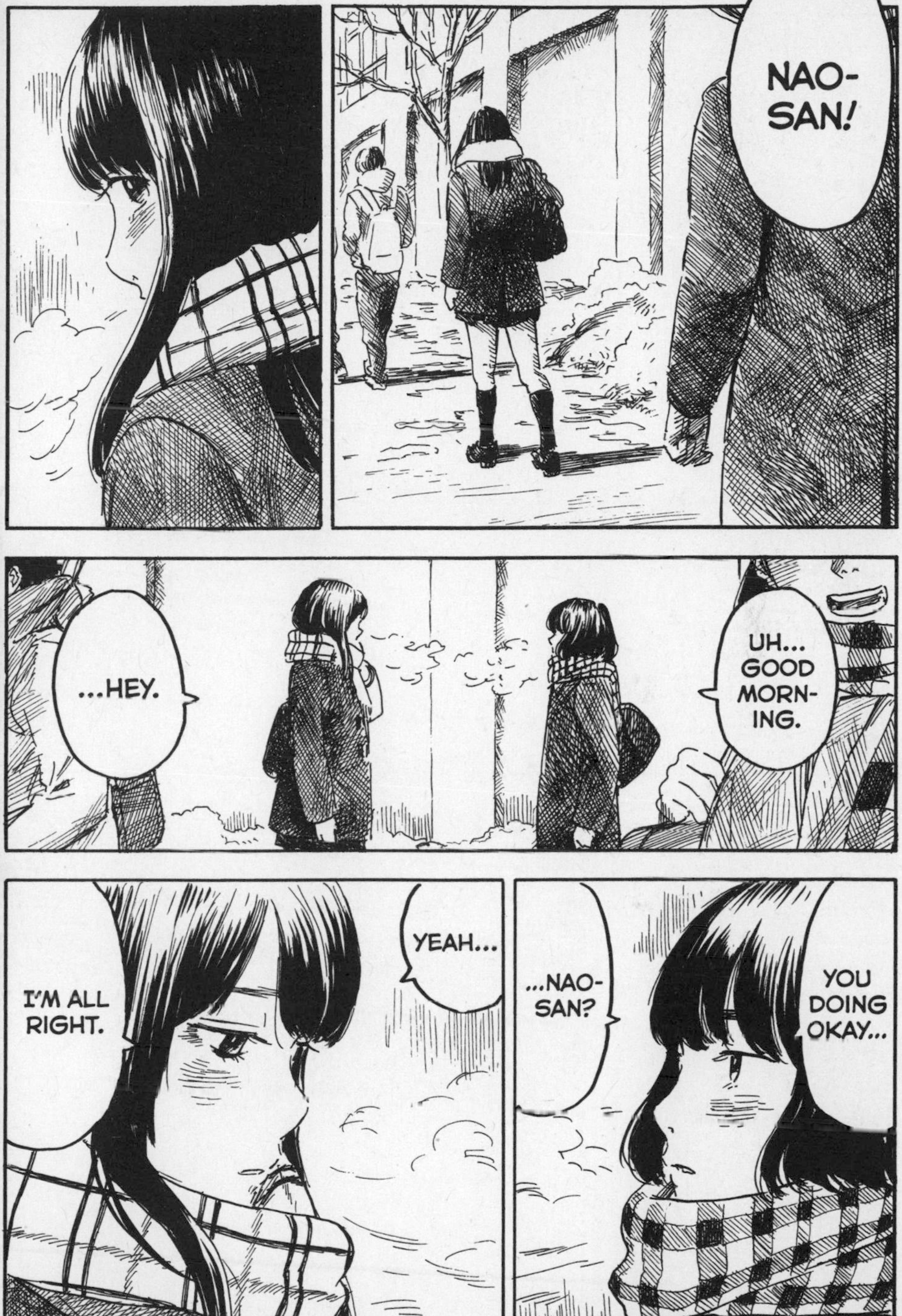
NAO-SAN!
UH... GOOD MORNING.
...HEY.
YOU DOING OKAY...
...NAO-SAN?
YEAH...
I'M ALL RIGHT.

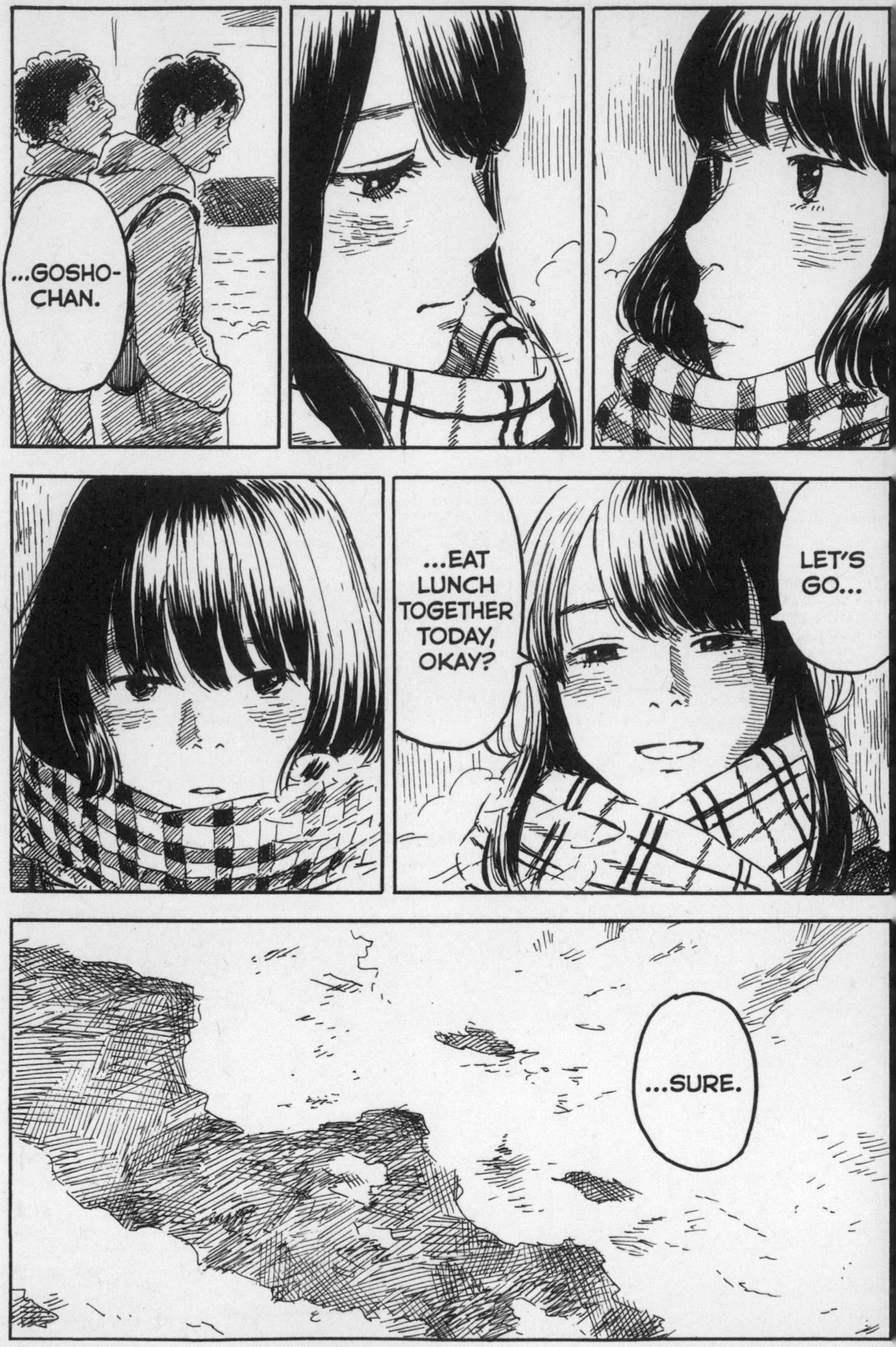
...GOSHO-CHAN.
LET'S GO...
...EAT LUNCH TOGETHER TODAY, OKAY?
...SURE.

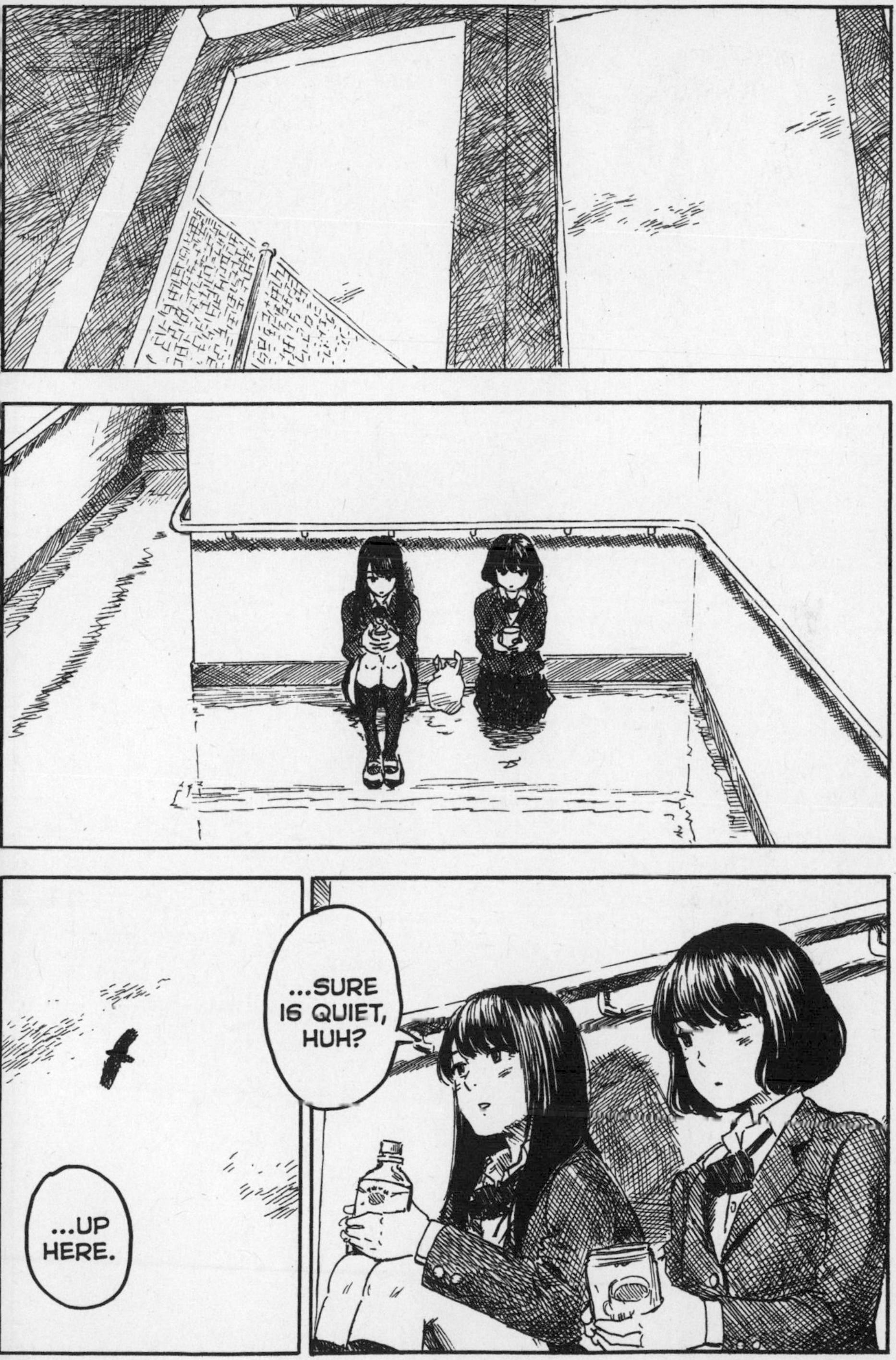
...SURE IS QUIET, HUH?
...UP HERE.

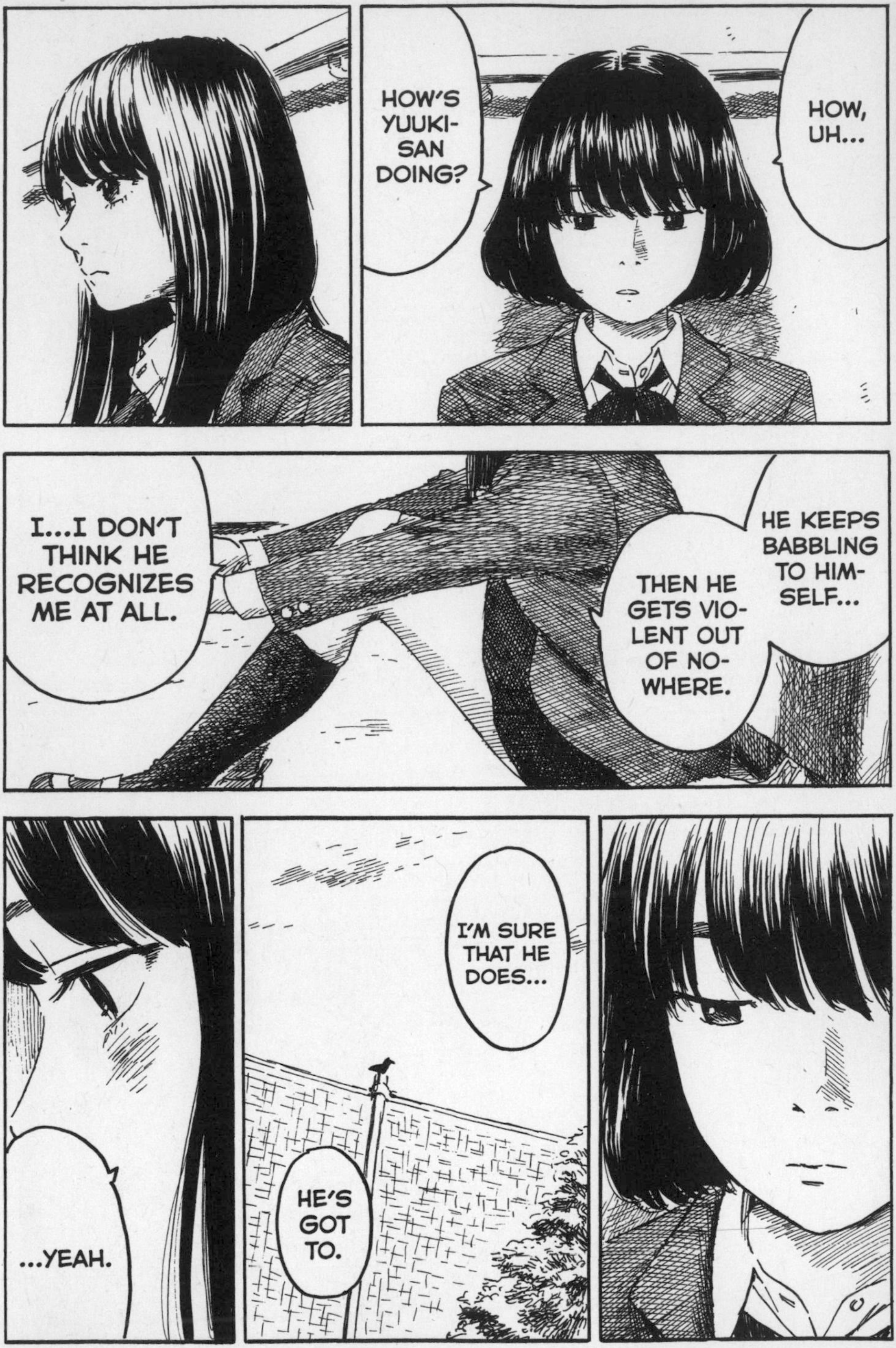
HOW, UH...
HOW'S YUUKI-SAN DOING?
HE KEEPS BABBLING TO HIM-SELF...
THEN HE GETS VIO-LENT OUT OF NO-WHERE.
I...I DON'T THINK HE RECOGNIZES ME AT ALL.
I'M SURE THAT HE DOES...
HE'S GOT TO.
...YEAH.

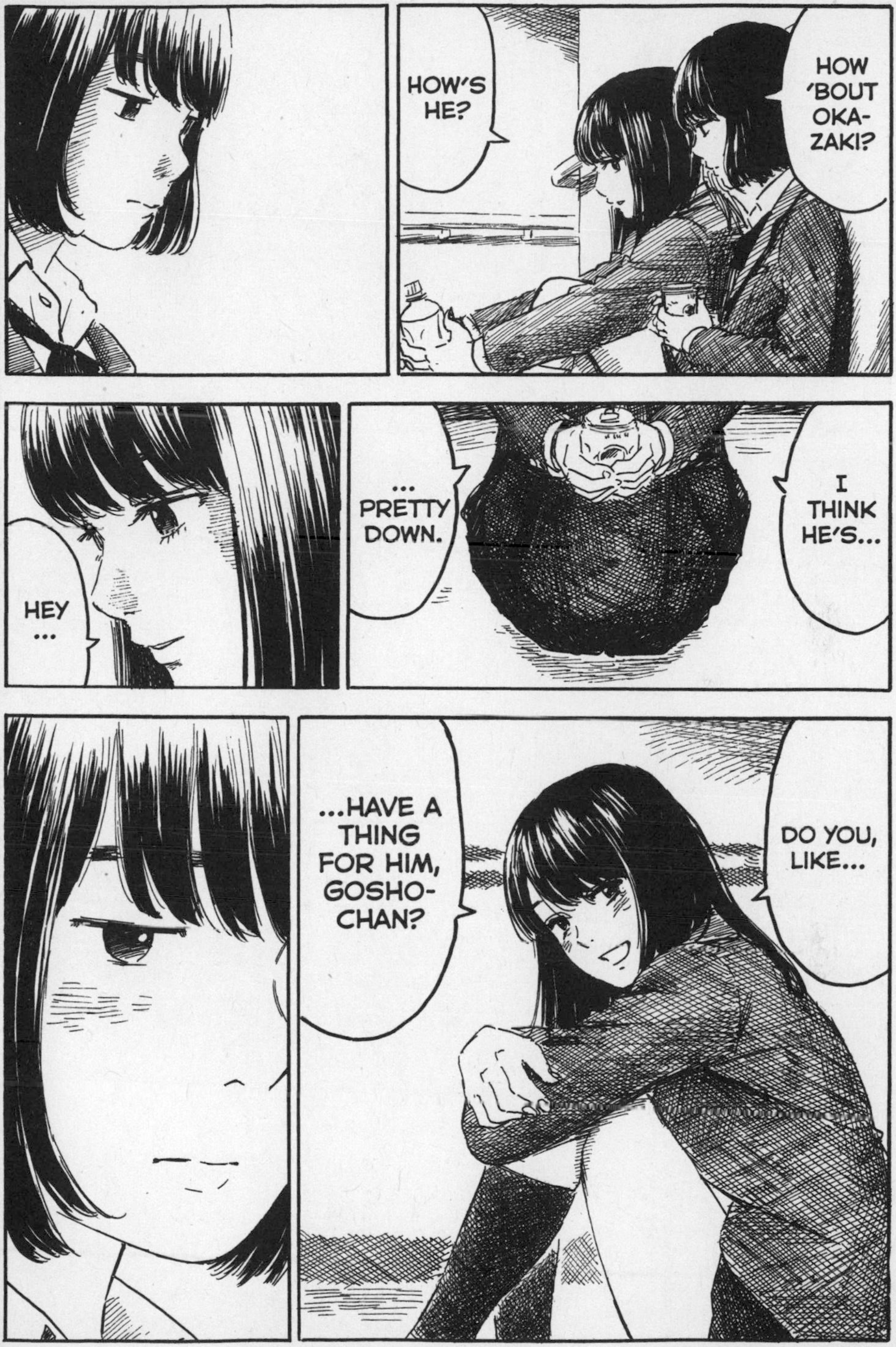
HOW 'BOUT OKA-ZAKI?
HOW'S HE?
I THINK HE'S...
... PRETTY DOWN.
HEY ...
DO YOU, LIKE...
...HAVE A THING FOR HIM, GOSHO-CHAN?

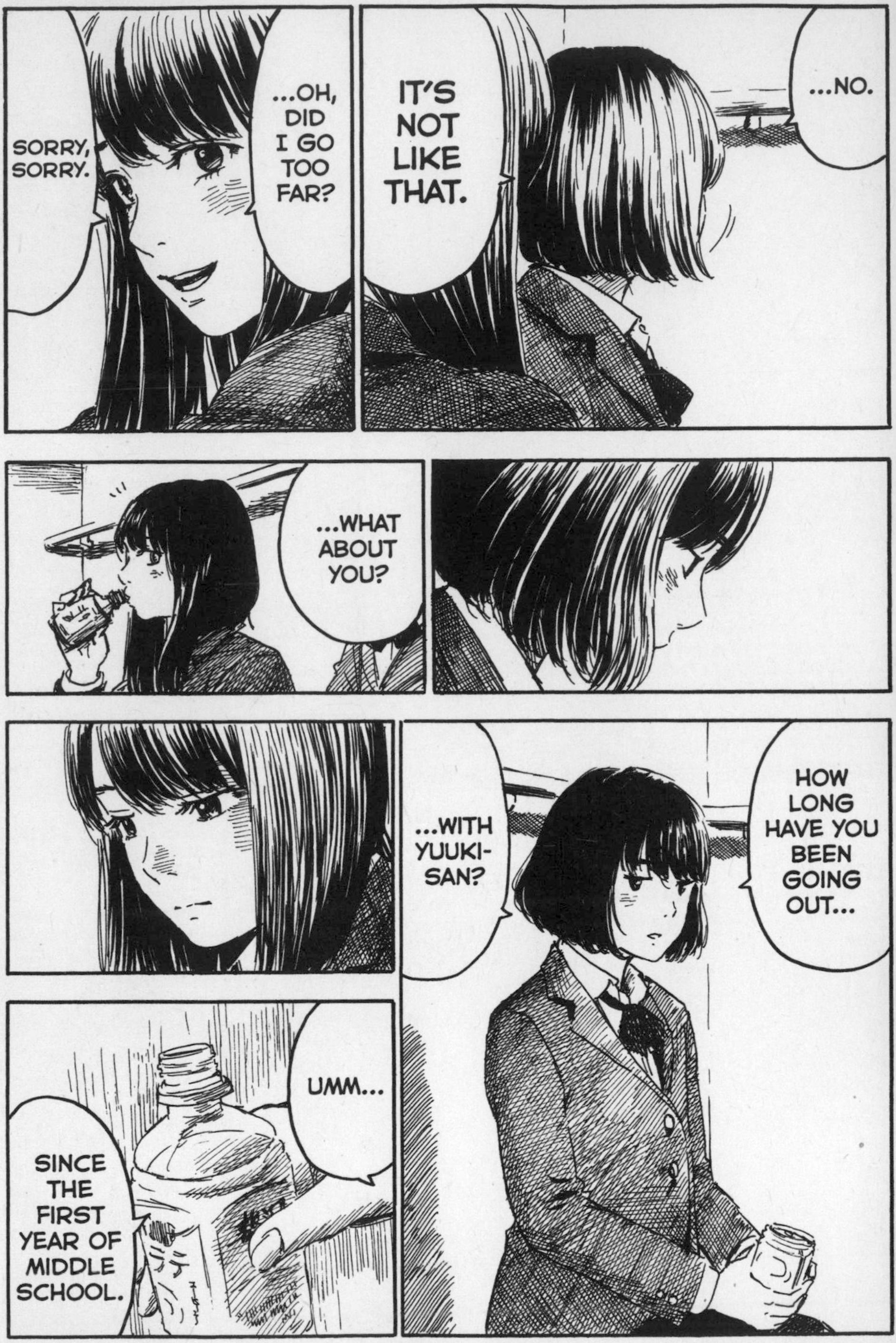
...NO.
IT'S NOT LIKE THAT.
...OH, DID I GO TOO FAR?
SORRY, SORRY.
...WHAT ABOUT YOU?
HOW LONG HAVE YOU BEEN GOING OUT...
...WITH YUUKI-SAN?
UMM...
SINCE THE FIRST YEAR OF MIDDLE SCHOOL.

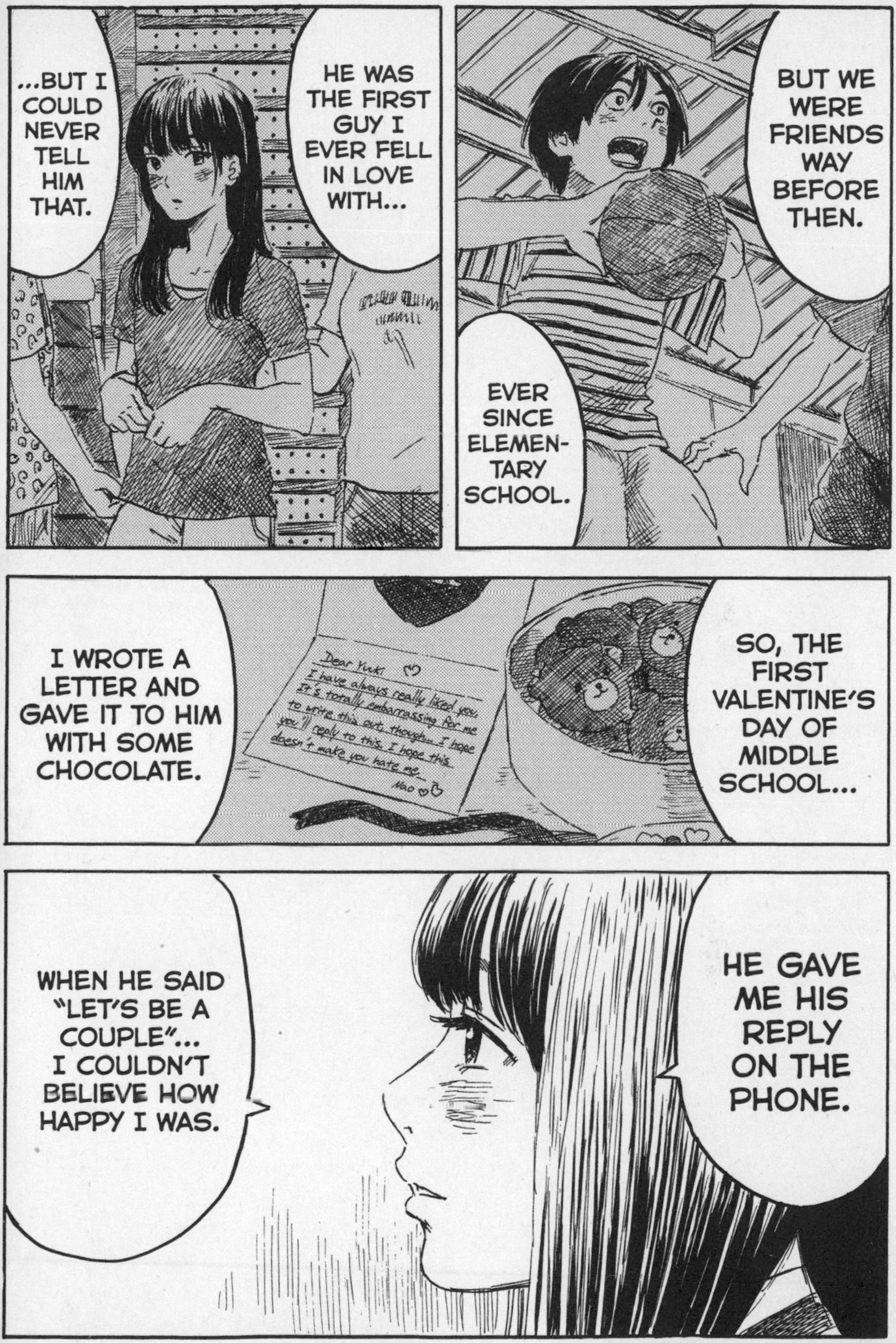
BUT WE WERE FRIENDS WAY BEFORE THEN.
EVER SINCE ELEMENTARY SCHOOL.
HE WAS THE FIRST GUY I EVER FELL IN LOVE WITH...
...BUT I COULD NEVER TELL HIM THAT.
SO, THE FIRST VALENTINE'S DAY OF MIDDLE SCHOOL...
Dear Yuki
I have always really liked you. It's totally embarrassing for me to write this out, though... I hope you'll reply to this. I hope this doesn't make you hate me.
Nao
I WROTE A LETTER AND GAVE IT TO HIM WITH SOME CHOCOLATE.
HE GAVE ME HIS REPLY ON THE PHONE.
WHEN HE SAID "LET'S BE A COUPLE"... I COULDN'T BELIEVE HOW HAPPY I WAS.

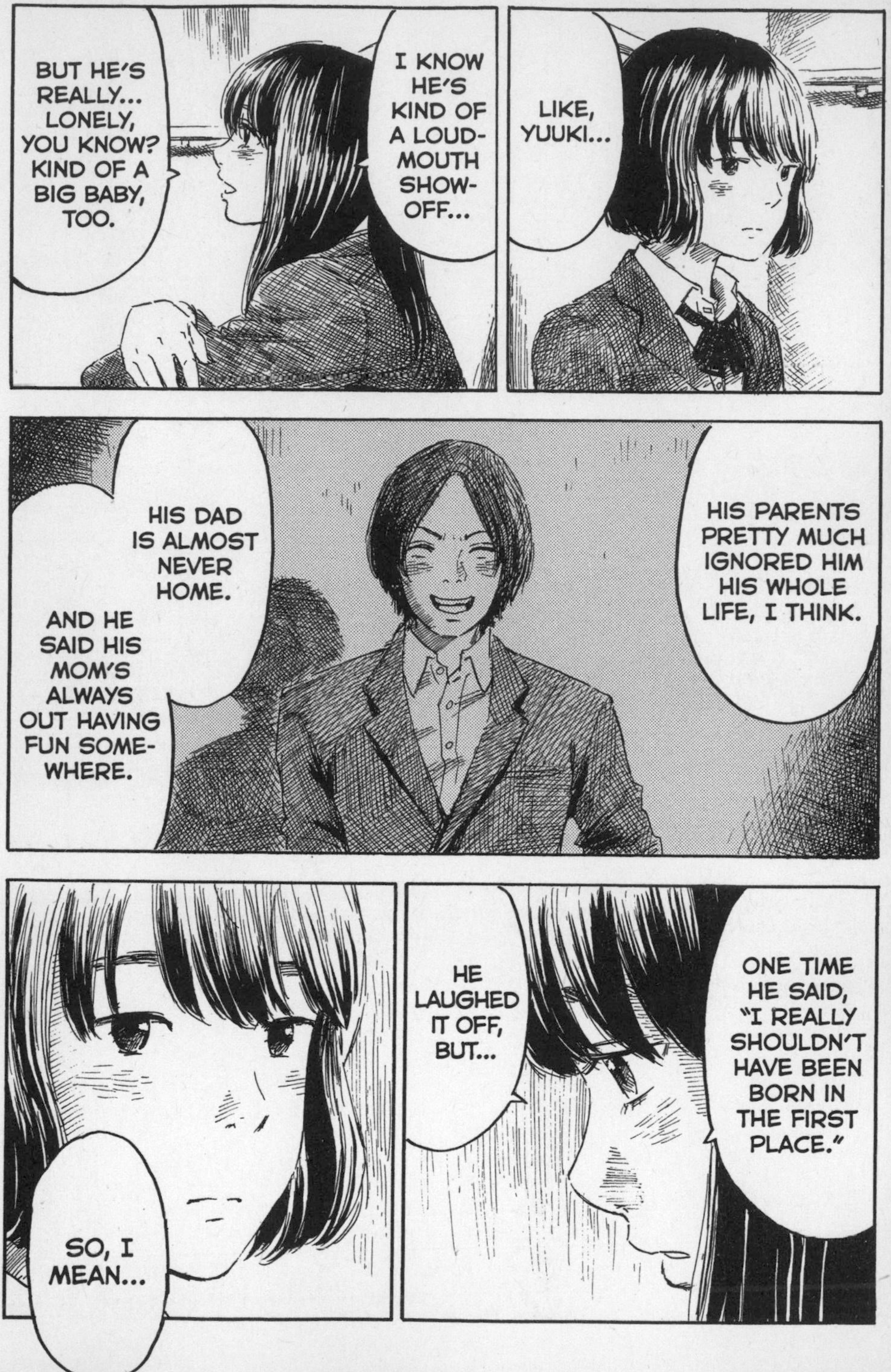
LIKE, YUUKI...
I KNOW HE'S KIND OF A LOUD-MOUTH SHOW-OFF...
BUT HE'S REALLY... LONELY, YOU KNOW? KIND OF A BIG BABY, TOO.
HIS PARENTS PRETTY MUCH IGNORED HIM HIS WHOLE LIFE, I THINK.
HIS DAD IS ALMOST NEVER HOME.
AND HE SAID HIS MOM'S ALWAYS OUT HAVING FUN SOME-WHERE.
ONE TIME HE SAID, "I REALLY SHOULDN'T HAVE BEEN BORN IN THE FIRST PLACE."
HE LAUGHED IT OFF, BUT...
SO, I MEAN...

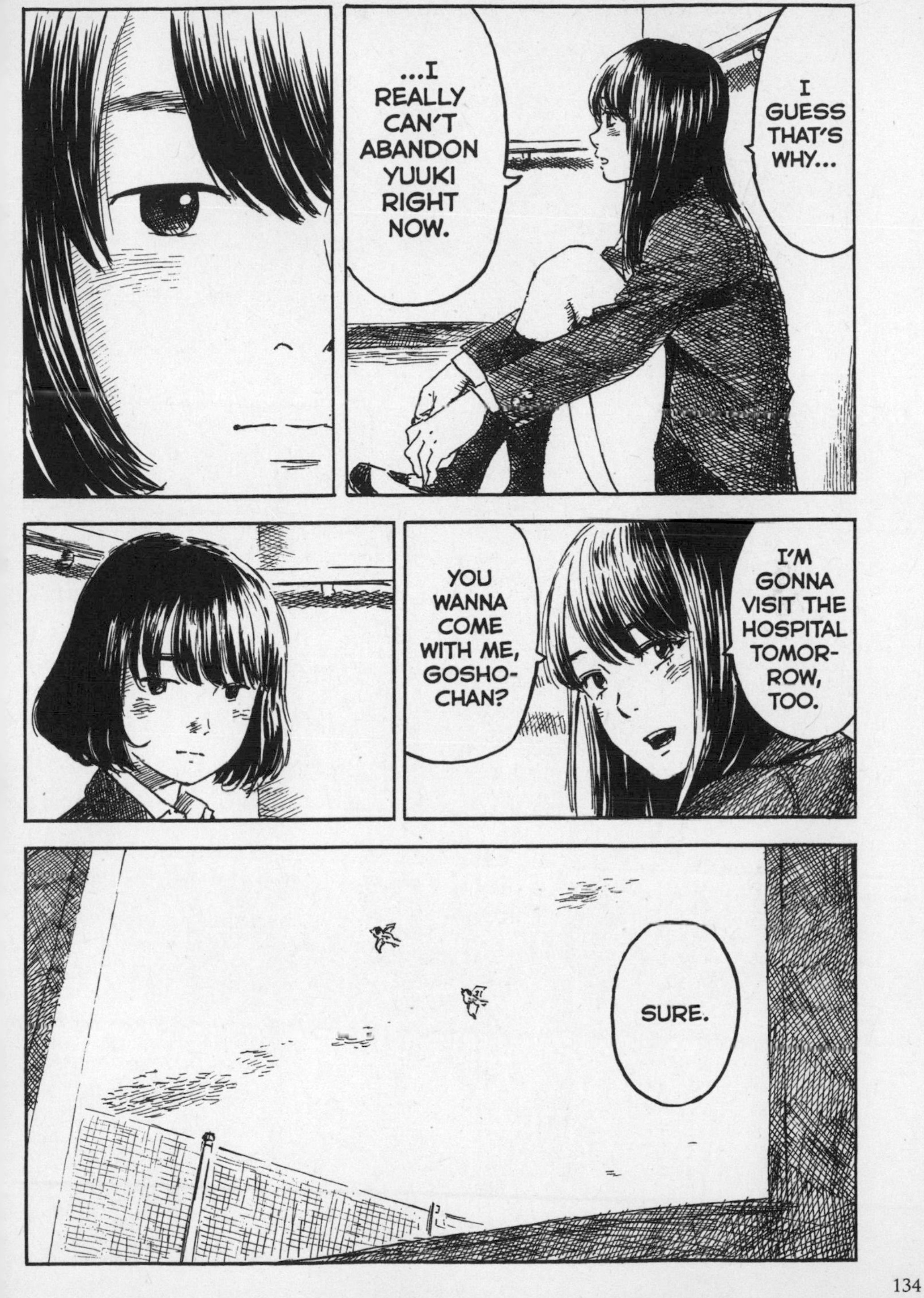
I GUESS THAT'S WHY...
...I REALLY CAN'T ABANDON YUUKI RIGHT NOW.
I'M GONNA VISIT THE HOSPITAL TOMORROW, TOO.
YOU WANNA COME WITH ME, GOSHO-CHAN?
SURE.

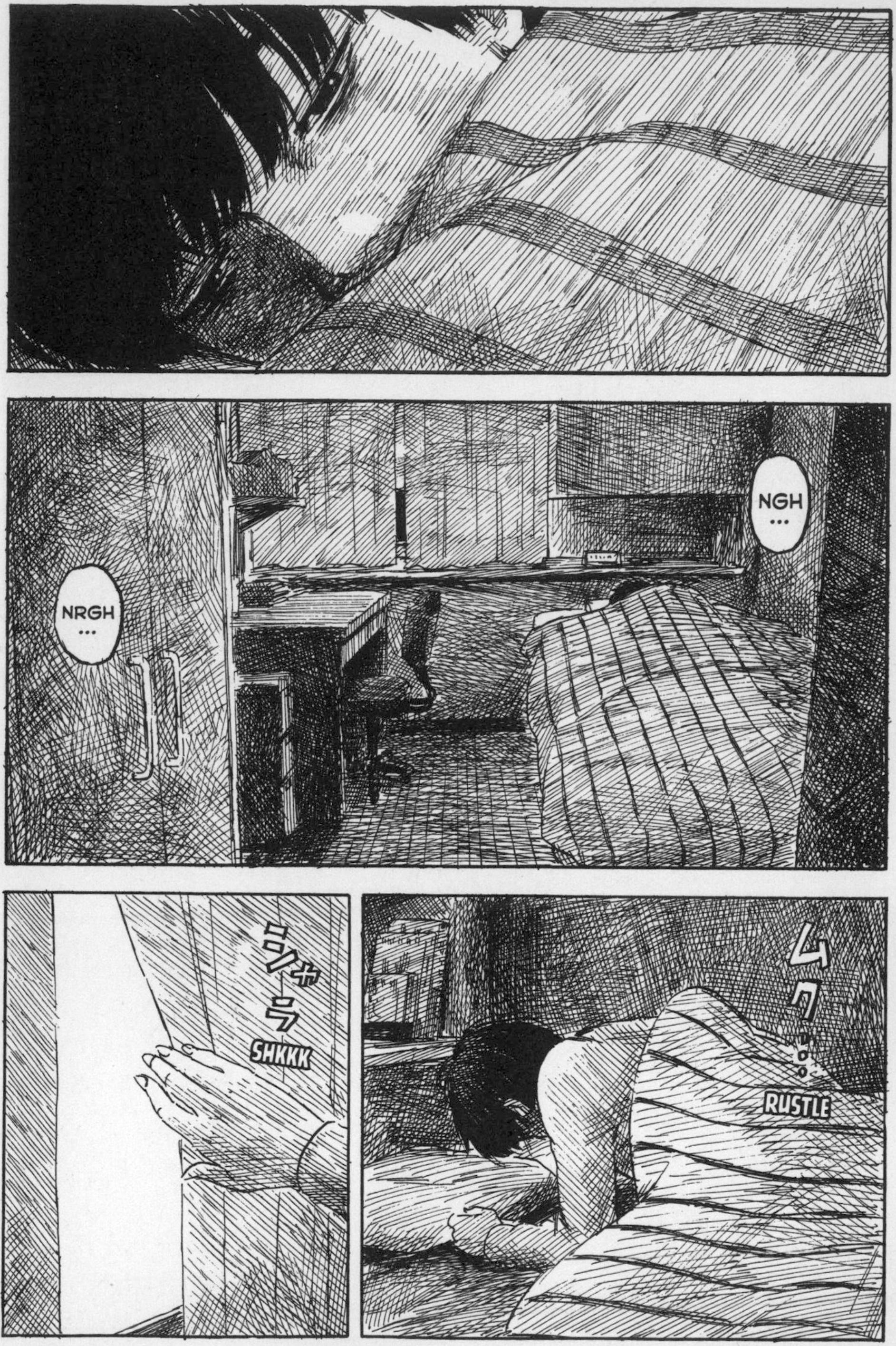
NGH...
NRGH...
RUSTLE
SHKKK

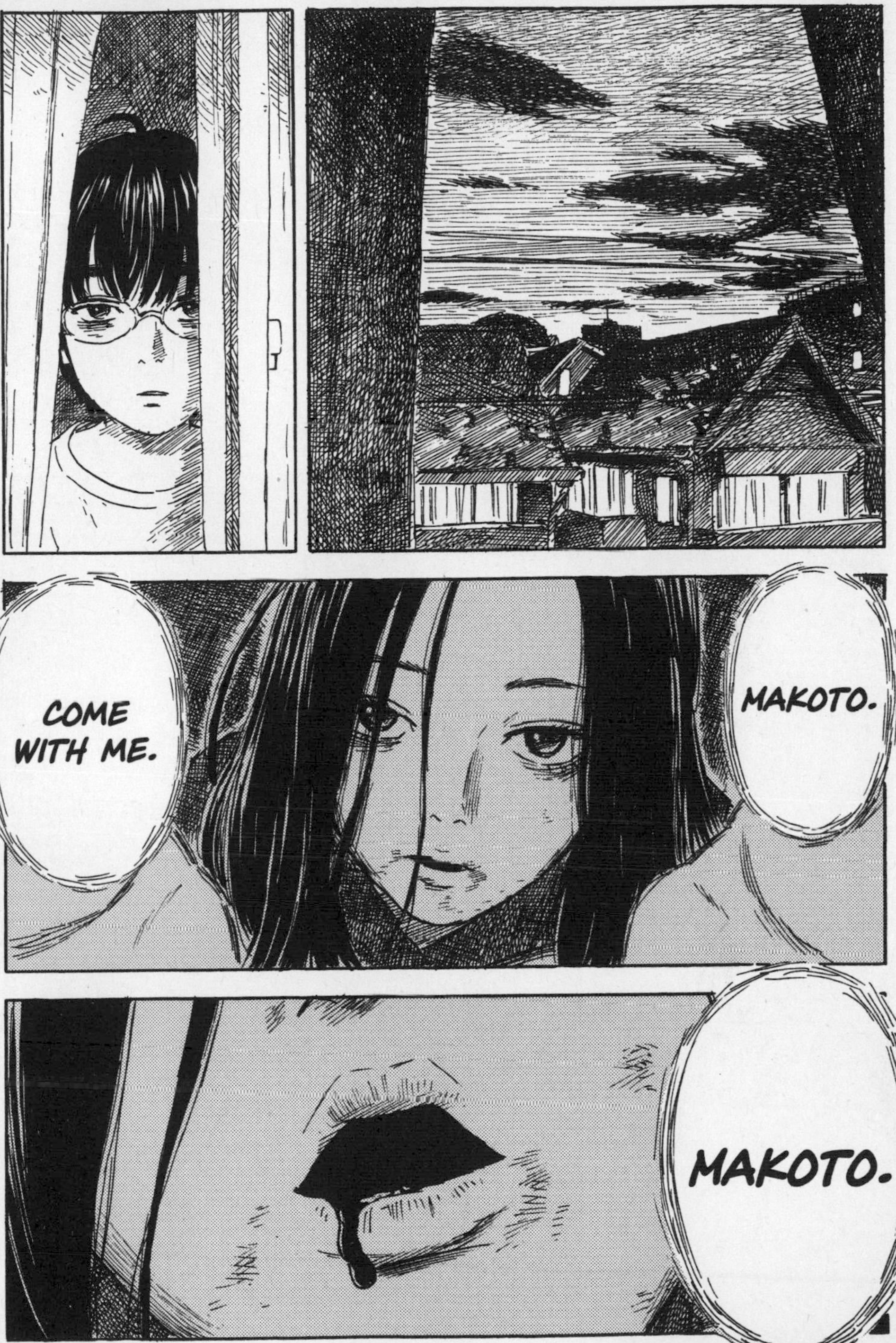
MAKOTO.
COME WITH ME.
MAKOTO.

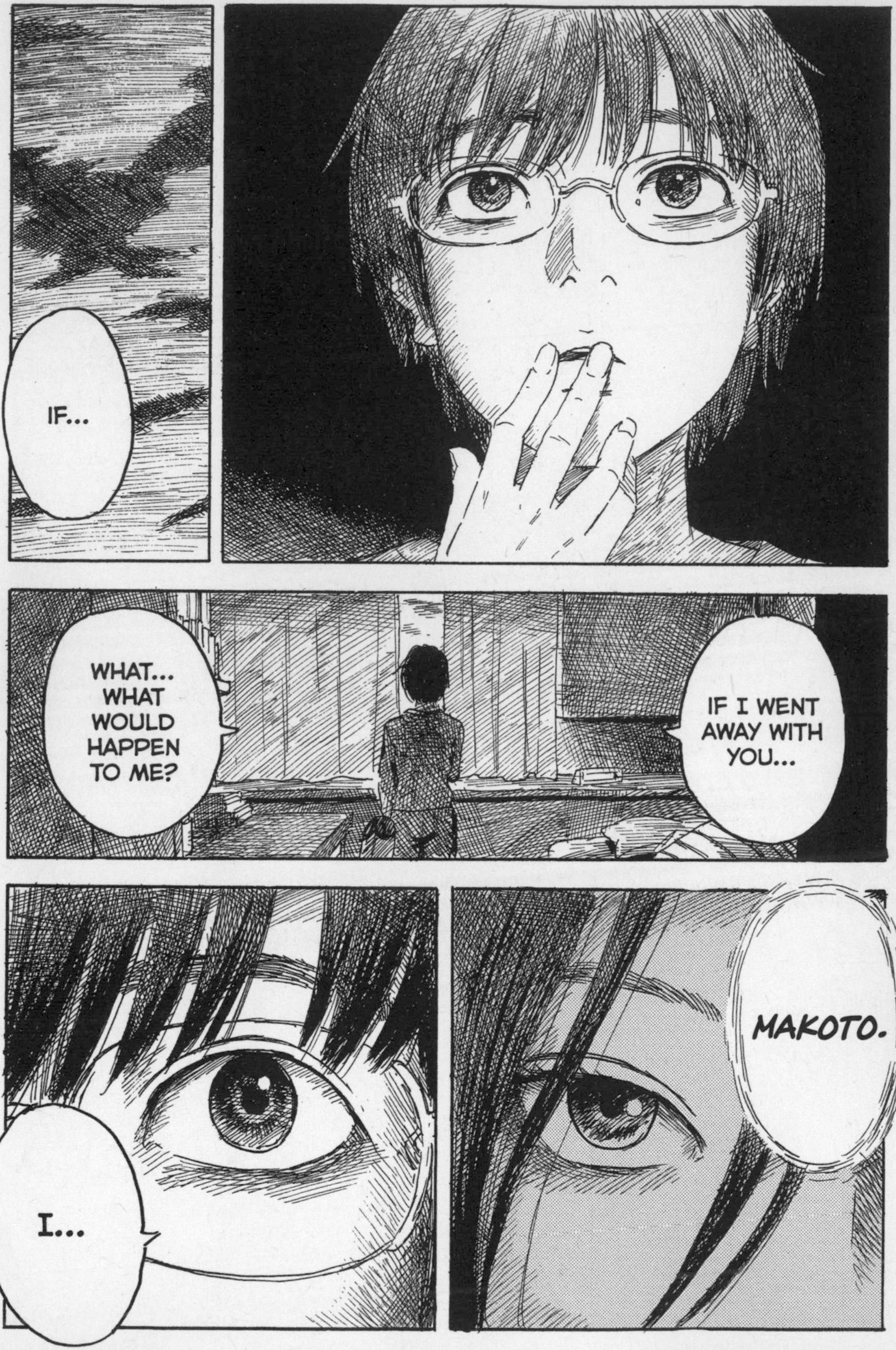
IF...
IF I WENT AWAY WITH YOU...
WHAT... WHAT WOULD HAPPEN TO ME?
MAKOTO.
I...

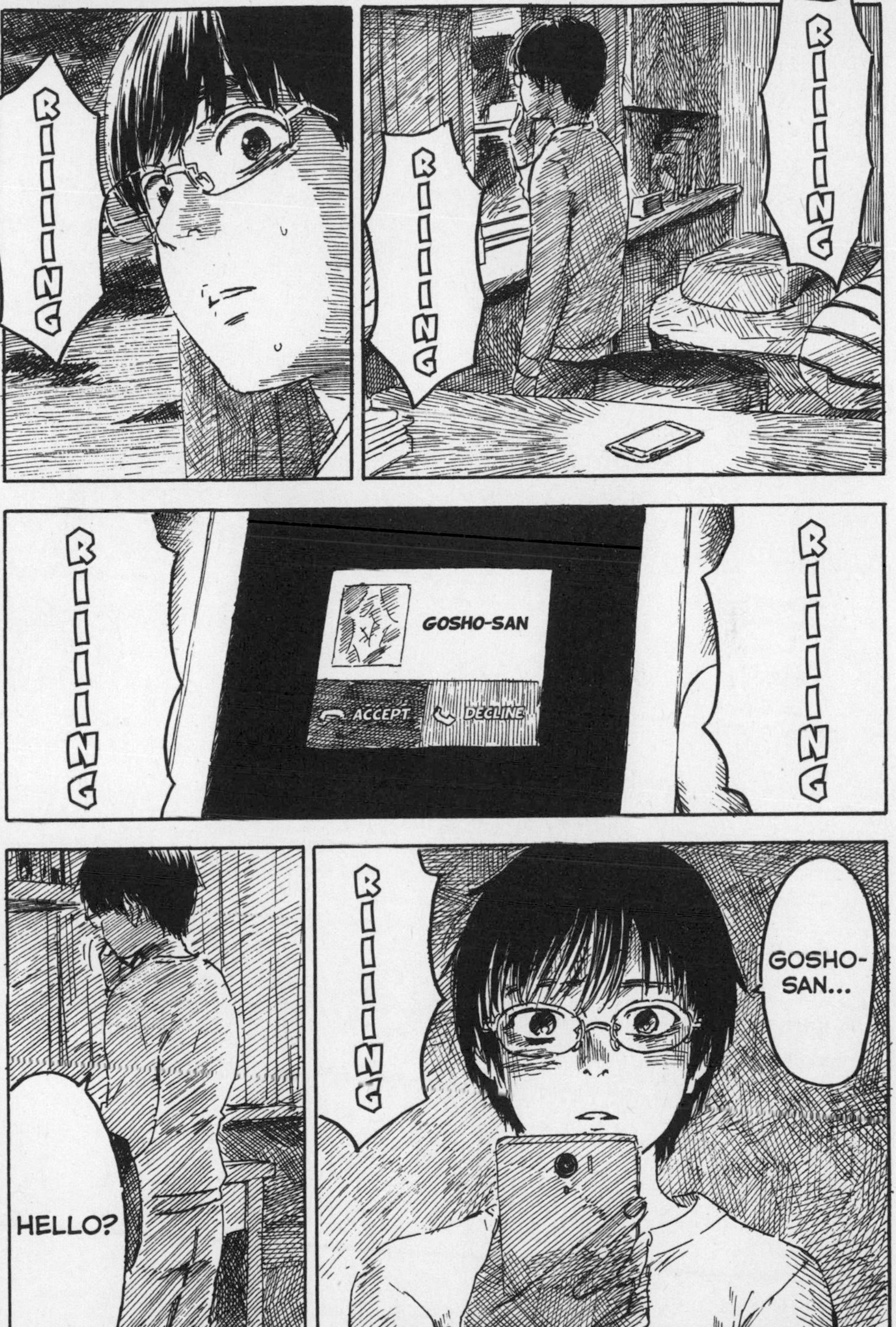

RIIIING
RIIIING
RIIIING
RIIIING
GOSHO-SAN
ACCEPT
DECLINE
RIIIING
RIIIING
GOSHO-SAN...
HELLO?

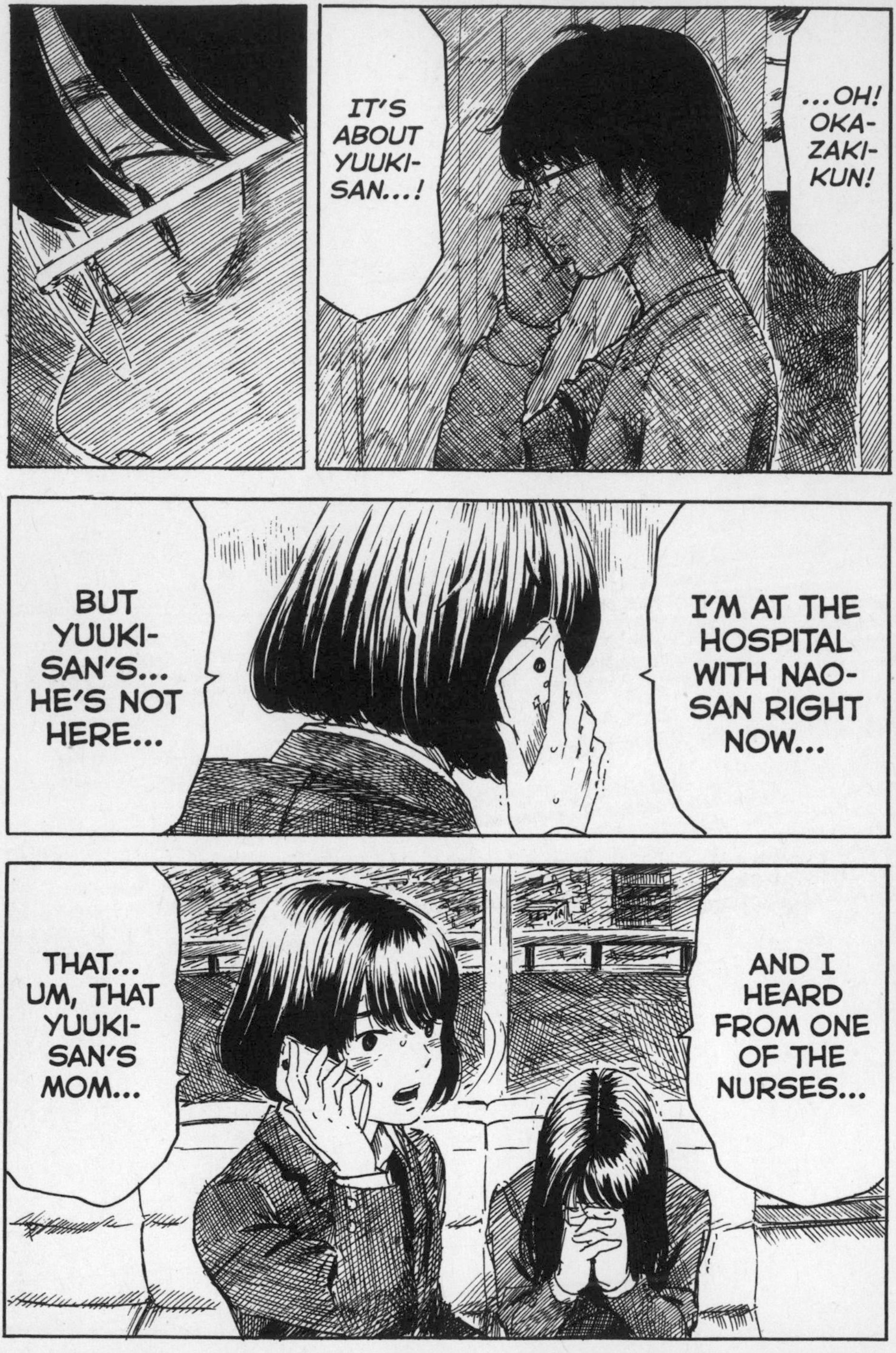
...OH! OKA-ZAKI-KUN!
IT'S ABOUT YUUKI-SAN...!
I'M AT THE HOSPITAL WITH NAO-SAN RIGHT NOW...
BUT YUUKI-SAN'S... HE'S NOT HERE...
AND I HEARD FROM ONE OF THE NURSES...
THAT... UM, THAT YUUKI-SAN'S MOM...

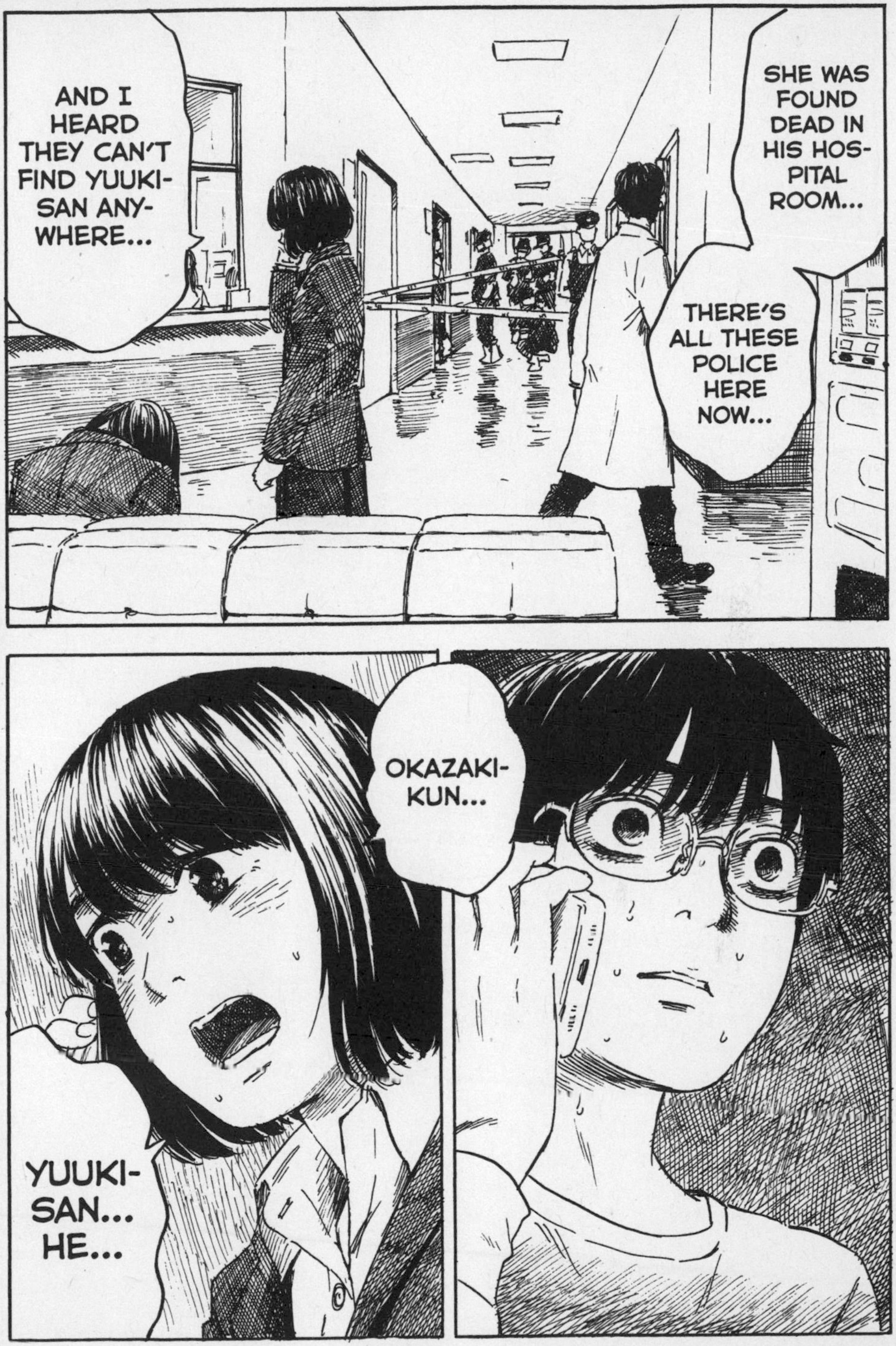
SHE WAS FOUND DEAD IN HIS HOS-PITAL ROOM...
THERE'S ALL THESE POLICE HERE NOW...
AND I HEARD THEY CAN'T FIND YUUKI-SAN ANY-WHERE...
OKAZAKI-KUN...
YUUKI-SAN... HE...

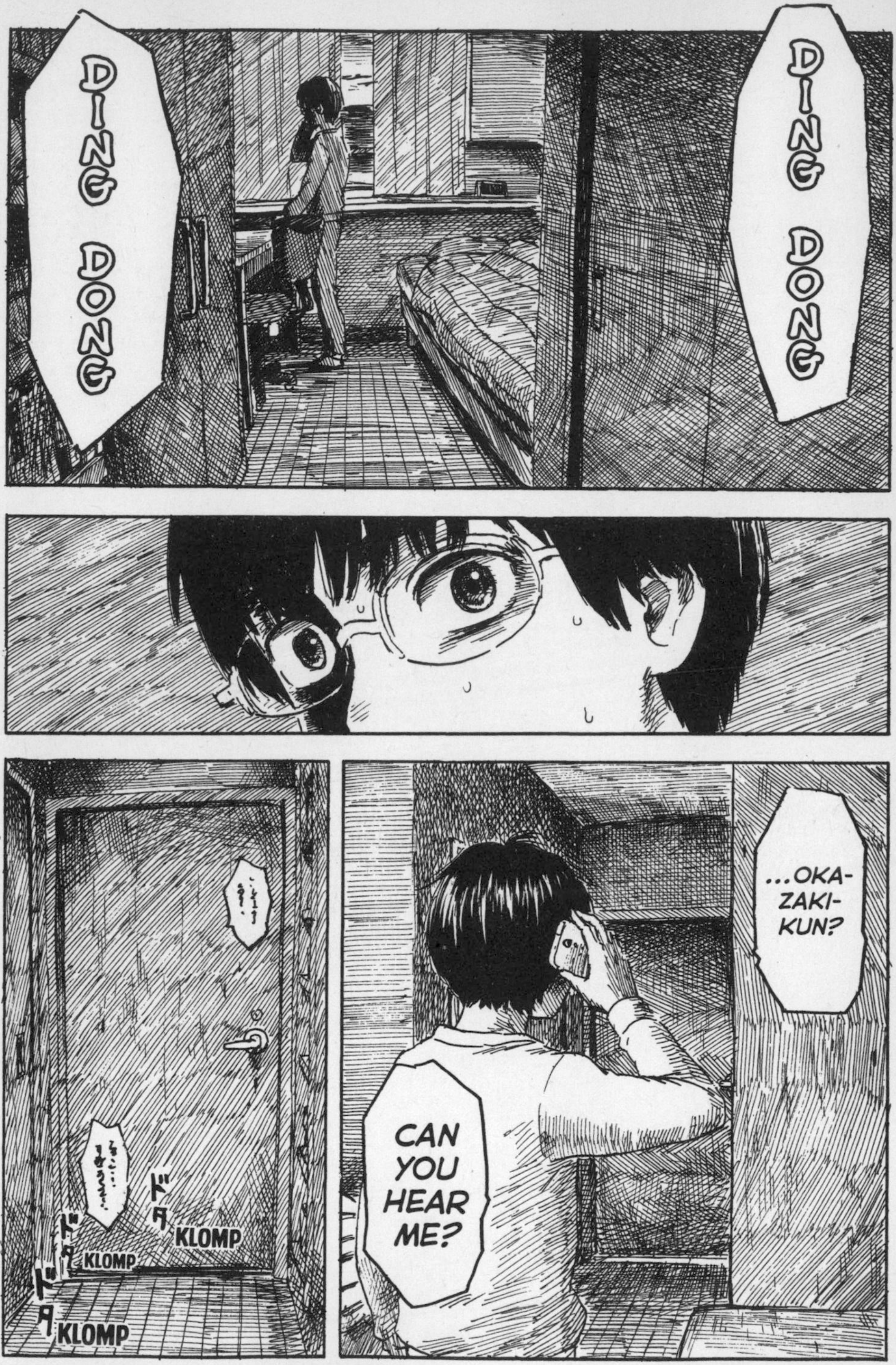
DING DONG
DING DONG
...OKA-ZAKI-KUN?
CAN YOU HEAR ME?
ドタ KLOMP
ドタ KLOMP
ドタ KLOMP

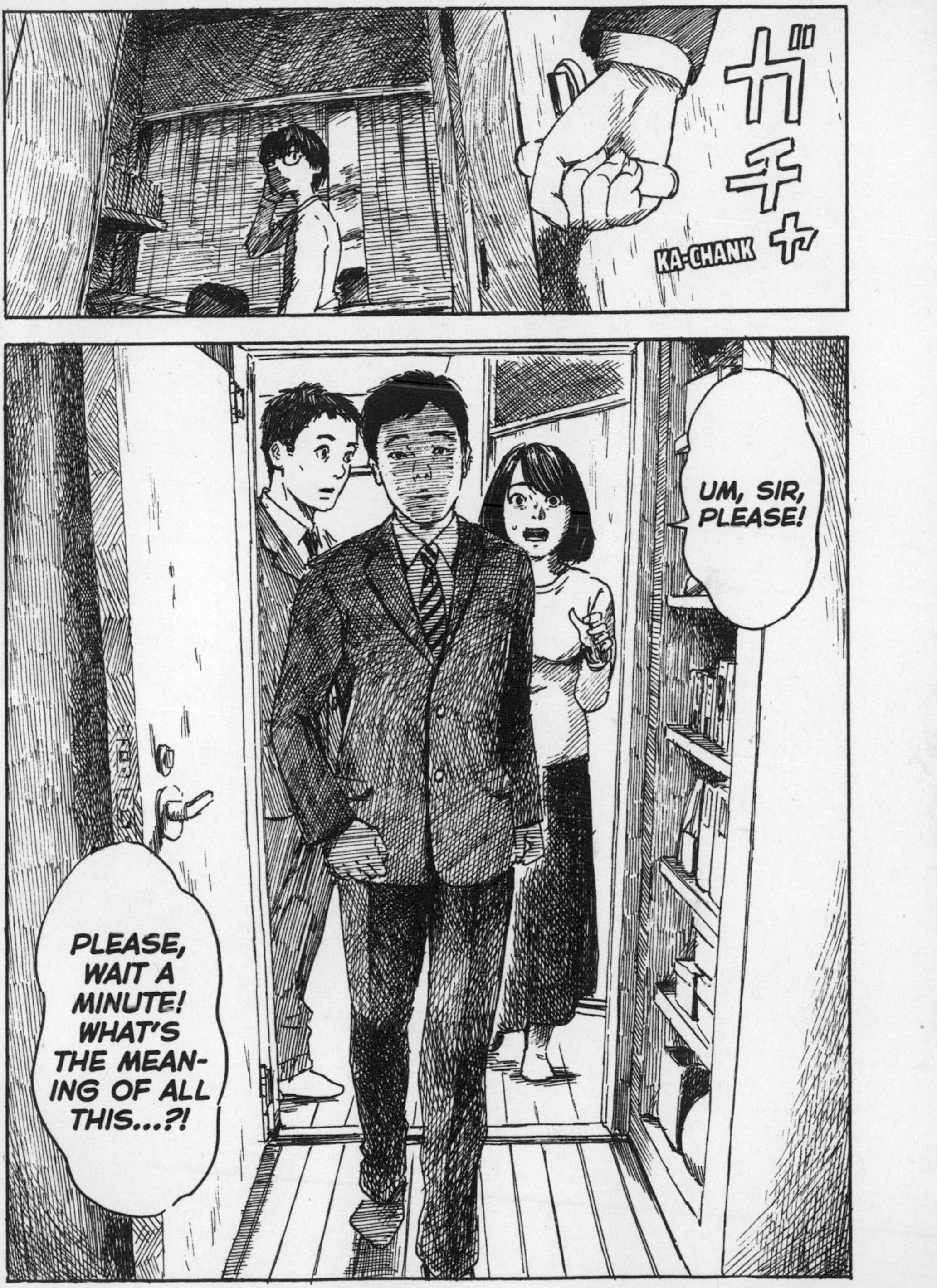
ガチャ
KA-CHANK
UM, SIR, PLEASE!
PLEASE, WAIT A MINUTE! WHAT'S THE MEAN-ING OF ALL THIS...?!

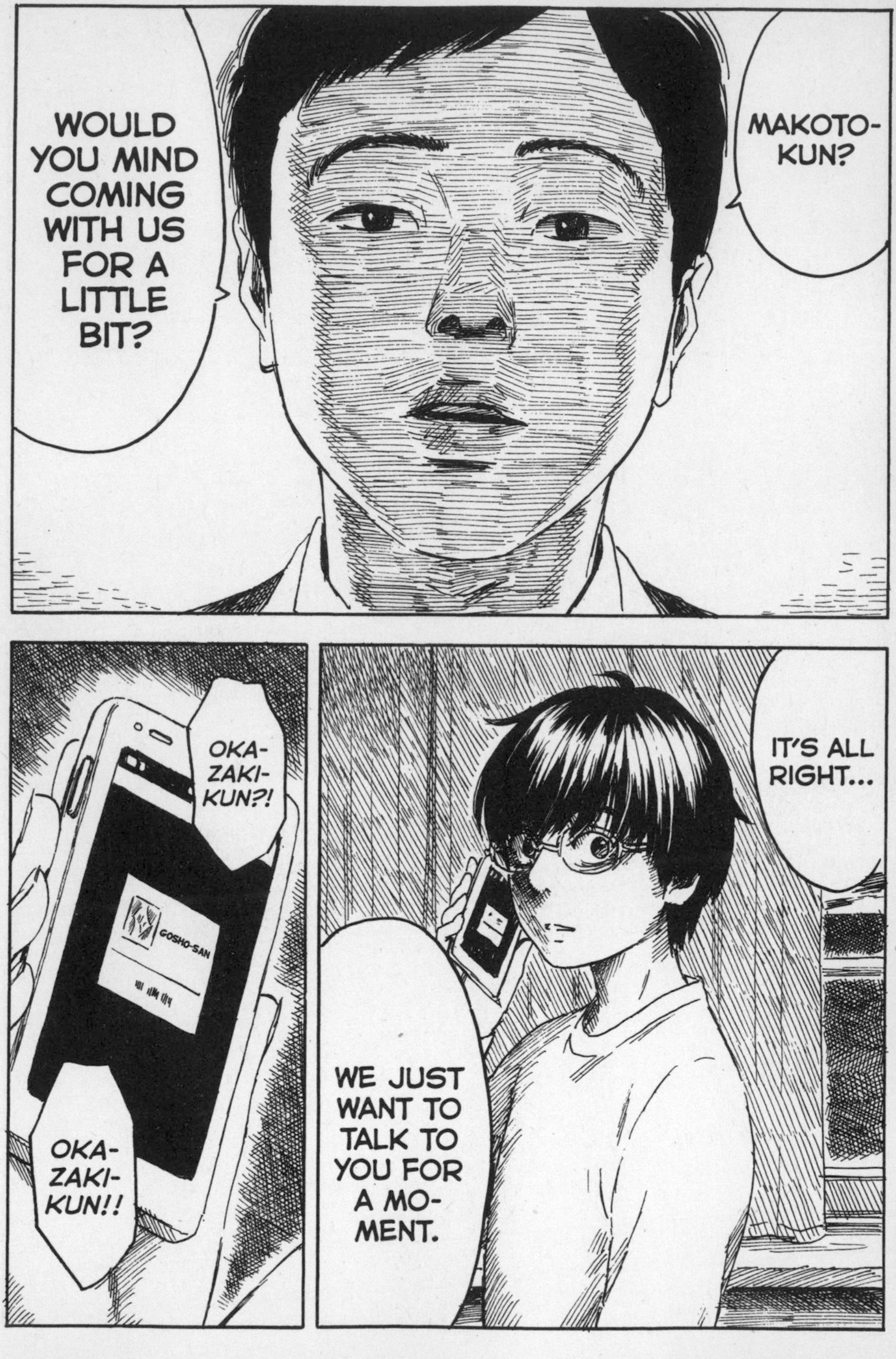
MAKOTO-KUN?
WOULD YOU MIND COMING WITH US FOR A LITTLE BIT?
IT'S ALL RIGHT...
WE JUST WANT TO TALK TO YOU FOR A MO-MENT.
OKA-ZAKI-KUN?!
GOSHO-SAN
OKA-ZAKI-KUN!!

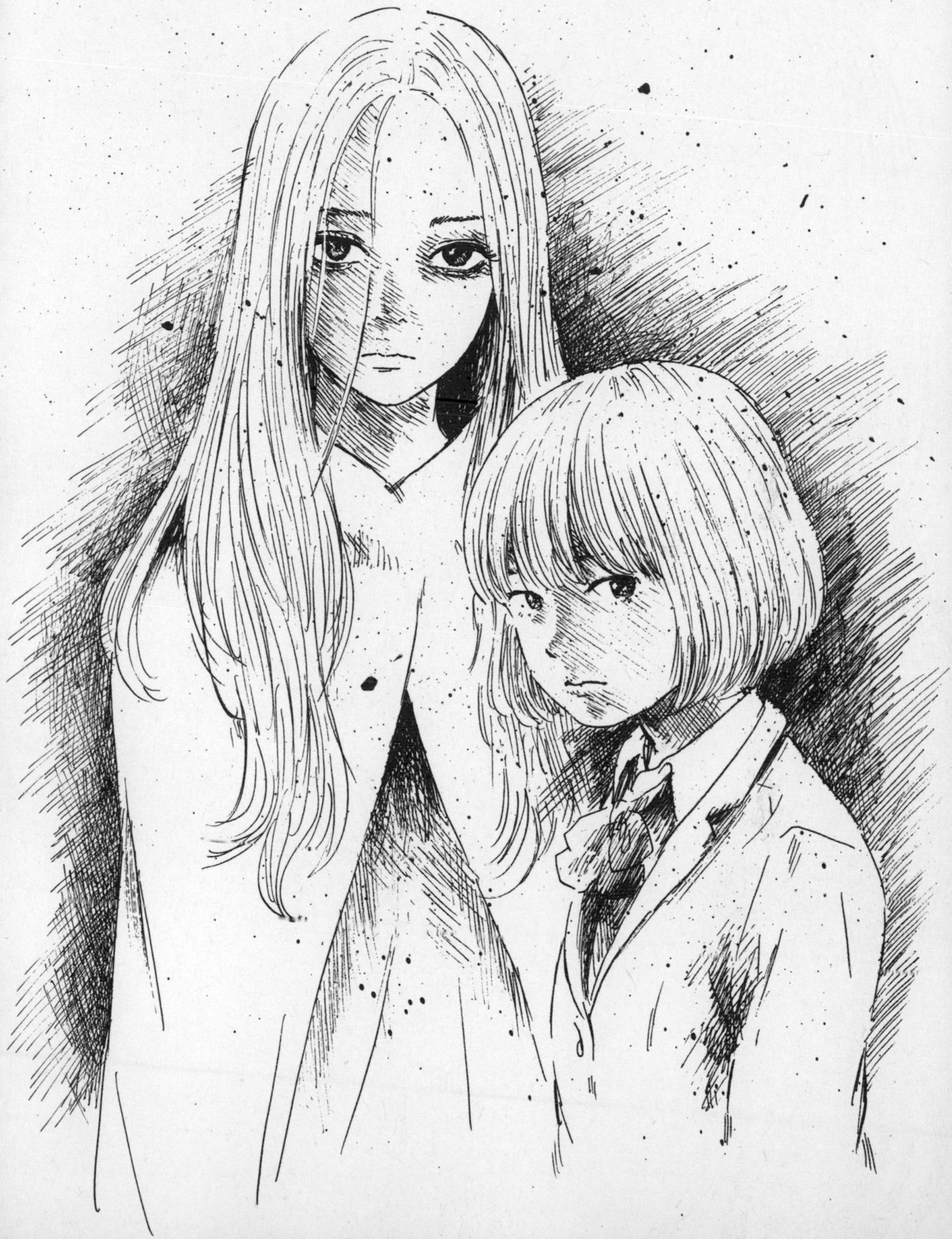

Chapter 15: Intersection

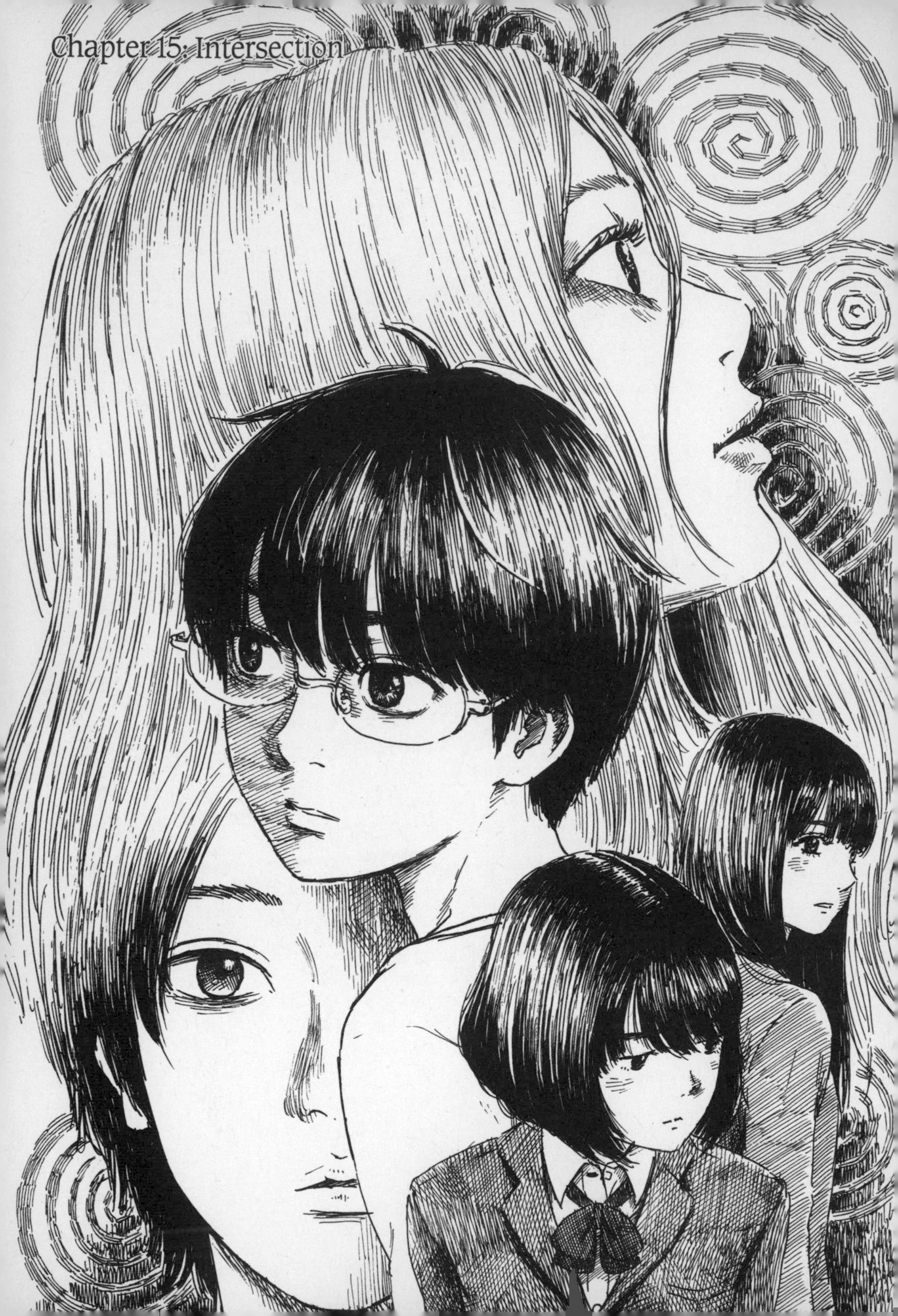

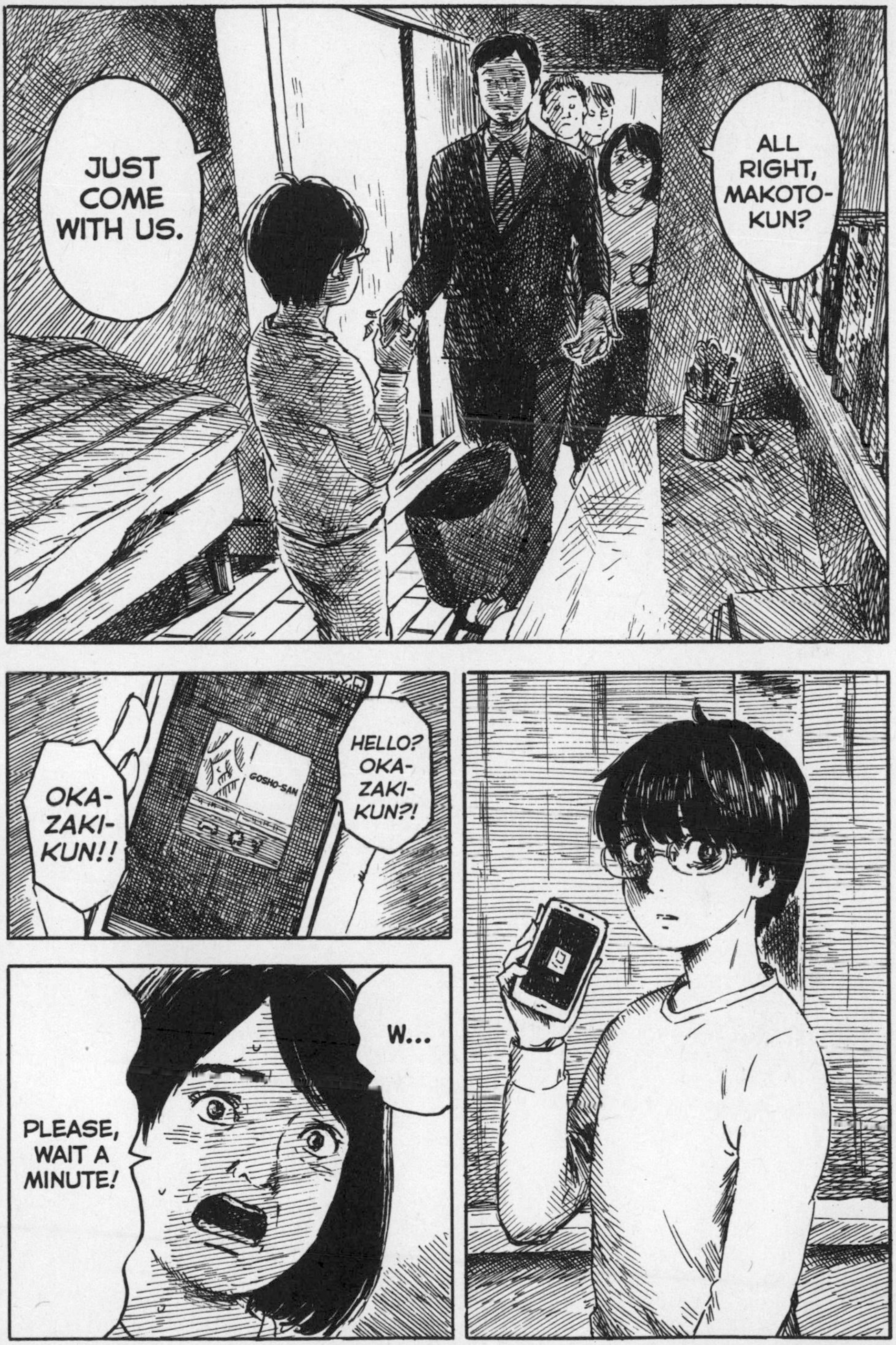
ALL RIGHT, MAKOTO-KUN?
JUST COME WITH US.
HELLO? OKA-ZAKI-KUN?!
GOSHO-SAN
OKA-ZAKI-KUN!!
W...
PLEASE, WAIT A MINUTE!

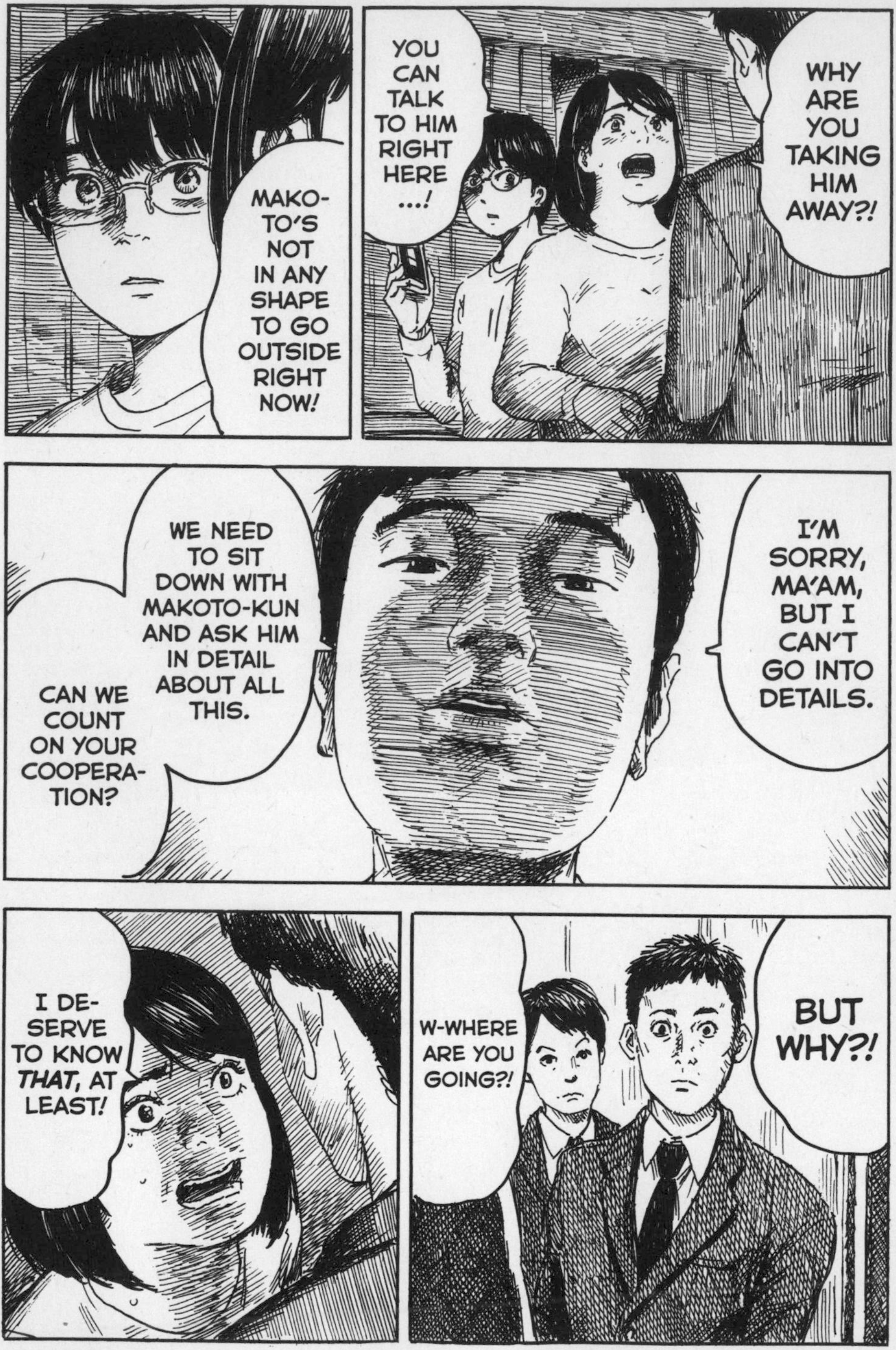
WHY ARE YOU TAKING HIM AWAY?!
YOU CAN TALK TO HIM RIGHT HERE ...!
MAKO-TO'S NOT IN ANY SHAPE TO GO OUTSIDE RIGHT NOW!
I'M SORRY, MA'AM, BUT I CAN'T GO INTO DETAILS.
WE NEED TO SIT DOWN WITH MAKOTO-KUN AND ASK HIM IN DETAIL ABOUT ALL THIS.
CAN WE COUNT ON YOUR COOPERA-TION?
BUT WHY?!
W-WHERE ARE YOU GOING?!
I DE-SERVE TO KNOW *THAT*, AT LEAST!

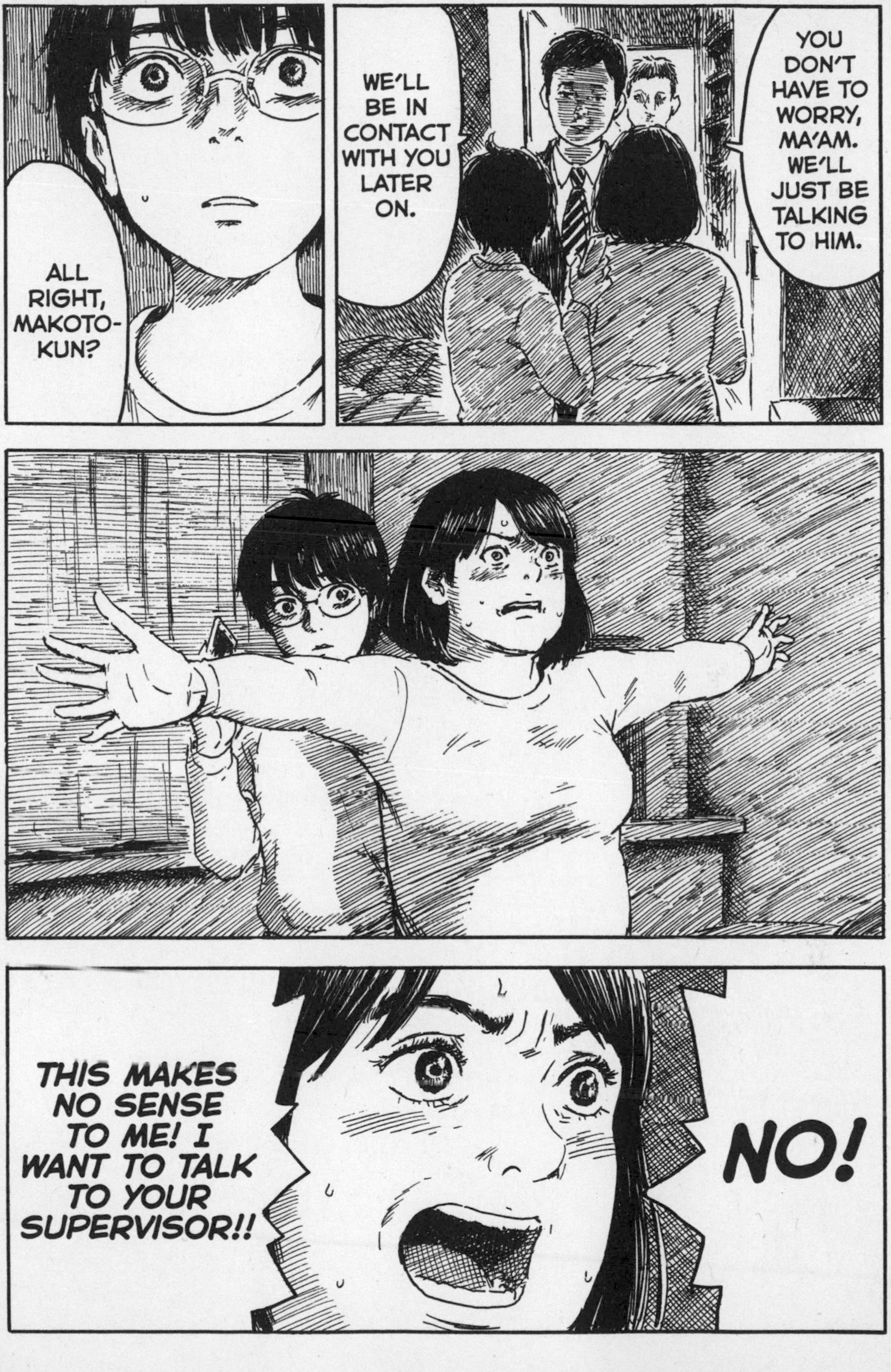
YOU DON'T HAVE TO WORRY, MA'AM. WE'LL JUST BE TALKING TO HIM.
WE'LL BE IN CONTACT WITH YOU LATER ON.
ALL RIGHT, MAKOTO-KUN?
NO!
THIS MAKES NO SENSE TO ME! I WANT TO TALK TO YOUR SUPERVISOR!!

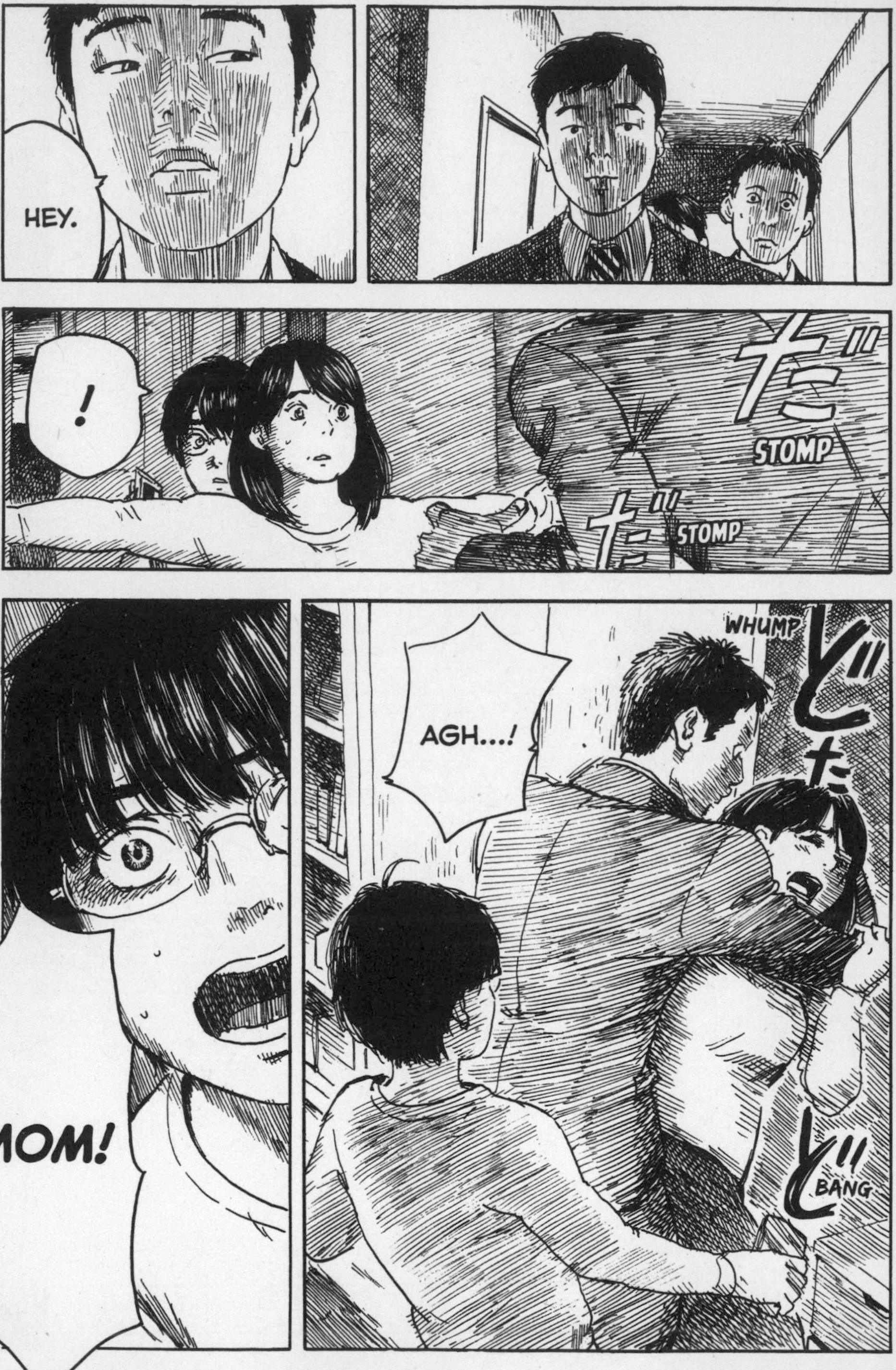
HEY.
だ
STOMP
だ
STOMP
!
WHUMP
どた
AGH...!
ど
BANG
MOM!

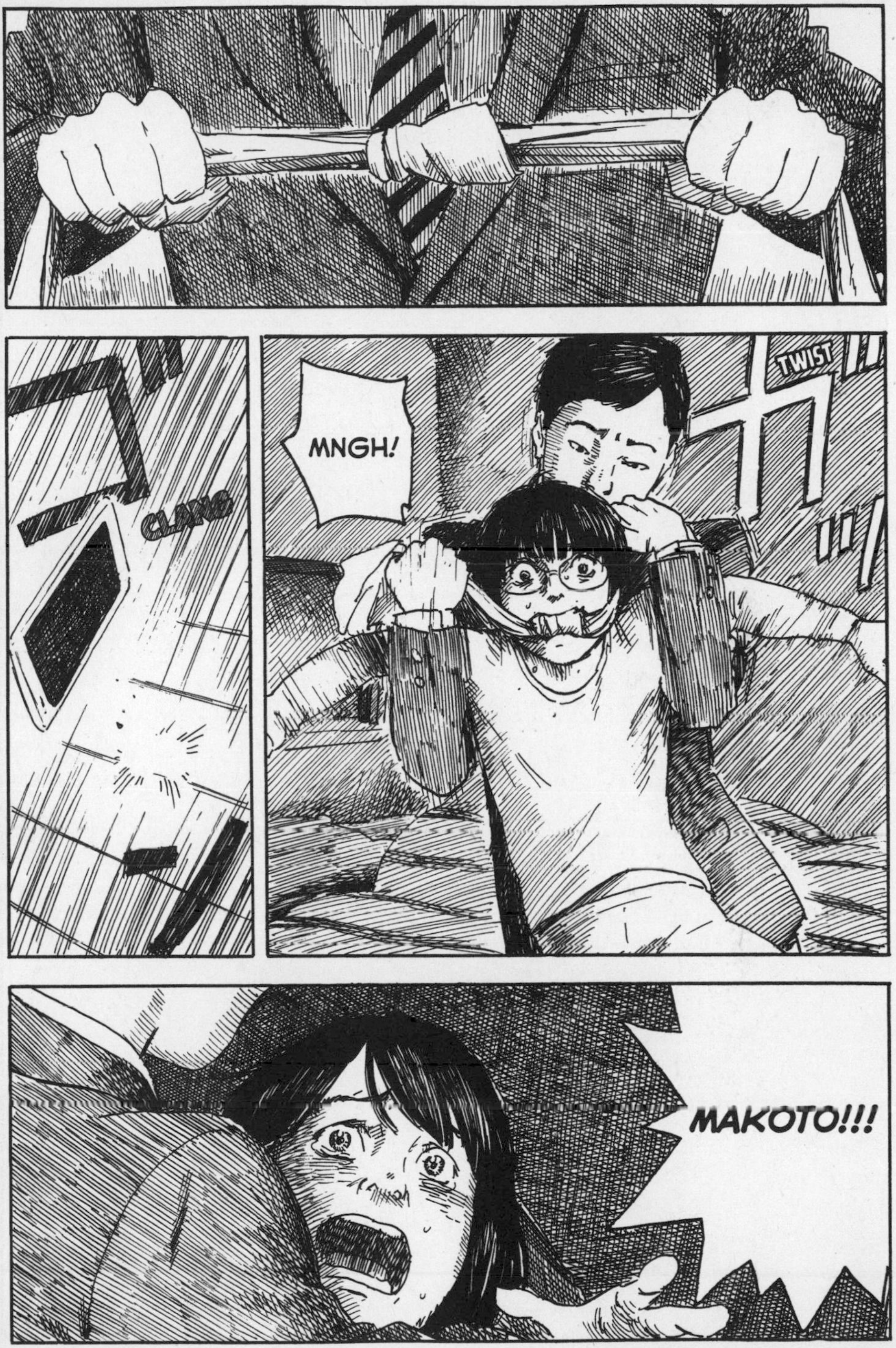
TWIST
MNGH!
CLANG
MAKOTO!!!

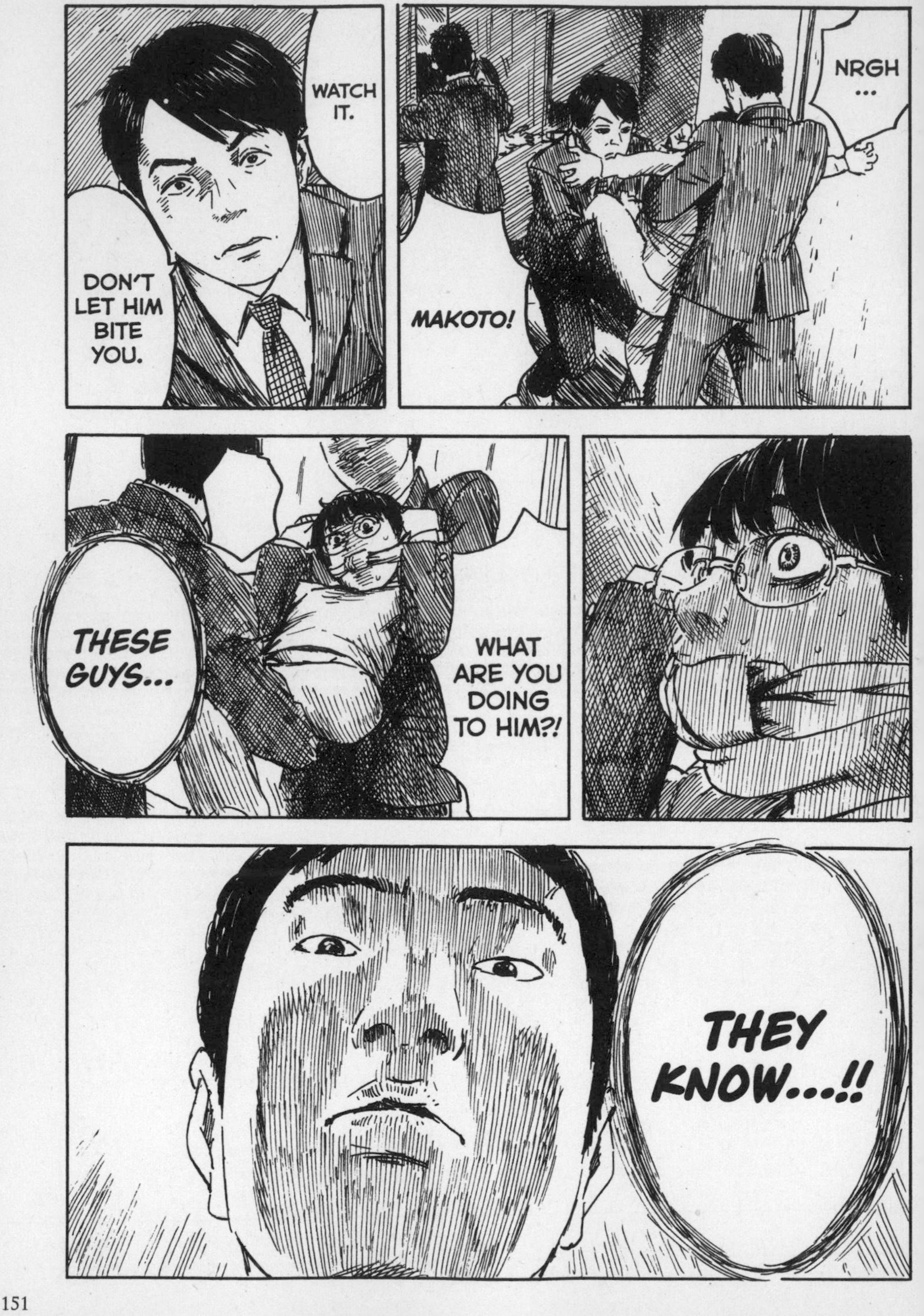
NRGH ...
MAKOTO!
WATCH IT.
DON'T LET HIM BITE YOU.
WHAT ARE YOU DOING TO HIM?!
THESE GUYS...
THEY KNOW...!!

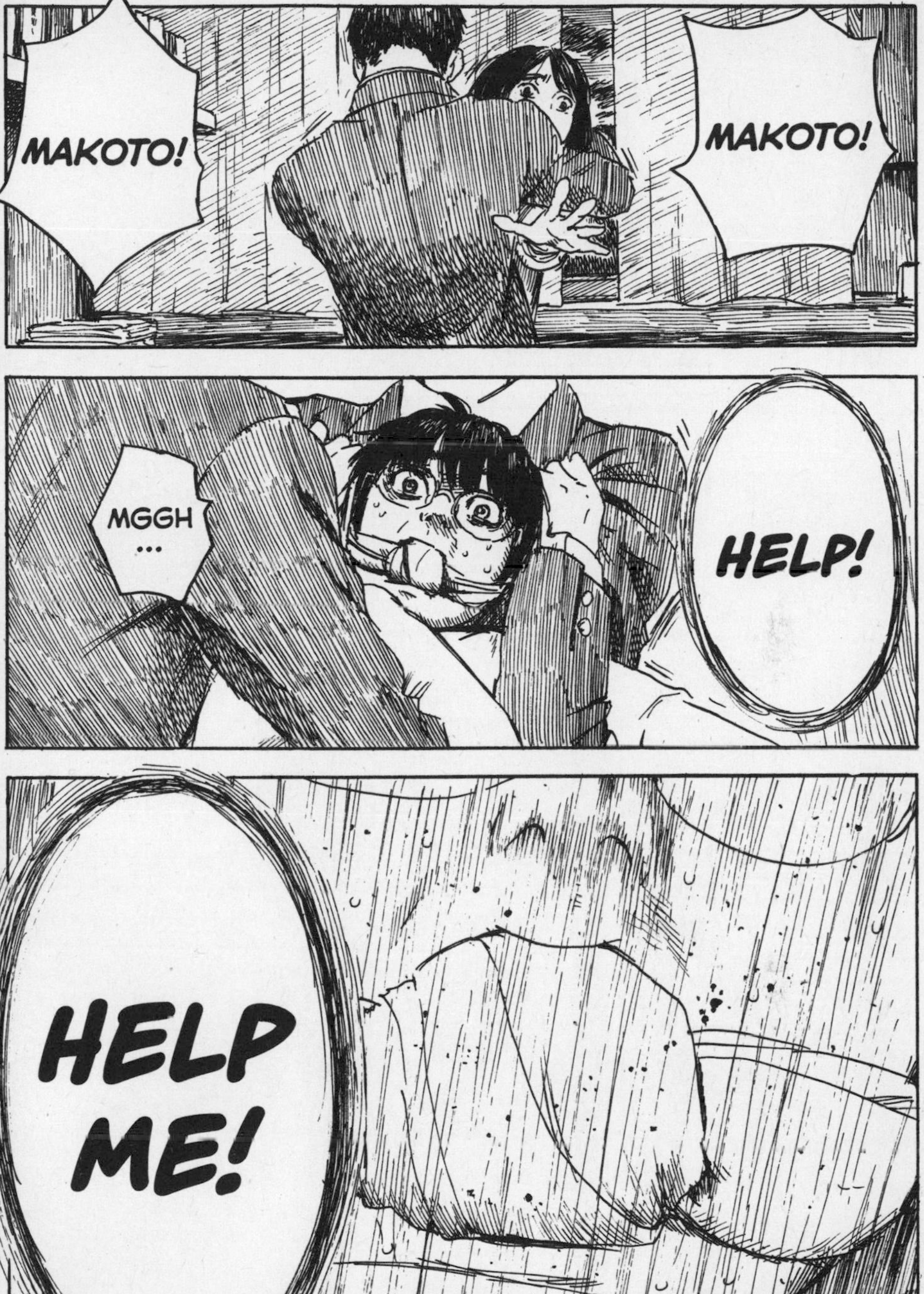
MAKOTO!
MAKOTO!
HELP!
MGGH ...
HELP ME!

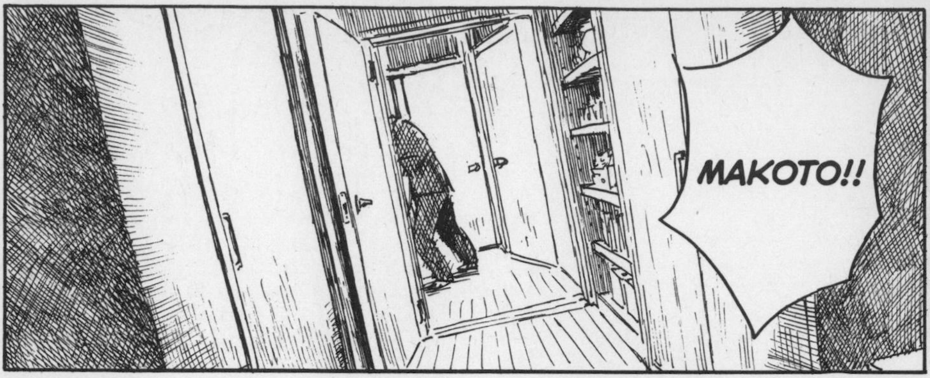
MAKOTO!!

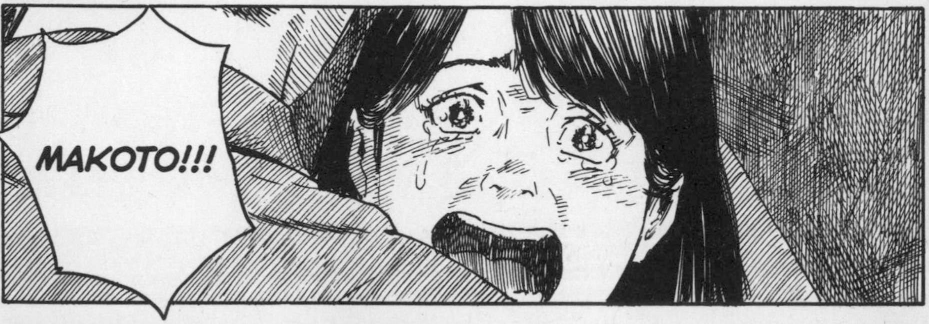
MAKOTO!!!

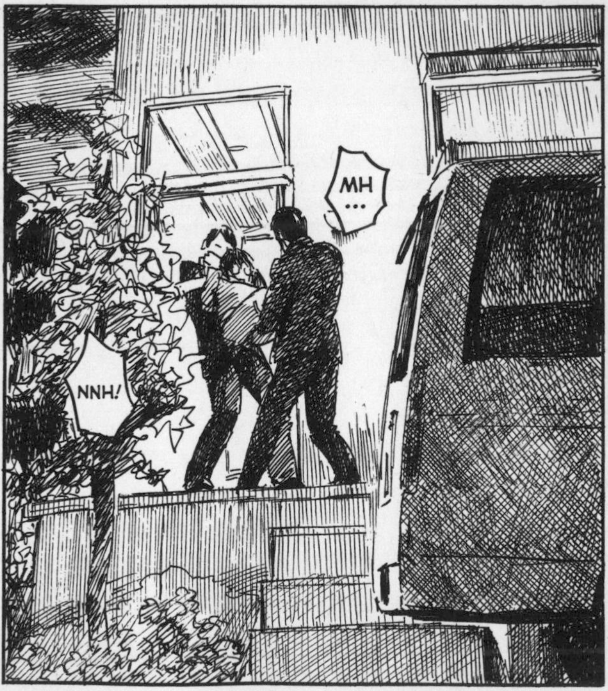
MH ...
NNH!

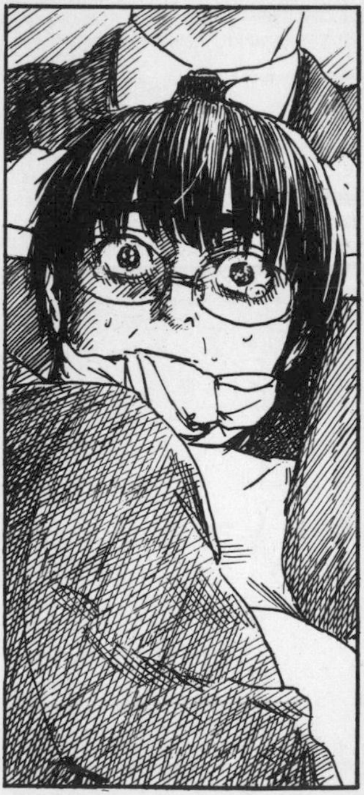

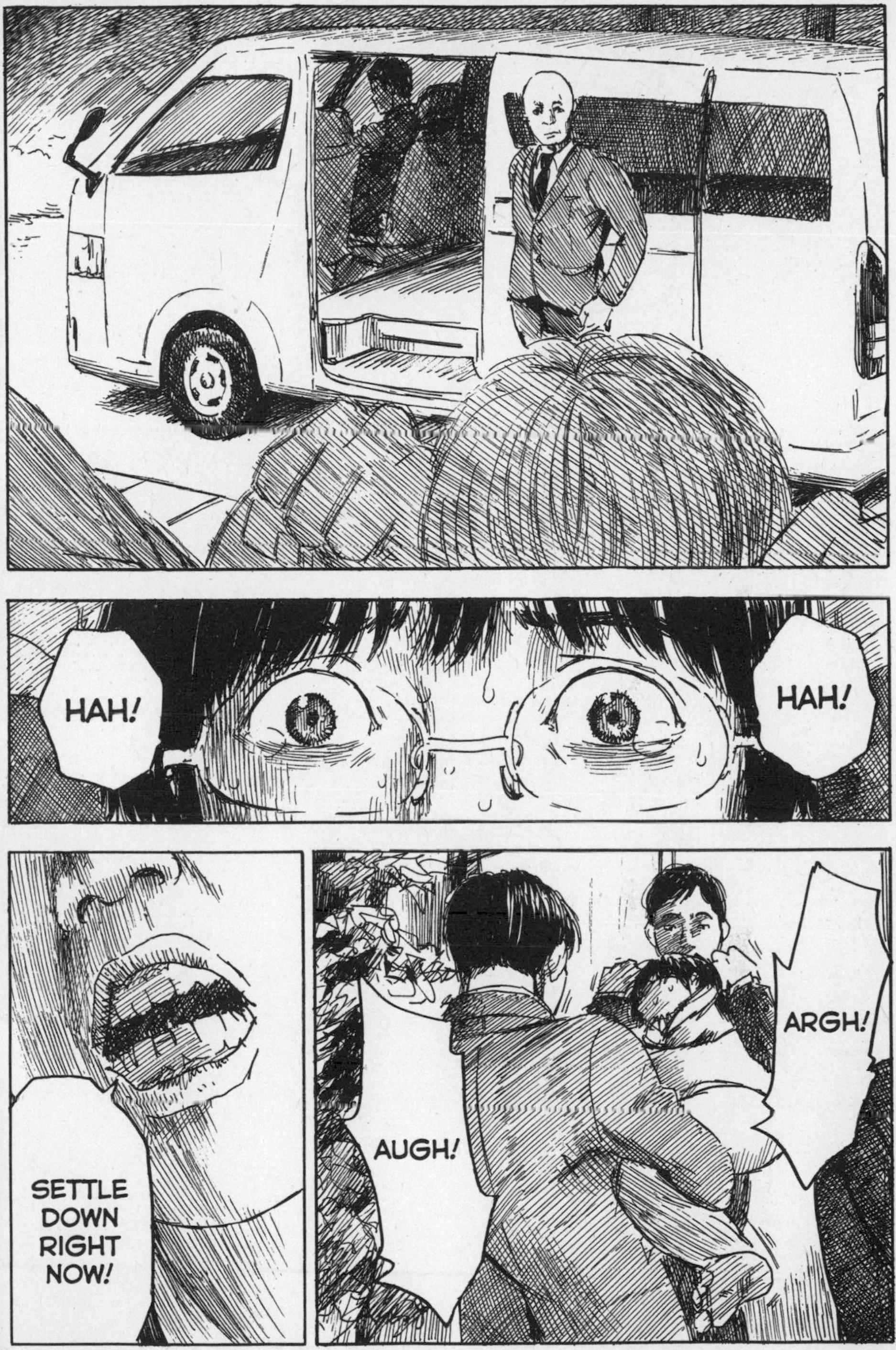
HAH!
HAH!
ARGH!
AUGH!
SETTLE DOWN RIGHT NOW!

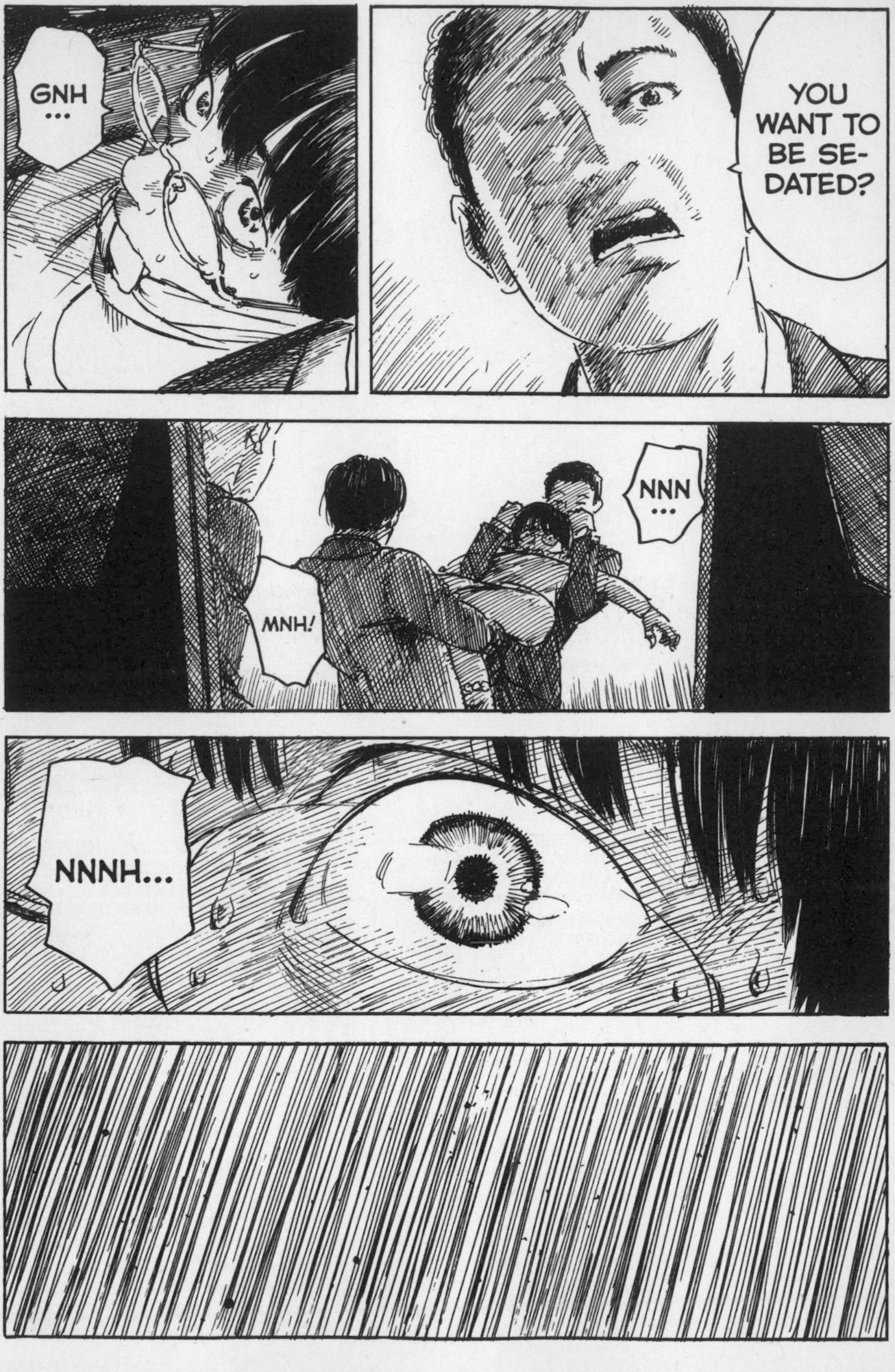
YOU WANT TO BE SE- DATED?
GNH ...
NNN ...
MNH!
NNNH...

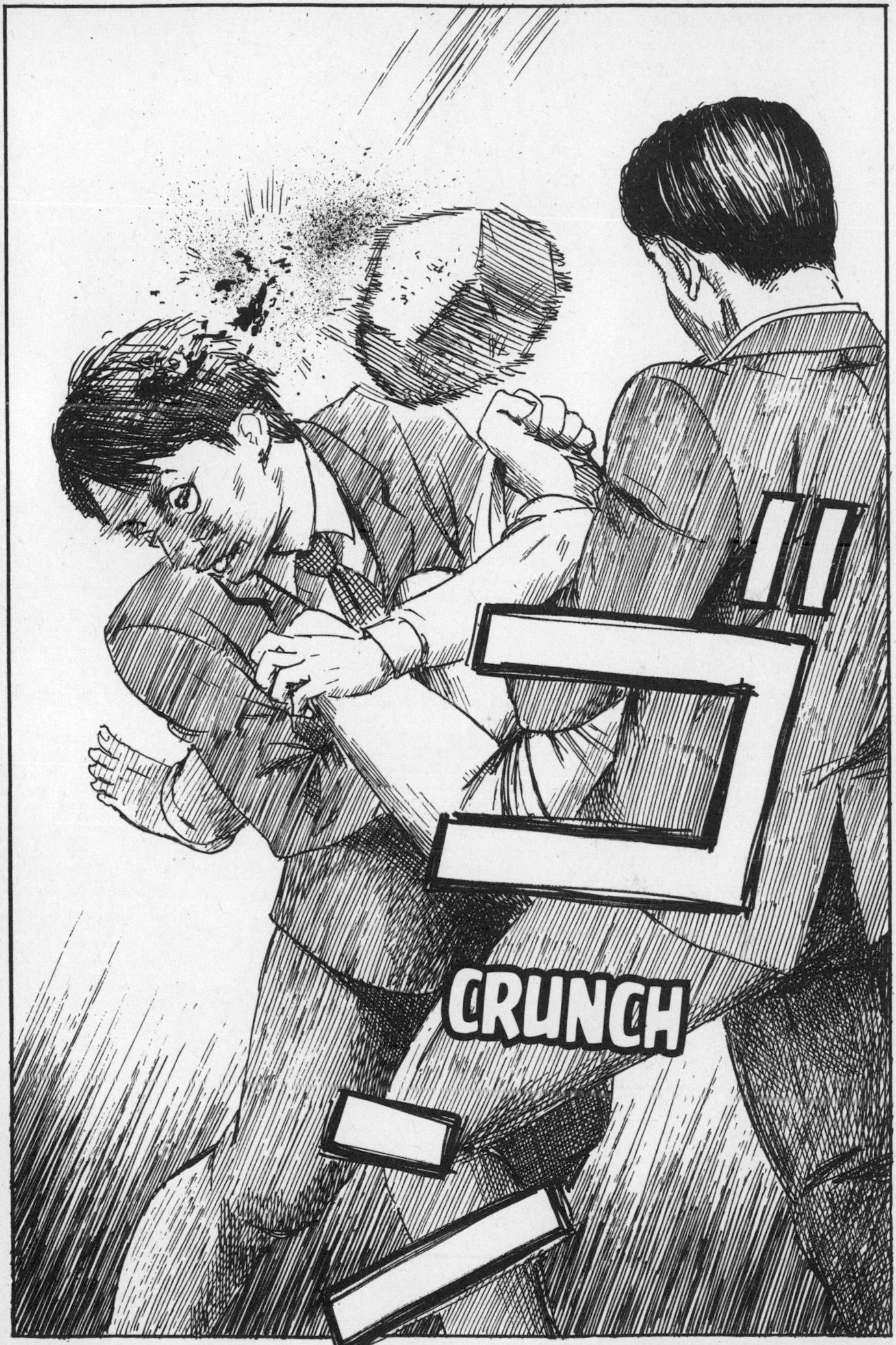
CRUNCH

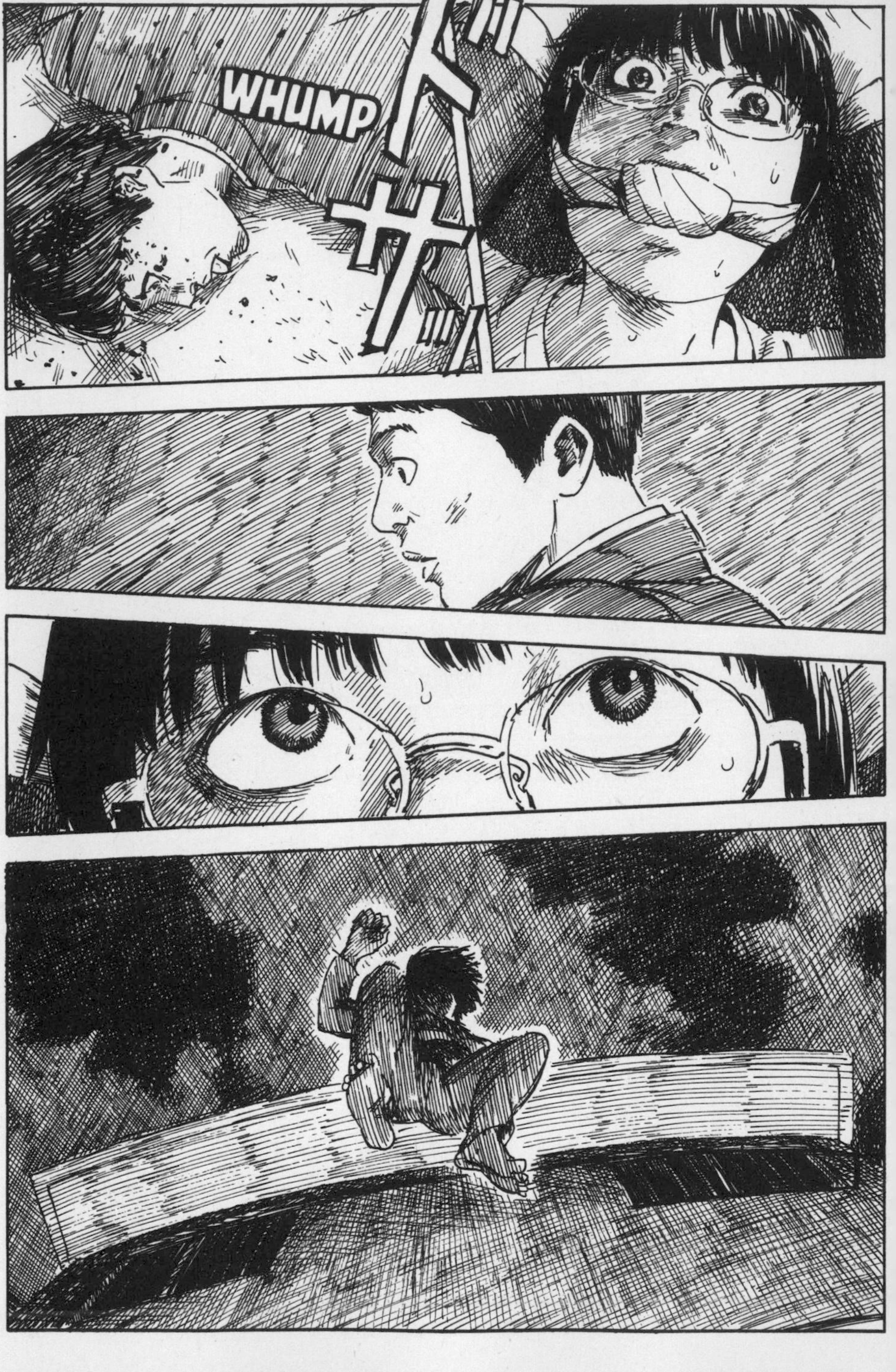
ドサッ
WHUMP

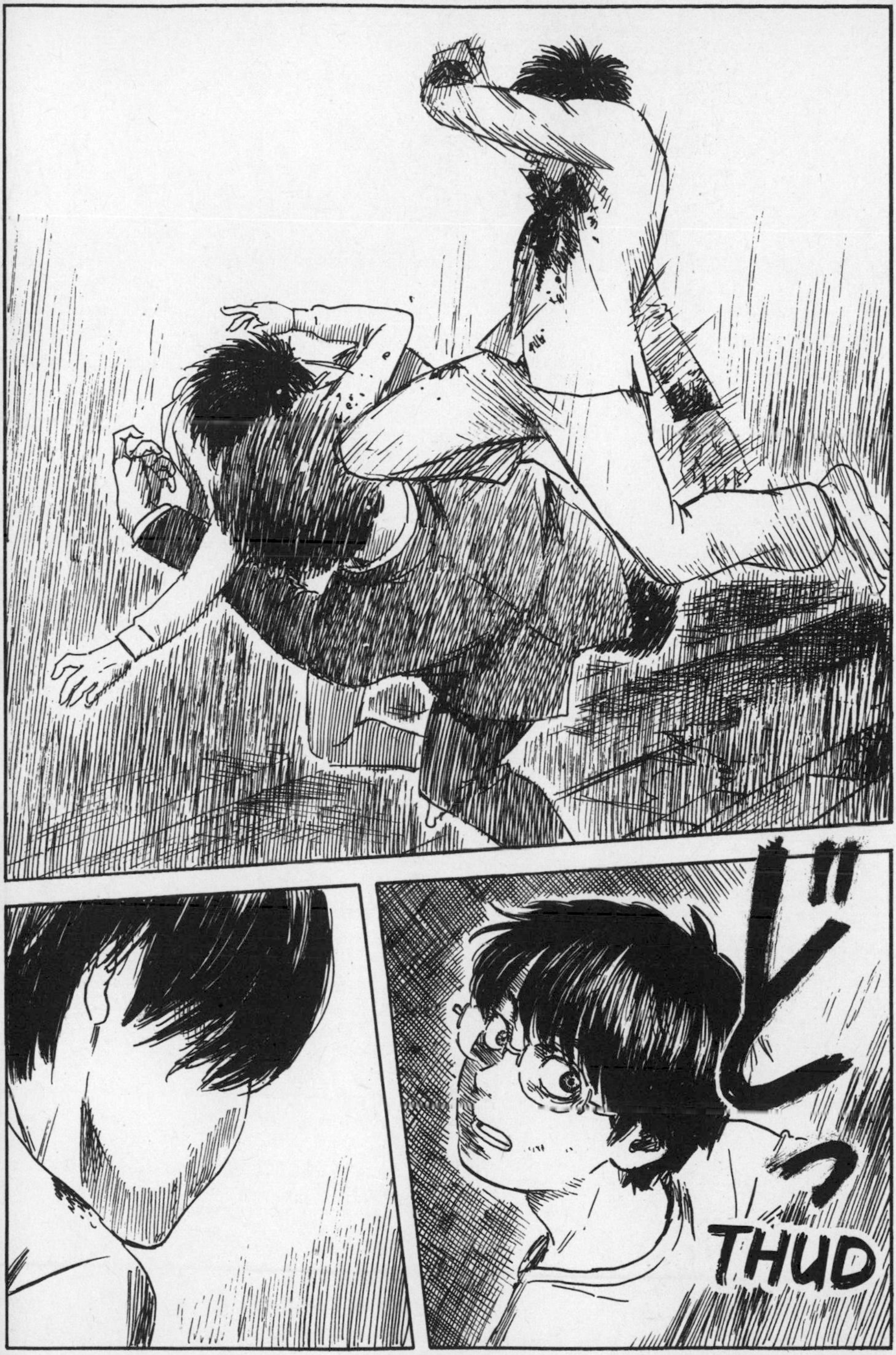
どっ
THUD

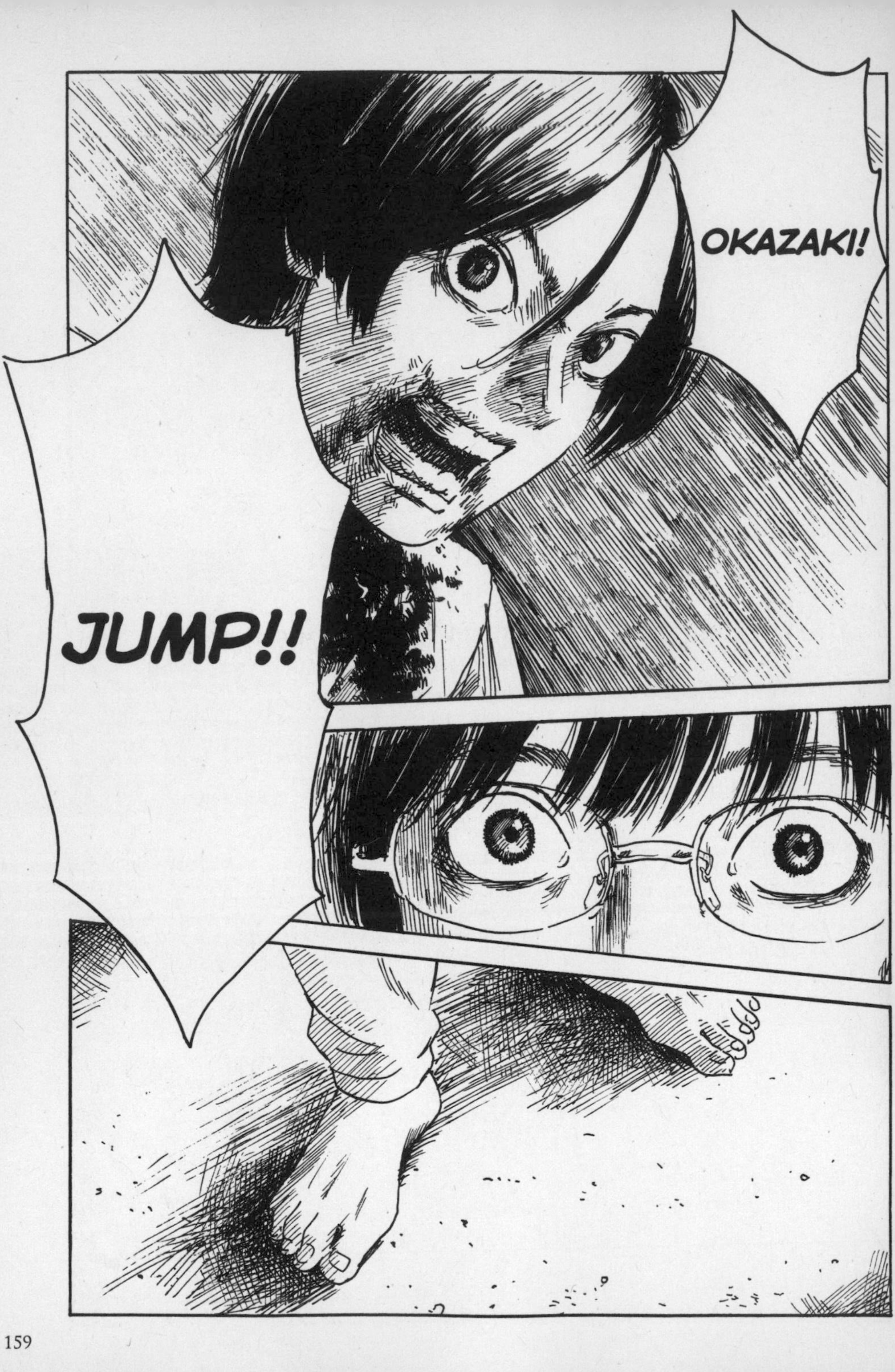
OKAZAKI!
JUMP!!

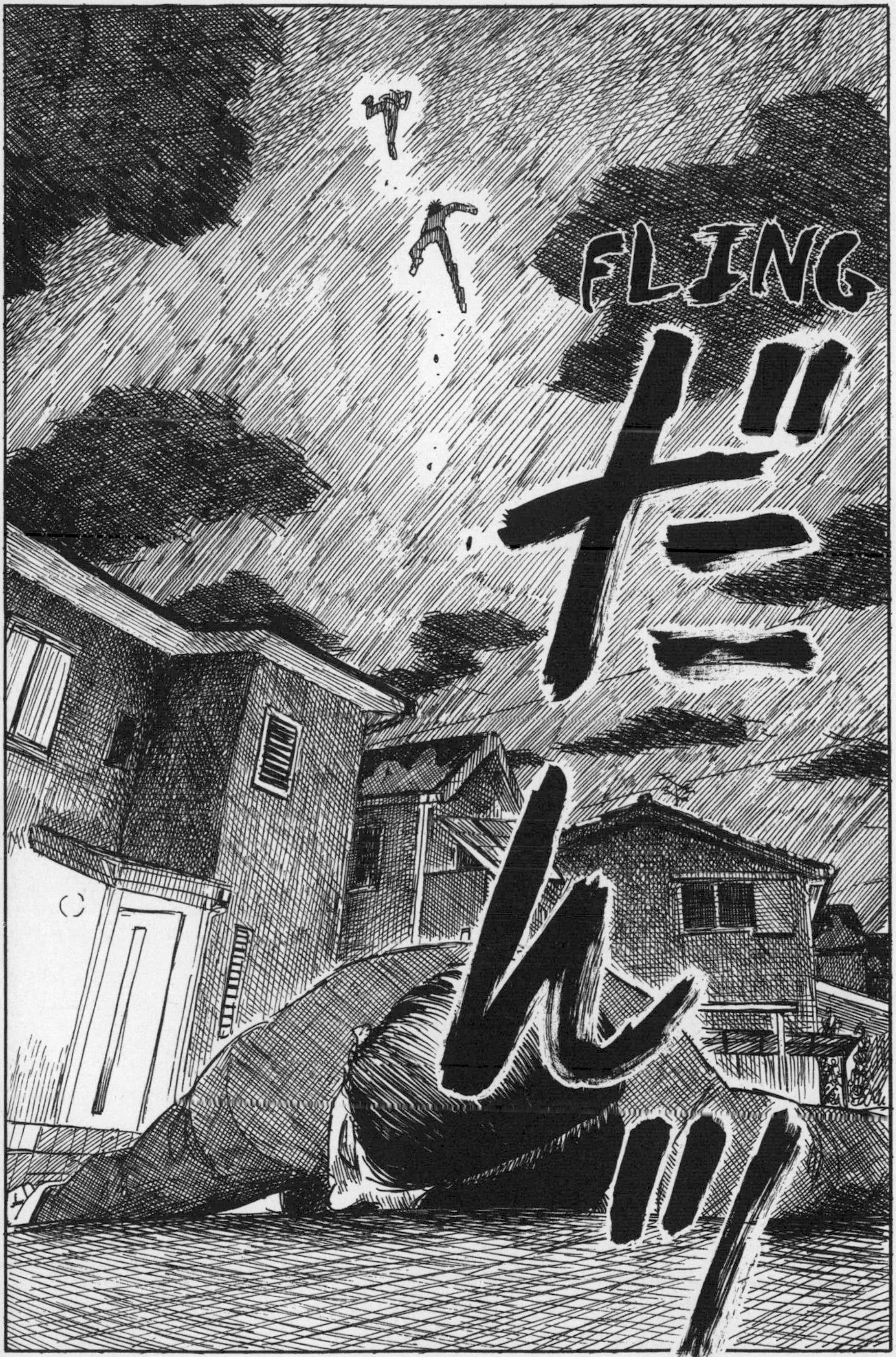
FLING
ずーん

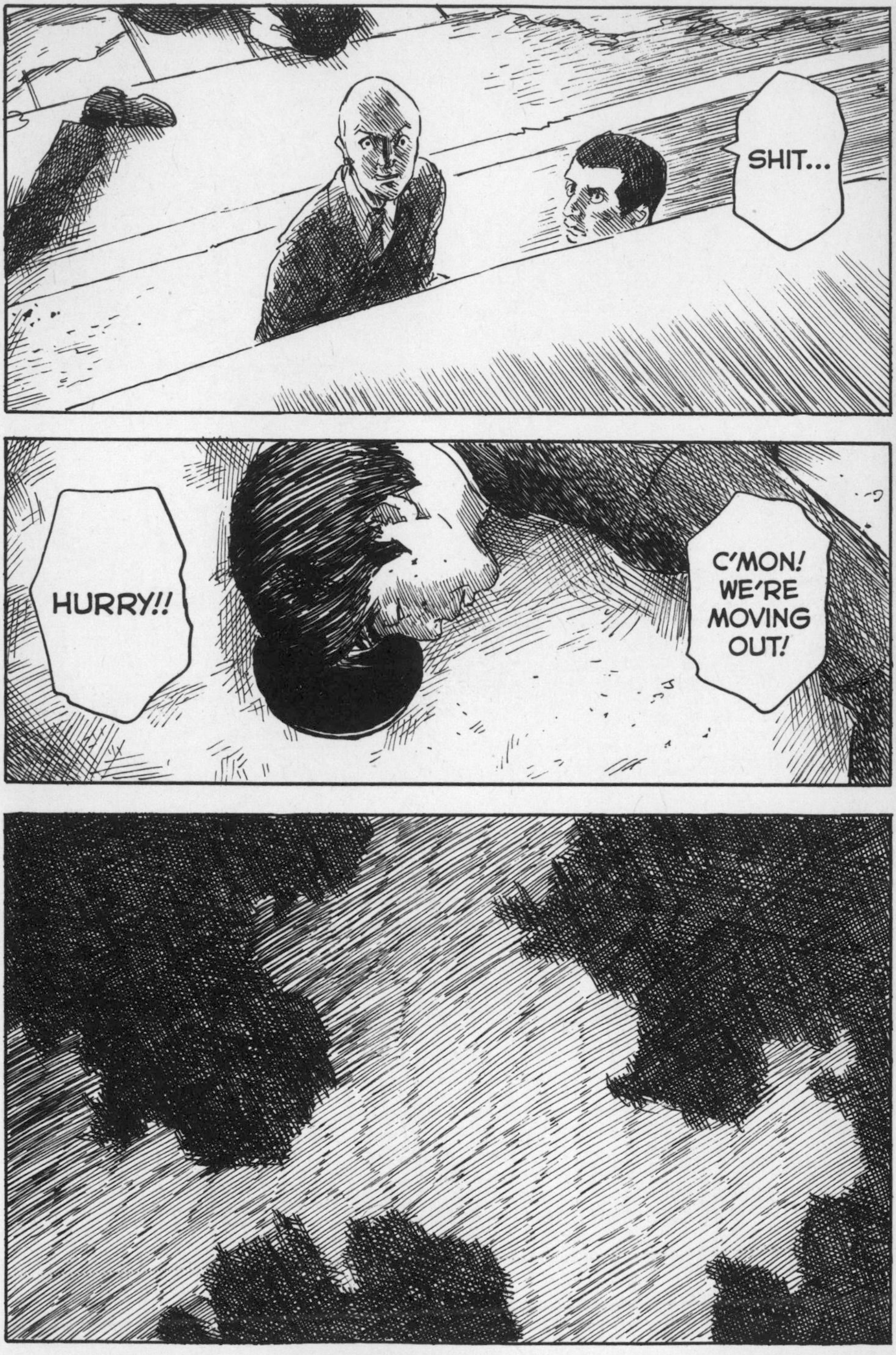
SHIT...
C'MON! WE'RE MOVING OUT!
HURRY!!

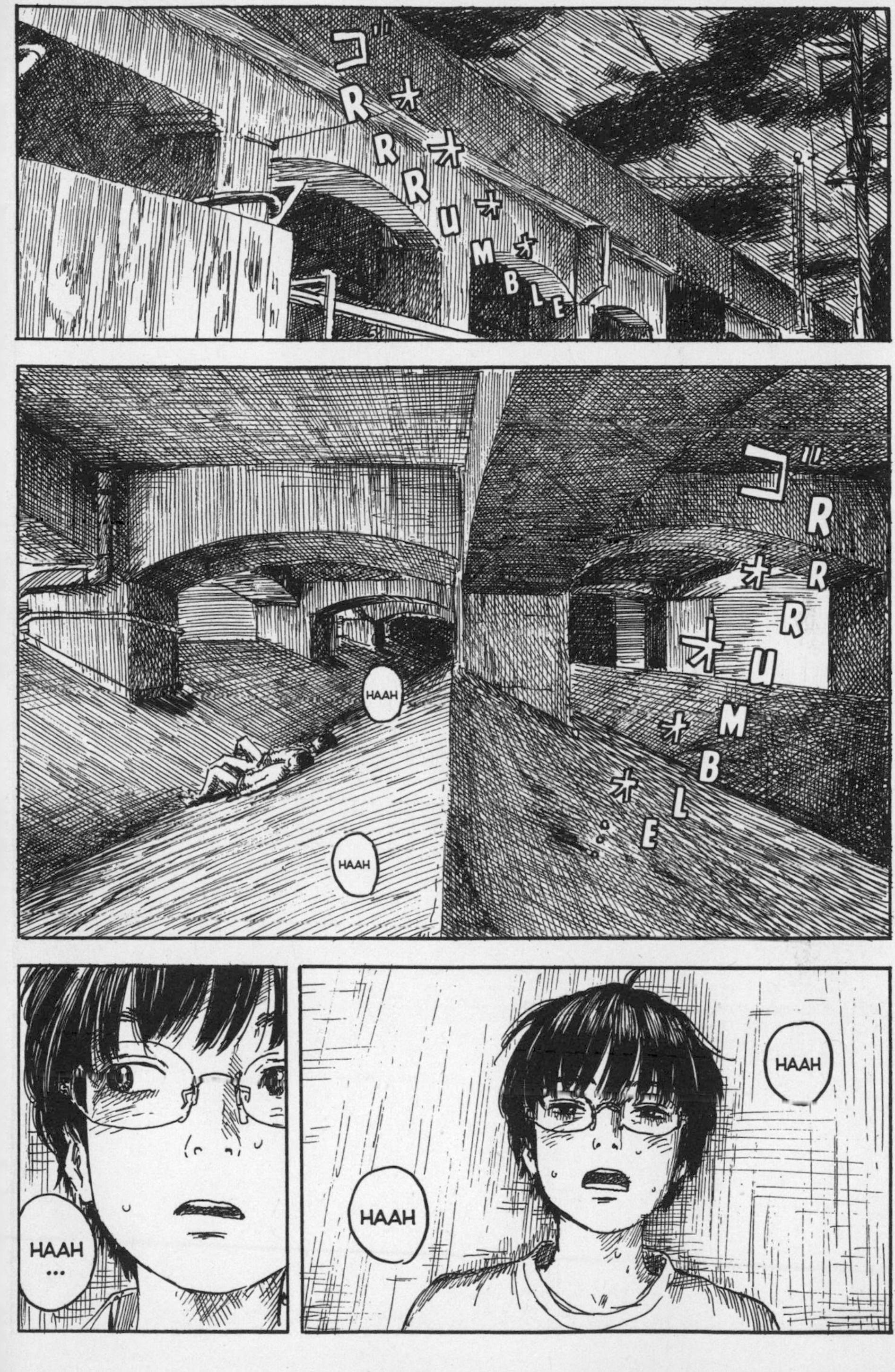
ゴオオオオ
RRRUMBLE
ゴオオオ
RRRUMBLE
HAAH
HAAH
HAAH
HAAH
HAAH ...

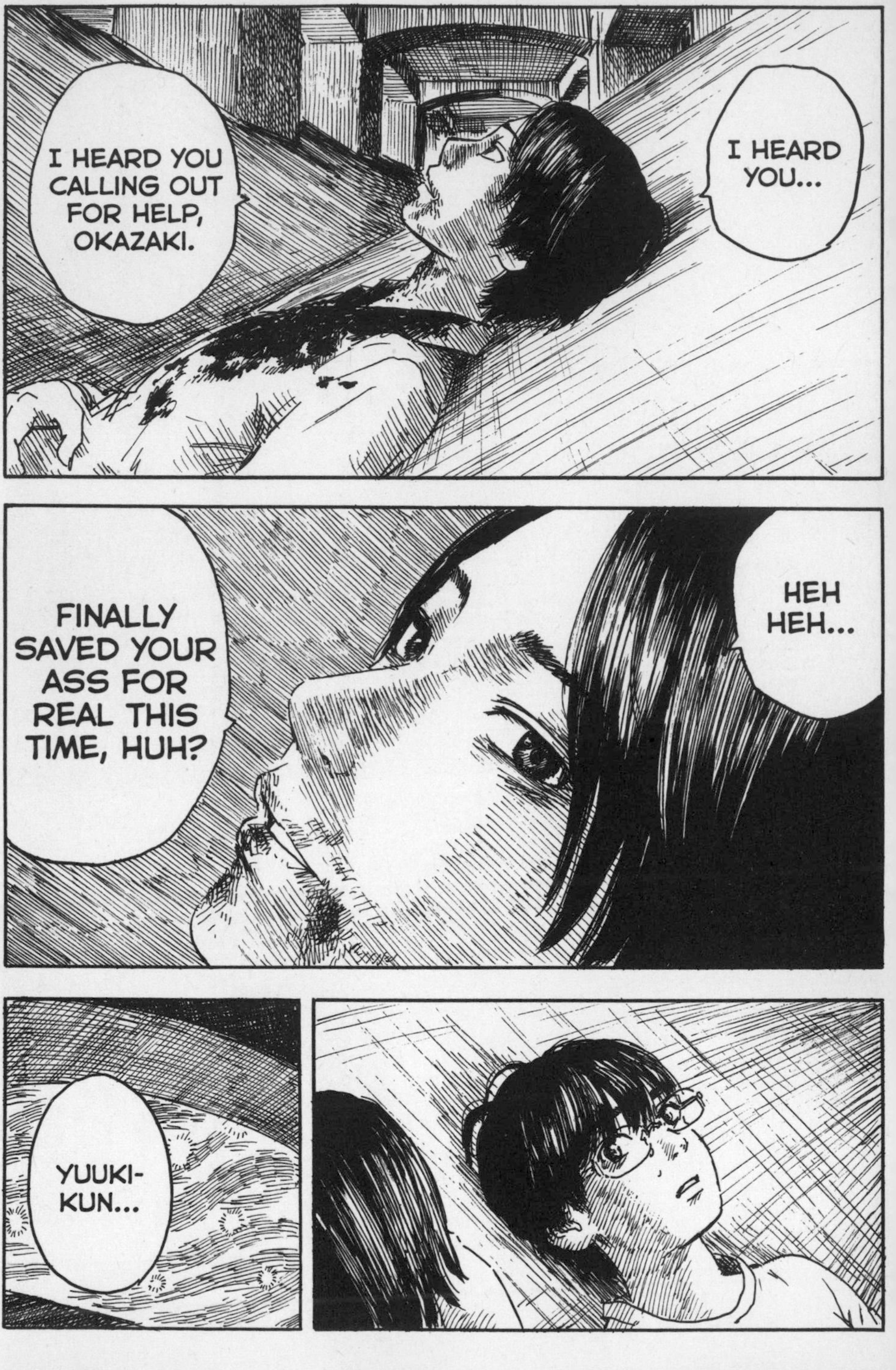
I HEARD YOU...
I HEARD YOU CALLING OUT FOR HELP, OKAZAKI.
HEH HEH...
FINALLY SAVED YOUR ASS FOR REAL THIS TIME, HUH?
YUUKI-KUN...

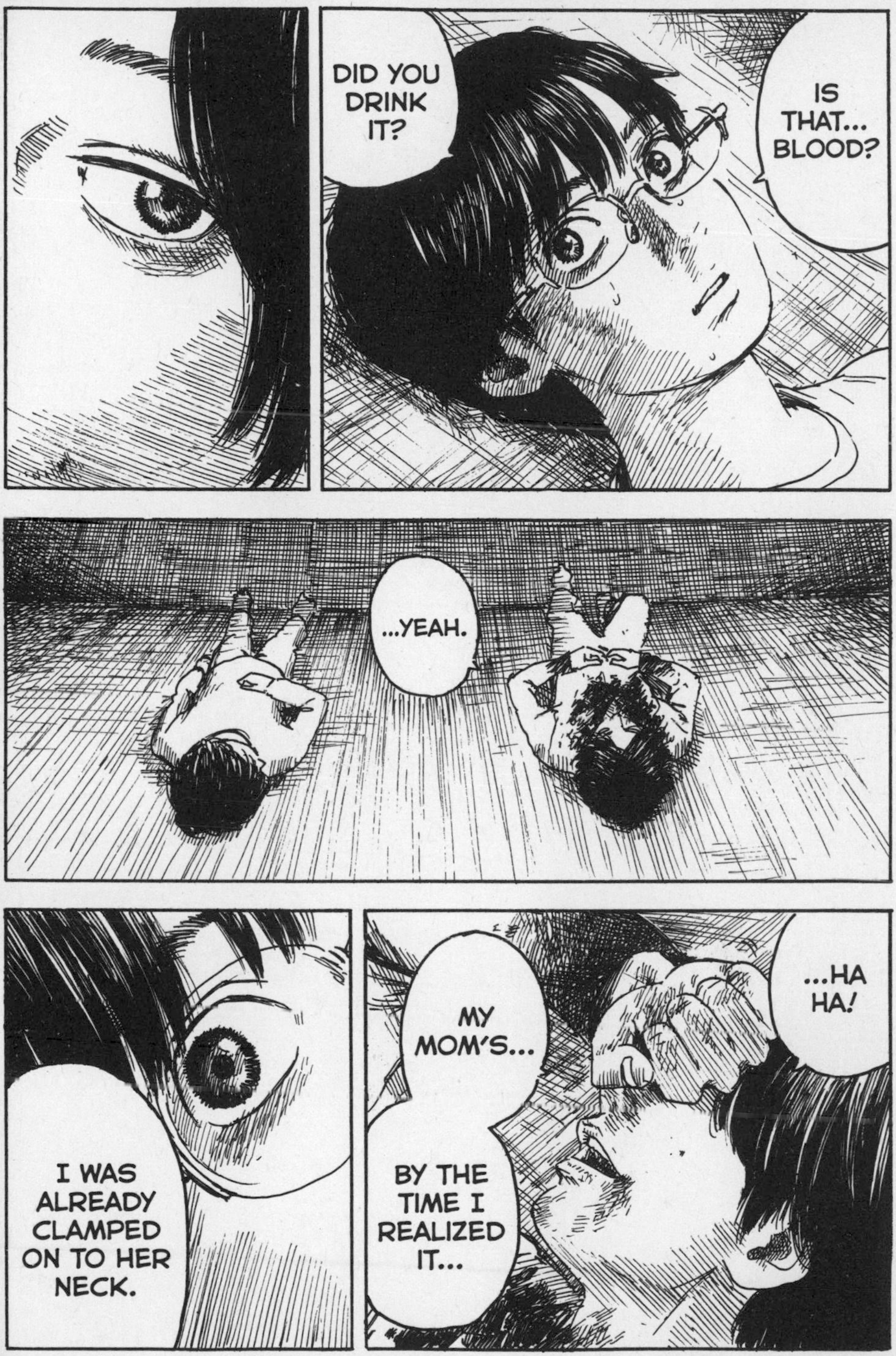
IS THAT... BLOOD?
DID YOU DRINK IT?
...YEAH.
...HA HA!
MY MOM'S...
BY THE TIME I REALIZED IT...
I WAS ALREADY CLAMPED ON TO HER NECK.

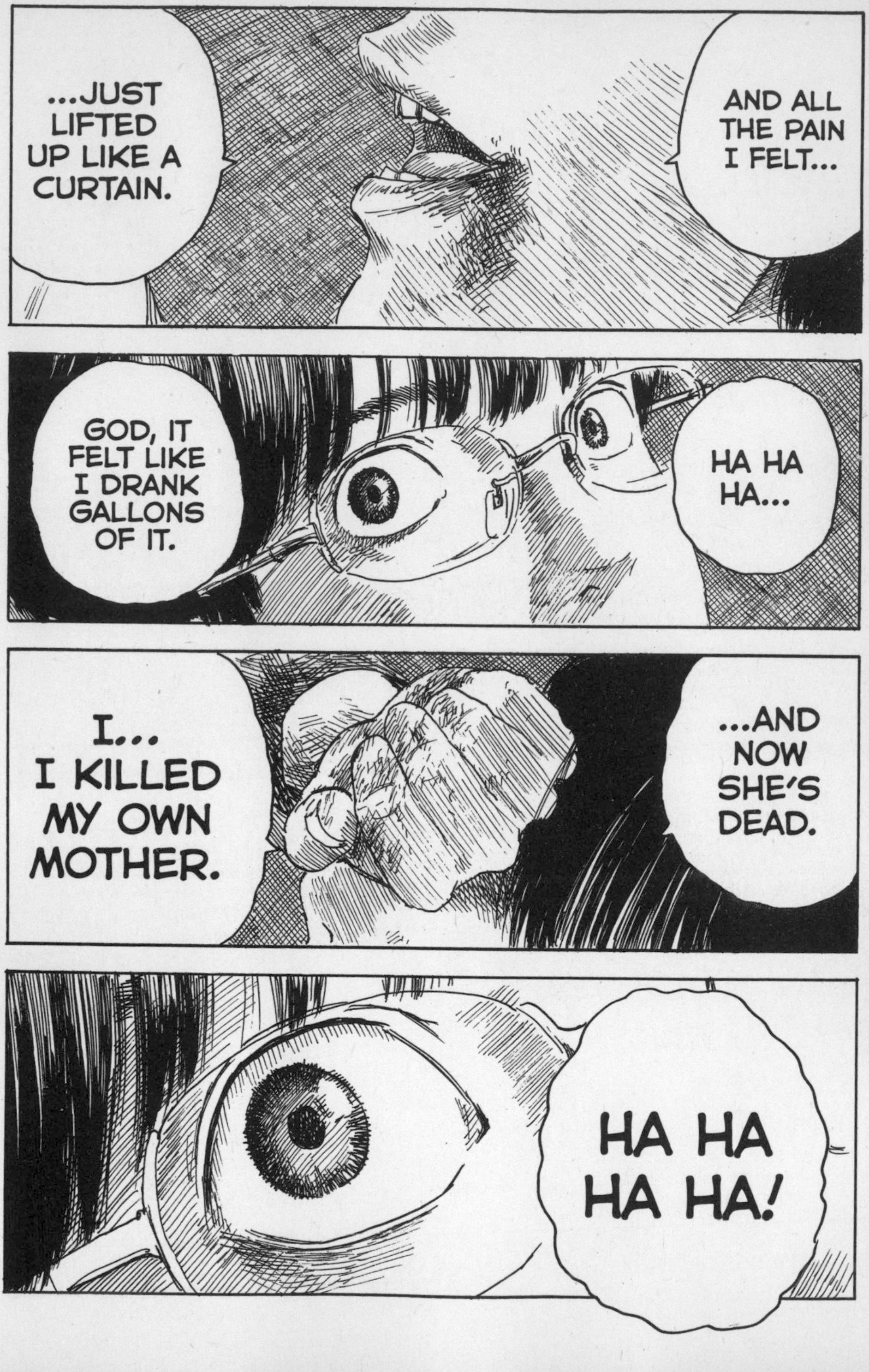
AND ALL THE PAIN I FELT...
...JUST LIFTED UP LIKE A CURTAIN.
HA HA HA...
GOD, IT FELT LIKE I DRANK GALLONS OF IT.
...AND NOW SHE'S DEAD.
I... I KILLED MY OWN MOTHER.
HA HA HA HA!

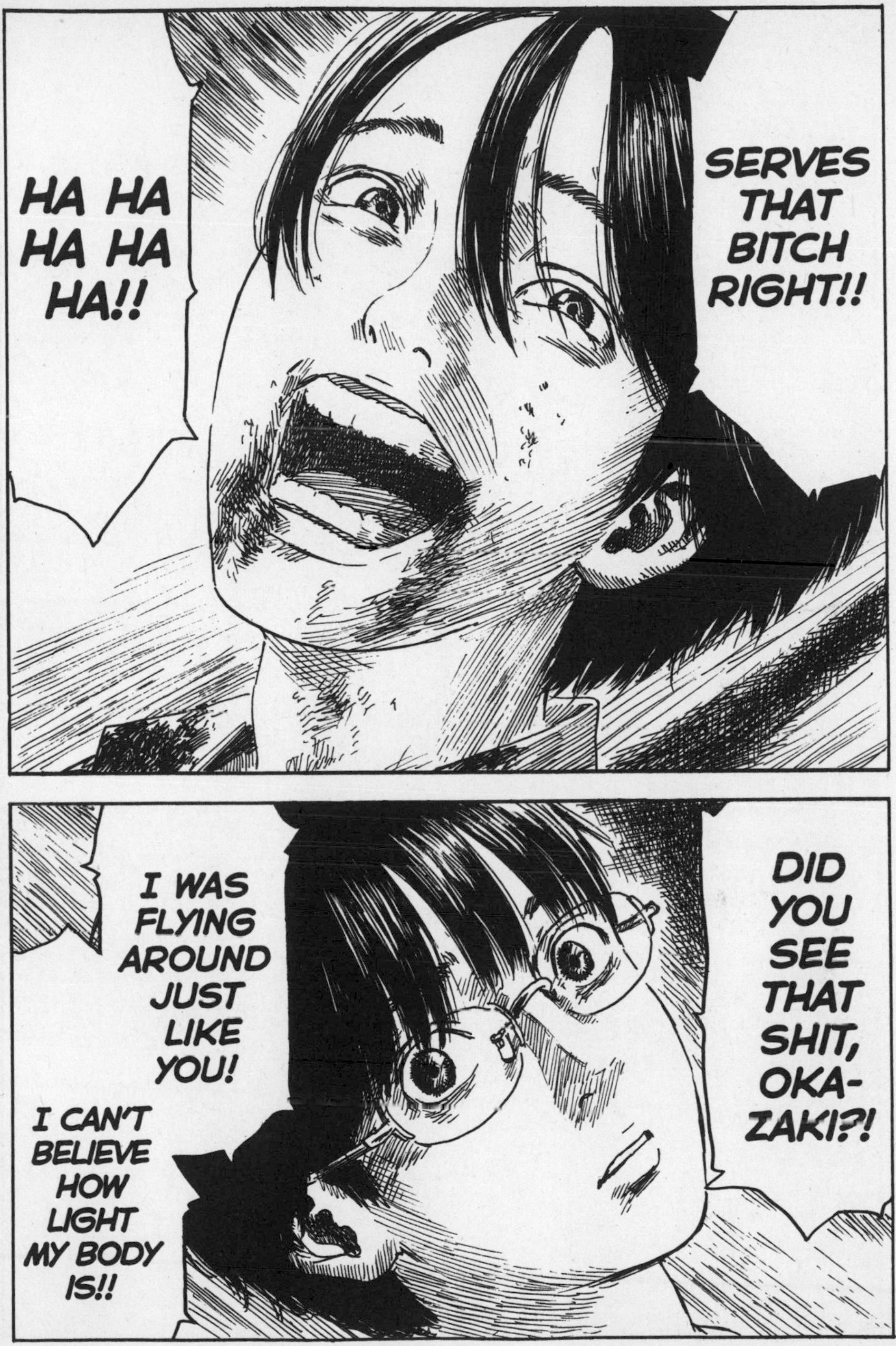
SERVES THAT BITCH RIGHT!!
HA HA HA HA HA!!
DID YOU SEE THAT SHIT, OKA-ZAKI?!
I WAS FLYING AROUND JUST LIKE YOU!
I CAN'T BELIEVE HOW LIGHT MY BODY IS!!

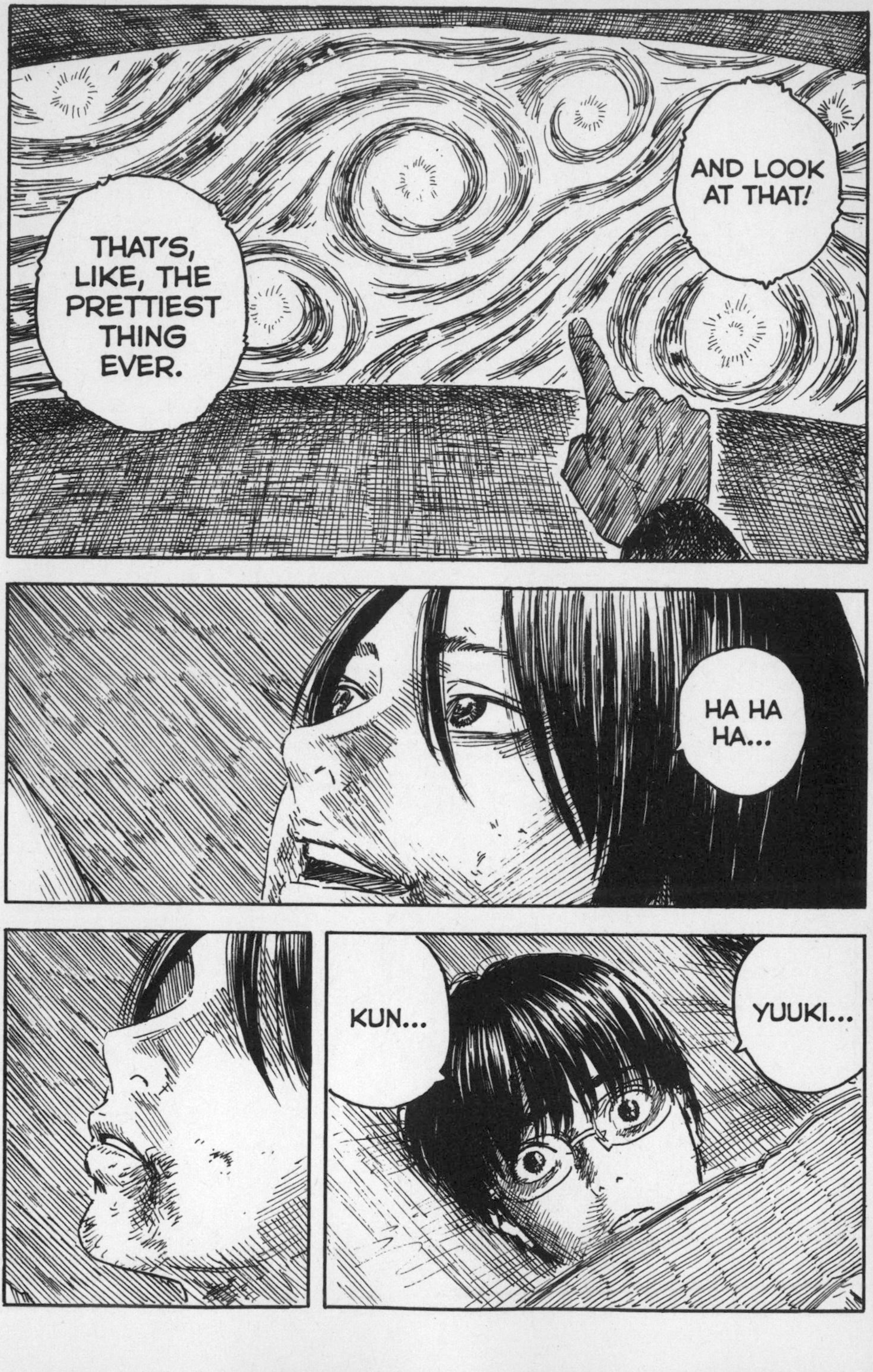
AND LOOK AT THAT!
THAT'S, LIKE, THE PRETTIEST THING EVER.
HA HA HA...
YUUKI...
KUN...

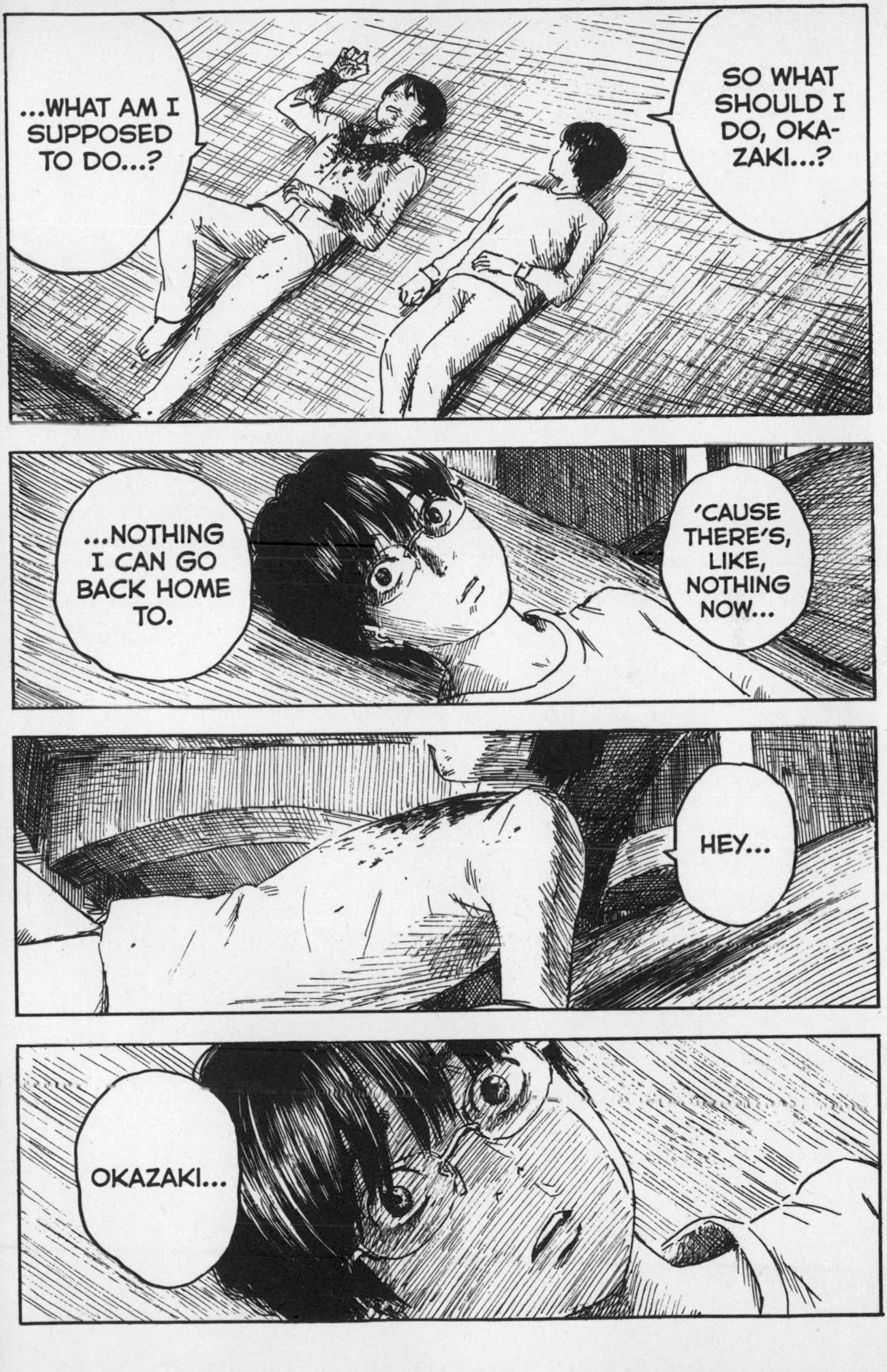
SO WHAT SHOULD I DO, OKA-ZAKI...?
...WHAT AM I SUPPOSED TO DO...?
'CAUSE THERE'S, LIKE, NOTHING NOW...
...NOTHING I CAN GO BACK HOME TO.
HEY...
OKAZAKI...

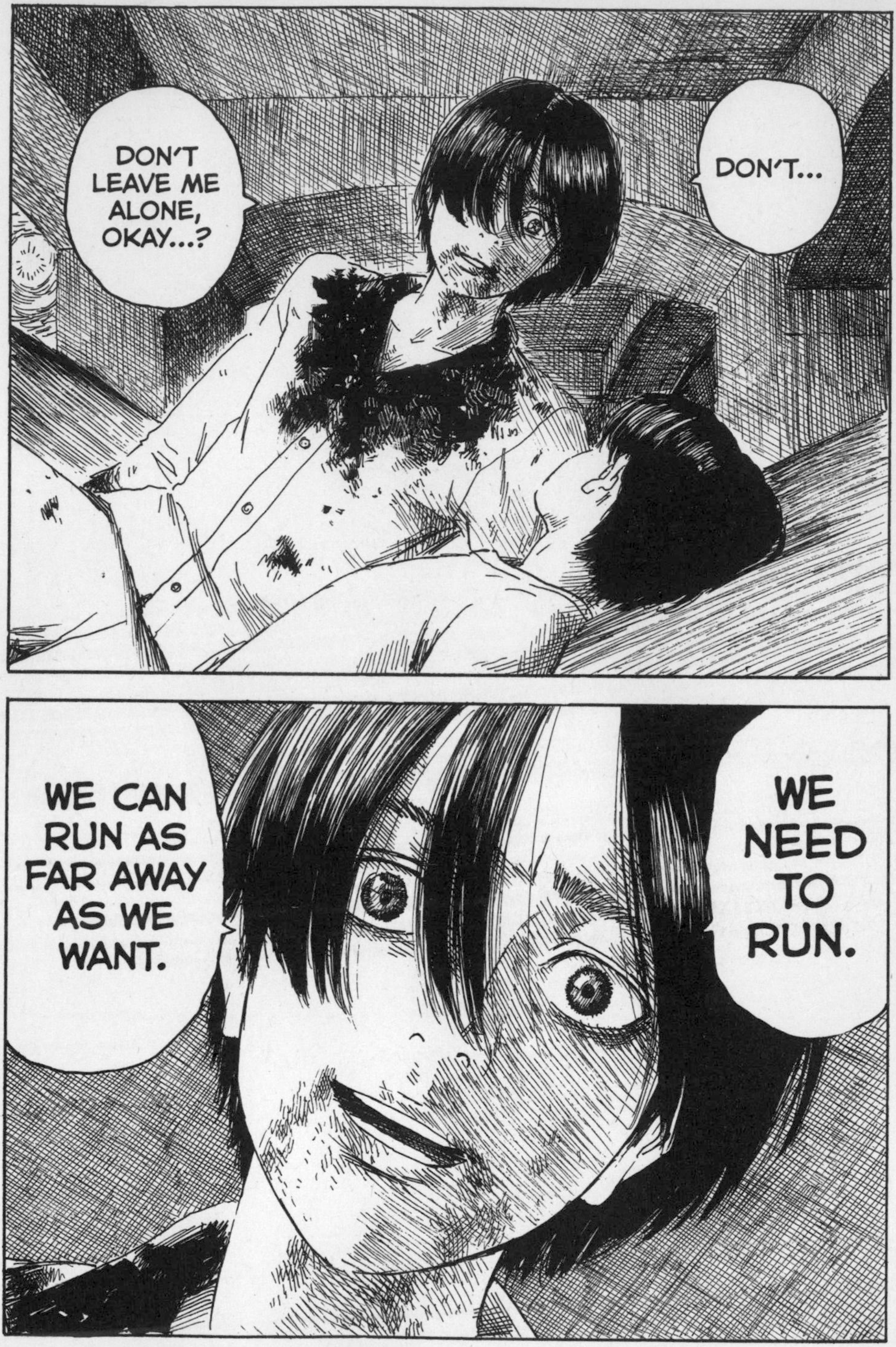
DON'T...
DON'T LEAVE ME ALONE, OKAY...?
WE NEED TO RUN.
WE CAN RUN AS FAR AWAY AS WE WANT.

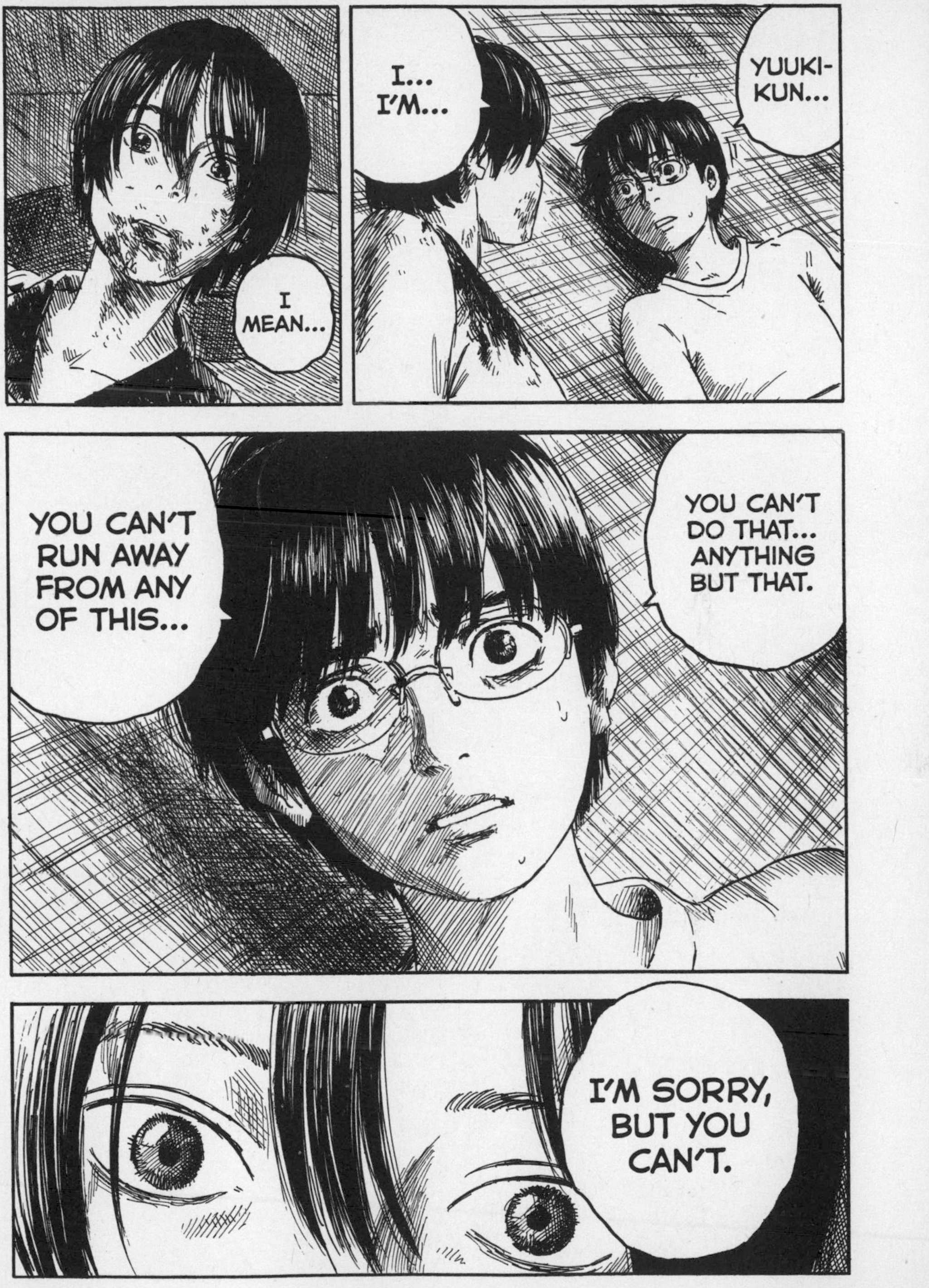
YUUKI-KUN...
I... I'M...
I MEAN...
YOU CAN'T DO THAT... ANYTHING BUT THAT.
YOU CAN'T RUN AWAY FROM ANY OF THIS...
I'M SORRY, BUT YOU CAN'T.

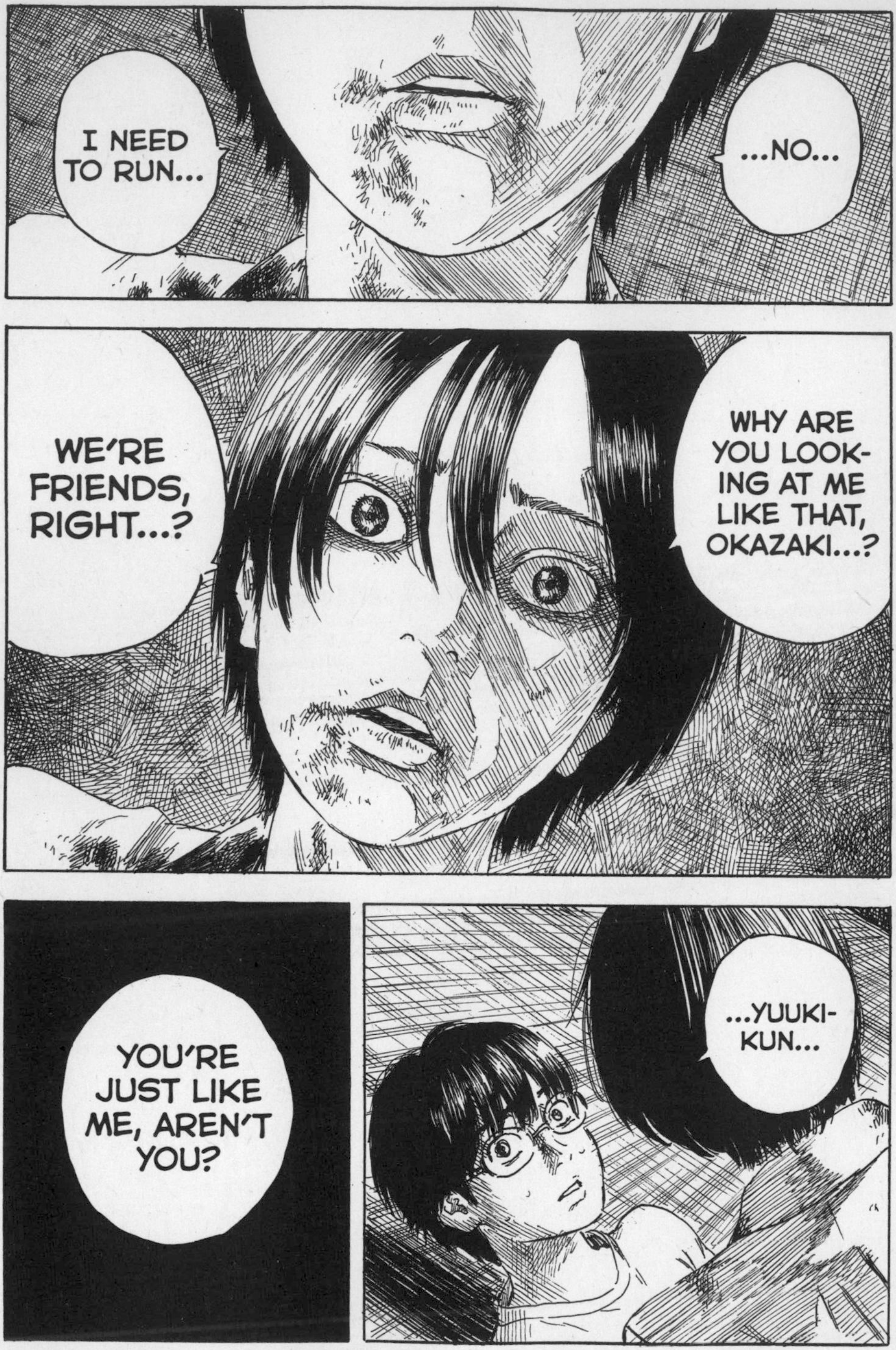
...NO...
I NEED TO RUN...
WHY ARE YOU LOOKING AT ME LIKE THAT, OKAZAKI...?
WE'RE FRIENDS, RIGHT...?
...YUUKI-KUN...
YOU'RE JUST LIKE ME, AREN'T YOU?

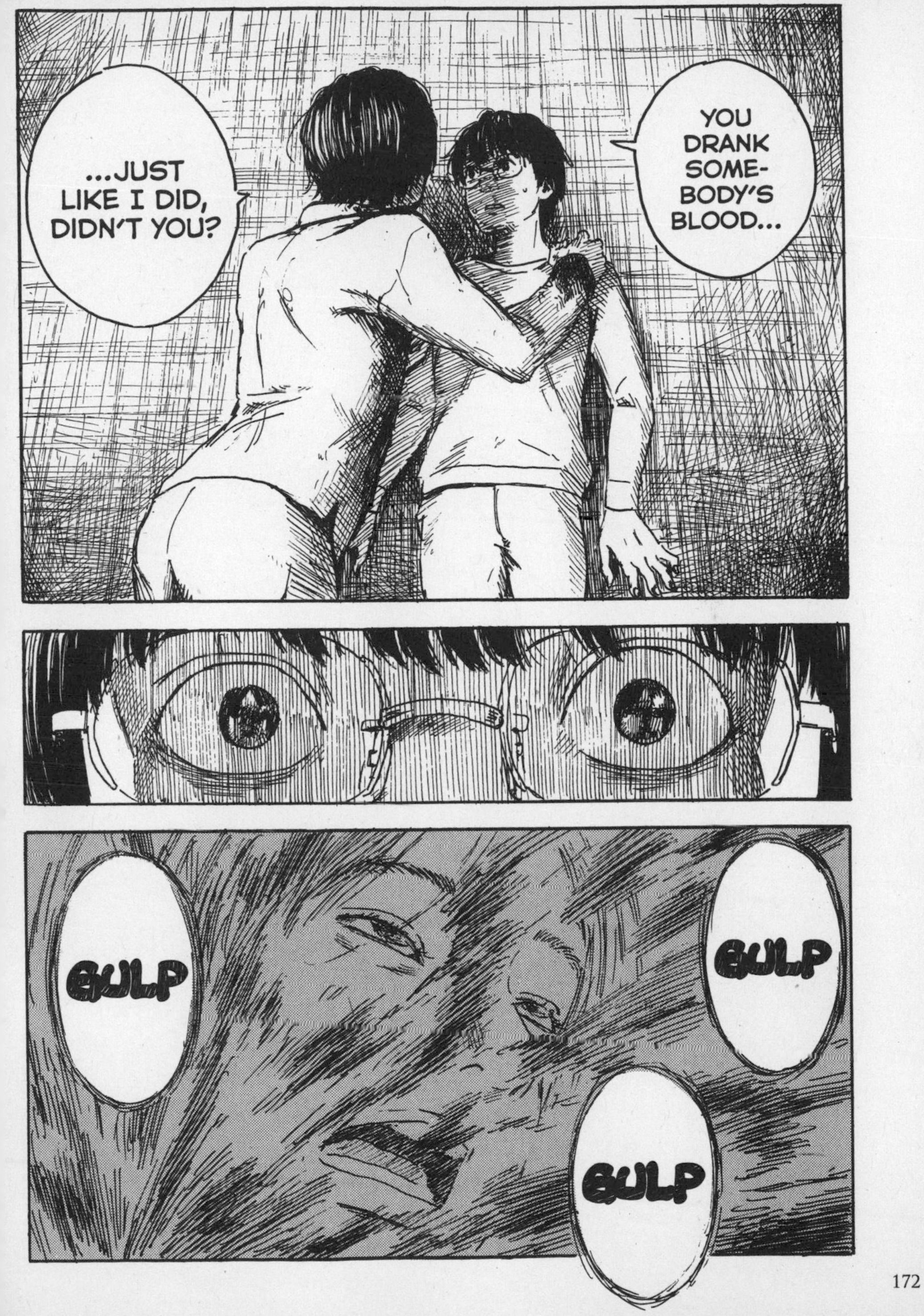
YOU DRANK SOME-BODY'S BLOOD...
...JUST LIKE I DID, DIDN'T YOU?
GULP
GULP
GULP

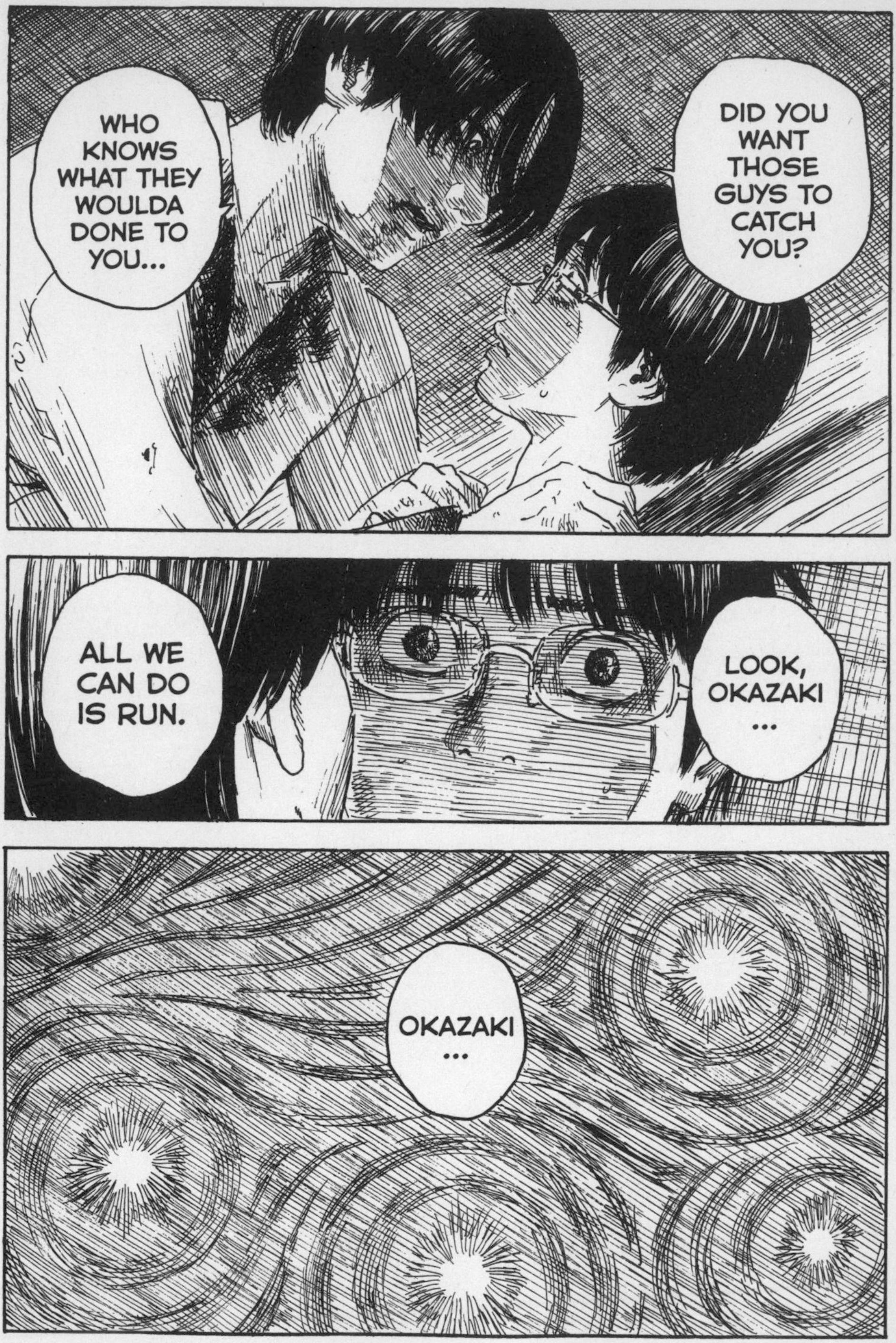
DID YOU WANT THOSE GUYS TO CATCH YOU?
WHO KNOWS WHAT THEY WOULDA DONE TO YOU...
LOOK, OKAZAKI ...
ALL WE CAN DO IS RUN.
OKAZAKI ...

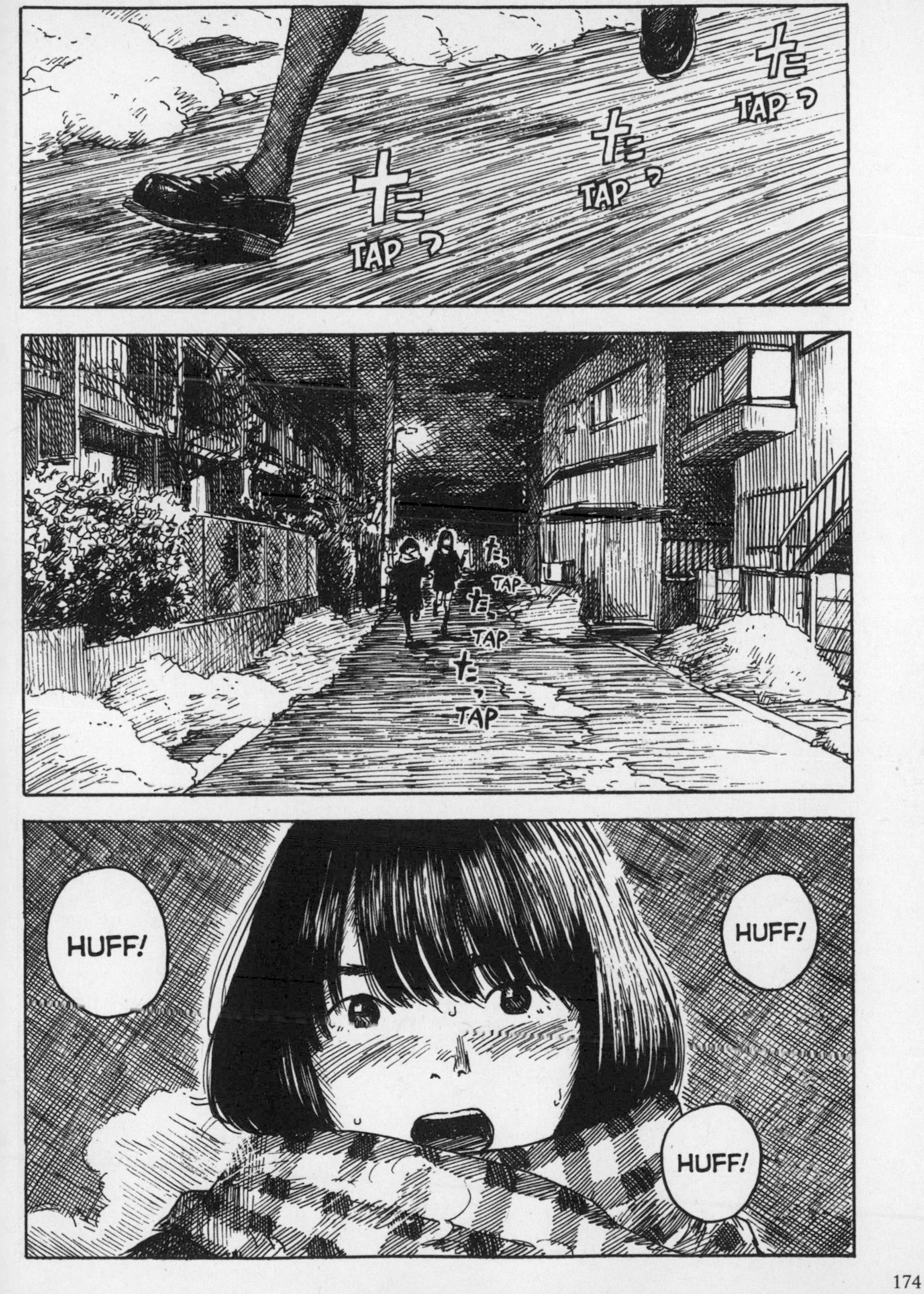
たっ
TAP
たっ
TAP
たっ
TAP
たっ
TAP
たっ
TAP
たっ
TAP
HUFF!
HUFF!
HUFF!

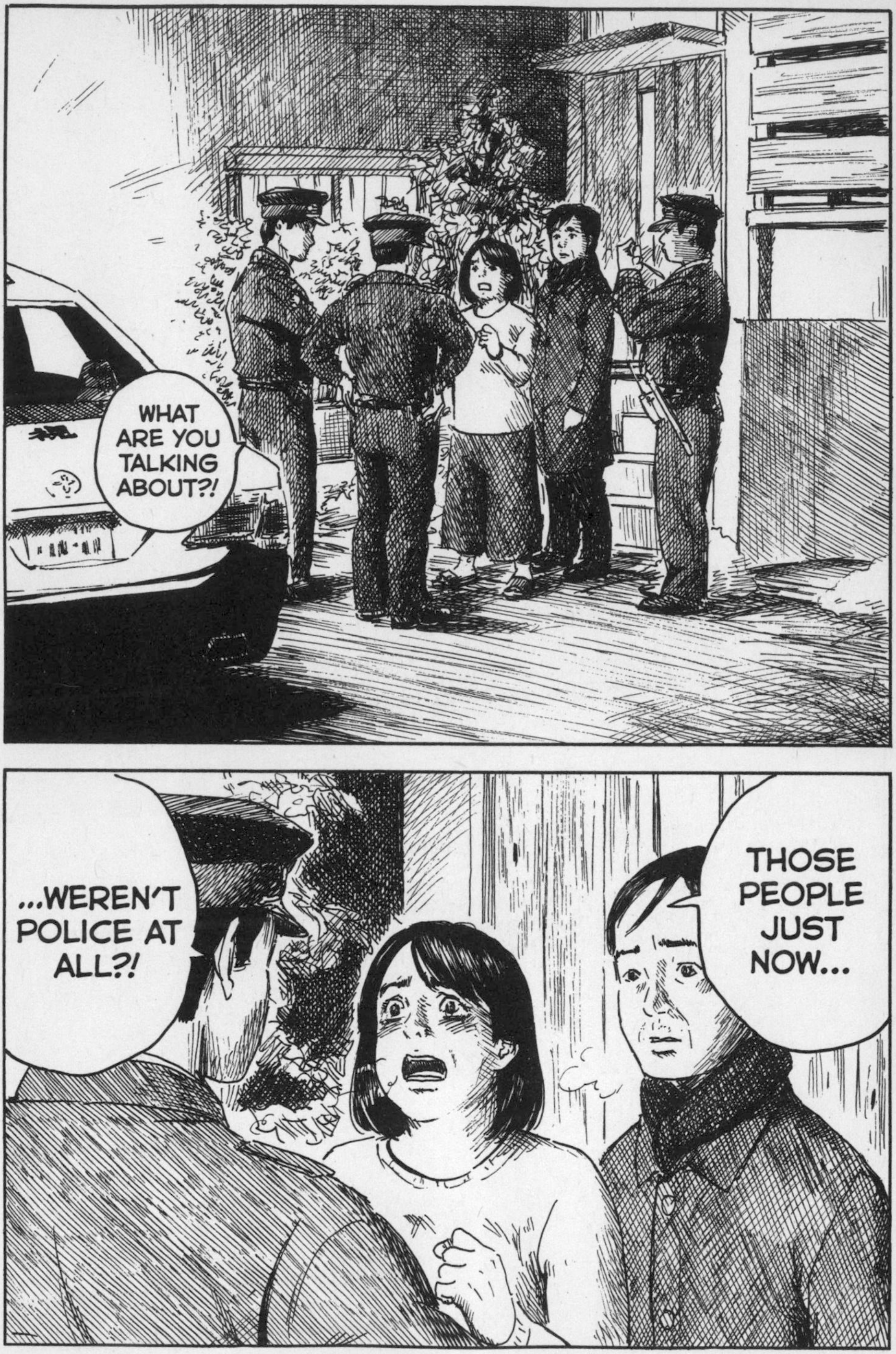
WHAT ARE YOU TALKING ABOUT?!
THOSE PEOPLE JUST NOW...
...WEREN'T POLICE AT ALL?!

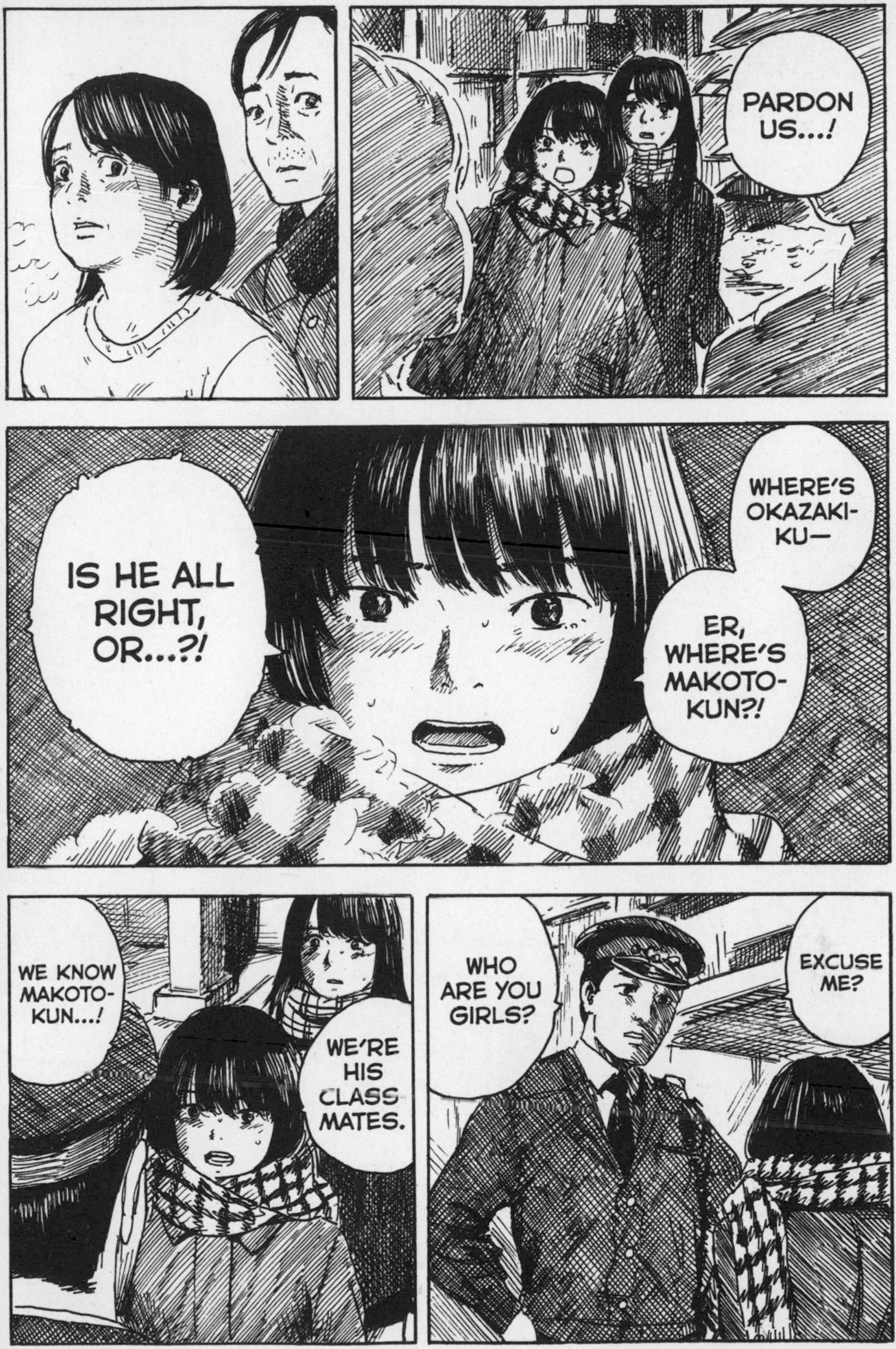
PARDON US...!
WHERE'S OKAZAKI-KU—
ER, WHERE'S MAKOTO-KUN?!
IS HE ALL RIGHT, OR...?!
EXCUSE ME?
WHO ARE YOU GIRLS?
WE'RE HIS CLASS MATES.
WE KNOW MAKOTO-KUN...!

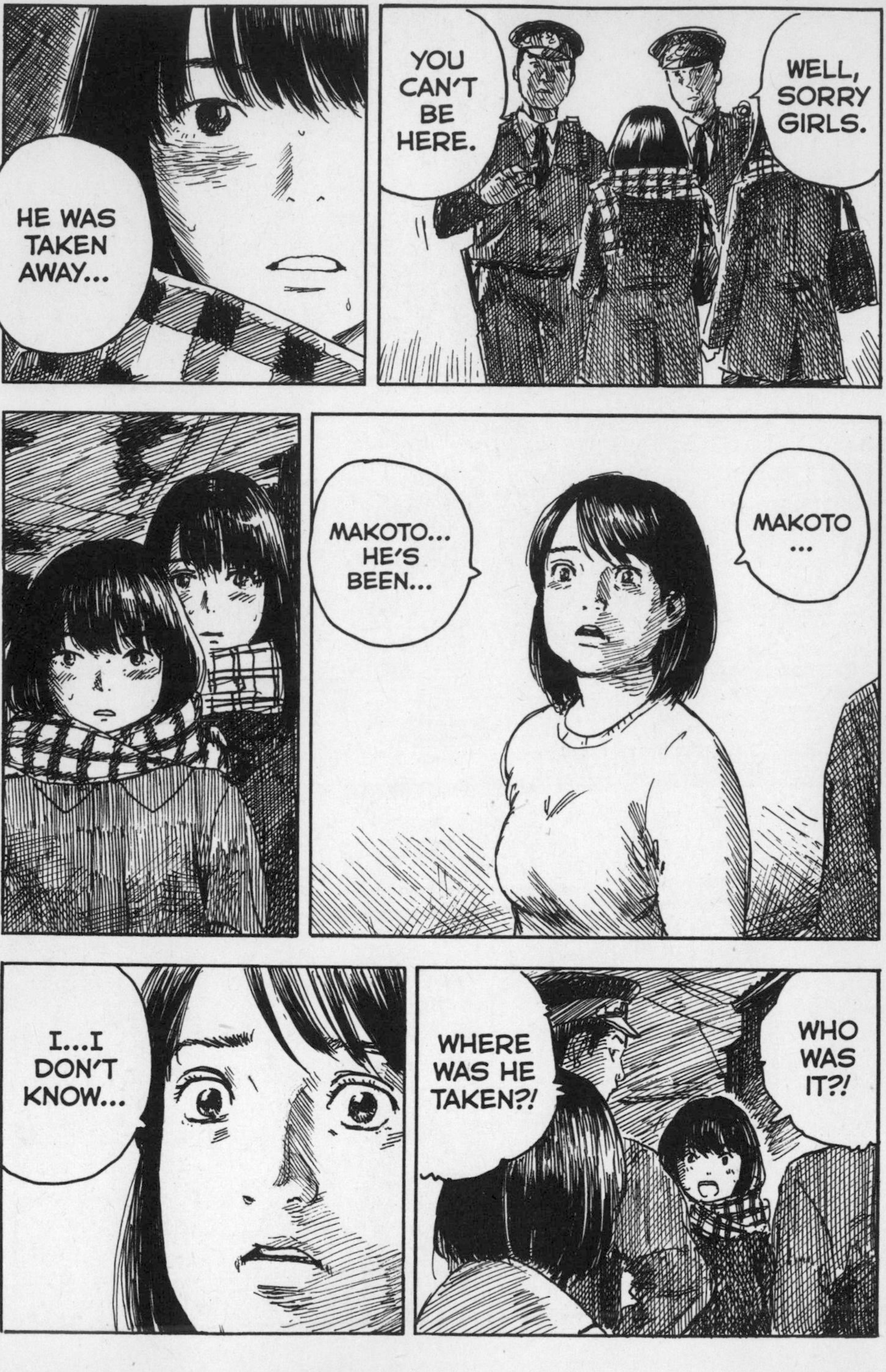
WELL, SORRY GIRLS.
YOU CAN'T BE HERE.
HE WAS TAKEN AWAY...
MAKOTO ...
MAKOTO... HE'S BEEN...
WHO WAS IT?!
WHERE WAS HE TAKEN?!
I...I DON'T KNOW...

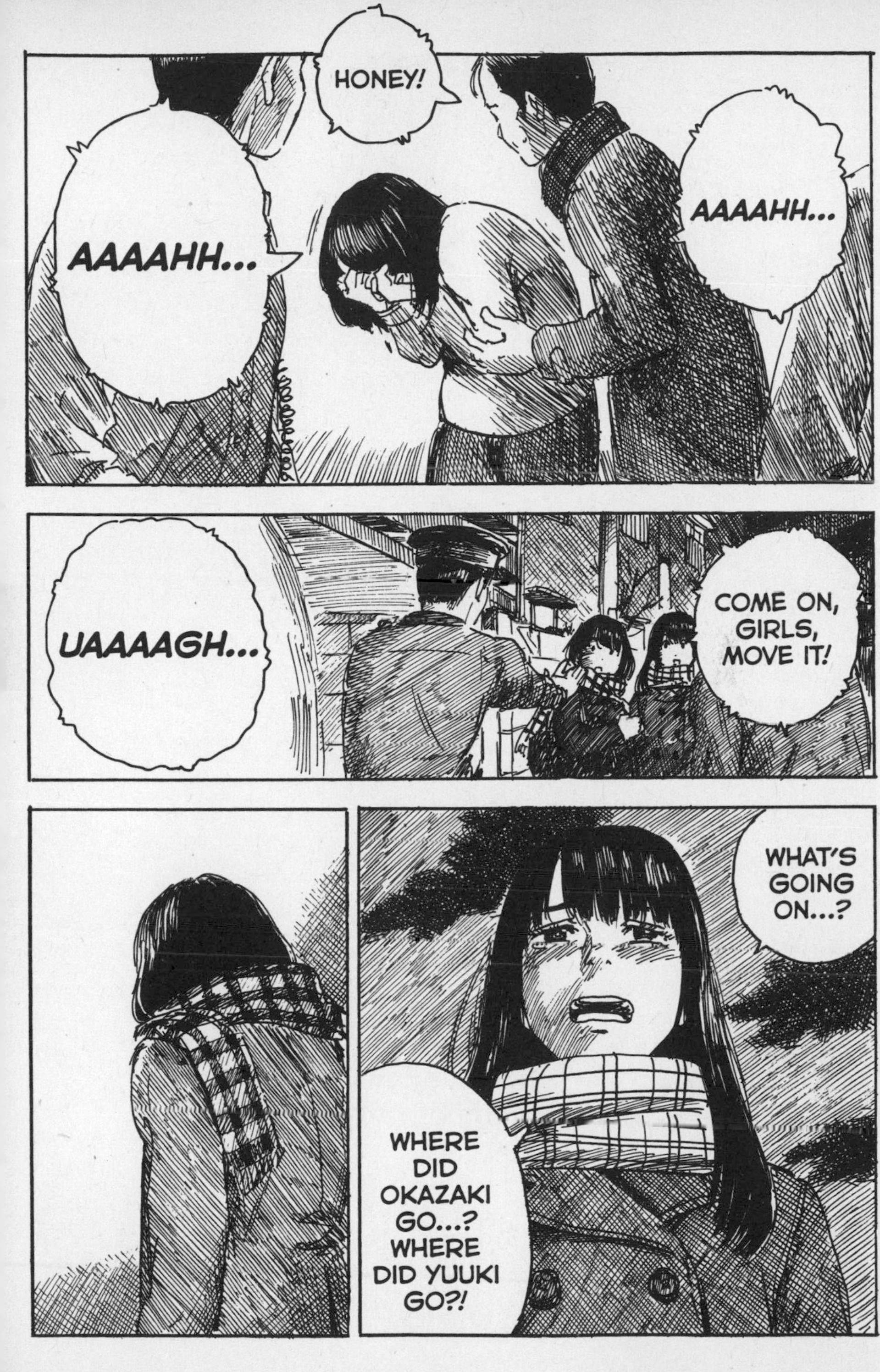
HONEY!
AAAAHH...
AAAAHH...
COME ON, GIRLS, MOVE IT!
UAAAAGH...
WHAT'S GOING ON...?
WHERE DID OKAZAKI GO...? WHERE DID YUUKI GO?!

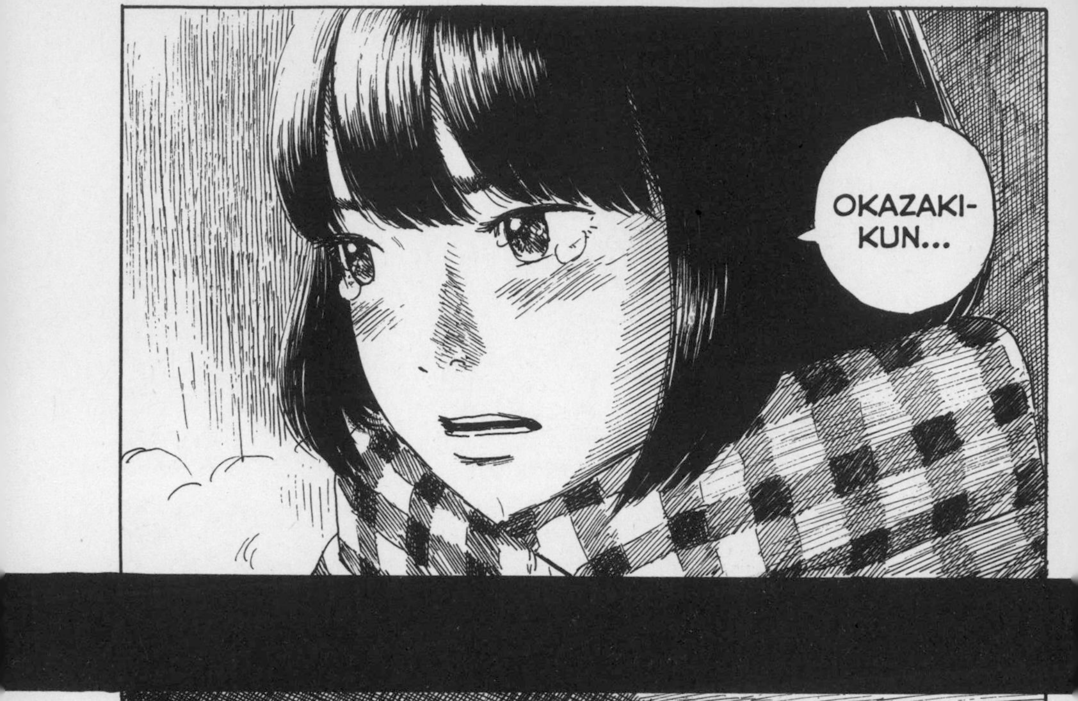
OKAZAKI-KUN...

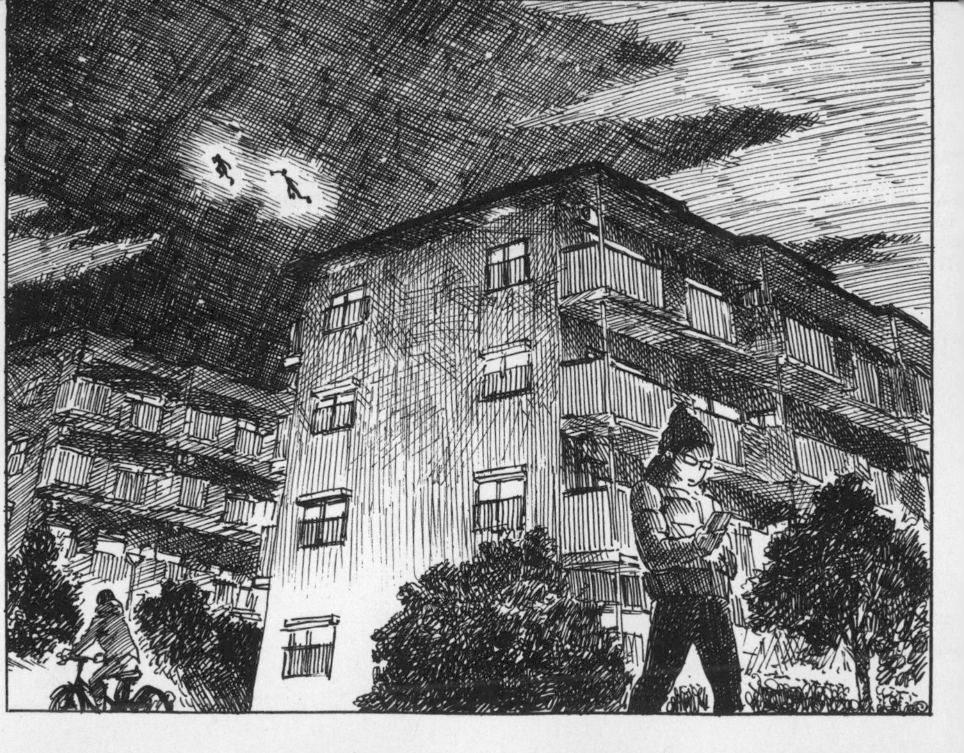

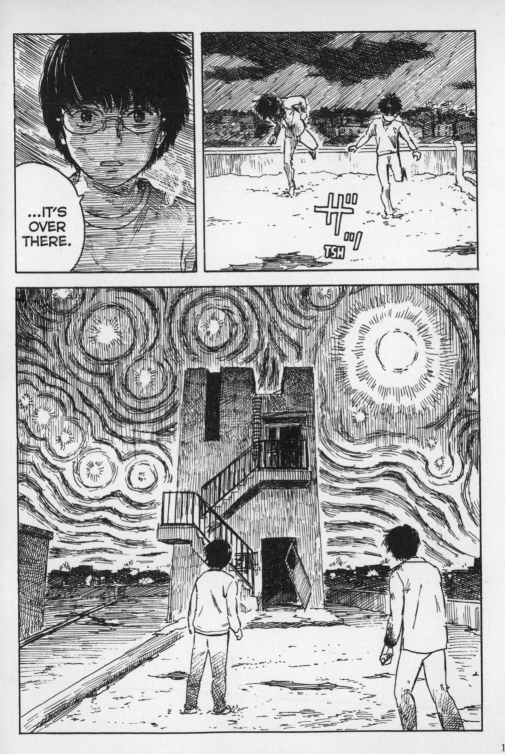

...IT'S
OVER
THERE.

ザ"
"ッ
TSH

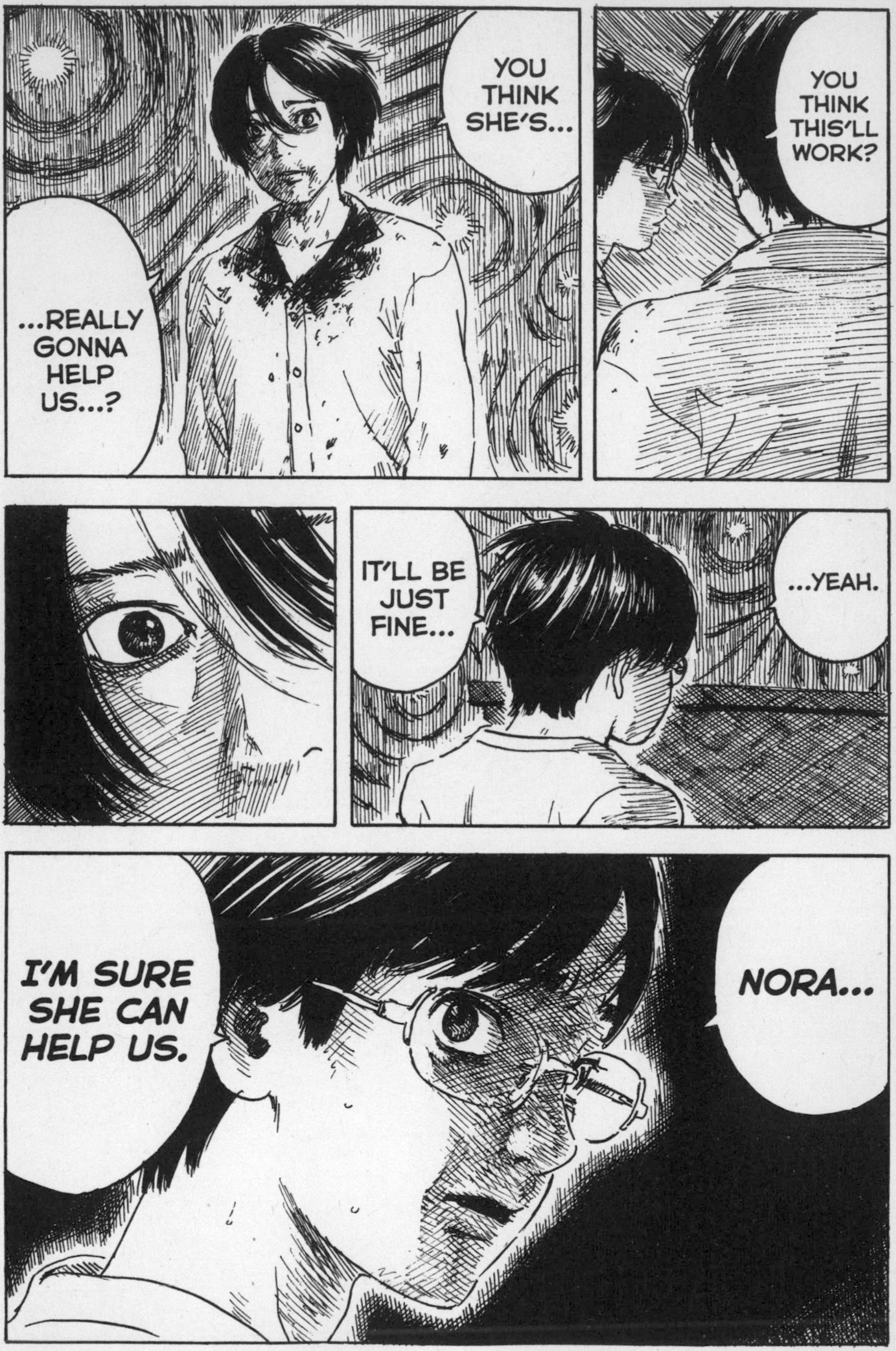
YOU THINK THIS'LL WORK?
YOU THINK SHE'S...
...REALLY GONNA HELP US...?
...YEAH.
IT'LL BE JUST FINE...
NORA...
I'M SURE SHE CAN HELP US.

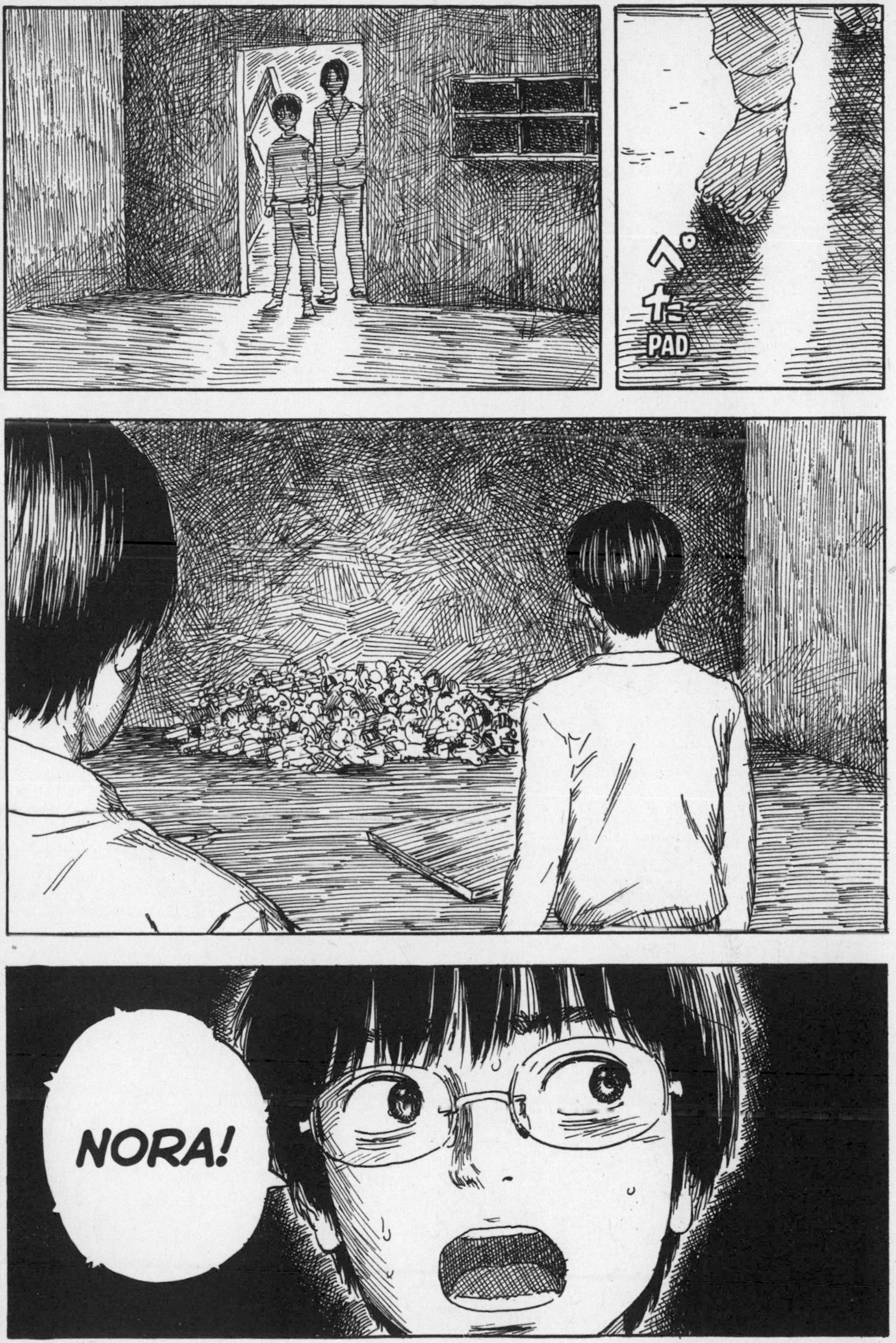
ぺた
PAD
NORA!

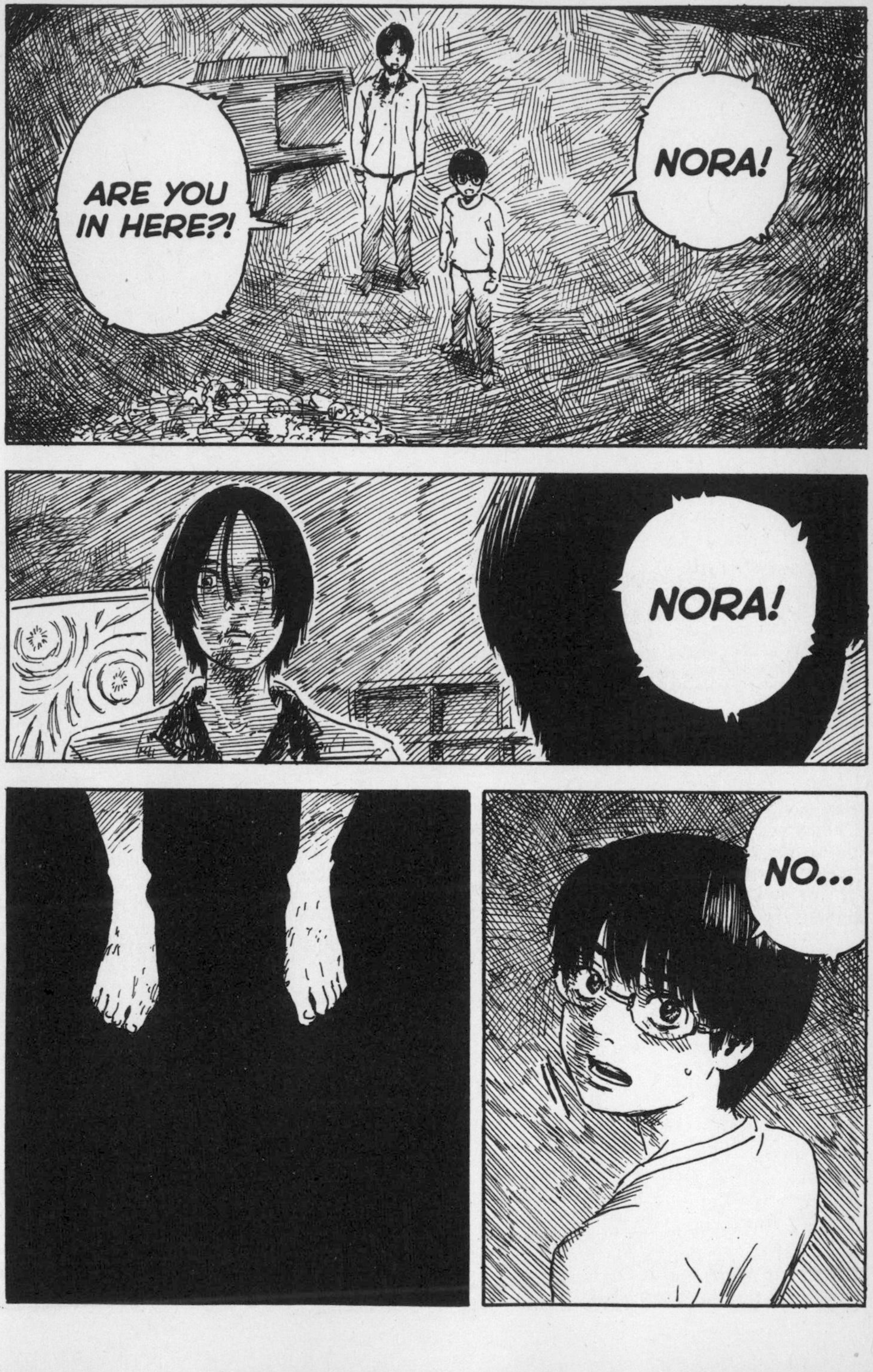
NORA!
ARE YOU IN HERE?!
NORA!
NO...

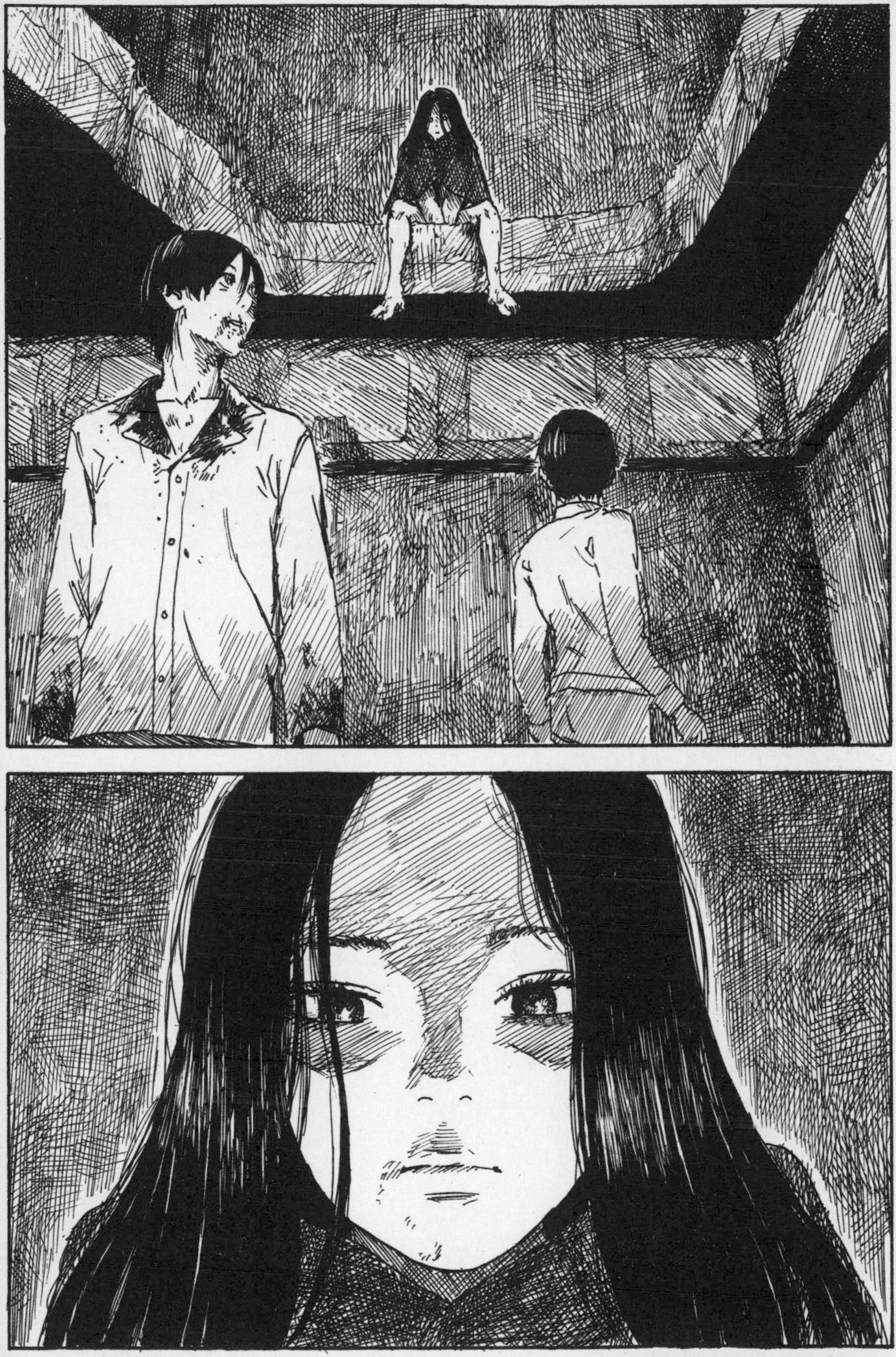

CONTINUED IN #4

HAPPINESS

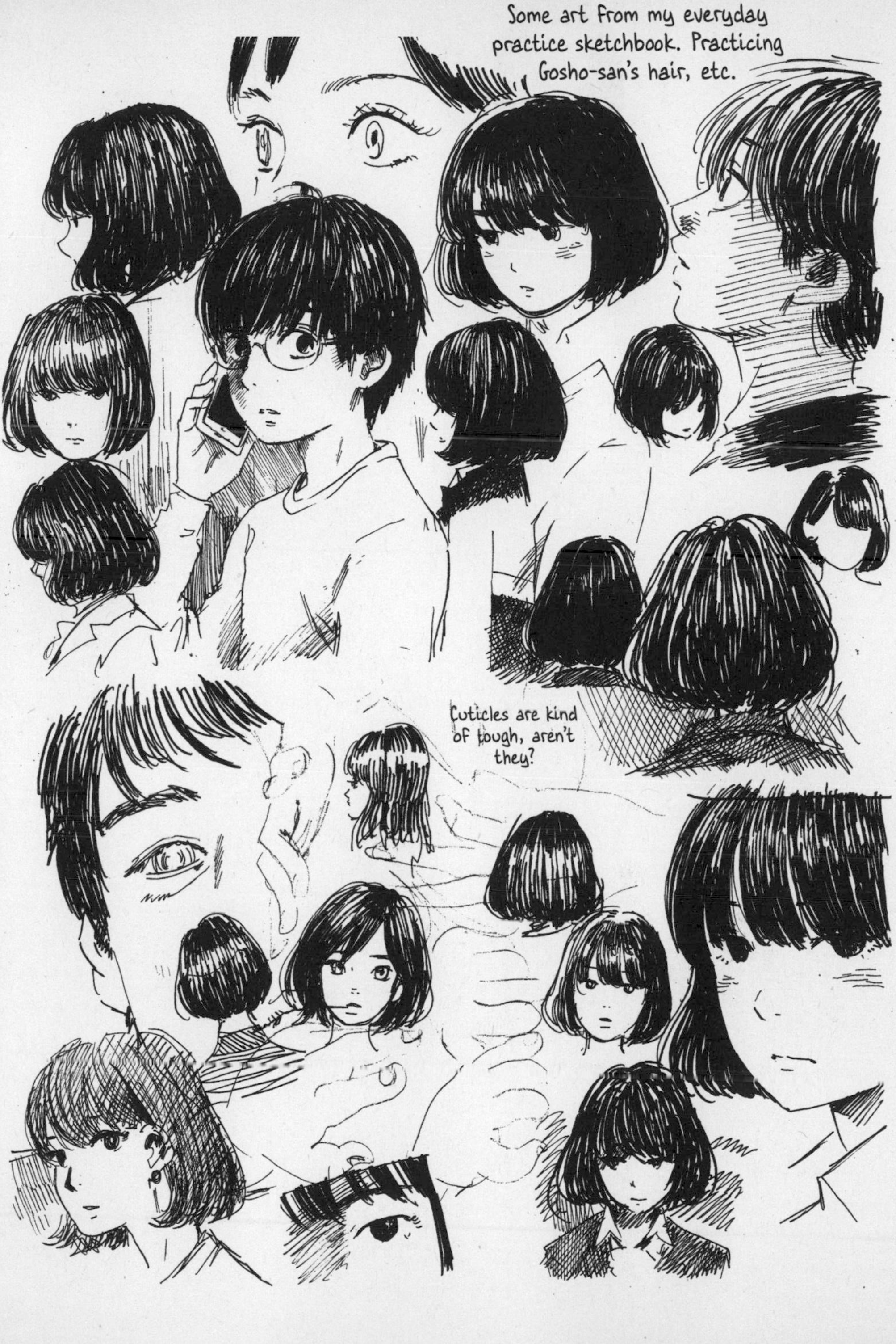
Some art from my everyday practice sketchbook. Practicing Gosho-san's hair, etc.
Cuticles are kind of tough, aren't they?

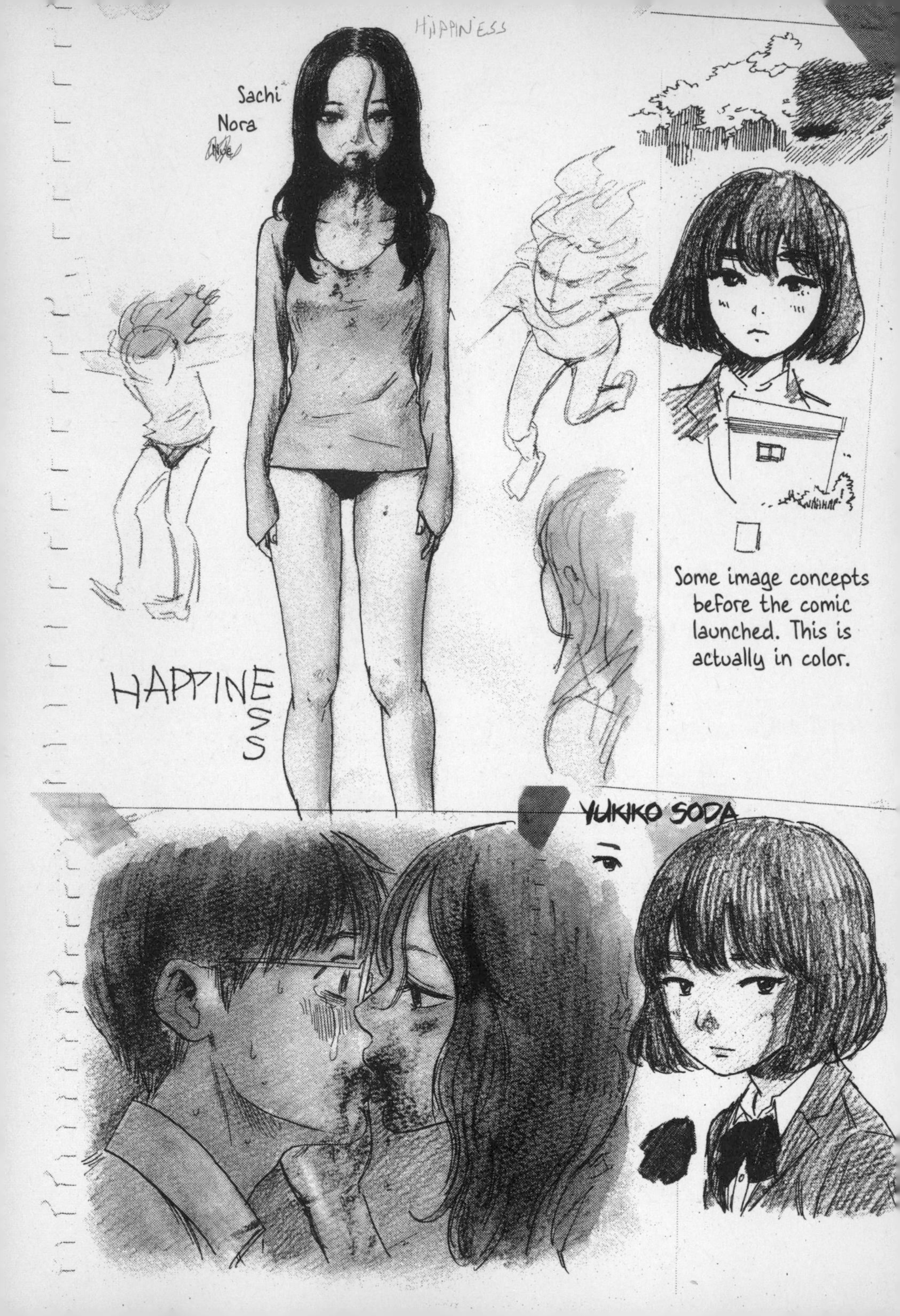
Sachi
Nora
HAPPINESS
YUKIKO SODA
Some image concepts before the comic launched. This is actually in color.

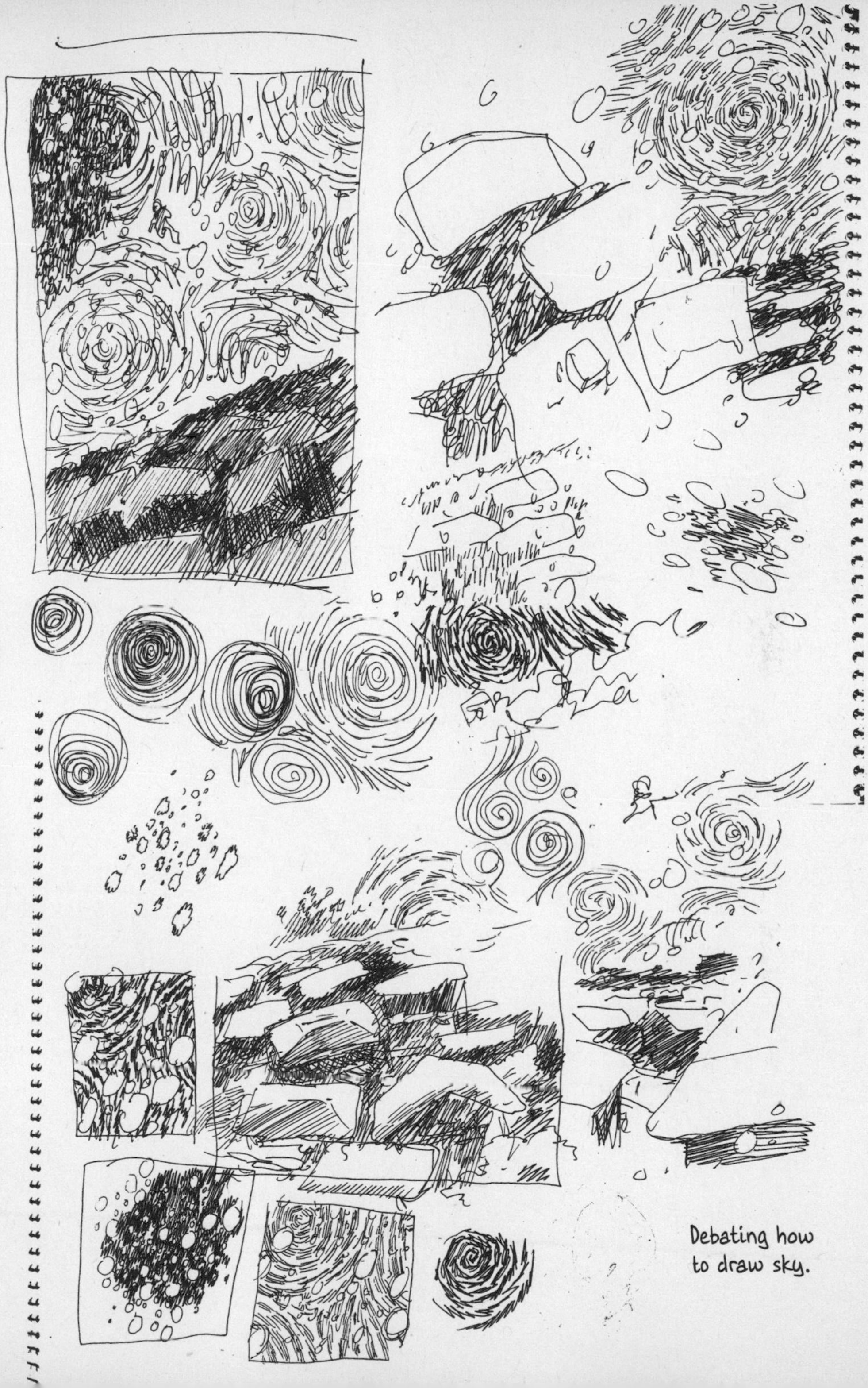

Debating how to draw sky.

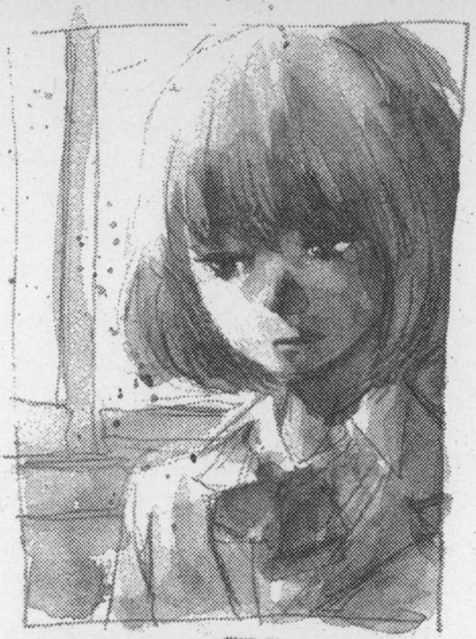

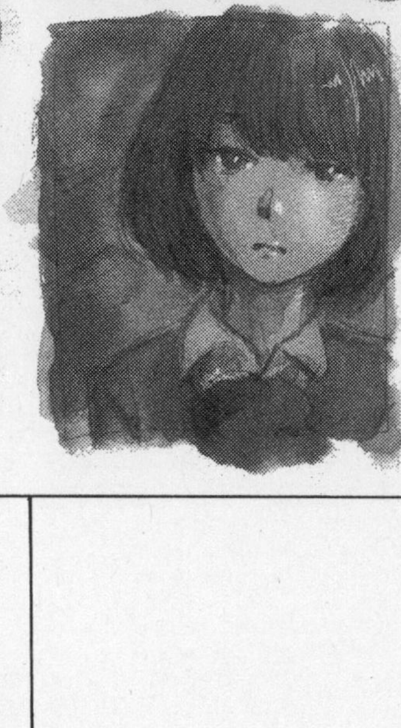

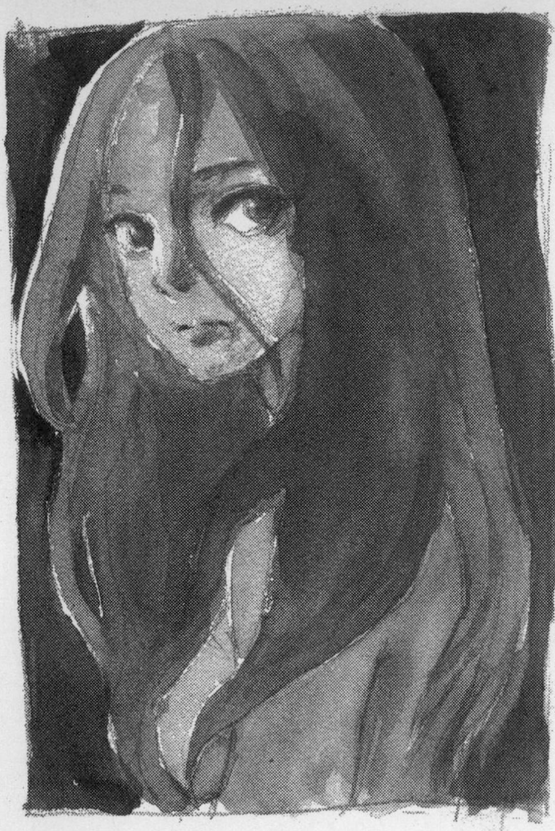

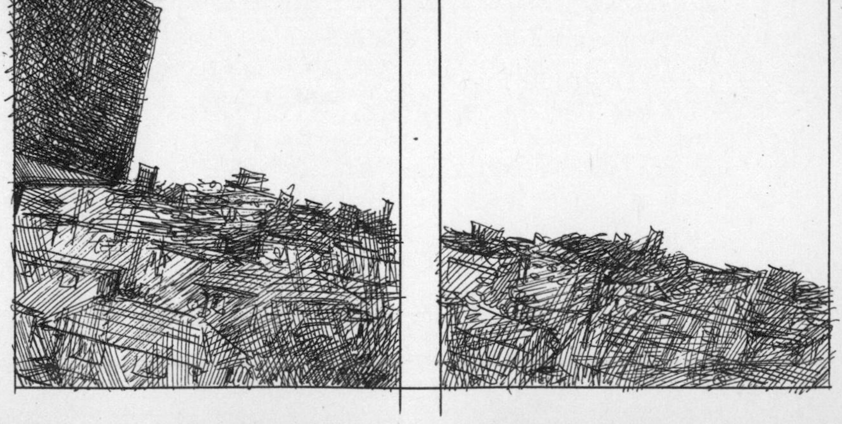

A rejected proposal for the Volume 3 cover.

Thank you very much! See you in the next volume.

Translation Notes

Shuzo Oshimi uses minute details in the contemporary Tokyo setting of *Happiness* to convey nuances of both story and character, many of which may be unfamiliar to non-Japanese readers. Here are brief notes on some of these details.

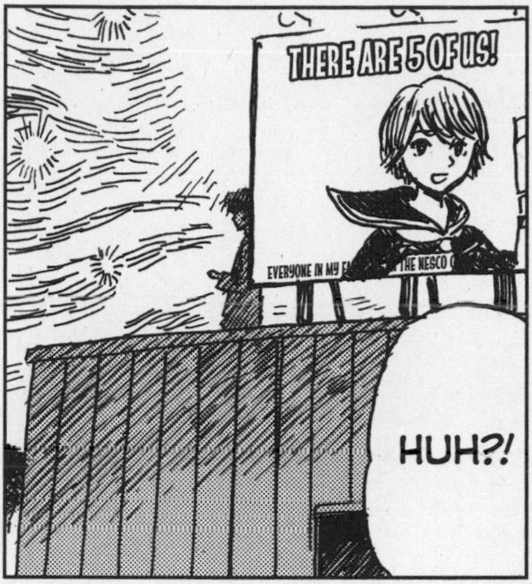
THERE ARE 5 OF US!
HUH?!

There are 5 of us!, page 7
This billboard is an homage to a short manga called *Lunn Flies into the Wind*, written by Osamu Tezuka (creator of *Astro Boy*, *Kimba the White Lion*, *Phoenix*, and countless other classics) and published in Monthly Shonen Jump magazine in 1979. It tells the story of a teenage boy who falls in love with a girl in a coffee advertisement he spots on the street (which looks exactly like this one), eventually seeing her as his only confidante in life. An anime version, also directed by Tezuka, was released in 1985.

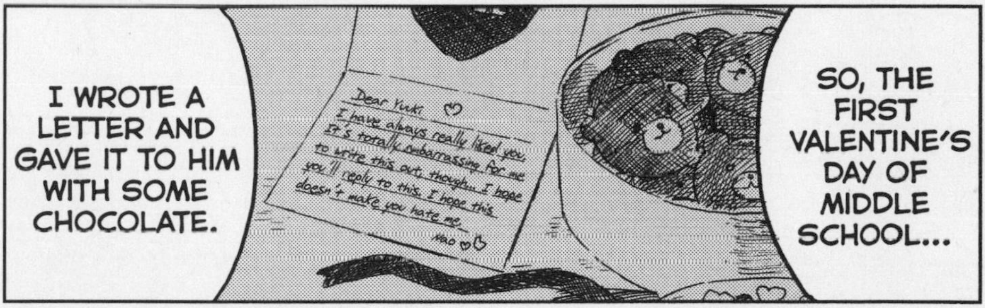
SO, THE FIRST VALENTINE'S DAY OF MIDDLE SCHOOL...
Dear Yuki ♡
I have always really liked you.
It's totally embarrassing for me to write this out, though... I hope you'll reply to this. I hope this doesn't make you hate me.
Nao ♡
I WROTE A LETTER AND GAVE IT TO HIM WITH SOME CHOCOLATE.

Valentine's Day, page 132
Valentine's Day was largely introduced to the Japanese public by candy makers and retailers in the 1950s and '60s. In Japan, it's traditional for women to give letters and chocolate to men on the big day, rather than the other way around. Men then repay the favor with chocolate of their own on March 14th, or "White Day", a holiday entirely invented by Japanese retailers.

HAPPINESS

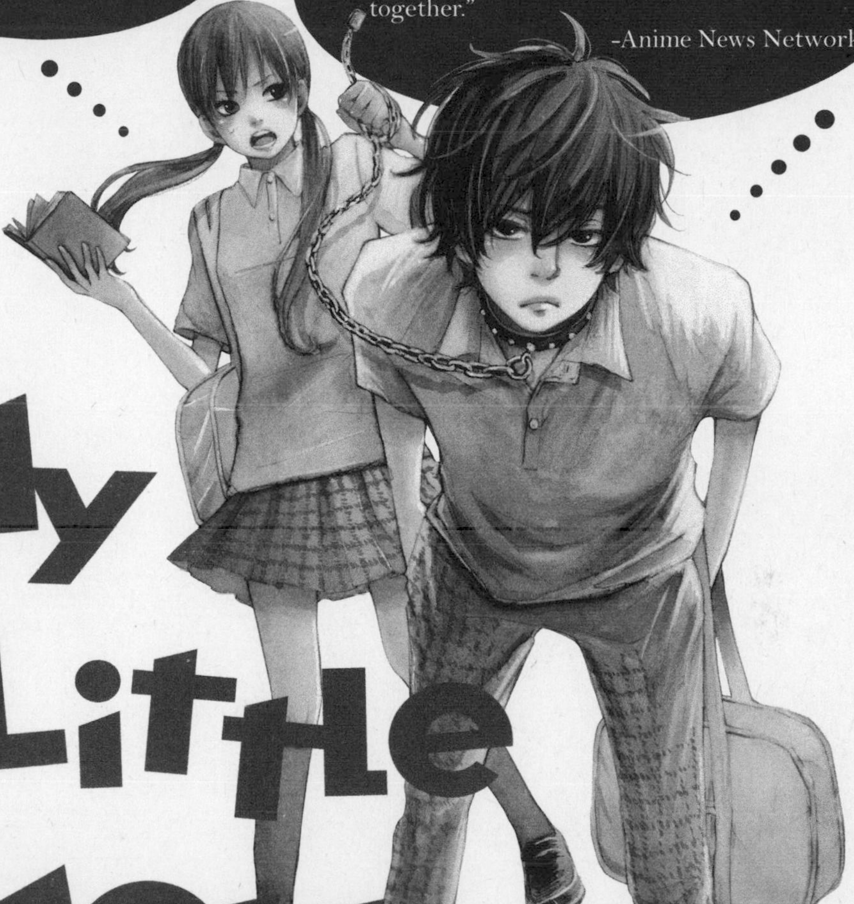

My Little Monster

OPPOSITES ATTRACT...MAYBE?

Haru Yoshida is feared as an unstable and violent "monster." Mizutani Shizuku is a grade-obsessed student with no friends. Fate brings these two together to form the most unlikely pair. Haru firmly believes he's in love with Mizutani and she firmly believes he's insane.

KC KODANSHA COMICS

INUYASHIKI

A superhero like none you've ever seen, from the creator of "Gantz"!

ICHIRO INUYASHIKI IS DOWN ON HIS LUCK. HE LOOKS MUCH OLDER THAN HIS 58 YEARS, HIS CHILDREN DESPISE HIM, AND HIS WIFE THINKS HE'S A USELESS COWARD. SO WHEN HE'S DIAGNOSED WITH STOMACH CANCER AND GIVEN THREE MONTHS TO LIVE, IT SEEMS THE ONLY ONE WHO'LL MISS HIM IS HIS DOG.

THEN A BLINDING LIGHT FILLS THE SKY, AND THE OLD MAN IS KILLED... ONLY TO WAKE UP LATER IN A BODY HE ALMOST RECOGNIZES AS HIS OWN. CAN IT BE THAT ICHIRO INUYASHIKI IS NO LONGER HUMAN?

COMES IN EXTRA-LARGE EDITIONS WITH COLOR PAGES!

Happiness volume 3 is a work of fiction. Names, characters, places, and incidents are the products of the author's imagination or are used fictitiously. Any resemblance to actual events, locales, or persons, living or dead, is entirely coincidental.

A Kodansha Comics Trade Paperback Original.

Published in the United States by Kodansha Comics, an imprint of Kodansha USA Publishing, LLC, New York.

Publication rights for this English edition arranged through Kodansha Ltd., Tokyo.

First published in Japan in 2016 by Kodansha Ltd., Tokyo, as *Hapinesu* volume 3.

ISBN 978-1-63236-392-3

Printed in the United States of America.

www.kodanshacomics.com

9 8 7 6 5 4 3 2 1

Translator: Kevin Gifford
Lettering: David Yoo
Editing: Paul Starr
Kodansha Comics edition cover design by Phil Balsman